A NEW ILLUSTRATED HISTORY OF

HER MAJESTY'S RAILWAY INSPECTORATE FROM 1840

IAN PROSSER CBE
& Eur Ing DAVID KEAY

EDITED BY NIGEL HARRIS

DEDICATION

This book is dedicated to the men and women who served the Railway Inspectorate from 1840 to 1990 and those who followed in Her Majesty's Railway Inspectorate, after 1990. Their patient and thorough investigations helped make our railway progressively safer for those who both work on it and those who use its trains. This history is also offered in memory of those who lost their lives in the mishaps reflected in these pages.

CONTENTS

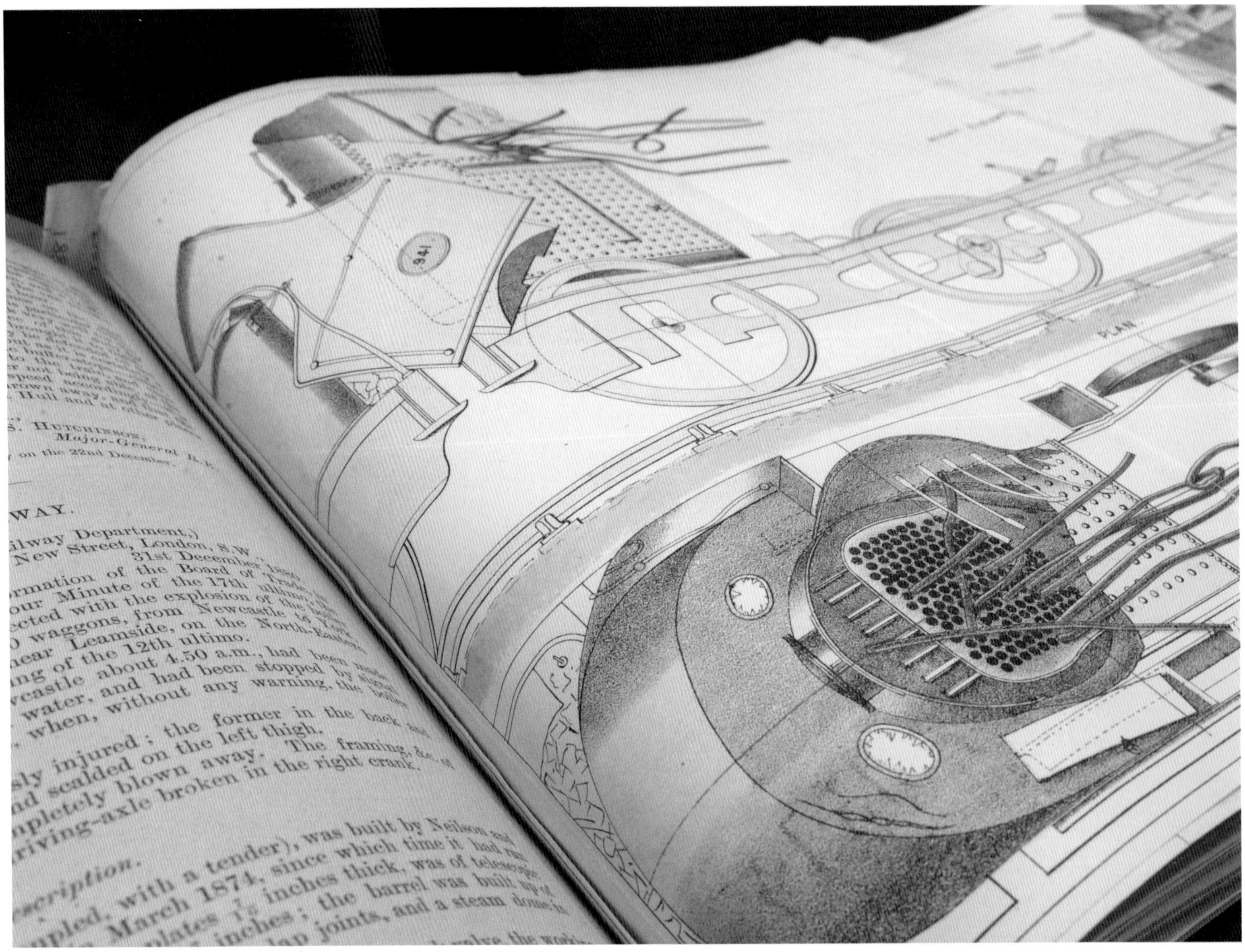

Published by Steam World Publishing,
Steam World, 4 Milnyard Square, Orton Southgate,
Peterborough, PE2 6GX
Telephone: 01733 363484
Email: steamworld@choicemag.co.uk

First published: November 2019
Designed by: Lucy Carnell
Printed in Poland www.lfbookservices.co.uk

British Library Cataloguing in Publication Data
A catalogue record for this book is available from the British Library.

ISBN 978-0-9927398-1-2

Above: ORR has a full set of rail accident reports in its London archive, which feature some quite beautiful graphics and artwork, painstakingly created during the investigation. This is just a single snapshot from one of the 1870s volumes. ***Clive Nicholls.***

Previous page: Four goods trains collided at King's Langley, on the West Coast Main Line, on March 13 1935, after a vacuum brake pipe failure caused the 4.55pm up express meat train to come to a stand on the up fast line. Aerial photographs are taken for granted today, but in 1935 it involved the photographer hanging out of an open biplane cockpit with a large, glass plate camera. This was an achievement in itself – but essential both for the media of the day, and the accident investigation. ***Getty Images.***

FOREWORD
BY MAJOR JOHN POYNTZ

Following an Army career of 35 years (I 'joined up' in 1955) in first the Royal Engineers and then Royal Corps of Transport, it was not only an honour but also a privilege to be appointed by the Railway Inspectorate in 1989 as an Inspecting Officer of Railways, to follow in the footsteps of my illustrious predecessors. I remained at the RI - and subsequently HMRI after 1990 - until I retired in 2006. I then then served HMRI for a further eight years as a heritage railways consultant, until 2014.

My Army career was not only rewarding and fulfilling in its own right, it was also a perfect preparation for a second 25-year career as an Inspector of Railways.

Between 1955 and 1969 I was fortunate to be stationed at the Longmoor Military Railway in Hampshire, where I cut my teeth on railway operations. From time to time, this railway life on the LMR was interspersed with visits to conflict zones such as Borneo and Cyprus. The most poignant experience at Longmoor was in 1956, when I witnessed the worst peacetime accident on a military railway. An LMS Stanier Class 8F 2-8-0 was hauling a passenger train when it passed a signal at danger and collided head-on with an LMS shunting locomotive hauling a rake of flat wagons between two brake vans. The leading brake van was full of soldiers: six were killed in the impact. I have therefore been around railway mishaps for my entire career, one way or the other.

I later spent many enjoyable years as the responsible officer for all British Army train movements in West Germany other than Berlin. This allowed me to experience the wide variety of European operating systems and the advance of technology in mainland Europe. From time to time, I was lucky to have the opportunity to drive the latest German locomotives.

This new history sets out a clear, detailed and very comprehensive picture of how successive generations of Royal Engineers played a key role in developing and shaping safety on Britain's railways, over 180 years. The Royal Engineers deserve more credit for this than I suspect they have had for this remarkable work, so this book plays an important part in putting this achievement firmly 'on the record.'

My two former colleagues, Ian Prosser CBE and David Keay knew RI/HMRI intimately from the inside, and they give fascinating insights into the powers of persuasion (and some of the frustrations!) of successive generations of Inspecting Officers. It is especially fascinating when highlighting their diligence in accident investigation and the absolute respect in which they were consequently held by railwaymen and women. I am delighted to see that HMRI, as part of the Office of Rail & Road, continues to build on this respect and credibility today.

It gives me great personal and professional pleasure to reflect that the diligence, skills and professionalism of the Royal Engineers and their successors have had such a profound influence on British railway safety, which has created the safest railway in the world.

I hope very much that this book provides the reader with a wider understanding of the role of the Inspectorate, not least through some previously unpublished material that graphically illustrates some of the major (and less serious) accidents. There are many important outcomes from these historic accidents. They remind us that these lessons of the past still need to be in the forefront of the minds of those engaged in the operation and management of today's railways and tramways. If we do not properly learn the lessons of the past, we run the risk of repeating its mistakes.

I very much hope that the reader will find this history as fascinating as I found my career. I am very proud to have played my part in the long history of the Railway Inspectorate.

Major John D. Poyntz,
Harrow. **September 2019.**

EDITOR'S INTRODUCTION
BY NIGEL HARRIS

Public railways using steam locomotives were invented in the north east of England with the opening of the Stockton & Darlington Railway on September 27 1825. Passenger railways followed almost exactly five years later, with the Liverpool & Manchester Railway opening, on September 15 1830.

Passenger trains had not even completed their first day in service on the world's first inter-city railway, before a fatality occurred - and a very high profile loss of life it was, too. Liverpool Member of Parliament William Huskisson was famously run over and within hours died from his injuries amidst the celebrations and razamatazz of opening day celebrations. George Stephenson himself drove the locomotive *Northumbrian* to rush the grievously injured Huskisson (he lost a leg) to hospital in Manchester, but in vain, given that Huskisson died the same day.

It is perhaps not surprising, therefore, that it was George Stephenson himself who fought so consistently a decade later for the creation of an empowered Railway Inspectorate to both inspect and approve new railways and investigate accidents.

I have always been fascinated by the forensic rail accident investigation reports that followed - they are wonderful documents from which much can still be learned today - even those from the earliest days, with their archaic language. This an interest that took root in 1968 (I was 11 years old) just as my love of toy trains (clattering three-rail 'OO' gauge Hornby-Dublo and Hornby tinplate clockwork 'O' gauge!) developed into a more mature interest in model railways, which in turn evolved into working as a volunteer (driver, eventually) on steam footplates on the Lakeside & Haverthwaite and Great Central Railways. This hands-on restoration,

Above: This 25mph fine weather derailment left 14 passengers dead, immediately south of Doncaster station, on March 16 1951. Only moments after leaving Platform 4 (one minute late) the 10.06am express to King's Cross (14 bogie coaches and a horsebox weighing 488 tons) hauled by Class A2/2 'Pacific' No. 60501 *Cock O' the North*, derailed on a badly maintained scissors crossover, approaching Bridge Junction. The engine and first two coaches passed safely beneath the bridge and remained on the track, but the following eight coaches all derailed after the third coach. The report explained how the derailed third coach (right foreground) was led to its left by diverging neighbouring rails: "while the front of the train continued to move forward onto the main line, thus tilting the third coach and taking it forward broadside until the middle of its body struck the pier of Balby Bridge. At this moment the engine was pulling the leading end of this coach to the right of the pier while the thrust from the rest of the train carried the trailing end to the left until the coach was virtually wrapped around the pier. The body was crushed against the brickwork and demolished and the underframe was bent into a U-shape; so far as could be ascertained, all the fatalities were in this coach." The RI report documents in detail the thoroughness of the investigation with regard to the condition of the crossover and how it failed. It also emerged that passenger trains routinely travelled over the 10mph speed restriction at around 20-25mph with the full knowledge of footplate crew and signalmen. Compared with today, it is astonishing how quickly lines were restored after this major incident. This derailment blocked the up main, up slow and two up goods lines, which were damaged for about 120 yards. Incredibly, the down goods line was cleared by 9.30pm on the day of the accident, whilst the down and up main lines were reopened to traffic at 11.00pm and 11.15pm, after an interruption of just 13 hours. The scissors crossover where the derailment happened was not reopened until 7.00am the next day while the two up goods lines were not cleared until 5.00pm on Sunday March 18 - just two days later. Consider that after the fatal Hatfield derailment of 2000, the East Coast Main Line remained closed for three weeks. *Alamy*.

maintenance and operating experience, incidentally, was enormously useful in sharpening my understanding of rail mishaps - especially from the driver's perspective.

This fascination was triggered on one of those seemingly interminable Sunday afternoons of the late 1960s/early 1970s, which those who lived through them may also remember with a sinking feeling! No shops were open. Little moved. Every Sunday then felt like Christmas Day does now: everyday life came to a standstill. At least one of the only two principal TV channels always seemed to be screening an afternoon Gregory Peck US Air Force war movie! There was little to look forward to after that, other than tinned cling peaches (in syrup) and a can of 'Carnation' evaporated milk for tea, a black-and-white BBC Dickens dramatisation at 5.30pm (Great Expectations, usually)... followed by Captain Pugwash and then 'Sing Something Simple' on the radio after 'Pick of the Pops' with Alan 'Fluff' Freeman... it was then all downhill to school on Monday morning.

It's hard to convey, now, just how excruciatingly tedious Sunday afternoons were.

To escape this stultifying boredom, my dad and I would often jump in our Ford Cortina and motor 'over the tops' into Yorkshire for an afternoon of steam on the Worth Valley Railway.

And it was there, in 1968, at Haworth station, that it happened. My dad shelled out five shillings (only 25p now, but not insignificant back then for a casual treat) in the souvenir shop for my much-prized, and now very tattered, Pan paperback copy of L.T.C. Rolt's classic *Red for Danger* - one of the finest railway books ever published.

I read it in less than a week and loved every word, even though I understood hardly any of its technicalities. *Red for Danger* had a profound impact on me. I was baffled by absolute block working, Automatic Train Control and continuous train brakes - but Rolt's transformation of formal accident reports into dramatic, beautifully crafted storytelling gripped me. I was hooked.

I've read *Red for Danger* repeatedly since 1968 and each time my advancing railway technical, operational and human knowledge enables me to understand more about accidents whose names are tragically etched into our collective consciousness...Armagh, Tay Bridge, Abbots Ripton, Hawes Junction, Harrow & Wealdstone...

My pre-teen eyes widened not just in horror, but in great sympathy (and empathy, though I wouldn't have understood that as a concept at the time, as an 11-year old) with Midland Railway Hawes Junction signalman Alfred Sutton, whose wretched mistake forgetting a pair of light engines standing at his down main line signals, caused the terrible 1910 disaster just north of Garsdale, in the high fells, in which 12 people died. They were burned to death in the splintered wreckage of wooden, gas-lit coaches.

When Sutton realised the full horror of what he had done, he turned to Driver George Tempest, who was in his box on the platform at Garsdale and said: "Go to Bence [the stationmaster] and tell him I am afraid I have wrecked the Scotch express..."

Those words haunt me still. It is impossible to conceive how the poor, wretched man felt - but what Rolt did, in taking the formal, technical language of railway accident reports and turning them into compelling prose, was ensure the human element was properly and powerfully captured and conveyed. Rolt made certain that a train-obsessed 11-year old would ever-after appreciate that human beings are as important as mechanical, system or operating failures. Rolt wisely and cleverly made sure that our interest in rail catastrophes wasn't prurient.

Even so, *The Times* was nevertheless cautious over enthusing about tragedy and in its review of *Red for Danger*, said: "At the risk of being thought callous, one must praise Mr Rolt for making death and disaster on the line most attractive reading."

The Listener really 'got it' too: "Intensely human story. A remarkable book."

It certainly is. And this history of Her Majesty's Railway Inspectorate, by two of its own men, honours the relatively small group of technical inspectors who produced those incredible accident reports. If you've never read one, you really should - their forensic examination of what happened and the skilfully-drawn, measured conclusions make powerful reading. No wonder Rolt was inspired. Dip into any one, but I'd recommend you look at the report by Lieutenant Colonel G.R.S. Wilson and Brigadier C.A. Langley into the fatal Doncaster derailment and bridge collision of 1951 (see page 4) which happened at just 25mph. The detail of the investigation into every aspect of the incident - including repeated recreated test runs - is a classic example of these superb reports. You can find many of them online at *The Railways Archive* (*https://www.railwaysarchive.co.uk*) - a superb resource, without which caption research for this book would have been ten times more difficult. I recommend following in my footsteps and using this book as a guide to which reports to delve into...I promise it will be time well spent!

We all ask and debate 'why' and 'what happened' as we pore over rail accidents. One of the first to appreciate these important questions was George Stephenson. He felt so strongly that accidents should be investigated and lessons learned that he wrote to the Board of Trade in 1841, urging rapid development of an investigative body to look into rail accidents in order to improve safety in this fast-growing new industry. That letter is reproduced in full on page 12. The Railway Inspectorate that it helped fully establish is 180 years old in 2020 and Her Majesty's Railway Inspectorate is now our second oldest great railway institution - only the British Transport Police as a national railway institution can trace its roots back further, to 1826, the year after the Stockton & Darlington Railway opened.

Co-author of this book and current Chief Inspector of Railways Ian Prosser CBE is surely unique in occupying a position effectively proposed by George Stephenson himself! Who else in the railway industry can make this claim?! The full story of how the Railway Inspectorate developed from 1840 is told in these pages with considerable expertise born of decades of front line HMRI experience,

Below: Railway Inspectors had been urging an end to gas lighting in passenger carriages since the Hawes Junction disaster of 1910. And yet, 30 years later, in 1947, with Nationalisation imminent, 10% of the 40,761 largely timber-built passenger carrying vehicles inherited by the new British Railways organisation on January 1 1948 was still gas lit. Of this total, 35,162 were available for traffic. This figure included rail motors. The sheer scale of the investment required to eliminate gas lighting is implied by this GWR carriage depot of the late 1920s/early 1930s. Collett 'bow enders' introduced in 1922 are prominent. A good number of much older clerestory roof coaches are also visible, especially the splendid example on the right. Over 100 coaches are stabled here. *CC Collection.*

RAILWAY AMALGAMATION—A PLEASANT STATE OF THINGS.

Passenger. "What's the Matter, Guard?"
Guard (with presence of Mind). "Oh, nothing particular, Sir. We've only run into an Excursion Train!"
Passenger. "But, good gracious! there's a Train just behind us, isn't there?"
Guard. "Yes, Sir! But a boy has gone down the line with a Signal; and it's very likely they'll see it!"

RAILWAY UNDERTAKING.

Touter. "Going by this Train, Sir?" *Passenger.* "'M? Eh? Yes."
Touter. "Allow me, then, to give you one of my Cards, Sir."

Media criticism about rail safety, or the power of big corporations, is by no means new. These mid 19th century cartoons from the popular press are significant because they capture the prevailing public, media and political mood of the mid-late 19th century.

Left: Captioned 'The Railway Juggernaut of 1845' this cartoon is a reaction to the 1840s 'Railway Mania'. A runaway speculative investment bubble saw 272 Acts of Parliament passed in 1846 alone, authorising an eye-watering 9,500 miles of new railway. One third of such railways were never built - but more than 5,000 miles of new railway were constructed in the 1840s.

Above: Safety was a major concern to a generation who had grown up with a galloping horse as the fastest mode of travel, for one person only, over short distances only. In RAILWAY UNDERTAKING, the top-hatted undertaker asks "Going by train, sir?" to which the distracted passenger replied: "M? Eh? Yes." The undertaker replies: "Allow me, then, to give you one of my cards, sir."

Left, Top: In RAILWAY AMALGAMATION a passenger asks: "What's the matter, guard?" and is told: "Oh, nothing particular sir. We've only run into an excursion train!" The passenger replies: "But good gracious, there's a train just behind us, isn't there?" to which the Guard responds: "Yes sir, but a boy has gone down the line with a signal and it's very likely they'll see it!" This was the path which led to the dreadful Armagh collision of June 12 1889 and the 'Lock Block and Brake' legislation passed as a direct consequence just 79 days later.

by Ian Prosser and David Keay. Ian and David tell the RI's story from investigating its first accident, which happened on August 7 1840, three days before it was formally established! Four passengers had been killed on the Hull & Selby Railway. Not every accident since then can either be covered or illustrated in this book, so the authors have chosen those that illustrate specific points, were major catastrophes which triggered major changes - or, with regard to the pictures, those which simply caught our eye! So, plenty of small and lesser known mishaps are also covered alongside 'the big ones' in words, photographs, trackplans and diagrams.

Some broad common themes run through the nearly two centuries of history in these pages. The three principal causes of death and disaster on the railway were:

- Mistakes by drivers.
- Errors by signalmen.
- Excessive speed.

The biggest problem for drivers was overlooking signals - especially crucial distants at caution, warning that the next stop signal was likely to be at danger. Drivers then came horribly to grief when it became impossible to stop before either colliding with another train, or derailing because of excessive speed.

Technology to support driver vigilance was slow to come in Britain - other than on the Great Western Railway. The GWR's Automatic Train Control (ATC) was a primitive, but highly effective precursor to the later BR Automatic Warning System (AWS) and then later still, the privatised railway's Train Protection Warning System (TPWS). Evidence for the life-saving success of GWR ATC is unequivocal and unarguable.

Between 1923 and 1947 (excluding the war years) there were just two fatal GWR train accidents, with a single passenger killed in each - an unparalleled safety record, largely as a consequence of ATC. Compare this with the series of fatal accidents on and around the LMS West Coast Main Line, which relied on driver vigilance alone. These included: Carlisle Canal (January 3 1931); Leighton Buzzard (March 22 1931, pages 70-73); Bletchley (October 13 1939, pages 77-78); Bourne End (September 30 1945, pages 79) and Polesworth (November 19 1951, pages 86-87). There were 56 deaths (and 227 injuries) in these five accidents alone, all of which could probably have been prevented by some form of GWR-style ATC.

That said, it would be wrong to believe that the LMS had 'sat on its hands' and done nothing. It had actively sought improvement via widespread installation of track circuits and block signalling control and also by replacing difficult-to-see semaphore signals (especially bad weather and at night) lit by paraffin, with brighter, electric colour light signals. Whilst this was indeed an improvement, accidents like those mentioned earlier at Bourne End (1945) and Polesworth (1951) still proved that without the further support of some kind of ATC, colour lights alone provided only marginal and inconsistent improvement. Even with colour light signalling, safe running still hung on the fragile thread of driver vigilance alone.

This very slow progress to assist drivers is surprising given that, in parallel, the proportion of accidents resulting from signalling errors was in steady decline, thanks to increasingly common track circuits and other applied technology. Track circuits made it impossible for the presence of a train on his 'patch' not to be clearly visible to the signalman, either by lights on his panel, or by instruments on the block shelf at eye level, above his levers.

In conjunction with the old faithful lever collar and further protection by Rule 55 (which required firemen to visit the signalbox and remind the signalman of his train's presence after a couple of minutes standing at a stop signal) Hawes Junction (1910)-style accidents declined steadily as a direct result. Of 29 fatal crashes between 1969 and 1989, only three were a consequence of signalling errors. Drivers, however, in the same period, were responsible for 15 accidents. This disparity of management approach is hard to fathom.

It is strange that drivers remained the 'poor relation' in terms of assistance by technology. As recently as December 4 1984, there was a fatal collision at Eccles (page 113) when a locomotive hauled Liverpool-Scarborough express collided heavily with the rear of an oil tanker train - on a route with no AWS. This was fully 32 years after Harrow, in 1952, when 112 people died and 340 were injured in the three train pile-up directly caused by lack of AWS. Given that it was a Labour Government which failed to make progress with AWS, there could be no suggestion that private profit was the obstacle.

Likewise with gas lighting. Fully 38 years after the terrible deaths by fire in gas-lit wooden coaches at Hawes Junction proved the horrific scale of the risk, fully one in ten of our coaches - more than 4,000 vehicles - were still gas-lit at Nationalisation in 1948. This despite the Hawes Junction RI report by Colonel Pringle, who said that our railways should be using electricity and not gas to light passenger coaches. Nearly two decades later, in 1928, roughly half the LMS and LNER passenger fleets were still gas lit, whilst on the SR it was one third. The GWR, significantly ahead in safety for drivers by providing ATC, lagged even more severely here: around two thirds of its carriages were still gas-lit as 1930 approached.

ATC was still the exception rather than the rule, other than on the GWR, so safe running continued to rely 100% on driver vigilance. Why did progress in driver assistance via ATC lag so far behind steady improvements offered to assist signalmen?

Maybe it was a hangover from the bizarre corporate belief of the 19th/early 20th century that effective, cheap measures like wooden lever collars costing pennies were not a good idea? These collars were a sturdy, bored wooden block which could be dropped over a signal lever, obstructing the release catch. It was a simple, but unmissable physical reminder to a busy signalman that a train was standing at the signal controlled by that lever, which couldn't be pulled without lifting the collar off. Had Signalman Sutton had a lever collar at Hawes Junction on that dark and fateful Christmas Eve morning in 1910, he might not have forgotten the two light engines standing at his down main line home signals. At this time, railway managers regarded lever collars as undermining concentration and encouraging complacency - they perversely believed that lever collars made it too easy for signalmen not to pay attention. It almost beggars belief now, but this cannot have been an objection rooted in cost: they really did believe that lever collars would compromise and not enhance safety!

Was the widespread slowness to adopt ATC another example of this fear of 'mollycoddling' drivers, who might thereby be encouraged to take their eye off the ball? The human cost was appalling. Of 1,093 train deaths in accidents between 1912 and 1952, 28% - nearly a third - might have been prevented by ATC. (see also pages 4-9)

That would have been 300 lives saved.

Another obstacle to safety investment was that railways actually had a pretty good general safety record, with only the occasional bad year. In 1842, there were 20m journeys but only one passenger death. Between 1916 and 1922, there were only eight passenger deaths a year on average - even in wartime.

There were no passenger deaths at all in 1925, leading even the RI's Sir John Pringle to comment that the case for ATC was "less urgent and that the expenditure involved could not be justified." Interestingly, in 1997 HMRI drew exactly the same conclusion about Automatic Train Protection. RI accident reports have frequently reflected this problem. For example, the 1968 fatal Hixon level crossing disaster (see pages 8-9) RI report notes: "There is no such thing as unbounded resources for every desirable reform."

Only a single passenger was killed on a train in 1930, with just 17 more in the next three years - to set this in context, this was roughly half of the death toll of 31 in the single terrible collision at Ladbroke Grove on October 5 1999. Did this relatively good safety record lull government and railway into a false sense of security? It certainly made it very difficult to justify heavy capital investment on ATC. This was especially the case in the 1920s/30s when railways were hit hard by massive (and unfair) competition from road haulage, plus a world economic slump - and with even aviation making its first inroads into the top-end of the express passenger market, too.

But there were also some very bad years. In 1928, for example, 48 passengers were killed in the worst peacetime year since 1906. Or 1947, the worst ever peacetime year for rail safety, with 88 passenger deaths.

The safety investment argument has often been muddied and politicised with the accusation (still levelled sometimes today) that the pre-1948 private companies focussed on profits rather than safety.

This argument collapses after 1948, when the Labour Government which had nationalised the utilities, created the National Health Service and removed the railways from private ownership in favour of state control, but failed to implement ATC nationwide and simply perpetuated private company policy.

In that worst ever year for peacetime rail safety - 1947 - when 88 lives were lost, none were on the GWR, where drivers had had ATC protection for many years. It could not have been more obvious that ATC saved lives and was urgently needed - yet all the new Labour Government did was make vague promises of reviews and 'consideration'. It kicked the can down the road. As late as 1986, the Railway Inspectorate's Major Freddie Rose was still urging widespread installation of AWS (as ATC had evolved into) in his annual report.

This was two years after the third major derailment on the 50mph very sharp curve through Morpeth station on the ECML - the others had been in 1926 and 1969. Here's another way in which the railway has changed beyond recognition, even since 1984: the 1984 Morpeth driver admitted in the investigation that on his way to work on the day of that crash he had downed a fifth of a gill of whisky, a pint of

Above: Other than on the GWR, where Automatic Train Control had been around since 1906, drivers had to rely entirely on their own vigilance to run safely by obeying fixed signals. But semaphore arms could be difficult to pick out (especially at night) and could come in confusing groupings. These are Lancashire & Yorkshire Railway electro-pneumatic signals at Southport Chapel Street's excursion platforms, on April 18 1951. Clearly identifying the signals beyond the signal box - which face both ways - demanded detailed knowledge and steely vigilance by drivers, even at slow speeds. *D. T. Greenwood/RAS.*

WYNNS

Facing Page and left: Level crossings of all kinds remain a major risk for railway and road/farm track/bridleway/footpath users alike. Amongst the worst fatal level crossing accidents on the electrified railway was this horrific collision at Hixon, on the West Coast Main Line between London and Manchester, on January 6 1968. The collision happened at 12.26pm, on an automatic half barrier level crossing installed the previous April, between the A51 and a former airfield, where Wynn's road hauliers were delivering a 120-tons electrical transformer. Hixon's barriers were triggered at 1,000 yards from the crossing, both by treadles and track circuits on the 85mph main line, meaning that a train arrived in a few seconds from the warning lights starting to flash. A 400-tons train would require just over 1,500 yards to stop. The Wynn's crew and its police escort were part-way over the crossing with their 162-tons, 32-wheel rig - which was more than 148ft long - moving at just 2mph, when the warning sequence started. The 11.30am 12-coach Manchester-Euston express, carrying 300 passengers, was just 1,000 yards away and bearing down on them at 85mph. On the curving approach to the crossing, the train driver would have seen the obstruction from around 400 yards - and he braked heavily. Leading Wynn's road tractor driver B.H. Groves saw the train approaching, yelled a warning and accelerated - as did, to his credit, rear tractor driver A.H. Illsley, despite this putting him into the path of the approaching express. They nearly succeeded - the train crashed into the rear 6-7 feet of the transporter, shearing the 'swan neck' securing the loaded deck to its rear wheels and flinging the 128-tons dead-weight transformer to its left, where it came to rest at the lineside. All three railwaymen in the locomotive died instantly as did eight passengers - and as terrible as this was, the report noted that had the train hit the transformer 'more squarely in the centre' the impact - and death toll - might have been much worse. Neither the police escort nor the Wynn's crew had stopped to telephone the signalman because they were unaware of the requirement to do so and failed to see the warning signs as they approached the crossing. While praising the drivers' valiant attempt to clear the crossing, the RI report also said that the leading tractor driver should have been aware of the requirement to stop and telephone the signalman and that he should have complied with this. But the real responsibility for the accident, said the RI report, was placed firmly on Wynns, BR, the police and the Ministry of Transport: the words 'failure', 'gravely at fault', 'wholly ignorant' and 'inept' are damning of all involved. The full report makes grim, but very educational reading - it's on *The Railway Archive.* It's sobering to note that in planning AHB crossings, both government and railway were seemingly obsessed with minimising the time the barriers were down (the safety margin) to deter cars zig-zagging round the barriers rather than considering the time an abnormal road load would take to clear a crossing. What made this especially damning was that Government, BR and Wynns all knew that an abnormal road load could not clear an AHB crossing safely in 24 seconds after a near carbon copy incident at Leominster on November 8 1966, when a huge road rig barely escaped a crossing before a train passed. *Alamy.*

Foster's lager and two cans of Tennent's lager - one of them extra strong! The RI's report clearly implied an entirely reasonable belief by the Inspector that the driver had dozed off.

Some of these themes continued into more recent history. Fatal accidents at Cowden (1994), Purley (1989), Southall (1997) and Ladbroke Grove (1999) were all driver errors - signals passed at danger. Clapham (1989) was a signalling technician's error. Potters Bar (2002) and Grayrigg (2007) were poor maintenance of points. Then there were more unpredictable accidents like Heck (2001) - a road vehicle incursion. Level crossings continued to cause concern, with major failings exposed by HMRI after the tragic deaths of teenagers Olivia Bazlinton and Charlotte Thompson at Elsenham, in 2005.

In the later 1990s, HMRI itself became the story, during its unhappy time as part of the Health & Safety Executive and that story is told candidly in these pages in detail, including Chief Inspector Alan Osborne 'blowing the whistle' in disgust and resigning in November 2003. This paved the way for Labour Secretary of State Alistair Darling to remove HMRI from HSE in 2006 and embed it in ORR where it remains in 2019. The authors are to be commended for their 'warts and all' approach to this turbulent time.

Reading this book, it is important to understand the incredibly challenging context in which the pioneering Railway Inspectors of the 19th century established their new role. The network was extended with breathtaking speed in the 1840s, when more than 250,000 navvies were furiously building our railways:

1841 1,556 miles of railway constructed
1845 2,746 miles
1850 6,621 miles
1890 20,073 miles
1914 23,701 miles

In the 19th century, Britain's railway companies were amongst the world's largest and most complex commercial concerns on the planet - consider them as having a similar transformative impact back then as Google and Facebook have had in the 21st century.

According to respected railway historian Terry Gourvish, the London & North Western Railway was capitalised at more than £29m as early as 1851. By 1894, that capitalisation had risen to £111,457,620, according to Bradshaw's Railway Manual that year. Of that, total £81,123,233 was in stocks and shares with the remainder in loans. Comparable figures were £82,726,271 for the GWR, £101,593,763 for the MR and £64,430.930 for the NER.

These enormous figures for the day give an indication of the major corporate power which the RI's handful of army engineer inspectors were ranged against. Britain's rail industry continued to grow rapidly in size, impact, power and complexity. By the time of the Grouping in 1923, there were more than 24,000 locomotives, 51,500 carriages, 722,639 goods wagons and nearly 700,000 staff, including 71,400 drivers and firemen and 24,000 guards.

Today's railway is much smaller in headcount and mileage - but use of the smaller 11,000-miles network is intense. On the last day of BR, around 800m people a year used trains: that figure has more than doubled in 2019, to 1.7bn. That creates a whole range of new risks for passengers and railway men and women (especially those on the track) before a train even runs, or anyone boards it.

In BR's days, there were 17 express trains a day from Euston, over the West Coast Main Line, to Manchester Piccadilly. In 2019, there are 47. The impact of such spectacular growth across the smaller network has been immense not only in terms of wear and tear, maintenance and renewal - but also in safety.

HMRI today, at ORR, is very different to the RI of the 19th/20th centuries and its own history very much mirrors that of the industry it has regulated for almost two centuries. This book is offered in gratitude, respect and tribute to successive generations of railway inspectors who strove to understand where it went wrong and how safety could be improved as a consequence.

It has been my privilege to work closely with an HMRI Chief Inspector and a former Deputy Chief Inspector, and their colleagues, in editing and illustrating this important book.

Nigel Harris,
Lincolnshire.

October 2019.

AUTHORS' PREFACE

IAN PROSSER CBE & Eur Ing DAVID KEAY

On August 10 2015, Her Majesty's Railway Inspectorate, part of the Office of Rail Regulation since April 1 2006, celebrated its 175th anniversary. As the Railway Inspectorate (the 'HM' prefix applied after the 125th anniversary in 1990), the organisation had been formed in 1840 'to provide for the due Supervision of Railways, for the Safety of the Public'. That is still its basic role today - HMRI acts as a watchdog for health and safety on behalf of the travelling public and the 175th anniversary year passed with no major railway mishap and happily, there have been no fatalities in train accidents for the 12th successive year in 2019.

Relatively soon after the introduction of railways into Britain in 1825, it became evident to Whitehall that professional advice was required to enable the Government to judge the various railway schemes brought before them for sanction. It therefore turned to the Board of Trade for this advice. The Board in turn looked to the Corps of Royal Engineers for a supply of suitably qualified methodical, disciplined men to act as their advisers as to how they should handle and manage this brand new transport technology.

Initially, an Inspector-General was appointed to examine and report on the projects submitted to the Board of Trade and he also had the duty, as an Inspector of Railways, to carefully examine all new lines after construction. Crucially, he also had the job of investigating and reporting to the Railway Commission on the causes of accidents. These three responsibilities - advice, inspection and investigation - have been

Above: The first step in the long march to the second-to-none passenger safety we enjoy today. In 1830, when stagecoach speeds were maybe 10mph at best, Stephenson's *Rocket* was capable of sustained running with hitherto undreamed of loads, at 30mph. Flat-earth prophets of doom warned that passengers would be unable to breathe and would suffocate! Although passengers had been carried on the Stockton & Darlington Railway from its opening in 1825, that was essentially a coal railway (See Chapter 1). People were effectively carried in goods wagons. The Liverpool & Manchester Railway, opened in 1830, was the world's first bespoke passenger railway and this was the design of its first carriages. *Experience* and *Traveller* were replicas built by the London Midland & Scottish Railway to celebrate the centenary of the LMR, in 1930. The only passenger vehicle builders in Britain in the late 1820s were stagecoach builders and these pioneer railway coaches comprise three dovetailed road stagecoach bodies, mounted on an underframe of about the size common for British goods traffic for another 150 years or so. Road traditions persisted: rooftop racks for luggage, with a precarious outdoor seat for the guard, reached via steps on the carriage end. Separate underframes carrying wooden (much later, steel) bodies persisted in UK carriage design until the BR Mk 1s of the 1950s. This resulted in many horrific deaths and injuries when, in accidents, coach bodies were detached, destroyed or the vehicles 'telescoped'. Then, of course, there was the fatally flammable combination of wooden carriages and gas lighting... *CC Collection.*

Above: With soaring demand, passenger carriages grew quickly in the 19th century, from four to six-wheels and finally bogie vehicles of up to 60ft in length, with timber-framed, panelled bodies mounted on separate steel underframes. The kinetic energy which rapidly dissipated in even relatively low speed collisions or derailments often led to complete destruction of the body, with a terrible human toll. On April 2 1937, recovery continues after a Southern Railway mishap at Battersea Park, London. This was long before the days of high-visibility protective clothing for railwaymen - although cloth caps, bowlers and trilbies were obligatory badges of status and role! There appears to be only one solitary hatless man on the right, between the track and bridge parapet opposite the carriage end! *Getty Images.*

CHIEF INSPECTORS/INSPECTOR GENERALS OF RAILWAYS, 1840-2019

Since its foundation in 1840, there have been just 25 Chief Inspectors, so this is a very elite and distinguished group. Until 1968, every Chief Inspector had been drawn from the ranks of Army engineers, whose expertise and discipline was second to none. Major Freddie Rose was the last ex-Army Chief Inspector to be recruited in 1968 and he served until 1982, when he stepped down from the top job, although he did not retire for another six years, until 1988.

The final Railway Inspector to be recruited from army ranks, in the Royal Engineers, was Major John Poyntz in 1989. In view of the long and proud tradition - and truly excellent service - rendered by no fewer than 18 ex-army Chief Inspectors, we invited Major Poyntz to write the Foreword (page 3) for this new history of the RI,which he served with distinction for 17 years. Even after retirement in 2006, John continued to consult with HMRI with regard to heritage railway safety matters, until 2012. John's Foreword is a fitting salute to all the army engineers who served the RI and HMRI before him.

The table below lists both final rank of the army CIs, and their rank at the time they led the RI.

1

2

3

4

5

6

7

8

9

10

11

12

13

14

15

16

17

18

19

20

21

22

23

24

25

CHIEF INSPECTORS/INSPECTOR GENERALS OF RAILWAYS, 1840-2019 (as at September 2019)

	Year joined Inspectorate	Appointed Chief Insp.	Left or retired	Years service
1: Lieutenant-Colonel (later General) Sir J. M. Frederic Smith	1840	1840	1841	1
2: Major-General (later General) Sir Charles W. Pasley	1842	1842	1846	4
3: Captain (later Field Marshal Sir John) Lintorn A. Simmons	1847	1850	1853	6
4: Captain (later Sir Henry) W.Tyler	1853	1871	1877	24
5: Colonel W. Yolland	1854	1877	1885	31
6: Colonel F. H.Rich	1861	1885	1891	30
7: Major-General C. S. Hutchinson	1867	1892	1895	28
8: Colonel Sir Francis Marindin	1877	1895	1900	23
9: Lieutenant-Colonel Sir H. Arthur Yorke	1891	1900	1913	22
10: Lieutenant-Colonel P. G. von Donop	1899	1913	1916	17
11: Colonel Sir John Pringle	1900	1916	1929	29
12: Lieutenant-Colonel Sir Alan H. L. Mount	1919	1929	1949	30
13: Lieutenant-Colonel G.R.S.Wilson	1935	1949	1958	23
14: Brigadier C. A. Langley	1946	1958	1963	17
15: Colonel D. McMullen	1948	1963	1968	20
16: Colonel J.R.H.Robertson	1958	1969	1973	15
17: Lieutenant-Colonel I. K. A. McNaughton	1962	1973	1982	20
18: Major C. F. Rose	1968	1982	1988	20
19: Robin J. Seymour	1988	1988	1993	5
20: Stan S.J.Robertson	1993	1993	1998	5
21: Vic Coleman	1990	1998	2001	11
22: Alan Osborne	2002	2002	2003	1
23: Allan Sefton	2001	2004	2006	5
24: Linda Williams	2004	2006	2008	4
25: Ian Prosser	2008	2008		11

Left: HMRI's collection of Inspectors reports, going right back to its first days in August 1840, are mostly still in traditional binders. Current Chief Inspector Ian Prosser CBE is keen to digitise this unique archive so they remain secure for future generations. *Clive Nicholls/HMRI-ORR.*

continued, largely unchanged, right up to the present day. This is a remarkable record of continuity and stability for a single organisation over 180 years. Right through the pre-Grouping period, the post-1922 'Big Four' era, the slightly less than half-century of British Railways experience from 1948 and finally the hectic churn of the post-1993 Railways Act second privatised period, the Railway Inspectorate has survived as a single entity with a consistent role. That is core to why the RI's 180th anniversary in 2020 is so very important.

It is important to distinguish between the responsibilities of the Inspectorate and the railways themselves, so far as safety is concerned. The railway companies are responsible, wholly and completely, for the safety of their passengers and workforce. It is for the railway companies to decide how trains should be operated, what equipment and materials should be used, what rules, procedures and methods should be adopted, how fast trains should run and what the staffing levels should be. The responsibility of the Inspectorate, so far as the safety of the operation of trains is concerned, has never been established by statute, but has rather developed and evolved as a consequence of the reports of successive 19th century Royal Commissions.

We would not wish to give the impression that all the improvements in railway safety have stemmed from the activities of the Inspectorate. That would be quite unfair to generations of railway managements and whilst it is true that in the 19th century the Inspectorate had to apply great pressure upon certain railway companies - including some of the largest and most powerful - in order to achieve desirable improvements, in the 20th century it was mainly the lack of finance, not a lack of willingness, which slowed progress. As a result, improvements have not always been made as rapidly as they ought to have been, particularly in providing more safety assistance to the driver. It is regrettable that successive railway managements and governments have dragged their collective feet, despite the Inspectorate's recommendations, especially regarding the fitting of Automatic Warning System.

Until the 1980s, Railway Inspecting Officers were appointed exclusively from army officers of the Corps of Royal Engineers. This practice began because when the Inspectorate was established in 1840, the Royal Engineers were really the only source of appropriately experienced and available engineers who also had the necessary degree of status and independence. The Institution of Civil Engineers had only just been formed but its members could not serve as Railway Inspectors because they were also heavily engaged in railway construction.

This practice continued and became a tradition, until the Royal Engineers ceased to have a Transportation Branch in 1965 on the formation of the Royal Corps of Transport and from that time the army's railway activities have very much declined. The practice of appointing Royal Engineers' officers as Railway Inspecting Officers has ceased because the supply of suitably experienced officers dried up. The Health & Safety at work Act 1974 had the effect of considerably enlarging the number of Railway Inspectors in the Inspectorate.

Virtually all rail/tramway accidents are reported to the Inspectorate. This enables a comprehensive watch to be kept on the general state of safety and on the development of trends, both good and bad.

Over the years, the Chief Inspector has issued an annual report on safety, setting out the year's results and trends, and giving details of the more important incidents together with his view of how the industry is performing and developing. These annual reports also contain valuable statistical data. Incidentally, the current Chief Inspector, Ian Prosser, is only the 25th individual to hold this prestigious and influential post since 1840 - another powerful indication of the RI's continuity and evolving presence in the world's oldest railway.

The story of the Inspectorate is a long relentless and sometimes elusive quest for improving safety in the running of passenger trains and trams in Britain - and occasionally Ireland, at least up to 1922. This story has been told in the context of the country's growing economic and industrial development of which the railways and tramways were, and still are, such an integral and important part.

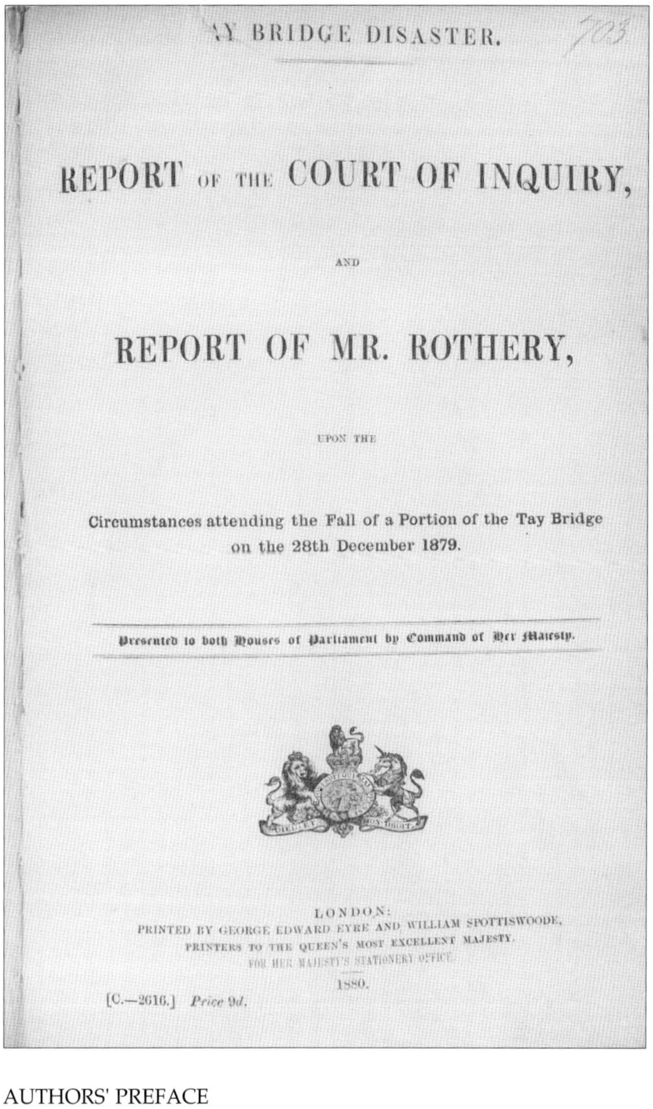

AY BRIDGE DISASTER. 703

REPORT OF THE COURT OF INQUIRY,

AND

REPORT OF MR. ROTHERY,

UPON THE

Circumstances attending the Fall of a Portion of the Tay Bridge on the 28th December 1879.

Presented to both Houses of Parliament by Command of Her Majesty.

LONDON:
PRINTED BY GEORGE EDWARD EYRE AND WILLIAM SPOTTISWOODE,
PRINTERS TO THE QUEEN'S MOST EXCELLENT MAJESTY.
FOR HER MAJESTY'S STATIONERY OFFICE.
1880.

[C.—2616.] Price 9d.

Left: Every rail accident investigated by the Railway Inspectorate led to a formal report: they make compelling reading. They detail the circumstances, sequence of events and an explanation of an accident, complete with the beautiful diagrams and artwork common before widespread use of photography. Some railway accidents were so terrible that their names will forever carry a terrible resonance: Armagh, Quintinshill, Hawes Junction, Harrow & Wealdstone and Ladbroke Grove, for example. One of the 19th century's most notorious catastrophes was the 1879 collapse, in a dreadful overnight storm, of the so-called 'high girders' of Thomas Bouch's Tay bridge - with a passenger train encased within them, which plunged into the river. This is the title page of the RI report, published by Her Majesty's (that's HM Queen Victoria) Stationery Office and priced at 9d! (4p) *Clive Nicholls/HMRI-ORR.*

Right: A picture which graphically illustrates the inherent perils of separate carriage bodies and underframes. This is the aftermath of the LMS West Coast Main Line crash at Bourne End, near Hemel Hempstead, in Hertfordshire, on September 30 1945. The 15-coach 4.23pm Perth-Euston express, hauled by 'Royal Scot', 4-6-0 No. 6157 *The Royal Artilleryman*, derailed after failing to slow down as required by fixed signals, and then taking 15mph points from fast to slow lines at 60mph. The upturned carriage underframe nearest the camera and the reared-up coach body sheared from its chassis imply their own stories of human misery - 43 lives were lost here. The driver had a reputation for conscientiousness, was highly experienced and had read a notice about the diversion over the 15mph crossover. Did he doze off - or was he simply tired and 'on autopilot' on the fast line after working for 26 days continuously, because of post-war staff shortages? Such fatigue is now much better understood and guarded against - also the Automatic Warning System (not fitted here at the time) would almost certainly have prevented this disaster. The crowd of men, women and children who are very close to the wreckage - including, in the centre, a schoolboy in cap! - appear to be a crowd of local 'gawpers'!
C.R.L. Coles/Rail Archive Stephenson.

Above: All railway crashes have played their part in developing rail safety, as lessons were learned and consequent RI recommendations hopefully implemented - although some were only acted on belatedly after several similar accidents claimed lives. Some accidents were so horrific that they became tragic milestones. The appalling three-train Quinstinshill-style collision in fog on the West Coast Main Line at Harrow & Wealdstone on October 8 1952 is one such crash. The driver of a southbound express ran past a distant signal at caution and then passed two stop signals at danger before colliding at speed with a suburban train standing in the platform. Within seconds, a double headed down express crashed into the wreckage at speed. The full story is in Chapter 6 (pages 90-95). A mixture of then-new all-steel BR Mk 1 and older LMS vehicles were involved and 112 people were killed. There were also 340 injuries, 88 of them serious. Almost lost in the sprawling wreckage, on the right of the picture, is one of the Stanier express locomotive tenders. *Getty Images.*

Facing page lower: Train crashes have always been big news, even in the pre-TV age, when photographers in biplanes secured images such as this for newspapers and cinema newsreels. This was the scene at Polesworth following the high speed (65-70mph) derailment of the 8.30am Euston-Liverpool express on July 21 1947. Five lives were lost; four in the crash and one later, in hospital. There were also 19 serious and 45 minor injuries. The engine crew were both uninjured and the driver went forward to protect his train, in accordance with his training and the rulebook. Fourteen coaches were derailed and while the first two were very badly damaged, the remaining vehicles fared reasonably well and although there was end damage to all, they did not 'telescope.' All four lines were blocked but the alert Polesworth signalman limited the disaster: worried that the down express train had not passed his box well after he expected it to do so, he stopped an up express which would otherwise have ploughed into the wreckage. A goods train approaching on the down slow was also stopped in time by the rapid action of an off-duty fireman travelling in the last coach. The derailed streamlined Stanier 'Pacific' is lying on its right side at the top of the picture: it travelled 400 yards after derailing. *Getty Images.*

Right: The horizontal diamond shaped white plate mid-way between the signal arms on the post (often known as a 'doll') indicates that these signals are protected by a track circuit which gave drivers an audible and visual indication as to the distant signal aspect in particular. On passing a distant at caution, the hooter and 'sunflower' display that suddenly appeared in front of him warned a driver to 'ease up' in readiness for the next signal being red. If he failed to cancel the warning, the train brakes were applied. Lack of AWS played a major part in the horrific Harrow & Wealdstone three-train collision (see pages 90-95) of October 8 1952, when 112 people died in the morning fog. Some routes were still not covered by AWS even as late as the 1980s. (see the Eccles rear-end collision of December 4 1984) Where there was no AWS to assist, unfailing signal sighting by an alert and vigilant driver was fundamental to ensure safety. In July 1942, the lampman at Ashton, Preston cleans the down main semaphore aspect glasses so that the oil lamp behind can shine clearly through the green or red glasses on this stop signal. *D.T. Greenwood/RAS.*

Chapter 1
THE BEGINNINGS 1825-1850

Above: Photography (albeit rather complex) became commercially available in 1839, widely accepted as the birth year of a practical photographic process. It was the work of Louis Daguerre, whose sharp, finely detailed 'Daguerrotype' pictures were the result of a few minutes of exposure in the camera. Henry Fox Talbot refined this metallic process in 1840, his paper-based process requiring much shorter exposures. This was, however, fully 15 years after the opening of the Stockton & Darlington Railway (September 27 1825) and a decade after the Liverpool & Manchester's opening (September 15 1830). The demonstration line at County Durtham's Living Museum of the North, combined with engineer Mike Satow's 1975 working replica of Stepenson's *Locomotion* has however enabled us to enjoy a visual flavour of the SDR's impact. On August 26 1983, the *Locomotion* replica rounds the curves at Beamish, with four replica chauldrons. *Nigel Harris.*

Facing page, top: *Locomotion* steams past with its short, joggling train of chauldrons, whose image remarkably remained familiar in the UK coalfields for another 175 years. The late 20th century BR 33-ton capacity HAA four-wheel merry go-round power station coal wagons were effectively bigger, air-braked steel versions of the NE chauldron. HAAs started running in 1966 and 11,000 were built at Darlington, Shildon and Ashford. All the the world's railways trace their DNA back to the SDR. *Nigel Harris.*

Facing page, lower: To an industrialising world accustomed to horsepower, canals and rutted roads, *Locomotion* must have seemed the wonder of the age. The *Locomotion* replica looks completely at home in the Beamish museum mine. But mechanised rail movement, pressurised steam and only rudimentary brakes brought risks, danger - and accidents. Fifteen years later, in 1841, George Stephenson urged the Board of Trade to take action - and this led to the formation of the Railway Inspectorate (see page 18). *Nigel Harris*

Railways had existed in Britain for many years in primitive forms, before the opening of the Stockton & Darlington Railway in 1825. This was especially true in colliery areas where wagon ways had been common for probably two centuries or more and as long ago as 1758 an Act of Parliament had been passed authorising the construction of a railway from Middleton to Leeds. The Surrey Iron Railway obtained its Act in 1801 authorising the construction of a railway from Wandsworth to Croydon, for the conveyance of coals, corn, merchandise and commodities, and worked by horses. The promoters had also originally envisaged a railway between London and Portsmouth.

Although early railways used horse traction, steam engines were already in existence. The inventor of a practical steam engine is generally held to have been James Watt, an instrument maker of Glasgow, who patented his invention in 1769, but this was a stationary engine and steam's application to railways was slow and confined to a few colliery lines. The development of the steam locomotive, which was to revolutionise not only 19th century Britain but also the rest of the world, was yet to come, in 1804; with Richard Trevithick's *Pen-y-Darren* locomotive the stage was set. The means were available and the money too. All that was needed was the catalyst.

There is some debate as to whether the passenger railway proper commenced in 1825 with the opening of the Stockton & Darlington Railway (SDR) or in 1830 with the Liverpool & Manchester. In its conception, the Stockton & Darlington was little more than a colliery railway, to be worked by horses, but even before it was opened the railway company obtained parliamentary powers to use 'locomotive or movable engines', thanks to the intervention of George Stephenson, who became Engineer to the Railway. The line opened on September 27 1825, when a procession travelled over the route, led by the company's only steam locomotive, George Stephenson's now famous

Facsimile of Letter from George Stephenson.

To the
Right Honble H. Labouchere,
President of the Board of Trade.

Sir,

Since my examination before the select committee on Railways I see the difficulties you have to contend with, from the opposing members to your Bill in bringing forward a measure for the management and better regulation of Railways. I am quite sure that some interference on the part of Government is much wanted. Perhaps I ought to be the last man to admit this (the whole system of Railways, and Locomotive Engines having been brought out by my exertions) but when I see so many young Engineers, and such a variety of notions, I am convinced that some system should be laid down, to prevent wild, and visionary schemes, being tried, at the great danger of injury or loss of life to the public. I consider it right that every talented man should be at liberty to make improvements, but that the supposed improvements should be duly considered by proper judges. Then the question follows, from the opponents to the Bill, who are those judges to be? I beg to lay before you my views on this point.

Suppose any Engineer has any improved plan for the better working of Railways to propose, he should submit his plan to the Engineer belonging to the Board of Trade, but before that Engineer should give his decision as to the utility of the scheme, he should have full power to call together the chief Engineers of the principal Railways of the Kingdom, and after the subject has been duly discussed, votes should be taken for and against the measure: the discussion should be laid before the Board of Trade, accompanied with the observations of the government Engineer, and if approved of should be then placed into his hands to carry out.

I should propose for the consideration of the different Engineers that the speed of Locomotives should not exceed forty miles per hour on the most favourable Lines, excepting on special occasions: curved Lines to diminish in velocity according to the radius. I am quite aware that this cannot be carried out to any great nicety, but still it would be a check upon the Drivers. Collateral Lines require government consideration is a very strong point of view.

Uniformity of signals is another desirable point.

As several persons are now turning their attention to the construction of self acting breaks, it will soon appear that great benefit and safety to travelling will be found by their adoption. In the mean time no train should be allowed to travel which has not two breaksmen and four coaches in each train should be provided with breaks to allow for contingencies. It is my opinion that no contrivance can be found out by which the breaks can be dispensed with.

Six wheeled Engines and carriages are much safer and more comfortable to the travellers than four; any person riding one hundred yards upon an engine or coach constructed upon this plan would discover the difference. The rim of all Railway wheels ought to be made the same width, and the axle trees for all coaches of a strength approved of by the Engineers, both wheels, springs, and axles should bear the government stamp, to being made of the best materials, as every practicable means ought to be made use of in order to have these made of the best iron.

All disputes between Railway Companies should be decided by the Board of Trade.

It appears to me that the above suggestions might be carried out with success, without interfering injuriously with Raily property. I hope that you will not consider that I am intruding by sending you these observations.

I am, Sir,
Your Most Obt. Servant,

(Sgd.) Geo. Stephenson.

Tapton House,
nr. Chesterfield.

March 31st, 1841.

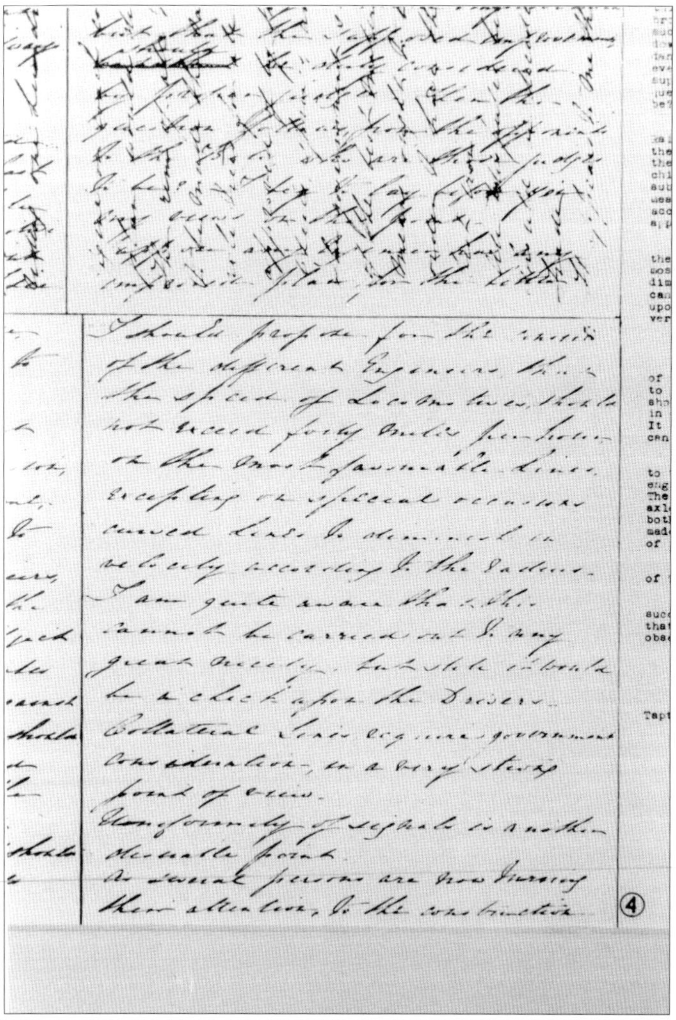

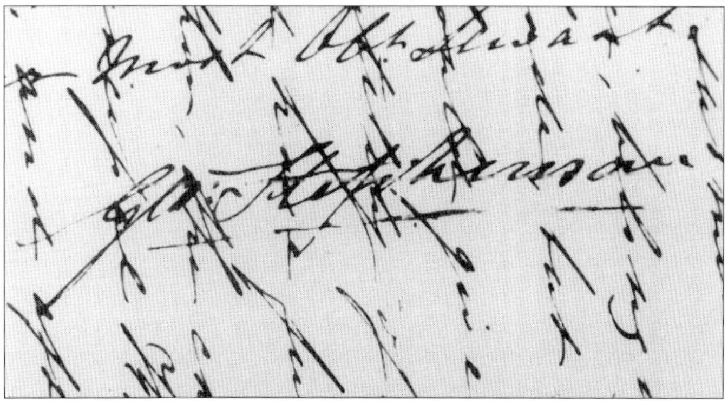

Facing page: Mechanised transport, high pressure boilers and increasing traffic, of increasing weight and faster speeds, all brought risks and mishaps in their wake and in 1841 George Stephenson wrote this letter to the Board of Trade urging the establishment of what became the Railway Inspectorate. It is still proudly displayed on the wall at today's ORR. *Clive Nicholls/HMRI-ORR.*

Left: Stephenson's original letter, which was partly conventionally written and partly cross-written. This was a common 19th century practice whereby a page would be rotated through 90 degrees and a second page effectively written over the first. This was intended to minimise postal charges, which were seen as expensive - so, nothing new there then! Combined with Stephenson's hand writing this makes the letter very difficult to read. *Clive Nicholls/HMRI-ORR.*

Left lower: George Stephenson's signature on his letter to the Board of Trade, of March 31 1841, which prompted formation of the Railway Inspectorate. *Clive Nicholls/ORR-HMRI.*

Locomotion No 1. The SDR owned the tracks and anyone who paid the SDR money could operate steam trains or horse drawn wagons. The separation of track and train is not a recent development! There was no timetable or central control and trains ran when required, resulting in fights between rival operators. In 1833, the SDR became the sole train operator and a signalling system was established to prevent collisions. However, by then a much greater railway had entered the story.

With the massive growth of the Lancashire cotton industry, the two important towns of Liverpool and Manchester were developing rapidly and the need for better transport facilities between them was becoming more and more pressing. After much hard work and persistence - and despite fierce opposition from landowners and canal interests - the promoters of the Liverpool & Manchester Railway obtained their Act in 1826. In order to decide upon the form of traction to be employed, a public competition was held at Rainhill in 1829, in which five steam locomotives competed. Eight conditions were prescribed for the locomotive trials, these included that the maximum weight must not exceed six tons, all wheels must be sprung and the cost had to be less than £550. To qualify for first place the locomotive had to reach 10mph. *Rocket*, manufactured by Robert Stephenson, the son of George was the winner; a world-changing event which established the steam locomotive as the best means of haulage, a position it retained for over a century. *Rocket* brought together a number of important innovations, the most important being the multi-tube boiler design, a design feature that continued in principle in all subsequent locomotives. The success of the Liverpool & Manchester was assured.

The line opened with great pageantry on September 15 1830 and was so successful that businessmen and promoters all over the country began to develop their own schemes. Plans already being developed received a great boost and there was an explosion of interest, as demonstrated by the number of railway bills that were introduced into Parliament in the 1830s - including amendments to existing Acts:

1831	15	**1836**	21
1832	11	**1837**	64
1833	12	**1838**	21
1834	16	**1839**	28
1835	21		

The number of Acts passed for new railways:

1831	5	**1836**	29
1832	4	**1837**	15
1833	5	**1838**	2
1834	5	**1839**	1
1835	8		

Among the more famous companies authorised in this period were:

1831	Sheffield & Manchester
1833	Grand Junction - London & Birmingham
1834	London & Southampton
1835	Great Western
1836	Eastern Counties
	Manchester & Leeds
	Midland Counties
	North Midland
	South Eastern
1837	London & Brighton - Manchester & Birmingham
1838	Edinburgh & Glasgow

Even though these were the great days of *laissez faire*, when it was felt that businessmen should be left alone to create wealth and not be fettered by laws and regulations, it was also, maybe surprisingly, a period when Parliament was very active in promoting social improvements, after the passing of the great Reform Bill in 1832. Lord Althorp introduced his Factory Act in 1833, which provided for paid inspectors to be appointed to see that the law was carried out. This provided a clear precedent for the subsequent formation of the Railway Inspectorate. Lord Ashby, who later became the Earl of Shaftesbury, devoted his long life to the improvement of the conditions of his less fortunate countrymen, resulting in Acts to prohibit the employment of children as chimney sweeps, and the employment of children less than 13 years of age - and women - in mines. The Municipal Corporations Act of 1835 placed the administration of towns on a proper footing and introduced a single type of town council, elected by male ratepayers. It was not surprising that the rapidly-developing railway system soon attracted parliamentary attention and it was felt that some control over the working of the railways was necessary in the public interest.

A Parliamentary Select Committee was appointed in 1839 to consider this question. There was a lively public debate between the great engineers of the day, George Stephenson in one corner fighting for Government oversight of new railways and Isambard Kingdom Brunel in the other corner fighting for no Government intervention. George Stephenson strongly supported the Government and recommended that all new works should be submitted to the Board of

Trade for their approval so as to 'prevent wild and visionary schemes being tried at the great danger of injury or loss of life to the public'. His original letter of March 31 1841, addressed to the President of the Board of Trade is in the Inspectorate archives.

Isambard Kingdom Brunel, the brilliant engineer of the Great Western Railway unsuprisingly opposed any form of Government interference, however, and went so far as to say that he preferred enginemen who could neither read nor write, as he did not consider they obtained the slightest knowledge of instructions by reading them!

The recommendations of the Select Committee led to the historic and very important Regulation of Railways Act of 1840. This short Act came into force on August 10 1840. It's opening words were:

'Whereas it is expedient for the Safety of the Public to provide for the due supervision of the railways ...'

It contained the following principal provisions:

1. No railway may be opened for the public conveyance of goods or passengers without a month's notice being given (Sec 1)
2. Returns of traffic, charges, and accidents causing personal injury are to be made by railway companies (Sec 3)
3. The Board of Trade may appoint persons to inspect railways (Sec 5)
4. Copies of railway bye laws are to be laid before the Board of Trade (Sec 7)
5. Railway servants found drunk on duty, or guilty of misconduct which might cause injury or obstruction, are liable to a fine or imprisonment (Sec 13)
6. Anyone obstructing trains or endangering safety is liable to imprisonment (Sec 15)

The Railway Inspectorate was thereby born, with powers to inspect any railway. The Inspectors were drawn from the Corps of Royal Engineers, a practice which continued until the 1980s. (see page 12) The first Inspector General of Railways was Lt. Col Sir J. M. Frederic Smith, and two other officers were appointed to assist him Lt. Col R. Thomson and Captain S. C. Melhuish. Sir Frederic Smith held office only until the following year, when he resigned to take up the position of Director at the School of Military Engineering, Chatham. Frederic Smith had been commissioned in the Royal Engineers in 1805 and was a veteran of many military campaigns. In 1845, he was appointed to the gauge commission reporting to Parliament on the practicality of a uniform track gauge throughout Britain. In addition to his role of Commandant at Chatham he was the elected parliamentary member for the town from 1857 - 1868.

The Inspectorate had no powers other than to inspect railways and they could do nothing if they found that a new railway had not, for instance, been built to a standard that would allow passengers to be carried safely, other than to use their powers of persuasion. A similar situation arose when unsafe working practices in the operation of railways were found. The Inspecting Officers had no powers to insist on changes, nor had they any powers to inquire into accidents, but they did carry out such inquiries without any authority, and their reports lay bare the very primitive operating methods of the day.

This was a matter of considerable importance by 1841 by which time there were no fewer than 1,556 miles of railway open and more than 20 million passengers were carried that year. After the mini railway mania of the middle 1830s, the promotion of new lines had subsided somewhat and in 1840, for the first time for several years, no new railway was authorised, and only one was authorised in 1841. There was a feeling that the railway map was reaching its peak and that the Inspecting Officers' duties would be mainly concerned with

Above: Railways developed quickly and within five years of the SDR opening locomotives looked very different indeed. Winner of the Rainhill Trials to find a locomotive for the opening of the Liverpool Manchester Railway on September 15 1830 was Stephenson's legendary *Rocket*. Its combination of a multi-tubular boiler, with very large heating surfaces and a blastpipe through which exhaust from the cylinders 'exhausted' in the smokebox to draw the fire through the tubes, enabled it to steam very well, allowing it to run at sustained speeds of up to 30mph. This *Rocket* replica was built by the London Midland & Scottish Railway (LMS) for the LMR's centenary in 1930. This shows *Rocket* in its original form: it's cylinders were later lowered to a near horizontal position, which not only lowered the centre of gravity, but also gave much smoother running. *Getty Images*.

Above: *Rocket* still hogs the limelight even today, but Stephenson's *Northumbrian*, built only a year after *Rocket* and also used on the LMR's opening day, shows the lightning speed of locomotive development. It was the last of Stephenson's *Rocket*-style 0-2-2s, but it was the first locomotive to have its firebox incorporated in the boiler and having a smokebox the same diameter as its barrel. It was therefore the world's first conventional locomotive boiler of the style which survived, albeit in superheated and in more sophisticated form, to No. 92220 *Evening Star*, the last steam locomotive built for British Railways, at Swindon, in 1960. *Northumbrian* is pictured here on September 14 1930, during the LMS Centenary celebrations for the LMR. *Rocket's* chimney is just visible on the left. Note *Northumbrian's* much less sharply inclined cylinders. This is how *Rocket* was subsequently modified. *Getty Images.*

accidents, and with making recommendations to improve safety.

The first railway accident which had the distinction of being investigated by the Railway Inspectorate occurred on August 7 1840, three days before the Inspectorate was formally established. Lt. Col Sir Frederick Smith inquired into the accident, which happened on the Hull & Selby Railway near Howden. A heavy casting which had been loaded on a wagon marshalled next to the engine fell off and derailed the following coaches. Four passengers were killed.

A month later, the up morning train of the North Midland Railway was derailed between South Wingfield and Ambergate, killing two passengers. The very next day a train overtook and collided with a train in front at Old Ford, near Bow, on the Eastern Counties Railway, killing a passenger. The driver was sacked and the Inspector, Lt. Col Thomson, recommended that there should be a school for enginemen; that there should be half-an-hour between trains starting and that mileposts should be erected at the lineside so that passengers could assess the speed of the train and complain to the railway company if they thought that it was excessive! If collisions were to be avoided in the absence of a signalling system it was essential firstly that trains ran to time and secondly that there was a sufficient interval of time between trains starting their journeys.

A collision on November 11 1840 in which two more passengers were killed occurred on the York & North Midland Railway at Taylor's Junction (also known as South Milford Junction) and added to the public alarm already being felt at the frequency of railway accidents. The 6.04pm passenger train from Leeds to York and Hull, via Woodlesford, Castleford and Burton Salmon was standing in the station at Taylor's Junction when it was run into by a following luggage train. Sir Frederic Smith recommended that no train should be allowed to pass or leave a station within 10 minutes of the preceding train, during which time a red flag or lamp should be displayed. There were no fixed signals at Taylor's Junction and the Inspector-General called for a statement from all railway companies showing which stations were provided with revolving signal lamps placed on posts. It transpired that the passenger train did not have a tail lamp and that the breaksman (the spelling 'brake' did not come into general usage until late in the 19th century) had ridden upon the top of the fourth vehicle and had shown his red handlamp towards the rear. Once again the importance of trains running to time was stressed.

When Captain Melhuish inspected the Birmingham & Gloucester Railway he discovered that down trains used Birmingham time whilst the up trains used Cheltenham time and that the clocks of those two towns varied by between 10 and 15 minutes. He recommended that all lines of railway leading to London should adopt London time, under the title of 'railway time'. This led quickly to the adoption of a standard time throughout the country and is just one way in which the railways not so much influenced modern Britain, as created it.

There were two other interesting features of note in 1840. Smoking was not allowed anywhere in trains or on railway premises and intoxication and trespass were a widespread problem, causing many deaths. Inebriated passengers often fell out of trains, or crossed the railway without taking care and were knocked down. Trespassers had not yet learned that a railway train is a very effective killer.

The Inspector-General soon became aware that the powers

conferred upon him by the 1840 Act were insufficient to enable him to supervise the operation of railways properly. In 1841 he reported on the measures which he thought were necessary, stating that whilst Government should not attempt to regulate matters of detail and take the management of the railways out of the hands of the directors and their officers, it was necessary that the Government should have the power of enforcing the observance of all precautions and regulations approved by experience and were obviously conducive to the public safety. He also said, in relation to the powers in the 1840 Act, that it was essential to prevent a new railway from opening if it was found to be unsafe or unsatisfactory.

As a result of this report and pressure from George Stephenson, Mr Gladstone, the newly-appointed vice-president of the Board of Trade, introduced another Bill, which became law on June 30 1842 and was entitled 'An Act for the better Regulation of Railways and for the Conveyance of Troops'. It amended most of the provisions of the 1840 Act and after just two years of experience it gave the Railway Inspectorate greater powers, which were to be largely unchanged for the next 30 years or so. In particular, Section 6 gave the Board of Trade power to postpone the opening of a new line if an Inspector reported that the opening 'would be attended with danger to the public using the same' by virtue of the works being incomplete, or the establishment for working the railway being insufficient. Section 8 gave the Board of Trade the power to demand returns of serious accidents whether causing personal injury or not. The Act also made provision for safety at level crossings, requiring the gates to be normally placed across the road, rather than across the railway, except where the Board of Trade authorised otherwise. These were important milestone powers for the Inspectorate.

The 1842 Regulation of Railways Act did not empower the Inspectors to inquire into railway accidents but to their great credit they continued to do so. It also contained no provisions for the recommendations of the Inspectors, following inquiries into accidents, to be enforced. The Government felt that such powers would take management of the railways out of the hands of the directors and place the responsibility for safety of operation fairly and squarely upon the Inspectorate and the Board of Trade. This was felt to be an unwarrantable interference in the running of the railways and a dangerous step for the Government to take, a point of view that has prevailed until the present day (except for the Lock, Block and Brake regulations in 1889 and the Railway Safety Regulations in 1999, that mandated the Train Protection and Warning System TPWS) and which has stood the test of time. This principle, that the railway companies should bear the full responsibility for the safety of operation of their trains, has been questioned frequently over the years but has always prevailed.

A large number of passengers were continually injured through such causes as slipping when getting in and out of trains owing to the lack of proper foot-boards, and falling out of 3rd class carriages, some of which were little more than open trucks.

Sir Frederic Smith severely criticised the design of these carriages in his report on a derailment in Sonning Cutting on December 24 1841. On this occasion, eight passengers were killed and 17 were injured when a mixed train of two 3rd class carriages and 17 wagons derailed at night after a bad bank slip in the cutting. Most of those killed or injured were workers returning home for Christmas having worked on the construction of the new Houses of Parliament. Sir Frederic pointed out that not only were the 3rd-class passengers liable to be thrown out of their carriages - as happened on this occasion - but in winter they were exposed to all the rigours of the climate on journeys lasting as long as 12 hours. As a result of this and similar criticisms in other reports a watershed clause was inserted in the Railway Regulation Act of 1844.

It stipulated that every railway company was obliged by law to run one train per day in each direction at a cost of not more than one penny per mile for the poorer class of traveller, in carriages provided with seats and properly protected from the weather, and designed to the satisfaction of the Board of Trade. These trains became known as 'Parliamentary trains' and they continued in use until 1883. Incredibly, the term nevertheless lingered in railway language for another century, remaining in use in some places even today.

Major General (later General) Sir Charles Pasley FRS was appointed as Inspector General in 1842. He had been commissioned in the Royal Engineers in 1798 and had an illustrious military career

Above: By 1838, locomotives had adopted the layout and outline they retained until *Evening Star* in 1960. This is the LMR's famous 0-4-2 *Lion*, built in 1838, on September 2 1930 in advance of the LMR centenary celebrations by the LMS, staged between September 12 and 20. The train comprises three replica first class coaches and three open third class vehicles. *Lion* famously won the starring role in the much-loved 1953 Ealing Comedy, *The Titfield Thunderbolt*. Getty Images.

Above: Given that workable photography only dated from around 1840, this 1844 portrait says a great deal about the mood, feel and appearance of the railway and its managers that the Railway Inspectorate was created to work with. The Great Western Railway's Daniel Gooch, then aged 28, stands alongside a model of his first design of locomotive - a Brunel broad gauge (7ft ¼in) 'Firefly' 2-2-2 tender engine. The model in this photograph survives in the National Railway Museum Collection. *Elton Collection/Ironbridge Gorge Museum Trust.*

having also started the School of Military Engineering. Sir Charles retired in 1846.

It is quite likely that attitudes in 1842 were influenced by a continuing reduction in the number of accidents. In the 20 million passenger journeys taken that year, only one passenger was killed that year while travelling by train. The railway companies were learning the importance of punctuality and fixed signals (mechanical signals in fixed locations) were steadily coming into use.

Stronger carriages were being built and there was a general adoption of the use of buffer springs to help to absorb impact in the event of a collision - crashworthiness is not new!

Provided that trains could be guaranteed to run on time and assuming that all the trains that ran were in the timetable, there would have been little need for a signalling system, but it was becoming very obvious that these two conditions were unattainable in practice. Locomotives were not sufficiently reliable and were sometimes overloaded; also, they broke down in mid-section between stations, or lost time in running. The safety system that developed consisted of two essential parts: first, there was the principle that a train should not be allowed to pass a station until the previous train had had sufficient time to get well clear and second, the principle that if a train broke down in mid-section the guard was to go back along the line at once showing a danger signal, such as a red flag or lamp, to warn the driver of a following train of the blocked line.

Primitive signals began to be erected at stations for the guidance of drivers - and staff were employed to operate them. After a train had passed, the signal was operated to show danger for a period of time, possibly five or ten minutes, then the danger signal was replaced by one showing 'all clear'. At some stations, on some lines, a caution signal was displayed for a fixed period of time before the 'all clear' was given. There were no fixed signals, a policeman gave the driver the different indications by means of hand signals. These policemen were properly sworn-in constables and were required to investigate accidents. They wore top hats and swallow-tail coats, and even though they were to be replaced by signalmen before many years had passed, their name still lives on today in the form of 'bobby', a term frequently still used by drivers when referring to signalmen. Another expression still used by drivers, which dates back to those early days, is the word 'board', used to describe a semaphore signal. Early signals were often wooden boards, which were turned to face the driver to indicate 'danger', and were turned end-on for 'all clear', which was sometimes indicated by a disc. These disc and crossbar signals were very popular for a time but fell out of general use over a century ago.

Detonators, which are small explosive devices clipped to the rail-head in an emergency and exploded by the wheels of a locomotive passing over them, were invented in 1841, and rapidly came into use to enable guards of broken-down trains to give an extra warning to drivers of following trains. They were especially useful in fog, when the red light from the guard's handlamp was easily missed by a driver peering ahead into the gloom. Fuse signals were also used from an early date. They were similar to roman candle fireworks and were placed on the track to indicate that a train had been stopped there in mid-section and had since moved on but may be somewhere just in front. Incredibly, 'dets' are still in use in 2019 as this book goes to press!

The first half of the 1840s was a period of consolidation. In 1841 there were 1,556 miles of railway open for traffic and 20.4 million passengers were carried that year. By the beginning of 1845 the mileage open had increased to 2,240, and passengers carried had risen to 30 million. These were small increases, compared with what was to follow. Only 10 Acts were passed for new railways in the first half of the 1840s and the Inspectors were only examining about 200 miles of new railway each year, prior to their opening.

So far as safety was concerned, in 1843 only one passenger was killed in a train accident (a collision at Barnsley on the North Midland Railway in fog; he was the only passenger on the train), whilst six were killed in 1844 in four separate accidents. On September 2 that year it is recorded that no fewer than 5,600 passengers travelled from Sheffield to Hull in four excursion trains. There was a minor collision between two of the trains and a passenger sitting outside one of the carriages was thrown off and killed. All the passengers had been put inside the carriages before the trains left Sheffield but some had climbed out on the journey to escape the crush.

There were two accidents in 1844-45 which were forerunners of mishaps which still happen today. A train ran into a cow on the line at Ryton on the Newcastle & Carlisle Railway; the engine was thrown down an embankment and the driver was killed. Nearly a century and a half later, in 1984, a cow caused the derailment of a push-pull passenger train (in 'push' mode) at Polmont on the Edinburgh to Glasgow line and 13 passengers were killed). A passenger was killed in another accident when an engine which was going to assist a train that had broken down ran into it, a type of accident also not unknown in the 1980s.

The electric telegraph was coming into widespread use by the mid-1840s as a means of giving information about the running of trains. It was first brought into use on the Blackwall Railway and on the Great Western between Paddington and Slough, but by 1845 it was in use on the whole of the London & South Western Railway and the South Eastern Railway, on most of the London & Birmingham Railway, and was being ordered or installed on other railways. Electric telegraph block signalling was first installed in 1844 on the Norwich-Yarmouth line. But perhaps the most significant comment on the year 1845 was that no fewer than 2,746 miles of new railway were authorised in that year's parliamentary session. That said, even that figure pales into insignificance compared with the 4,538 miles which were authorised the following year, even though a lot of the mileage authorised was never actually built. The railway mania was about to engulf the country, as illustrated by the enormous expansion of railways which took place in the second half of the 1840s:

Year	Mileage of railway open for traffic	No. of passengers (million)
1846	3,142	
1847	3,945	44
1848	5,127	58
1849	5,996	64
1850	6,621	67

Despite the massive increase in mileage and traffic, the number of passengers killed in train accidents from causes beyond their own control remained low. Nine were killed in 1848, five in 1849 and 12 in 1850. These figures are all the more remarkable since the new railways were largely run by staff with little or no experience and that some of the more impecunious lines could afford neither proper safety appliances nor adequate staff.

In 1848, the Inspectorate consisted of Captains Simmons, Harness, Laffan and Wynne. They were kept extremely busy not only inquiring into accidents and inspecting new lines, but also inquiring into all manner of disputes between railway companies and between railway companies and local authorities. In 1848, they examined and sanctioned the opening of 1,191 miles of railway, in 116 separate inspections. The worst accident in 1848, in fact one of the worst to date, occurred on the Great Western Railway at Shrivenham on May 10 when five people were killed. The porters "were moving wagons in the sidings, and one of the wagons, a horse box, inadvertently fouled the up main line. The policeman had already cleared his signals for a West Country to Paddington express, which was approaching at 55-60mph. It consisted of three first-class carriages, three second-class carriages and a luggage van, hauled by an eight-wheeled

STATISTICAL SUMMARY 1841-1850

Year	Mileage of railway open for traffic	No. of passengers (million)	No. of passengers killed in train accidents, through no fault of their own
1841	1,556	20.4	1
1842	1, 717	21.4	1
1843	2,036	25.6	6
1844	2,240	30.4	6
1845	2,536	33.8	4
1846	3,142	N/A	3 (last 6 months)
1847	3,945	44	14 (first 6 months)
1848	5,127	58	9
1849	5,996	63.8	5
1850	6,621	66.8	12

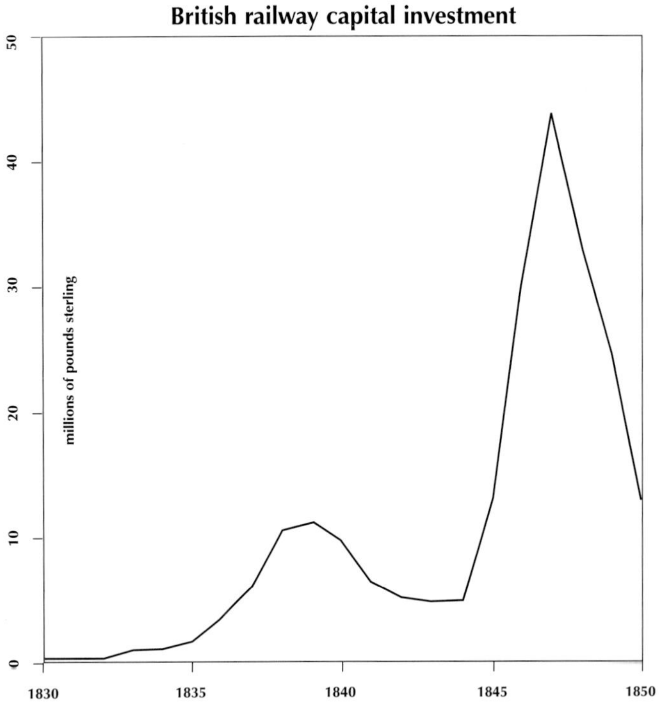

Railway investment in the United Kingdom from 1830 to 1850.

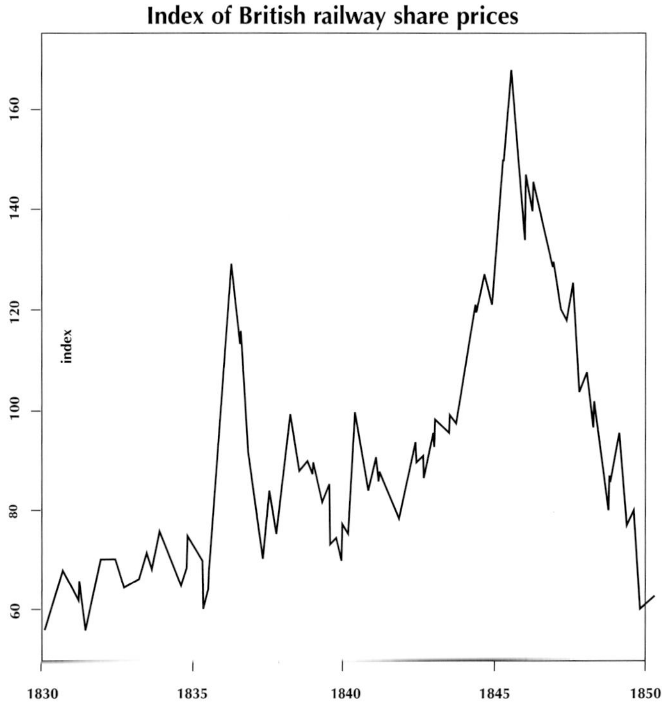

Railway share prices in Britain from 1830 to 1850.

wheeled engine. The express crashed into the horsebox and smashed it to smithereens, then became derailed. The carriages piled up in a heap. There were three important lessons to be learned from this accident:

- There were no trap points or scotch blocks to prevent vehicles in the sidings from escaping on to the main line.
- The fixed signal was not interlocked with the sidings points.

The braking system in use on the express was inadequate for such a high speed. The only brakes available apart from those on the engine and tender, were hand brakes operated by brakesmen riding in the train. It was to be many years before continuous braking systems came into general use.

A similar accident occurred on the same railway at Wootton Bassett, not many miles away, in 1850. An excursion train returning to Bristol at 10.45pm and running at 25-30mph, collided with a horsebox which had run away, out of a siding. The magistrates found the policeman on duty guilty of neglect for not examining the vehicles in the sidings and ensuring that they were secured. He was sent to prison for his offence. Following these two accidents the GWR decided to provide short dead-ends or scotch blocks at all locations.

The new railways were immensely popular with the working classes, who used them in large numbers. Excursion trains were very frequently run, but they were more than ordinarily prone to accident for a number of reasons.

Owing to the enormous crowds who sometimes used them, the trains were often of great length, overpowering the engines provided. They did not run to a fixed timetable and therefore they were particularly vulnerable. However, partly because of the low speeds at which they ran, some of the accidents had their comic side, though no doubt they were frightening at the time to the passengers. For example, a Whitsuntide excursion in 1849 returning from Liverpool to the East Lancs Railway came to a stand near Burnley because the engine was underpowered. As it had been travelling very slowly, the following regular passenger train caught up and collided with it at low speed. The guard of the regular train ran back to protect his own train, but he did not get far enough to prevent a third train, a return excursion from Preston, from colliding with the regular train. The return excursion from Liverpool consisted of 32 carriages with an engine at each end! There were no serious injuries.

By the late 1840s, the railway mania had burnt itself out. Just 16 miles of new line were authorised by Parliament in 1849, and only eight miles in 1850. There were more than 60,000 railway employees, but in addition 104,000 workmen were employed on building new lines, a figure which itself showed a sharp drop from the quarter of a million employed on new construction just a year or two earlier.

By the end of 1850 there were 6,621 miles of railway open, consisting of 5,132 miles in England and Wales, 951 miles in Scotland, and 538 miles in Ireland. The duties of the Inspectorate and the provisions of the Regulation of Railways Acts, applied equally to Ireland until the Irish Free State was formed in 1922.

In the space of ten years the Inspectorate was firmly established and well respected by the railway companies and Parliament. The inspectors made a real change to the safety of the railways in the British Isles approving the construction of over 5,000 miles of new railways and investigating many serious accidents.

Major changes in operations, rolling stock and equipment came directly from the recommendations in the Inspector's accident reports, such as electric block signalling.

CHAPTER 2

LOCK, BLOCK AND BRAKE 1851-1889

Above: This was the railway overseen by the RI in the second half of the 19th century: four-coupled steam locomotives and timber-built, gas lit coaches, controlled by line of route signalboxes managing blocks of route, connected by telegraph wires and with trains controlled by oil-lit semaphore signals. This is the North Eastern Railway at Gaisgill, a few miles east of the West Coast Main Line at Tebay, on the spectacular line over the Pennines to Darlington, via Barnard Castle and Stainmore. This featured one of Tay Bridge designer Sir Thomas Bouch's spindly, towering viaducts at Belah, which survived until demolition in the 1960s, after line closure in 1962. This line once carried coke from the NE, to feed the iron and steelworks at Barrow in Furness. The locomotive is '901' class NER 2-4-0 No. 167, one of the last express designs by Edward Fletcher. They came in two varieties: Class 901 (7ft diameter driving wheels) and Class 1440 (6ft driving wheels) and were regularly used over Stainmore. No. 167 was one of 55 '901' 2-4-0s built between 1872 and 1882. This shows No. 167 following the fitting of a larger boiler and cab in 1906. Gaisgill closed to passengers on December 1 1952 and this Tebay-Ravenstonedale section is now the A685. Keep your eyes peeled and you actually drive past Gaisgill station on the trackbed, past where the platforms used to be. The station building survives. *CC Collection.*

At the beginning of 1851, the Railway Inspectorate consisted of just four senior staff: Captain Simmons (Inspector-General), Captains Laffan and Wynne, and Lt Galton. Britain's passenger rail industry was just 21 years old, taking the Liverpool & Manchester opening of 1830 as its 'ground zero' year; the Stockton & Darlington Railway of 1825 was effectively a colliery railway. This quartet firmly established a philosophy and pattern of work for the Inspectorate which was to remain in place - more or less unchanged - for more than 100 years. They are as important as they are largely unknown!

These men were pioneers, especially in the very new field of accident investigation, which they carried out with great thoroughness and purpose, despite the lack of any real statutory authority for this role. It is far too easy from the sophisticated viewpoint of today, to look back on their work as being Victorian and quaint, but this would be very wrong. The railway was the technological wonder of the age. Previously, transport had been very slow and very 'low tech' - horses and carts making painfully slow, jolting progress on rutted roads or not much faster, if a smoother journey, on canal boats. The railway changed this rather sedate

Above: A picture which powerfully captures the catastrophe of the 1879 Tay Bridge collapse. The 'high girders' of the bridge's central section - which enclosed trains in a cage - collapsed beneath the passenger train, which left Wormit on the southern shore at about 7.05pm, bound for Dundee, during a violent storm on the night of Sunday December 28 1879. All 59 souls aboard perished during the plunge, or by drowning; only 46 bodies were recovered. Wrought iron cross-bracing of the bridge structure was too weak to withstand the silvery Tay's high winds. There were also failings in bridge design, iron casting quality and maintenance, all of which lay within designer Sir Thomas Bouch's remit. Having lost the Forth Bridge contract, he died within the year, a broken man with his reputation in tatters. Thereafter, British bridge designs had to be capable of withstanding wind loadings of 56 pounds per square foot. *Alamy.*

Right: A very dramatic graphic produced in 1880 for the popular press, purporting to show how the full extent of the disaster was discovered by a railwayman who crawled out to the edge of the precipice to discover a yawning gap where the high girders used to be. (See also pages 35-36) *Alamy.*

world very quickly, fundamentally and in ways those in the largely agricultural way of life that had survived for hundreds of years with little change, could never have dreamed of in the first quarter of the 19th century. The railway had started to create the world we know today and it's impact presented massive new challenges which these men confronted and managed with both confidence and courage. Think of America's NASA organisation grappling with the new technology of space travel from the late 1950s and you'll get a hint of what it must have been like for the early RI. And there were only four of them!

As these men retired, or returned to active military service, they were replaced by four more officers from the Corps of Royal Engineers, each one of whom eventually became the Chief Inspecting Officer (previously known as Inspector-General). All four new officers served for more than 20 years and their collective contribution to the improvement in the safety of railway passengers was incalculable. When the first of the four, Lt Henry Tyler, joined the Inspectorate in 1853, railway operating and signalling methods were, to say the least, primitive. Accidents, injuries and deaths were frequent. By the time

Above: The locomotive which plunged into the Tay in December 1879 - North British Railway Wheatley 4-4-0 No. 224, of a class of six dating from 1871. This express engine was spare on the day of the disaster but was called on because the rostered engine for the 1.30pm mail train from Dundee to Burnisland - '88' class 0-4-2T No. 89 *Ladybank* - failed. No. 224 worked the southbound mail without incident, but then departed at 5.20pm with the doomed northbound train. Both driver and fireman died in the collapse into the Tay at around 7.13pm. Examination after the disaster revealed that the locomotive's regulator was still open and no brakes had been applied - catastrophe overwhelmed the driver so swiftly he had no time to react: his engine was still working as the bridge collapsed. In April 1880, No. 224 was recovered - with difficulty, on the third lift - after two failed attempts. The engine stood on the bank of the Tay before being towed - on its own wheels - to Glasgow's Cowlairs Works, for repair; it was, after all less than a decade old. The 4-4-0 had been protected inside the 'cage' of high girders. No. 224 worked for a further 45 years and was eventually withdrawn in 1914. It was forever after the 1879 disaster known by railwaymen as 'The Diver' and drivers refused to take it over the second Tay bridge, opened in 1887. However, on December 28 1908, the 29th anniversary of the collapse, No. 224 once again hauled the evening mail to Dundee, where it arrived safely. No. 224 also had the distinction of being Britain's first inside frame/cylinder 4-4-0. *Alamy.*

the last of the four, Major-General Hutchinson, retired in 1895, the railways had developed into a highly-organised, well-disciplined and responsible industry, with, generally, a more proper regard for safety. However, this change was not achieved without a struggle, setbacks and friction between Inspectorate and industry. It is our view that the major contributions made by this largely forgotten quartet have not had the recognition they so richly deserve. We are happy to put this right!

It's important to keep a sense of perspective about the relative dangers of the era, too. Even though accidents were frequent and the primitive operating methods conjure a rather ramshackle impression, it is very important to stress that our railways were never dramatically unsafe. Even in those primitive years of the 1850s, the average number of passengers killed in train accidents, from causes beyond their own control, was only about 20 a year, which cannot be considered 'serious' in the grand scheme of things, when considered against the enormous number of passengers carried each year - 85m in 1851, nearly doubling to 150m within just eight years, by 1859. To set that latter figure in its proper context, the UK population at that time was 21m; it is around 63m today. Astonishingly, our railways were carrying the equivalent of eight times the entire population within just 30 years of *Rocket's* triumph at Rainhill. That is a truly astonishing trajectory to reflect upon. Today's railway, in comparison, carries c27 times the entire UK population.

The railway companies were inevitably reluctant to spend large sums - and certainly no more than they had to - on improving safety. They had to consider their owners, who were the shareholders and the first duty of the directors was to them. Shareholders had invested very significantly in railway companies in the expectation of dividends. If those dividends were unsatisfactory, their investment would decline or even cease so it is important to remember that profit wasn't a dirty word - and it still isn't. Without it, there would be no cash at all today for any safety improvements - or anything else - including workers pensions. Companies would wither and die.

Decisions about how much to spend on safety were always difficult and never became easier. This was (and still is) an area where the Railway Inspectorate played such a vital role in establishing standards of safety and, where necessary, applying pressure to persuade foot-dragging railway companies to comply. Less prosperous lines could barely afford to do so; the more prosperous could - and indeed ought to have spent more than they did. The four Inspectors who led the way in these crucial developments and testing times were:

- Lt H. W. Tyler .... 1853-1877 .... 24 years
- Lt-Col W. Yolland .... 1854-1885 .... 31 years
- Capt F. H. Rich .... 1861-1891 .... 30 years
- Lt-Col C. S. Hutchinson ...... 1867-1895 .... 28 years

Captain Sir Henry Whatley Tyler KCB
Chief Inspecting Officer: 1871-1877

Henry Tyler was the eldest son of the Deputy Lieutenant of Gloucestershire. He joined the Royal Military Academy in 1842, at the age of 15. After training, he spent four years in the Caribbean, in St Lucia, as private secretary to the Civil Governor and was one of several Royal Engineers specifically employed in the great International

Exhibition of 1851, sometimes described as 'The Crystal Palace Exhibition.' A collection of permanent exhibits which he established there, later became the nucleus of the Natural History Musuem.

In 1852, Tyler married the daughter of Lt-Gen Sir Charles Pasley and at the same time was appointed engineer to the Colony of Victoria, in Australia. He never actually reached there, however, owing to ship breakdowns and he accepted the appointment of Inspector of Railways in London, in 1853, at the early age of 26.

In 1867, Tyler spent his leave making an inspection of the Grand Trunk Railway of Canada and spent his following year's leave constructing the first railway in Greece, hiring six brigands to police it. In 1875-76 he was chairman of the English Channel Tunnel Commission - and so far from regarding such a tunnel as a menace to our insular isolation, he held that if only we could induce a hostile army to enter a pipe 30 miles long and 30ft in diameter, it would be worthwhile spending £3m on the construction for that sole purpose!

In 1871, he inspected the International Bridge over the Niagara River in America and also reported on the Metropolitan water supply for the East End of London. In 1872, he gave evidence on the Euphrates Valley Railway scheme and in 1871 inspected the Erie Railway. The next year he was inspecting railways in Romania and Bosnia whilst on his annual leave - a very adventurous busman's holiday!

Tyler was the approving Officer for the Festiniog Railway between 1864 and 1870, allowing passenger services on the narrow gauge railway. The tightest curve on the railway at 2.4 chains is still named Tyler's Curve in honor of his encouragement and enthusiasm.

Tyler resigned his appointment as Chief Inspector of Railways in 1877, receiving a Knighthood for his services and he became chairman of the Westinghouse Brake Company, in England. Tyler was Conservative MP for Harwich between 1880-85 and for Great Yarmouth from 1885-92. He died in 1908.

Throughout his long life Tyler combined great energy and zest with a very focused lucidity of thought, accompanied by very clear, sharp judgement. He was one of the very few Inspecting Officers to leave before attaining 65 years of age and he was a major loss to the Inspectorate. Had he remained, his influence on railway safety would in all likelihood have been even more profound than it already was. This is one of the great 'if only' questions of railway history.

Colonel W. Yolland
Chief Inspecting Officer: 1877-1885

Colonel Yolland was commissioned in the Royal Engineers, becoming a Lieutenant Colonel in 1855 and a Colonel in 1858. He served for 31 years in the Railway Inspectorate, including eight years as Chief, this is a record unlikely ever to be broken. Sadly, he died in service in 1885 just before he was due to retire. Col Yolland was a charismatic and rather fiery character who had a considerable influence on railway safety during its formative years. He doggedly sought improvements to the locking of points and the fitting of continuous train brakes which, just four years after his death, were mandated as compulsory by the 1889 'Lock, Block and Brake' Regulations, of which we will hear more soon.

Colonel F. H. Rich
Chief Inspecting Officer: 1885-1891

Colonel Rich joined the Royal engineers in 1840, aged 19 as a Second Lieutenant becoming a Colonel in 1873. He was seconded to the Board of Trade in 1861 and served in the Railway Inspectorate for 30 years, the second longest serving officer, becoming a Colonel in 1873. He served in the Railway Inspectorate for 30 years, the second longest serving officer.

Rich investigated more than 250 railway accidents. One notable accident was at Staplehurst, in 1865, when a South Eastern Railway Folkstone-London boat train derailed while crossing a viaduct where a length of track had been removed during engineering works, killing ten passengers and injuring 40 more.

The author Charles Dickens was travelling on the train and he tended the victims, some of whom died while he was with them. The experience affected Dickens greatly; he lost his voice for two weeks and afterwards was always nervous when travelling by train, using alternative means when available.

Amongst the new railway lines and other works that Rich inspected prior to opening were Ribblehead Viaduct (May 1876) and the Severn Tunnel (November 1886).

Major General Charles Scrope Hutchinson
Chief Inspecting Officer: 1892-1895

Charles Hutchinson was commissioned in the Royal Engineers in 1843. For many years, he was based at the Royal Military Academy at Woolwich as an instructor and later as Professor of Fortifications. In 1867, he was appointed as an Inspector of Railways, by which time he had reached the rank of Lieutenant Colonel. He retired from the Army in 1877 with the honorary rank of Major General.

Charles Hutchinson was a most influential and effective inspector and conducted no fewer than 6,500 railway and tramway inspections, travelling 1,250,000 miles on duty. He conducted 1,100 inquiries into accidents, a remarkable record.

From 1876 to 1879, he was heavily engaged in providing technical advice to several select committees of the House of Commons and House of Lords, established to consider the use of steam traction for street tramways. In this role, he travelled extensively around Europe where steam traction had already been adopted. Charles Hutchinson also has a claim to fame in that he was instrumental in removing the famous and oft-quoted need for a person with a red flag to walk in front of a locomotive on the highway, a requirement of the Locomotive Act of 1865. This led eventually in 1896 to the full repeal of the Act which gave everyone full freedom of the road.

One of his colleagues in the Board of Trade wrote of Charles Hutchinson: "He had a passion for work, in the execution of which he displayed a zeal, amounting to enthusiasm. He never spared himself, and often after a comfortless night journey in cross-country trains, he would snatch a hurried breakfast at some dreary railway buffet and begin a long day's work of inspection at eight o'clock in the morning, much to the surprise and not always to the joy of the railway officers, who wondered how in the world he got there. He gained the warm friendship and respect not only of his colleagues but also of all the officers of the railways in the United Kingdom with whom he was brought into contact in the course of his official duties."

For four decades, the most important battle to significantly enhance railway safety was fought on three principal fronts. This has since become known as 'lock, block and brake'. 'Lock' referred to the interlocking of signals and points, through which it became impossible for an unsafe or conflicting combination of route and signalling to be made; also the securing (or locking) of facing points so that they could not be moved as a train passed over them. Facing points are track switches that change the passage of an approaching train between diverging tracks. If the movable blades are not securely clamped against the outer stock rails, wheel flanges could possibly get between them and open the tapered rail 'switch', thereby allowing the train to try and travel in both directions at the same time. Or, the wheels could be trapped in the narrowing space between the switch rails, resulting in a catastrophic derailment. (See also page 33) Recent fatal high speed examples include Grayrigg (February 23 2007) and Potters Bar (May 10 2002).

There are four principal requirements for safety so far as points are concerned:

- The tapered point blade must lie tightly against the stock rail so that wheels of the train are deflected and guided to follow the correct route.
- Points and the signals must be interlocked so that a signal can only be 'cleared' for the direction in which the points are lying.
- Once the junction signal has been 'cleared' to allow a train to pass, it must be impossible to move the points.
- As the train passes over the facing points they must remain locked so that it is impossible for them to move under the train even if the signalman has put the junction signal back to danger.

'Block' describes a space-interval signalling system of 'blocks' of route, in which only one train can run at any one time. In 1851, the use of the time-interval system which had been introduced when railways first started running, was widespread and routine. Generally, the policeman (or signalman) gave a danger signal for five minutes after a train had passed, in order to prevent the next train from following its predecessor too closely. He would then display a caution signal for five minutes more as a warning to the driver of a following train that another train was not far ahead; he would then show an all-clear signal.

With the benefit of hindsight, the fatal flaws are obvious. If a train broke down in mid-section, after passing the 'Bobby' but after the train had passed beyond his sight and hearing, there was a clear risk that a following train would run into it. Also, if a train ran more slowly than the time interval was intended to provide a safety margin for, the same risk arose. A means was needed of maintaining a protective separation between trains so that they could not collide - and this led to the slow evolution of a signalling system known as the 'absolute block' system, which on traditionally signalled routes survives today as a proven and very safe method of train operation.

'Brake' referenced train braking systems. In retrospect it is astonishing that the primitive braking systems in use in the early

CONTINUED ON PAGE 32

Above: One of the collapsed high girders from the Tay Bridge collapse of December 1879, raised and dragged ashore, for salvage. The relatively lightweight and rather spindly cross-bracing is clearly shown. *Alamy.*

Below: Approaching the raised section of the 1887 'new' Tay Bridge on February 21 2019, as seen from the cab of an LNER southbound HST from Dundee, bound for Edinburgh. *Nigel Harris.*

Facing Page Top: This February 21 2019 view from within the 'high girders' of the 1887 Tay Bridge shows how much more robust the heavily rivetted steel structure is, compared with the wrecked section shown above, after the December 1879 collapse. Note the very sharp change of gradient, for the run down to the Tay's southern shore at Wormit. *Nigel Harris.*

Facing Page lower: The lessons learned from the Tay Bridge collapse of December 1879 were well and truly incorporated into the massive steel construction of the Forth Bridge, started in 1882, just three years after the Tay collapse, and opened on March 4 1890. This February 21 2019 view, from an Edinburgh-bound LNER HST, really emphasises the scale of the extensive steel cross-bracing over the Forth: they really were taking no chances. *Nigel Harris.*

CONTINUED FROM PAGE 29

days of railways lasted in service as long as they did. The only brakes available to those early drivers, apart from putting their engines into reverse gear and opening the regulator, were manually-applied screw handbrakes on the engine's tender and also on those carriages on the train which were accompanied by guards or 'breaksmen'. They rode outside the carriage (a hangover from road stagecoach practice) and they physically screwed on their brakes in response to the driver's brake whistle, this is why some locomotives were fitted with two whistles of differing tone - one was the driver's instruction to warn the guard to screw on his brake, the other was to use to warn of his approach to those on or about the line in front of his train.

Despite the increasing weight and speed of trains during the 1850s and 1860s, few real improvements had been made to train braking systems, even by 1870. Considering train weights and speeds had increased dramatically in that time it almost beggars belief that the railways were still relying on two handbrakes applied to a couple of wheelsets on trains weighing 50 to 200 tons, running at maybe 50mph. Mishaps were inevitable: it was impossible to control these faster, heavier, trains properly or stop quickly with such primitive brakes.

Primitive operating methods were not the only cause of accidents. Boiler explosions, with their very obvious hazards, were common. The relevant section in L.T.C Rolt's classic *Red for Danger* is fascinating, if horrifying, required reading on this subject. Possibly the most destructive example Rolt quotes being Midland six-coupled goods engine No. 356, which exploded in Colne Yard. A woman lying in bed fully a quarter of a mile away was hit on the leg by the potentially deadly shrapnel of a fragment of flying boiler plate. Pieces of No. 356 were still being recovered from surrounding fields weeks later. The locomotive's boiler pressure had been increased from 120 to 140lbs per square inch - something that Captain Tyler described in his report as 'unwise'.

Early safety valves could be screwed down by drivers, who realised that the extra pressure created more power for their engines: but this also led to boiler explosions. The safety measure that eventually emerged was very simple: safety valve adjusting rings and collars were secured with a tamper-proof 'excise' type wire and lead seal, attached when the boiler was formally tested and passed fit for service in works and at depots. If this wire seal was missing, it gave an instant indication of tampering. Like the wooden lever collar slipped over a signal lever to remind a signalman a train was standing at that signal, this was a safety device which cost only pennies but which had a very significant impact on improving safety. From the earliest days, the evidence was clear that significant safety advances do not always require major financial investment.

Broken wheel tyres and axles were often a cause of serious derailment in the early years, sometimes resulting in multiple deaths and numerous injuries. This problem was exacerbated by flimsy wooden rolling stock which either disintegrated into matchwood in collisions, or caught fire from the onboard bottled gas lighting - or both. As engineering technology developed, these causes of accidents declined in both frequency and impact.

10,870 route miles by 1861

In 1851, there were 6,890 miles of railway open for traffic, with 85m passengers carried each year. By 1861, mileage had increased to 10,870, carrying 174m passengers. By 1871, it was 15,376 miles and 375m. In addition to this very significant traffic, goods (and it is only in relatively recent times that the term 'freight' has taken over in Britain) was even more important than passengers in terms of revenue - £26.5m for freight as against £20.6m for passengers in 1871. Very few railways were built specifically with passengers in mind - goods was traditionally the first priority...usually coal.

This explosive growth sparked a time of great prosperity in industry: Britain was still the world's pre-eminent nation, a situation that would not have been possible without the railways. Not for nothing was Britain known as 'the workshop of the world'. The whole life of the country had come to depend on the iron road and as a result, commercial use of roads and canals steadily declined. Little wonder, therefore, that railways and the safety of passengers were very much in the forefront of the public and parliamentary mind.

It might be believed that in the 1850s workers had neither the time, energy nor disposable income to take an excursion or travel by train at all - but this was not the case. Horse-racing, for example, regularly drew immense crowds, with thousands tavelling by special train, as illustrated by the circumstances of an accident at Sutton Tunnel, near Frodsham, on the Birkenhead Lancashire & Cheshire Junction Railway on April 30 1851. After the Chester Cup Race, no fewer than 9,000 passengers arrived at Chester station for trains heading in the Warrington direction. The station master despatched seven trains, of which the first and second got through without mishap. The third train, however, was too heavy for its locomotive and it stalled near Sutton Tunnel, so the fourth excursion was brought up behind to push it along. The combined load still proved too much, even for both locomotives. This very heavy, labouring cavalcade struggled slowly into the tunnel but speed kept falling and eventually the two trains came to a dead stand, leaving 2,000 passengers stranded in the eerie smoke-filled darkness. It was pitch black because there were no lights in the carriages but worse still there was no tail light at the rear of the propelling train. The guard should have walked back along the line and laid explosive detonators to protect his train by warning the driver of an approaching train, to which he would also be duty-bound to give an emergency stop signal - but he failed to carry out these crucial duties.

The station master at Frodsham, even though he had seen the two trains struggle into the tunnel, nevertheless allowed the fifth excursion to follow, only five minutes later. Disaster was inevitable. The fifth train entered the tunnel at speed, to the terror of the stranded passengers inside, as the full realisation of their impending doom became horribly clear. There was no escape. In the appalling crash in the confined space of the tunnel, six passengers were killed.

But what of the sixth excursion, which was close behind and which was also allowed by the Frodsham station master to proceed? Would it too plunge into the tunnel and add to the chaos, with 3,000 passengers milling around in darkness? Fortunately not. The guard of the fifth train quite properly - and to his very great credit - rushed back along the line on foot, frantically waving his handlamp in a danger signal which was seen by the driver of the sixth train, who successfully stopped before reaching the wreckage of the three wrecked trains in the tunnel.

Capt Laffan was not sparing in his criticism. He recommended that:

- The block telegraph should be installed between the stations at each end of the tunnel and no train should be allowed to enter the tunnel until the previous one had passed through it safely and reached the other station.
- More staff and engines were needed. In a period of rapid expansion

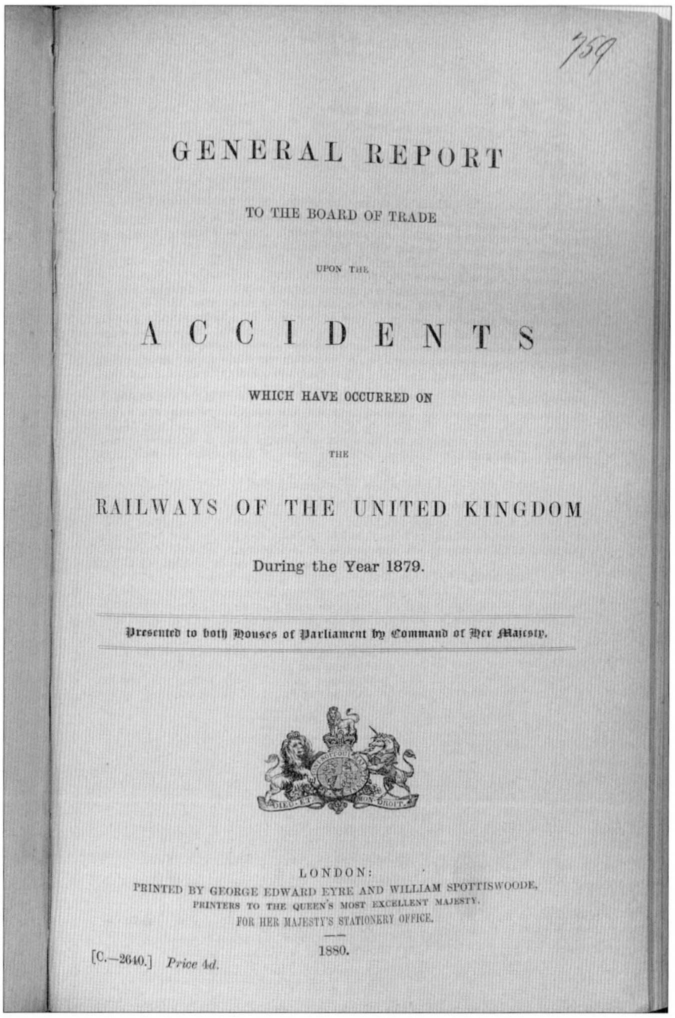
759

GENERAL REPORT

TO THE BOARD OF TRADE

UPON THE

ACCIDENTS

WHICH HAVE OCCURRED ON

THE

RAILWAYS OF THE UNITED KINGDOM

During the Year 1879.

Presented to both Houses of Parliament by Command of Her Majesty.

LONDON:
PRINTED BY GEORGE EDWARD EYRE AND WILLIAM SPOTTISWOODE,
PRINTERS TO THE QUEEN'S MOST EXCELLENT MAJESTY.
FOR HER MAJESTY'S STATIONERY OFFICE.

1880.

[C.—2640.] Price 4d.

Above: The 1879 volume of the General Report to the Board of Trade covering all railway accidents that year - it would have included the Tay Bridge collapse of December 28. Published in 1880, it cost 4d!
Clive Nicholls

suitable and experienced staff were hard to come by and the resources of both rolling stock and men could be overwhelmed on a small railway company by such a popular event as the Chester Cup Race.

- Lights should be provided in the carriages of trains when passing through Sutton Tunnel.
- The five-minute time interval in operation at Frodsham was too short.

Serious accidents in tunnels were not unknown and there was to be another one at Clayton Tunnel on the London Brighton & South Coast Railway, ten years later on August 25 1861. Again, excursion trains were involved, but this time the electric telegraph was already in use through the tunnel. Even so, 23 people died and 176 were seriously injured in what was Britain's worst railway disaster up to that time.

A fatal collision at Lewisham on the South Eastern Railway on Sunday June 28 1857, in which 12 passengers were killed, demonstrated yet again that the installation of the electric telegraph did not in itself guarantee safety. The technology had to be accompanied by a proper working system, operated by competent staff, if it was to enhance safety effectively. This accident also clearly showed once again the inadequacies of the distant signal as operated at the time.

Concern about the level of safety on the railways was as a consequence often expressed in Parliament. In 1853, the Cardwell Committee considered whether it was desirable to give the Board of Trade power to enforce the application of an Inspecting Officer's recommendations (an issue which has been raised at intervals ever since) but decided that the balance of advantage lay in leaving responsibility with the railway companies.

The question of the provision of communication between passengers and those in charge of a train was a very live issue at this time and a House of Commons Select Committee, established in 1857 to inquire into the causes of railway accidents, recommended the provision of such equipment. However, the railway companies' response was lukewarm and they had eventually to be compelled to fit such apparatus by the Regulation of Railways Act 1868 on all trains travelling more than 20 miles without stopping. The Act stipulated that the type of apparatus provided had to be approved by the Board of Trade.

23 passengers killed in 1865

As trains were by now such an integral and indispensable part of everyday business, industrial and social life, it is not surprising that railway matters were always well to the fore in the public mind. The need to make the railways adopt the block system of signalling, together with the interlocking of points and signals, was often urged, but the Devonshire Royal Commission of 1865 pointed out that only 23 passengers had been killed that year in accidents beyond their own control, from 252m passengers carried. The argument was that as no other mode of locomotion known to man had shown a more satisfactory result, they were not prepared to suggest any alteration in the law. They did however recommend that Inspecting Officers should have the power to require the attendance of officers and servants of railways as witnesses at accident inquiries and to require the production of books and documents. Both these provisions were incorporated in the 1871 Regulation of Railways Act, together with a provision for the holding of inquiries into accidents, a well-considered and effective practice which was followed until 1996, when legislators decided that Inspectors inquiries were unnecessary for the modern railway and reliance would be placed upon members of the legal profession invited by the Minister to oversee any public inquiry following a major accident.

In retrospect, it is surprising that more parliamentary attention was not devoted to the question of train brakes. Thirty years after the opening of the Liverpool & Manchester Railway in 1830, and notwithstanding the rapid development of longer, heavier and more frequent trains, the same crude handbrakes were still in use. Even by 1870 there had been little real improvement. Whilst poor braking systems were not in themselves the direct cause of accidents, they frequently caused the consequences of mishaps to be much more severe than they might otherwise have been.

Even though there were plenty of accidents to occupy the time of the four Inspectors, they were also often called upon to consider other matters. In 1863, Col Yolland reported on railway schemes proposed for London and its suburbs and referred to an earlier Royal Commission report using language that is still very relevant to the situation today. He described "...the urgent necessity now generally admitted to exist for relieving the overcrowded streets of some portion of their traffic ... and the connection of the railways north of the Thames with those south of the Thames."

Although Col Yolland was an outspoken firebrand, he also had enormous prescience. He was referring in the above quotation to the authorisation of the Farringdon to Blackfriars section of line, reopened to passengers in 1988 with great success by British Rail under the brand-name 'Thameslink'. It is now difficult to believe that BR had actually closed this one rail route under the river in the late 1960s (it was a freight only line) and the track was lifted in 1971. It is impossible to conceive of life without it today, when there are plans to run 24 trains an hour over it everyday, in each direction.

Other matters engaged the attention of the Inspectorate. In 1865, Tyler prepared a report on the Mont Cenis Railway under the Alps, proposed by Brassey & Co, railway builders, then in 1866 he carried out an inspection of the railways and ports of Italy, with reference to the use of the Italian route for the conveyance of the 'eastern mails'.

The Inspectorate's normal work also continued to develop in parallel, given that the promotion and building of railways was still in full swing. In 1864, no fewer than 294 Bills were presented to parliament envisaging the construction of 3,099 miles of new line. The year 1865 was even busier, with 348 Bills for 4,270 miles. Many of these Bills were rejected and many more miles of authorised line were never actually built. But safety remained the Inspectors' chief concern.

The fast Irish Mail trains were the pride of the London & North Western Railway, bearing in mind that at this time the whole of Ireland was governed from London and so the carriage of mails and passengers was very important. The up train was in trouble at Tamworth on September 14 1870. The North signalbox had an up distant signal, an up outer home signal and an up inner home. The signalman had set his facing points for the platform loop line as he was expecting a goods train, but when the train arrived it was, to the signalman's consternation, the night-time Irish Mail. The distant and outer home signals were both showing a white light, meaning 'all right', and it was not until the hapless driver saw the junction signal set for the platform loop that he realised that his fast-moving train was about to turn onto the diverging route into the platform. With wheels screeching on the rails in protest, 'the Mail' took the points at nearly 50mph, ran through the loop and then into the dead end siding at its far end. Driver and fireman both hung on grimly as their train rapidly approached the stop block, which it demolished at 15mph before plunging into the River Anker. Both enginemen lost their lives and a passenger was killed. There were 11 vehicles on the train and Fay's brake was in use on the last three. It was better than nothing, but not much, and in any case its use depended upon the brakesman hearing the driver's brake whistle before operating a screw mechanism on the brake, which applied cast iron shoes to the wheels. It was an unreliable and cumbersome system.

Distant signals

Tyler inquired into this accident and came across a situation practically unknown in those days: the North Box signalman declined to make any statement without taking the advice of his solicitor! Tyler made the following recommendations, which underpin the theme of 'lock, block and brake':

- Two arms on the distant signal, or the outer home, would have given the driver an earlier 'two yellows' warning of the way the points were set.
- If a proper block system had been in force the signalman would have known which train to expect.
- A more efficient brake would have enabled the train to stop safely, short of the stop block.

There was at this time (maybe not surprisingly in the light of experience) a great dislike and distrust of facing points: this was not without good reason. Facing points could be very dangerous without proper locking and interlocking and they had already caused many serious accidents. This dislike was to affect track layouts until well into the 20th century, causing trains to have to set back and propel trains off the main line into sidings. (see also page 29)

Tyler's comments on the distant signal are very interesting. The idea of having two arms on the signal in order to give the driver advance warning of the way the facing points ahead were set was of great importance and was subsequently adopted on a wide scale. A distant signal with two arms became known as a 'splitting distant', but these gradually disappeared in later years and we reverted to the original practice of having only one arm, with the distinction that the arm was only lowered when the junction ahead was set for the higher speed route. There was a great deal of confusion about the role of the distant signal. It was originally designed to protect a train standing at the station (or home) signal in the days before the block system was installed, but it was increasingly coming to be regarded as a repeater signal for the home signal. However, it was still at that time classified as a danger 'stop' signal and carried a red light, which it continued to do for the next 50 years when it was changed to yellow.

Until 1867, most railway companies had adopted the following

Right: Locomotive boilers of the 19th century generated pressures which could overwhelm the engineering, maintenance and operational standards of the day - with the catastrophic outcome of boilers exploding. Violent explosions could be the result of poor design, maintenance or operations. In the early days, drivers had quickly realised that the relatively feeble pulling powers of their engines could be boosted by screwing down their Salter safety valves, which were easily tampered with. The increased boiler pressure did indeed boost power - at the risk of boiler explosions, however. It is not known what caused this catastrophic explosion at Bridge of Dun on the Caledonian Railway, on March 23 1872 - but the enormous potential for destruction of the power harnessed by steam is horrifically clear. *HMRI-ORR.*

Rule for distant signals, which were then known as 'auxiliary' signals:

'When a train is stopping at a station, or when there is any obstruction thereat, the main and auxiliary signal must be at Danger, and any coming engine or train must be brought to a stand at the auxiliary signal, when the engineman will open his whistle, and afterwards proceed with caution towards the station.'

Enginemen very frequently failed to carry out this rule, either because they couldn't see the signal until they were too close to stop at it, given the inefficient brakes in use, or because they could see that the line ahead was clear. The railway companies connived at this irregular practice and were censured by the Inspecting Officers whenever it caused or contributed to an accident. The superintendents of the companies therefore agreed to an amendment to the rule, relieving the driver of the need to stop at the distant signal if he could see the way ahead to be clear. If not, the driver was still expected to stop at the distant signal; this was, therefore, only a slight improvement in practical terms. The standard arrangement for semaphore signals was:

- Arm horizontal, red light at night - Danger, Stop
- Arm lowered 45°, green light at night - Caution
- Arm close to the post, white light at night - All right

The Great Western, already showing unmistakable signs of individuality, continued to use disc and crossbar signals. One or two other railways also had their own individual systems such as the double disc signal used on the South Western Railway.

1870 was a bad year, both for the LNWR and for the railways as a whole. No fewer than 66 passengers were killed, in several separate accidents. On the LNWR, five passengers were killed and many were injured when a North Eastern Railway goods train collided with the up Scotch Mail at St Nicholas Crossing, a flat crossing just south of Carlisle. The NER driver was drunk and failed to stop at the stop board. Seven passengers and the driver were killed at Harrow when the 5.00pm express from Euston to Liverpool and Manchester crashed into the back of a train of empty wagons in fog. The driver was not keeping a proper lookout, but even so the signalling system and the operating methods were unsatisfactory.

However, the worst accident of the year occurred at Stairfoot, on the Manchester Sheffield & Lincolnshire Railway, on December 12. Fifteen passengers were killed and 59 injured, when part of a goods train being shunted and made up on the main line at Barnsley, ran away down an incline and crashed into a stationary train.

But back to Yolland. After inquiring into a collision at Brockley Whins on the North Eastern Railway between Sunderland and Gateshead on December 6 1870, in which five lives were lost, which resulted from the absence of interlocking between points and signals, he tore into the directors of the NER:

"Nothing", he said, "can more plainly exhibit the entire absence of responsibility that exists on the part of the railway directors, their officers and servants, for the occurrence of preventable disastrous accidents, than what has taken place with reference to this very serious collision, because it appears to me that the company's management is wholly to blame for this accident.

"It is now nearly 15 years since I first called attention to the danger in allowing facing points to be inadvertently moved to the wrong position, and how, by interlocking the points and signals this class of accident might be altogether avoided."

Had it been left to Yolland, he would have tried to persuade the Board of Trade to obtain statutory powers to compel railways to adopt certain safety measures, but that would not happen for a further 20 years. Tyler counselled caution and suggested to a Select Committee in 1870 that if the practice of holding inquiries into accidents were to be legalised, and if reports on such accidents were promptly published, he thought that public opinion would so act upon the companies that "we shall get all that is required." He was over-optimistic, but the result was the passing of the Regulation of Railways Act 1871, an important milestone in the holding of inquiries.

Even so, by 1871, only slow and poor progress had been made towards 'lock, block and brake'. Locking of facing points and the interlocking of points and signals, was proceeding, but only at a snail's pace. The block system, too, was being introduced without any apparent urgency, and even then some of the systems in use were less than satisfactory. The LNWR, for example, used a system of permissive block which allowed a second train to proceed into an already-occupied section, a bad practice on passenger lines which resulted in several accidents. Little progress had been made on the question of train brakes. There has to be some sympathy for Yolland's view and many more lives were to be needlessly lost before the railways reluctantly came into line.

Between 1872 and 1889, the railways of Britain underwent a transformation. The mileage of line open soared by more than 25%, passenger journeys almost doubled whilst goods tonnage soared by two-thirds. But despite the railways becoming busier than ever, the average number of passengers killed each year in train accidents was reduced from 40 in the 1870s to 28 in the 1880s and declined to single figures in 1885 and 1886. This was an achievement which clearly illustrated the cumulative effect of the gradual adoption by the railway companies of the interlocking of points and signals, improved braking systems and the block system of signalling. The number of collisions involving passenger trains more than halved from a high of 155 in 1877 to a low of 73, ten years later. This was a major improvement.

Such progress was very satisfying to Captain Tyler, who had been appointed Chief Inspecting Officer in 1871 and to his three Inspecting Officers, Col Yolland, Lt-Col Rich and Lt-Col Hutchinson.

Captain Tyler was the first one of the quartet to leave the Railway Inspectorate in 1877, when, at the invitation of Westinghouse, he became Chairman of the Westinghouse Brake Company, in England. He was replaced by Major Marindin RE. Col Yolland died in service in 1885 after 31 years and even today retains the distinction of being the longest-serving Inspecting Officer in the history of the Railway Inspectorate. He had been the scourge of recalcitrant railway companies and his tongue never lost its cutting edge, nor his pen its acid. Col Yolland was not replaced. Perhaps their Lordships at the Board of Trade considered him irreplaceable. Tyler and Yolland had made a perfect pair - Tyler unvaryingly courteous whilst Yolland was fiery and outspoken. By the time Yolland died it seemed that the battle had been almost won, but new dangers were beginning to emerge and there would be new campaigns to be fought.

The railway companies had been unaccountably slow in adopting better train brakes and their persistent justification was that they couldn't find a suitable system. In 1874, a Royal Commission under the Chairmanship of the Duke of Buckingham and Chandos was therefore appointed to inquire into the whole question of the safe working of the railways and as part of their review they arranged for brake trials to be held in June 1875 near Newark, on the Midland Railway line from Nottingham. Cols Hutchinson and Yolland were present. Eight railway companies participated, and eight different brakes were tested, including the LNWR Clarke & Webb chain brake, the LYR with Fay's brake, the GNR with Smith's vacuum, and the Midland and the LBSCR with the Westinghouse brake. The results were inconclusive, with each patentee perhaps inevitably believing that his own brake was the best available. A great opportunity to standardise on the Westinghouse air brake for Britain's railways was consequently lost. This enormous mistake was not to be corrected until almost a century later. Most of the other brakes failed to meet the Board of Trade's Requirements, issued in 1876, that the brake should operate on all vehicles on the train, that it should be capable of being controlled both by the driver and the guard, and that it should be applied automatically in the event of a train breaking in two.

The 1874 Royal Commission had to consider whether the evidence submitted to it justified giving the Board of Trade greater powers to require railway companies to adopt certain equipment in the interests of greater safety, but they were emphatic that the responsibility for the safety of operation must remain with the railway companies. They pointed out that if the Board of Trade had the power to interfere and impose conditions there would be a concurrent transfer of responsibility and accountability from the railway companies to the Board. "We desire to record our decided opinion that any change which would relieve the railway companies from the responsibility which now rests upon them to provide for the safety of their traffic would be undesirable," they said.

The Board of Trade Requirements already mentioned first saw the light of day in 1858 and were issued as a brief guide to railway companies of the standards that the Railway Inspectorate would require when approving new works. The Requirements have been updated at intervals ever since.

The railway companies themselves were nevertheless busily engaged in improving their working arrangements in other areas and several very important Rules and Regulations date from this period. In 1876, for example, the first new Standard Rule Book was adopted by all companies. It specified the classic fish-tail arm for the distant signal to clearly and immediately distinguish it from the home signal.

Tyler left the Railway Inspectorate in 1877 and one of his last inquiries was into a derailment at Morpeth on March 25 that year. The 10.30pm from Edinburgh to King's Cross became derailed whilst negotiating the sharp left-hand curve just south of the station at a speed of 25mph. Five passengers were killed and 17 injured. On this occasion faulty permanent way was blamed but Tyler commented, with some foresight: "It would obviously be better if a deviation line could be constructed, to avoid the use of so sharp a curve on a main line." However, the wealthy and prosperous North Eastern Railway failed to heed his advice, which was a great pity. At the very least, the continued existence of the sharp curve demanded in perpetuity that all fast trains should slow down; it also sowed the seeds of a further four serious derailments in later years, notably in 1969,1984,1992 and 1994.

The Midland Railway was by this time becoming a force to be reckoned with. It had extended its main line to its new Gothic cathedral of a hotel (the Midland Grand at St Pancras) and the Barlow train shed (the biggest enclosed and unsupported space in the world at the time) at St Pancras in 1868 and was, in 1875, on the point of opening its spectacular new main line over the northern fells between Settle Junction and Petteril Bridge Junction, on the outskirts of Carlisle.

The Midland was also rapidly adopting the block system of signalling and had already equipped 627 miles out of 975, with a further 176 miles in process of being equipped. It was also starting to use the Westinghouse air brake, but not quickly enough for Col Yolland, who, upon reporting on a derailment at Wennington, on the Skipton to Lancaster and Carnforth line, on August 11 1880, in which eight passengers were killed and 23 injured, said: "If the train had been fitted with a good continuous break it would have stopped before the bridge and saved eight lives. It is all very well for the Midland Railway Company now to plead that they are busily employed in fitting up their passenger trains with continuous breaks, but the necessity for providing more break power was pointed out by the Board of Trade to all railway companies more than 20 years since; and with the exception of a very few railway companies that recognised that necessity and acted upon it, it may be truly stated that the principal Railway Companies throughout the Kingdom have resisted the efforts of the Board of Trade to cause them to do what was right, which the latter had no legal power to enforce, and even now some of those Companies are still doing nothing to supply this now generally acknowledged necessity."

Col Yolland's last inquiry took place in January 1885, into the circumstances of a collision on the North Staffordshire Railway near Stoke-on-Trent, between the 9.15am LNWR express from Manchester to Birmingham and a North Staffordshire goods train. There were clear signs that new era of railway working was quickly emerging but that further refinements were still urgently needed. Yes, the block system was in operation but the signalman had still accepted the express whilst he was still shunting the goods train and he did not have the necessary quarter of a mile overlap clearance in his signalling. The driver of the express failed to stop at the home signal but because his train was equipped with the vacuum brake the consequent collision took place at low speed and there were no serious injuries to passengers, although the unfortunate driver lost his life. Col Yolland had just inquired into another collision caused by the signalman giving the 'Train out of Section' bell signal to the previous signalman before the train had actually cleared the section and he repeated Maj-Gen Hutchinson's recommendation that there should be some apparatus, operated by the train, to prevent the signalman from acting prematurely. As always, Yolland was looking to the future, and considering new ways of improving safety.

Improvements were now coming thick and fast. The Great Western Railway, notwithstanding its already good reputation for safety, also did not finally approve the general adoption of block signalling and interlocking until 1877, whilst the LNWR in 1886 moved some way towards adopting the automatic vacuum brake. There was still a lack of standardisation in the colour of the lights used in signals at night; red was universally accepted to mean 'danger', but some companies continued to use white for the all-right signals, whilst others used green. The need for standardisation was especially urgent and important at junctions between different companies, where there could be a potentially confusing mixture of green and white 'all right' signals.

The worry about safe working during fog was also becoming a critical issue and several companies were starting to experiment with audible signals (either electrical or mechanical) as a means of helping drivers, but nothing suitable evolved in those early stages.

In order to obtain an impression of the size and general activities of the railways in the Golden Jubilee year of 1887, it is interesting to compare them with the situation 100 years later in 1987 and today:

	1887	1987	2016/17
Mileage of line open	19,578	10,345	9,881
Passengers killed in train accidents	25	3	0
Railway staff killed	422	32	1
Passengers (million)	734	710	1,700
Freight (million tons)	269	c.125	79.4
Collisions involving passenger trains	73	20	3
Passenger train derailments	49	20	3

Note the 1887 figures include the whole of Ireland

Today's railway is half as big as it was then and while it carries nearly twice as many passengers there is less than half as much freight. In 1887, total revenue was almost double the working expenditure.

The two most serious accidents in terms of lives lost in the 1870s and 1880s, were the Tay Bridge collapse of 1879 and the Armagh runaway and collision of 1889. The Tay Bridge disaster is noteworthy for support expressed by Joseph Chamberlain, then President of the Board of Trade, for the Inspecting Officer who had inspected the bridge prior to its opening, Maj-Gen Hutchinson. The bridge had opened for traffic on June 1 1878, after great efforts by the East Coast Group of companies, as it considerably shortened the distance from Edinburgh to Dundee and Aberdeen and strengthened their joint competitive position with the West Coast companies.

On the night of December 28 1879, a great storm blew up along the Firth of Tay. The evening North British train from Edinburgh, with 74 or 75 passengers on board (according to the ticket collectors) was making its way slowly across the bridge when observers suddenly saw the lights of the train fall from the bridge and then vanish. The whole central section of the slender bridge, with the train inside its box of girders, had collapsed into the sea, blown down by the force of the westerly gale. The subsequent Court of Inquiry was held by Col Yolland, W. H. Barlow (President of the Institute of Civil Engineers) and H. C. Rothery (Wreck Commissioner).

When Maj-Gen Hutchinson had inspected the new bridge in 1878 it had been tested by using six engines all coupled together. Hutchinson recommended a speed restriction of 25mph and expressed some reservations about the effects of wind when a train was crossing. His fears were not unfounded. Much public and press criticism was subsequently directed at Major General Hutchinson, but he was cleared of blame by Joseph Chamberlain (President of the Board of Trade during William Gladstone's second administration, 1880-85) who said:

"My Lords desire, in the first place, to state that they have always placed entire confidence in Major-General Hutchinson. No more competent, conscientious, and intelligent officer could be found to whom to entrust the inspection of the structure in question, and they are of opinion that his conduct of that inspection has not been such as to forfeit their confidence."

He then went on to comment on the perennial question of the extent to which the Government should interfere in the running of the railways, and whether it should have greater powers. These questions are as relevant today as they were nearly a century and a half ago - as witnessed by the Williams Review into precisely this question yet again in 2019.

"It may appear to some that the present state of things is one which cannot be logically defended and that the Board of Trade ought to be entrusted with further powers. The experience of a great number of years has, however, shown that the present system does not work unsatisfactorily, and a little consideration will show that the public safety and convenience would not be promoted by such a change.

"In the first place, if the Board of Trade were to be held responsible for the designs of railway structures and for the supervision of their execution, they must employ a staff as experienced, as numerous, and probably as highly remunerated, as the civil engineers by and under whom these structures are now designed and executed .... If any public department were entrusted with the power and the duty of correcting and guaranteeing the designs of those engineers who are responsible for railway structures, the result would be to check and control the enterprise which has done so much for this country, and to substitute for the real responsibility which rests on the railway engineer the unreal and delusive responsibility of a public office ... to say nothing of the necessary evils of double management." This important clarification of the Inspectors role has consistently prevailed ever since.

The other tragic accident occurred near Armagh, on the Great Northern Railway of Ireland, on June 12 1889. A very heavy Sunday school excursion of 15 carriages, packed with almost 1,000 passengers, stalled on a steep gradient. The train crew decided to divide the train (a common practice in those days) and take the first five carriages to the top of the gradient, put them into a siding, and then return for the others. Unfortunately, the rear ten carriages were not properly secured on the gradient and the train was not equipped with the continuous automatic brake. A jerk from the engine during the uncoupling process was sufficient to set them rolling backwards down the hill. The runaway carriages gathered speed very rapidly, to the mounting terror of their unfortunate occupants. They were unfortunate in more ways than one because the line, which was single, was not being worked on the block system but on the old fashioned time interval system. By now, another train, this one lightly loaded, was already making its way up the bank towards the runaway now rushing towards them, at a good speed. Disaster was inevitable. It was merely a question of how many would be killed. The final death toll was 80, of whom 22 were children, with a further 260 injured. It was the worst accident up to that time in the entire 60 years or so of passenger railway history, as marked by the opening of the Liverpool & Manchester Railway in 1830.

This terrible accident, caused both by the lack of an automatic continuous train brake and the absence of a safe system of signalling, was the last straw so far as the Railway Inspectorate was concerned. For more than 20 years its Inspectors had argued, cajoled, harangued and used every means at their disposal in an attempt to persuade the railway companies to adopt those valuable safeguards, and in truth, by now all of the companies on the British mainland had done so, or had plans in place. But on a number of occasions Col Yolland had pointed out that the Board of Trade had no power to compel railway companies to adopt the automatic continuous brake and the block system of signalling and he had consistently suggested that such powers should be available.

Now, although posthumously, his wish was to finally be granted - although the deaths of 78 passengers, including 22 children, was a fearsome price to pay. Parliamentary and public opinion had been deeply stirred by the vision of all those children so horribly killed at Armagh and a short Bill was hurriedly introduced, which quickly passed through Parliament and received the Royal Assent. The Act, known as the Regulation of Railways Act 1889, came into force on August 30 and became known as the 'lock, block and brake' milestone legislation. The Act contained the following important provisions:

Section 1

The Board of Trade may order a railway company:

1: to adopt the block system on passenger lines,
2: to provide for the interlocking of points and signals on passenger lines,
3: to provide, and use, on passenger trains, continuous brakes complying with the following requirements:

- Must be instantaneous in action
- Must be capable of being applied by the driver and the guard
- The brake must be applied automatically in the event of an accidental train division
- The brake must be capable of being applied to every vehicle in the train
- Must be in regular use in daily working
- Must be of durable character and easily maintained

At long last, the battle for continuous train brakes with some foot-dragging railway companies had been won and within a few years all railway companies had complied with the Act. 'Lock, block and brake' was now a national standard. The railways were now approaching the zenith of their importance in the social, business and industrial life of the country and a few facts and figures may help to set in context the sheer size and scale of the late 19th century British railway undertakings. The largest, most important and most prosperous company was, by any standards, undoubtedly the London & North Western which was the largest Joint Stock company in the world giving a minimum of 6% return on shares between 1876 and 1897. The Great Western and the Midland vied for second place, with the North Eastern in fourth place. In 1889, the total paid-up capital of all the railway companies was £877m. Total revenue for the year was £78m and working expenditure was £40m (52% of total revenue - a proportion which had hardly changed for 20 years).

Traffic details were:

	No. of passengers or tons of freight Traffic (million)	Revenue (£million)
First class	30	3
Second class	63	3
Third class	682	20
Season tickets		2
Coal and minerals	212	23
Merchandise	86	17
Livestock		1

These figures highlight two outstanding factors - that the passenger business was overwhelmingly third class and that the coal and minerals business alone was worth almost as much as the country's entire passenger traffic.

One final point. The term 'block' has been used frequently in relation to block telegraph, block signalling, absolute block and so on. The term refers to a system of signalling in which adjacent signalboxes are in communication with each other by telegraph wires, enabling signalling messages to be sent between them, and thereby along the line of route, by Morse-style bell codes. This allows one signalman to operate an indicator in the next signalbox ahead to show whether the section between the two signalboxes is clear on the line concerned. This allows a train to be 'passed on' from box to box quickly and safely. It also incorporates a procedure in which a signalman will not allow a train to pass his signalbox until the man at the next signalbox has given permission for it to proceed. The

Above: The aftermath of the dreadful runaway and collision at Armagh, on June 12 1889. A very heavily overloaded Sunday school excursion was unable to climb this gradient and stalled. It was divided and the front half restarted, leaving the rear half of the train on the steep incline. It overcame the stones placed between its wheels to help the primitive brakes hold it, ran away and collided at speed with a following train despatched on the very dangerous time interval system. 80 people died, about a third of them children and 260 more were injured. It was the worst rail disaster of the 19th century, the worst rail disaster in Europe at the time and to this day it remains the fourth worst in the UK. The disaster at Armagh led directly to the so-called 'lock, block and brake' Regulation of Railways Act of 1889 which the RI had been demanding, for many years. *Alamy*.

term 'block' is reputedly derived from the block of wood which was used in early days to hold over the operating handle of the telegraph instrument.

Memorandum of some of the Requirements of the Inspecting Officer, 1858

At the Stations

- Platforms to be not less than six feet wide, and when raised, the descent at the ends should be by means of ramps, and not by steps.
- Clocks to be provided in a position where they are visible from the line.
- Signals and distant signals in each direction to be erected.
- The lever handles of switches and signals to be placed in the most convenient position, and to be brought as close together as possible, so as to be under the hand of the person working them. The switches to be provided with double connecting rods.
- No Facing Points, except on single lines or at double junctions. In the case of Facing Points at junctions, it is most desirable that the signals should be connected with the points so as to be worked in conjunction with them, and to indicate whether they are open or shut.
- Sidings, if falling towards the line, or on a level, to be provided with locked chock blocks, or locked points, leading into a blind siding.
- Turntables for engines to be erected at terminal stations.

As Regards the Line Generally

- No standing work above the level of the carriage steps to be nearer to the rail than 3 feet 6 inches, where the carriages are not above 7 feet 4 inches in width, outside measurement.
- The interval between adjacent lines of rails, and between lines of rails and sidings, must not be less than 6 feet.
- When stations occur on, or immediately contiguous to, a viaduct, a parapet wall on each side, 3 feet high, should be built, with a hand railing or a fence on the top sufficient to prevent passengers from falling over the viaduct in the dark.
- At all level crossings of turnpike roads or of important public roads, the gates must be so constructed as to be capable of closing across the Railway as well as across the road.
- A fixed signal, either attached to the gate or otherwise, to be placed at every level crossing and when the level crossing is so situated that an approaching train cannot be seen for a sufficient distance, distant signals will be required.
- Main and distant signals for each line are required, at all junctions.
- Where the lines are single, an undertaking will be required, to be signed by the Chairman and Secretary of the Company, that the line shall be worked in such a manner that only one engine in steam, or two or more when coupled together and forming part of a train, shall ever be upon the single line, or upon defined portions thereof at one and the same time.

CHAPTER 3
THE GOLDEN AGE OF RAILWAYS 1890-1914

Above: At the turn of the 20th century, Britain's private railway network (about 120 companies) was approaching its zenith - a glorious period of pre-eminence, glamour, power and impressive image. This powerful period was choked off by the Great War after 1914 and these glory days never really returned, other than very briefly during the streamlined years of the later 1930s. In 1900, most passenger trains were hauled by four-coupled locomotives of the 4-4-0 wheel arrangement whilst virtually all freight was handled by 0-6-0 tender engines. This was the railway which the RI was responsible for supervising in good times and then investigating when it all went wrong. It is impossible not to be impressed by spectacles like this: an immaculate early 20th century crack passenger train. This is a Midland Railway nine coach clerestory express, hauled by 4-4-0 No. 2633, a 1901 three-cylinder Smith compound which used high pressure steam in the middle cylinder and low pressure exhaust steam in the two outside cylinders. Subsequently rebuilt for easier driving, this design was very economical and 195 were built for the LMS after the Grouping of 1923. Pioneer No. 2631, later No. 1000, survives in superheated form in York's National Railway Musuem. *CC Collection.*

In the two decades before the First World War, the railways reached the zenith of their power and prosperity, and the year 1890, following the Regulation of Railways Act of the previous year, marked a watershed in their progress. They came of age and donned a mantle of respectability. They still continued to grow from 20,073 miles of line open in 1890 to 23,701 miles in 1914 but the building of new lines was now coming to an end and would have done so even without the upheaval of war and its aftermath. The lines already open became even busier. Between 1890 and 1914 both passenger and freight traffic almost doubled, but the improvement in safety systems already achieved meant that there was no corresponding increase in passenger fatalities - indeed, the reverse was the case. In the 10 years from 1880 to 1889 no fewer than 249 passengers lost their lives in train accidents; from 1900-09 only 169, while in both 1901 and 1908 not a single passenger was killed in a train accident. This was a high water mark in safety which was not to be repeated for more than 40 years, until 1949. Had it not been for a number of disastrous high-speed derailments on curves the position would have shown even greater improvement.

The power and prosperity of the railways reflected the situation of the country as a whole. Britain was still the most powerful nation on earth. Coal and steel production easily outstripped any other countries and British steel and capital were used to build railways all over the world. In 1890, UK foreign trade stood at £740m. The nearest rivals were: Germany £367m, France £311m and the USA £320m. British shipping was pre-eminent on the high seas and the

mercantile marine was several times larger than any other nations. All this industrial activity provided the railways with their prosperity, but it was a reciprocal process; Britain's industrial progress could not have been achieved without the railways, whose tentacles and sinews reached into almost every corner of the land and influenced almost every aspect of national life.

This enormous enterprise - the railways of Britain - was watched over on behalf of the travelling population by a small band of Inspecting Officers of the Board of Trade. In 1890, it had consisted of Col Rich (Chief), Maj-Gen Hutchinson and Major Marindin. Col Rich retired in 1891, after 30 years' service, Maj-Gen Hutchinson retired in 1895 after 28 years, whilst Marindin, now Col Sir Francis Marindin, died in service in 1900 of pneumonia, contracted during a long and tiring day's inspection of new lines on the London, Brighton & South Coast Railway. He had been created Knight Commander of the Order of St Michael & St George at Queen Victoria's Diamond Jubilee. It was truly the end of an era. The new Inspecting Officers were:

- Major (later Lt-Col) Yorke 1891-1913
- Lt-Col Addison 1895-1899
- Lt-Col von Donop 1899-1916
- Major (later Col) Pringle 1900-1929
- Major (later Lt-Col) Druitt 1900-1918
- Both Yorke and Pringle were subsequently knighted.

Lt-Col Sir H. Arthur Yorke KCB
Chief Inspecting Officer: 1900-13

Arthur Yorke had joined the Royal Engineers in 1866 at the age of 17. His mother was the daughter of General Sir Alexander Campbell and his brother was the Fourth Earl of Hardwicke. During his army career he was engaged in the 1879-80 Afghan War and then in the Nile Expedition of 1884-85. He was promoted to Lieutenant-Colonel in 1894. Yorke joined the Railway Inspectorate in 1891, becoming Chief Inspecting Officer in 1900 on the premature death of Sir Francis Marindin. He was knighted on his retirement in 1913.

Lt-Col P. G. von Donop
Chief Inspecting Officer: 1913-16

Pelham von Donop was the son of Vice-Admiral E. P. von Donop and entered the Royal Military Academy in 1869, obtaining a commission in the Royal Engineers in 1871. His younger brother was also an army man, becoming Major General Sir Stanley von Donop. Pelham von Donop was a remarkable sportsman - he was a member

Above: This was the later 19th century secondary railway goods traffic that the RI worked with. This is thought to be a Thomas Wheatley North British Railway 0-6-0, of which 88 were built between 1867 and 1875. This was a busy and inherently dangerous (for staff) railway of mixed trains, extensive marshalling at wayside stations and yards, fly shunting, hand-operated points, shunting poles and still-rudimentary brakes. *Getty Images.*

of the RE team which won the Football Association Cup in 1875; a fine cricketer (again in 1875, he scored a century in a remarkable game against I Zingari, when the RE team amassed 726 for eight wickets), and he won championships at tennis.

His army career took him to many parts of the British Empire and he was in charge of the Sudan Railways during the 1884-86 campaign. He came to the Railway Inspectorate rather later in life than others, not being appointed an Inspector of Railways until 1899 when he was 48 years old. Despite all that had gone before, it was said of him that he now commenced 'what perhaps may be called the most valuable part of his official career'. He was Chief Inspecting Officer from 1913 to 1916, when he retired at the age of 65. He died five years later.

Colonel Sir John Wallace Pringle CB
Chief Inspecting Officer: 1916-29

John Pringle, the son of General Pringle, was commissioned in the Royal Engineers in 1883. He saw service in India and Burma for six years, then spent two years surveying the Uganda Railway, returning to India for a further five years. He came home in 1898 and was appointed an Inspector of Railways in 1900, becoming Chief Inspecting Officer in 1916, a post he held until 1929.

During the first two years of World War 1 he was Deputy Director of Railway Transport, Home Defences.

John Pringle was made a Companion of the Order of the Bath in 1921 and knighted in 1925.

During the postwar period of Sir John Pringle's service with the Railway Inspectorate the inspecting team was never more than three strong, partly reflecting the reduction in new works inspection duties in the changed economic conditions.

He was chairman of the Railway Electrification Committee, set up in 1927 to review the types of electrification that might be permitted on British railways. The Committee recommended the adoption of two types: third rail of 750V dc and overhead of 1,500V dc (with permission to use 3,000V dc in special conditions).

He was also chairman of the Departmental Committee set up in 1928 to consider the extension of the system of automatic train

Above: At Swindon, 15 miles of crude sidings were laid, using interlaced 'sleepers' to hold the spiked rails to gauge. Non-convertible locomotives awaited scrap. The engine on the left is thought to be a Dean passenger tank, built for South Devon. Its bunker is full of good quality coal and the baffle plate (or flame scoop as it's sometimes known) from the firehole, has been thrown into the bunker by its last fireman. The impressive outside-framed Gooch 'Rover' 4-2-2s appear intact, clean and in very good order, each complete with its single gauge glass and pressure gauge; the cabside nearest the camera bears evidence of its last polish. Connecting rods lie dumped in the tender - doubtless to make towing easier. There were 24 'Rovers', 20 being built new in 1873. Driving with lever reverse must have been challenging! *CC Collection.*

Above: It is interesting to compare the problems faced by today's railway to maintain and enhance its infrastructure with the late 19th century Great Western Railway's massive, initially incremental but later big project conversion of its extensive 7ft¼in gauge network, first to the very complex mixed gauge and finally to standard gauge. The scale of the final phase, when the last 177 miles of main line were converted to standard gauge over a single weekend in May 1892, is breathtaking. The Victorian RI thus had to contend with mixed gauge train operations and infrastructure for a long period and then a drawn out conversion, culminating in a truly massive weekend project. This is Didcot in broad gauge days as a down express passes, hauled by what appears to be a 7ft 2-2-2 'Single,' built as a convertible. *CC Collection.*

Above: An up express passes Cholsey & Moulsford, hauled by a Dean 2-2-2 'Single'. Brunel's broad gauge is clear to see, with longitudinal baulks beneath the rails and widely spaced 'sleepers'. The final broad gauge trains ran on Friday May 20 1892 with all remaining 7ft gauge locomotives and stock being moved to Swindon for conversion or disposal. On May 21/22, 177 miles of broad gauge between Exeter and Truro were converted to standard gauge (including all branches) by 4,700 workers. The work was completed on time and on Sunday the overnight 'Night Mail' ran all the way from Paddington to Penzance. The complexity, sheer amount and detail of advance planning and lineside preparation for this project is truly mind-boggling. Imagine such a project today... *CC Collection.*

Above: This night accident at Maudland, Preston, on August 13 1896, killed a single passenger, but it was spectacular, controversial and resulted in slowing down Anglo-Scottish express passenger timings until 1932. Its impact was significantly out of proportion to the human toll - and this was because the so-called 'Races to the North' of the previous summer between East and West Coast main lines caused great public and media disquiet and this accident validated those safety fears. Both locomotives - 2-4-0s No. 2159 *Shark* and No. 275 *Vulcan* derailed immediately north of Preston station after taking a 10mph curve at around 40mph. Preston station is beyond the Fishergate bridge in the right distance. (See also page 49) *Alan Middleton Collection.*

control (later known as the Automatic Warning System) which had been developed by the Great Western Railway. The Pringle Committee reported in 1930 and recommended the extension of ATC as well as the provision of more powerful signal lights and further controls to prevent signalmen's errors. Pringle died in 1938 at the age of 75.

The main requirements of safe signalling and braking systems had been implemented by 1890, but there were still several fundamental flaws in the manner in which our railways were operated. In particular, insufficient regard was paid to human aspects, resulting in a number of spectacular accidents from the following causes:

- Drivers wrongly passing signals at 'danger' at high speed.
- Drivers running round curves at too high a speed.
- Signalmen forgetting the presence of a train or light engine standing on the main line near their signalbox.

These three major causes of accident did eventually lead to the adoption of improved safety systems and equipment but it was a long, slow process, which had hardly been completed even a century later. Many of the improvements needed were fairly simple and cheap, but were nonetheless resisted by some of the railway companies as though safety were a 'macho' business and the men ought not to be 'mollycoddled' by such protective safety devices.

Some of these points are illustrated by the fatal accident at Norton Fitzwarren at 1.24am on November 11 1890. A down goods train had been shunting and was finally set back on to the up main line to await a path before proceeding on its journey. The signalman then forgot all about this train and when he was offered an Ocean Liner Special from Plymouth to Paddington by the signalman at Victory signalbox, a mile to the west, he not only accepted the train but offered it forward to Silk Mill signal box, 1,500yd to the east. He then cleared all his signals for it, with his lines blocked by the goods train. The Special, consisting of only two eight-wheeled composite coaches and a brakevan, was coming fast down a gradient and crashed head-on into the standing goods at a speed of between 50 and 60mph. The 50 passengers on the train had only just landed from the Cape of Good Hope: ten were killed.

The signalman had been at Norton Fitzwarren for 27 years, yet he made a simple human error (it is also thought he was unwell) and just forgot about the goods train. Colonel Rich, in one of his last inquiries, recommended that signalmen should be provided with a very simple device rather like a metal disc, inscribed 'Train Waiting', which could be slipped over the lever of the signal protecting a standing train, to prevent the lever from being pulled over by the signalman in a moment of forgetfulness. This variants of the lever collar is such a cheap, simple and effective solution it is surprising that it hadn't been introduced before - the reality is that yet again the idea had been resisted by many railway companies, who felt that it might cause signalmen to relax their vigilance. Perhaps they were right and in any event, signalmen sometimes didn't bother to use the lever collars even where they were provided. This omission occasionally had fatal results, but on the other hand you cannot prove a negative and we will simply never know how often a collar placed over a lever stopped the signalman from wrongly pulling the signal in a careless moment.

One interesting linguistic and technical snippet from this period - the accident reports from about 1888 start to use the spelling 'brake' instead of 'break'.

Parliament was seriously concerned at this time about the number of people killed whilst crossing the line at level crossings and the Inspectorate therefore compiled a report showing that in the five years from 1888 to 1892, 369 people had been killed, as follows:

- On public carriage roads 141
- On private or occupation roads 98
- On footpaths 106
- On footpath and occupation roads combined 24

CONTINUED ON PAGE 44

The 1896 Preston accident, looking west across Maudland Junction, from the east Preston station is to the left. The lines vanishing away into the murk ran to Blackpool and the spire of Preston's famous St Walburge's Church is dimly visible. No. 2159 *Shark's* dome is on the extreme right while No. 275 *Vulcan* is in full view, in front of its overturned six-wheel tender. In addition to speed, a contributory factor was the absence of leading bogies on the 2-4-0s to steer these LNWR locomotives into curves. The picture also tells a story about the complexity, sighting problems and interpretation difficulties of late 19th century semaphore signalling. Note the men watching from the crossbars of the telegraph pole behind *Vulcan's* tender and those sitting on the ridge tiles of the factory roof behind *Vulcan* itself. They had probably emerged from the open skylight on the roof behind, from which the picture on page 40 may also have been taken. Oddly, there appears to be a very smartly dressed lady, in long skirt, white blouse and straw 'boater' immediately behind the loaded coal wagon in the right foreground. Note also the 'gawpers'perched precariously on the telegraph pole crossbars, in the centre of the picture! (see also page 49) *Alan Middleton Collection.*

Above: Shrewsbury, October 15 1907. An LNWR overnight sleeping car/ mail train derailed after approaching the 10mph, 610-feet radius curve into Shrewsbury, from Crewe, at 60mph. LNWR 'Experiment' 4-6-0 No. 2052 *Stephenson*, built the previous year - derailed and ploughed up the track for 75 yards before rolling onto its right side and rapidly decelerating, whereupon its train piled up behind it. Driver and fireman were both killed and so the cause of their reckless approach remains a mystery. Did the driver doze off? We shall never know - but the propensity to drowsiness amongst shift workers is now much better understood. Note the terrible damage to the timber-bodied clerestory-roofed carriage, whose side has been sliced away. The bowler hat was very much the badge of authority amongst the very dapper managers at the scene. *Getty Images.*

Above: This wider 1907 view at Shrewsbury clearly indicates how the leading right hand corner of the leading clerestory carriage was torn away as it rode over the overturning tender as it rapidly slowed. The destruction of the rear of the carriage helps explain the passenger death toll of 11, together with three Post Office staff and two guards. Two sets of metals were destroyed for 140 yards. There were 33 other pasenger injuries. The 15-carriage train left Crewe eight minutes late at 1.20am, but the driver ran over the 18½ miles from Whitchurch to Shrewsbury at an average speed of 60mph regaining five minutes. This was the last of three high speed passenger derailments in just a year, the others being at Salisbury and the mysterious and unexplained high speed derailment at Grantham, both in 1906. *Getty Images.*

Above: This tangled mass of scorched steel and charred debris is all that remains of the burned out carriages in which nine passengers perished, during the notorious Hawes Junction disaster of Christmas Eve, 1910. The story of how a northbound Settle-Carlisle Midland express smashed into the back of two ambling light engines running northbound on the same track, near Grisedale Crossing, just north of Moorcock Tunnel, has been detailed many times, but most compellingly by L.T.C. Rolt in his iconic Red for Danger. Briefly, Hawes signalman Alfred Sutton had no fewer than five engines under his control on that stormy Christmas Eve and in this very busy spell he had forgotten about the two light engines sitting on the down main line, close to his box, awaiting a clear road to Carlisle. When the overstretched Sutton cleared his signals for the down express, the pair of light engines he had forgotten assumed the cleared signals were for them - they moved off at just 25mph for Carlisle. A simple, cheap, collar placed over the red lever controlling the signal the light engines were waiting at, as a reminder for the wretched signalman, could have prevented this terrible tragedy - but the MR did not like these devices and had resisted RI pressure to adopt them. Signalmen often were inconsistent in their use and some companies believed this undermined their alertness and was a risk in itself. The light engine crews were not blameless: they stood on the main line for at least 13 minutes, but failed to either carry out Rule 55, to remind the signalman of their presence, or even blow their whistles to attract his attention. As they steamed north, they were rapidly caught by the fast-running express. After the collision, coal gas (for carriage lighting) escaping from storage cylinders at 85 pounds per square inch, ensured the wreckage was consumed by fire. In his RI report, Colonel Pringle recommended stronger gas tanks with automatic shut-off valves to stop gas escaping if the pipe from the tank was severed. "But," he added "I still hold that electricity is the more desirable and should be adopted wherever possible." It was a recommendation which would be repeated many times in the next few years, before gas lighting was finally abandoned. An especially horrific fact is that some of the 12 who died were still conscious when the raging fire reached them - but desperate staff could not extricate them because of a lack of tools. The terrible toll accelerated the installation of track circuits at hundreds of other places on the MR, just as the terrible Harrow & Wealdstone accident in 1952 much later finally accelerated the wider installation of the Automatic Warning System on BR main lines. *Getty Images.*

CONTINUED FROM PAGE 41

In comparison there were two fatalities at railway crossings in 2018-2019. In their report to the House of Lords, the Inspectors detailed the proposals which the Railway Companies had in mind for dealing with this problem, which included the building of a large number of footbridges and a number of road bridges. Under the Railways Clauses Act 1863, the Board of Trade could subsequently require a railway company to erect, at its own own cost, a bridge in place of a level crossing, if this appeared necessary for public safety. Level crossings had always been a bone of contention between the railway companies and the public - and continued to be so. They still are today and remain a potential catastrophic risk for the railway and its users and those who cross its tracks.

Fog, combined with the lack of any automatic warning system for drivers, made a potent and dangerous combination. One of the last inquiries held by Major General Hutchinson concerned an accident at Castle Hills Junction on the East Coast Main Line at 3.06am on October 4 1894. The double-headed first portion of the 10.40pm Edinburgh to King's Cross express ran past all the signals at danger at the previous signalbox - Wiske Moor - in fog and failed to slow down at the distant signal at Castle Hills Junction. It collided with an almost stationary mineral train at 40mph. The front part of the express was severely damaged but as fate would have it, no passengers were killed. Eight passengers had been killed in a collision at Thirsk only two years previously when travelling in the second portion of the up Scotch express, and Hutchinson recommended that the line between Darlington and Thirsk should be 'duplicated' (converted from two tracks to four) in view of the heavy traffic. There had been no fog signalmen on duty and the signalman at Wiske Moor had been slow in putting warning detonators on the line at his signal box. The provision of detonator-placing equipment, worked by a lever in the signalbox, might well have prevented the accident, yet some railway companies were - yet again - very slow to provide such valuable (and simple, very cheap) safety devices.

CONTINUED ON PAGE 49

Above: Accidents from this era at Grantham (1906), Shrewsbury (1907), Hawes Junction (1910) or Preston (1896) have become notorious, as did Harrow & Wealdstone (1952) or, in more recent years, Ladbroke Grove (1999) and Hatfield (2000). But the RI (after 1990, HMRI) routinely investigated hundreds of far less serious incidents which might have either missed the news or only featured in a minor way. But lessons were always highlighted by the RI (whether or not they were learned and implemented by the railway companies) such as here at Vauxhall on August 29 1912. A light engine bound from the Motive Power Depot at Nine Elms to Waterloo collided with the rear of the 11.37am Aldershot-Waterloo, standing at the platform. The dangers of 'telescoping' are clear - fatalities were highly likely. There was one death in this incident and 48 injuries. The driver and fireman were also both injured. *Getty Images.*

Above: London & South Western Railway 4-4-0 No. 312 was the light engine involved in the Vauxhall collision (top) of August 29 1912. Running tender first, the driver's vision would not have been good over the high eight-wheel tender, whose rear two axles derailed in the impact. The carriage underframe appears to have ridden over small tender buffers and caused the impact damage to the rear of the steel tender tank. The other end of the rear coach telescoped into the rear of the penultimate carriage. The pre-Great War Edwardian era was a high point of the rail industry and this locomotive was in immaculate external condition in green, lined in black and white. *Getty Images.*

Above: Ditton, London & North Western Railway, September 17 1912. A common refrain in RI investigations was the need to assist drivers with unambiguous signalling on complex, busy track layouts, which tended to have towering, confusing, complex gantries of semaphore arms. Such layouts eased congestion - but they brought dangers too. (They were still doing so at Ladbroke Grove, in 1999, nearly a century later). At Ditton Junction, near Widnes, there were eight parallel running lines in 1912 and when the 5.30pm Chester-Liverpool express was signalled to cross from fast to slow metals, the driver misread signals, believing he had a clear run on the fast line. He approached the 15mph crossover at 60mph. Catastrophe followed. *Getty Images.*

Above: After derailing at a mile a minute, the 'Precedent' 2-4-0 rolled onto its side at Ditton and led its entire train off the rails, wrecking both down and slow lines over a considerable distance. The 2-4-0 halted when it collided with a brick overbridge with such force it 'broke its back', the boiler ripping free of the firebox throatplate. The six coaches shot over the derailed engine and tender and ended up in a pile of wreckage beyond the bridge, where fire broke out - just as at Hawes Junction two years before - fuelled by ruptured gas pipes. Driver, fireman and 13 passengers perished, most burned to death. *Getty Images.*

Above: Recovery at Ditton, 1912. Not only did the 'Precedent' lose its firebox, but at the front, the smokebox was also destroyed in the bridge collision. The tender lies some distance away, facing in the opposite direction. "There is, said Colonel Yorke, "no record of any previous accident in which the engine has broken its back, as in this case, and rarely has there been such wholesale destruction of rolling stock." *Getty Images.*

Above: The tender awaits recovery, doubtless for scrapping. The twisted remains of the 2-4-0 cab lie to left of the wheels. Colonel Yorke criticised both the driver's road knowledge and also the 'inconsistent and confusing' signalling, where there were muliple distant signals, depending on the route set. The RI recommended single distants, regardless of route. *Getty Images.*

Above: Burnt out wreckage from the double southbound sleeping car trains rear end collision of September 2 1913 lie by the lineside, about three quarters of a mile north of Ais Gill Summit, on the Settle-Carlisle line. The 'sleepers' were the 1.35am and 1.49am departures from Carlisle: both suffered poor steaming on the 'Long Drag' from the Border City because of poor coal sourced locally by the MR to cut costs. The first train - which qualified for a pilot engine but none was available - laboured increasingly, short of steam on the 'Long Drag' until it stalled at the point of subsequent collision. The following train also suffered poor steaming, leading to the distracted driver misreading the Mallerstang distant (he had been out of the cab on the framing oiling 'on the move' as was MR custom at the time) which he glimpsed from the running boards, as he emerged from Birkett Tunnel. Back in the cab, he became preoccupied helping maintain steam pressure and water level (the injectors were failing at low pressure) and he missed the stop signals. Seeing and hearing his approach, the guard of the stalled first train dashed back to try and stop him, but its driver was so busy helping the fireman that by the time he did see the guard's warning and the stalled train's red tail lamp, he could not stop and ran into it at about 30mph. The rear van was demolished after which the engine wrecked the carriage beyond: gas-fuelled fire broke out again (just as it did at Hawes in 1910) and 14 passengers died either in the crash or in the fire; two died subsequently from injuries. There were 38 serious injuries in the second train. *Getty Images.*

Above: On September 15 1913, MR General Superintendent Sir Cecil Walter Paget (appointed in 1907 - his title would today be Chief Operating Officer) seemingly seeks to avoid the camera lens during the Ais Gill accident inquiry. In his report, Col Pringle reviewed the day's embryonic systems of automatic train control and cab signalling - and the subject was covered in the media nearly a century before the very similar debate about automatic train protection after the Ladbroke Grove disaster of October 1999, when 31 people died. Pringle was lukewarm about the GWR ATC, saying it needed prolonged trials before it could be widely recommended. Sadly, the Great War intervened and halted progress: after the war, the GWR ATC principles were unanimously accepted by the industry. But progress was still very slow - 30 years later, the 1952 the Harrow & Wealdstone double collision in fog could have been averted by train control, but no Automatic Warning System was yet fitted, even on the West Coast Main Line, nearly 40 years after the 1913 Ais Gill disaster which had first highlighted the urgent need for such a system. *Getty Images.*

Above: So intense was the 1913 blaze at Ais Gill that, just as with the Hawker *Hunter* jet crash and fire at the 2015 Shoreham air show, many remains were never found. Relatives wait at Kirkby Stephen to identify victims. Then, as now, the news media took an intense interest. The 1910 Hawes Inspector, Col Sir John Pringle (who also reported on Ais Gill in 1913) had recommended that track circuits be installed at Hawes Junction to protect the high numbers of movements on and off the turntable. The MR went much further and installed track circuits at more than 900 similar locations - so railway companies were not always slow in adopting RI advice. As the 1913 fire proved, however, the MR had indeed dragged its feet regarding gas lighting in its carriages. *Getty Images.*

CONTINUED FROM PAGE 44

Over the decades, both East and West Coast night expresses have been involved in many accidents and in 1896 it was the turn of the West Coast Main Line. Shortly after midnight on August 13 the first portion of the 8pm from Euston, the down 'Highland Express', double-headed by four-coupled engines Nos 2159 *Shark* and 275 *Vulcan*, became totally derailed whilst travelling at 40mph over the curve to the north of Preston station. All except three coaches were damaged beyond repair, but as there were only 15 or 16 passengers on the entire train the death toll was low, only one passenger losing his life. The speed restriction over the curve was 10mph but it was widely disregarded. This was during the period known as 'the races to the North' between the East and West Coast routes.

Lieutenant Colonel Yorke, who inquired into the accident, might have had more to say if he had known how frequently high speed derailments were to occur in the next few years.

Railway accidents attracted just as much media attention in those days as they do today and a great deal of prominence was given in the press to suggestions that mechanical contrivances were needed, working in conjunction with the semaphore signals, to make it impossible for a driver to pass a signal at 'danger' without becoming aware of it. On the other hand, Lieutenant Colonel Yorke thought that this provision might cause drivers to pay less heed to signals and he was worried about the reliability of such equipment. In other words, Yorke seemed to see all the problems whilst appreciating none of the advantages. He envisaged having the apparatus at every signal and failed to realise the value of having the equipment at distant signals only. It is a pity that he was so lukewarm because he was in a position to give a great impetus to the development of what became known as Automatic Train Control, or ATC for short. Fortunately for the Great Western, a group of its officers did recognise the need for ATC at distant signals and work started on the development of a suitable system from 1906.

The first year of the 20th century began very auspiciously. For the first time ever, not a single passenger was killed in a train accident, which was a remarkable tribute both to railway engineers and operators. Bearing in mind the absence of many modern safeguards it could not have been achieved without a very high standard of discipline and devotion to duty, and pride in their particular railway company, by railwaymen of all grades.

That said, 1901 saw an accident which had ominous overtones for later years. On December 23 an electric train of the Liverpool Overhead Railway came to a stand with an electrical defect, approaching Dingle station, on the underground section. Electrical arcing then set fire to the train and fierce flames, fumes and smoke were driven by the wind into the station, which was also consumed by fire. All passengers were safely evacuated but six railwaymen died in the very rapid spread of the fire once it had gained a hold. Lieutenant Colonel Yorke investigated the accident and in view of the lethal nature of such fires and the speed with which they spread, recommended that as little wood as possible should be used in underground stations on electrified lines.

The biggest railway in 1903, in terms of train miles run, was the LNWR, with 47.6m, but it was very closely challenged for that position by the Midland, with 47.5m. The Great Western ran 46.6m, and the North Eastern ran 30.1m. That gave a total for these four alone of 171.8m miles.

The year 1904 saw the first of a remarkable series of four high-speed derailments in as many years, which ended as abruptly as it had begun. The cause, or causes, of the accidents remain a mystery to this day, as all four drivers were killed. In two cases, the signals were showing all-clear; in the other two they were at danger. The speed in every case was about 60mph.

Lieutenant Colonel Yorke inquired into the first crash, which took place at Aylesbury, on the Metropolitan & Great Central Joint line, at 3.38am on December 23. The 2.45am down GC express from Marylebone was coming fast down the seven mile-long falling gradient from Wendover, mainly at 1 in 117, in dense fog. Its driver should have reduced speed for the curve over the trailing junction with the line from Princes Risborough but he failed to do so and an exceptionally destructive derailment took place. The engine, four-coupled No. 1040, mounted the down platform, followed by three or four coaches, whilst two coaches came to rest on the up platform. Sister engine No. 1042, heading a Manchester to Marylebone express, came into slight collision with the wreckage, which was described by Yorke as one of the worst cases of the destruction of rolling stock in a derailment that he had ever known. Fortunately the train was mainly run for the conveyance of news and parcels and it had only three passenger coaches, which were very sparsely occupied by only eight passengers. The driver and fireman of engine No. 1040 were both killed, together with two railway servants, who were travelling 'on the cushions' as passengers.

Two years were to elapse before the next case, at Salisbury, in 1906, on the LSWR. The weekly boat express left Plymouth for Waterloo late on the evening of June 30 with five bogie-coaches conveying 43 first-class passengers who had just been landed by company's tender at Stonehouse Pool from the America Line steamship, the *SS New York*. Although the two rival companies, the Great Western and the LSWR, concerned in the Plymouth to London ocean liner traffic would have denied any suggestion of racing to see who could achieve the shortest journey time, there is no doubt that there was great keenness and rivalry between the train crews and some high speeds were attained. At 1.57am the 'Ocean Liner Express' approached Salisbury at about 60mph, headed by 6ft 7in 4-4-0 No. 421. Probably none of its passengers knew anything about the 30mph speed restriction through the station and were therefore not at all worried when the brakes did not go on. The guard was worried but he acted too late to be of any use. The train tore through the station to the amazement of the few staff on duty, but could not hold the rails over the curve at the east end and it overturned into a catastrophic derailment, colliding violently with a milk train moving in the opposite direction on the next line. The death toll was the highest for many years; 24 passengers were killed - over half the complement - and four locomen. Maj. Pringle inquired into the accident but had no particular recommendations to make, indeed it is difficult to know what he could have suggested that would have avoided such an accident, given the available technology.

The circumstances of the Salisbury accident attracted a great deal of public attention - so many first-class ocean liner passengers meeting their deaths in the middle of the night in a mysterious accident. Imagine, then, the impact on the public imagination of an even more mysterious accident at Grantham less than three months later.

The 8.45pm express from King's Cross to Edinburgh was booked to stop at Grantham at 11.00pm, and consisted of four brake and mail vans, six coaches and sleepers, and two more brakevans, headed by Atlantic locomotive No. 276.

All the signals were cleared for the train at Grantham South and Grantham Yard signalboxes, but the North box signalman had not cleared any of his signals for the express. His junction facing points were fatally set for the Nottingham branch, over which a 15mph speed restriction applied, as he was anticipating a train from that direction. The signalman at the South signalbox saw the express approach, and suddenly realised, to his concern, that it was going too fast to stop at the station. As the train passed his box, he clearly saw the driver and fireman 'standing looking out of their respective glasses'. The thought of possible derailment did not cross his mind because he was unaware that the junction to the north of the station was set towards the branch. The signalman at the North box was much more concerned. The train swept by his signals at danger and swung off through the junction towards the branch. It was too much to hope that a train travelling at over 50mph could safely negotiate a curve designed only for 15mph. The engine and five coaches plunged to destruction down a bank, then a relatively new hazard manifested itself. All except two vehicles were gas-lit, and fire broke out in the wreckage to add to the horror. Eleven passengers and a Post Office attendant, together with the driver and fireman, were killed.

Lt-Col von Donop, who inquired into the accident, concluded 'It is feared therefore that the primary cause of this accident must for ever remain a mystery'. He also said 'I consider that the accident points, as previous railway accidents have already done, to the unsuitability of gas as an illuminant for railway vehicles'. However, the main cause of the accident was the passing of signals at 'danger', and the express could just as easily have collided with another train as become derailed. It is a pity that von Donop failed to make any recommendation about the provision of apparatus to assist drivers in paying obedience to signals. By now, the Great Western was already conducting trials with its ATC apparatus on the Henley branch. Grantham has gone down in history as a high speed derailment, rather than as a signal passed at danger, even though the driver had no reason to reduce speed for the main line, for which he might reasonably have expected the facing points to be set. But even if he had forgotten about the booked station stop at Grantham he should still have stopped at the signals at the North signalbox.

TABLE 2

Regional details	England & Wales	Scotland	Ireland
Length of line open 1912	16,223	3,815	4,403
Originating passengers 1913	1,083m	120m	30m
Originating goods tonnage 1913			
Merchandise	58m	11m	3.6m
Coal, coke	191m	35m	1.3m
Minerals	60m	11m	0.7m

TABLE 1

Passenger traffic 1913	Receipts	Originating passengers
First Class	£4m	26.5m
Second Class	£1m	12.9m
Third Class	£36m	937.0
Workmens tickets	£2m	257.0
Season tickets	£5m	-
Mail	£1m	-
Parcels	£9m	-

Goods traffic 1913	Receipts	Originating tonnage
General merchandise	£33m	73m
Coal, coke	£23m	227m
Minerals	£9m	72m
Livestock	£2m	-

Notes:

1: Net revenue in 1913 was £53.3m.

2: The basis of counting journeys/tonnage was altered after 1912. Before 1913, each railway counted all journeys and tonnage as originating, even though some were taken over at junctions from other companies. From 1913, they were only counted once, at the actual originating point, and this should be borne in mind when comparisons are made with earlier years.

The last of the four accidents was of a rather similar nature. On October 15 1907 the 1.20am LNWR express from Crewe, headed by 'Experiment' class 4-6-0 No. 2052 *Stephenson*, approached Shrewsbury at 60mph, passed all the signals at danger at Crewe Bank signalbox and was derailed on the sharp curve beyond. The train of 15 vehicles was almost completely wrecked. Eleven passengers, three Post Office workers and four railway servants were killed. There were about 70 passengers on the train. (see also page 43)

Lt-Col Yorke took this inquiry. He considered that the driver may have dozed off, and discussed the possible use of ATC-type equipment, but once again he was lukewarm about the idea - despite the fact that it could have prevented both the Shrewsbury and the Grantham accidents, as well as many others. It is a measure of the public concern at these four accidents that the Rt Hon David Lloyd George was present at the Shrewsbury inquiry in his capacity of President of the Board of Trade.

A significant feature of these four accidents is that they all occurred during the night:

- Aylesbury 3.38am
- Salisbury 1.57am
- Grantham 11.04pm
- Shrewsbury 2.08am

Many years later the pattern of derailments on curves was to be repeated:

• Lincoln	12.49am	June 3 1962
• Morpeth	1.31am	May 7 1969
• Paddington	6.11am	November 23 1983
• Morpeth	12.40am	June 24 1984

It is significant that many of the accidents happened during the night hours and it is fortunate that most of the trains concerned were lightly loaded. It only serves to emphasise the need to assist drivers to counter the effects of drowsiness or inattention. In the next few years many companies were to experiment with ATC apparatus but the First World War put paid to most of these developments. It is a great pity that the 68 companies were not given a greater lead by the Inspectorate. By the time that lead was given the mood had changed and times were harder.

1908 was the second year in which no passenger was killed in a train accident, and only one was killed in 1909, which must have done much to tip the balance against heavy expenditure on safety equipment.

The railways were at their height in the years before the First World War. It was a position of power and prosperity that they were never to regain. After the war, costs rose enormously and competition from road transport started to be a major factor. In 1913 the paid-up capital of the companies was £1,334 million, and the average rate of interest on their ordinary stock was 4.6%. Traffic figures and receipts were as shown in accompanying Tables 1 & 2.

CHAPTER 4
TROUBLED YEARS: 1915-1929

Above: Britain's worst train crash was the multiple collision at Quintinshill on May 22 1915, ten miles north of Carlisle, near Gretna Green, on the West Coast Main Line - in which 215 soldiers and nine passengers perished. Signalling errors caused the crash, which was made much worse by fire, fuelled yet again by ruptured gas tanks. This old 12-wheeler has been incinerated to its frames. This horrific collision and fire was fully five years after Hawes Junction (1910) and two years after Ais Gill (1913) where acetylene gas tanks, wooden carriages and fire had previously combined to lethal effect. Many further deaths by fire were to come before gas was eliminated from passenger carriages. Unbelievably, this did not happen until BR days. *Getty Images.*

On August 4 1914, Britain declared war on Germany. That date was a watershed in many aspects of our national life and the effect on the railways was particularly marked. Never again would they reach such heights of power and influence as they had in the Edwardian years up to the Great War. From the early beginnings of railways until the very day that war was declared, their history had been one of continual expansion and growing traffic. All that came virtually to an end on August 4 1914, when the building of new railways ceased overnight, never to be resumed until the building of HS1 (announced in 1991 opened on November 14 2007), other than on a very small scale.

When the war ended, the railways faced a much bleaker, tougher and troubled future. The costs of labour and materials increased considerably while the railways' virtual monopoly of inland transport was seriously and successfully challenged by road transport, aided by the Government's action in dumping on the market, at a cheap price, tens of thousands of surplus lorries and motorcycles. Worse still, the railway's ability to fight such competition was hampered by the upheavals of the Grouping, when 120 individual railway companies were forcibly combined into four major groups (the Great Western, Southern, London Midland & Scottish and London & North Eastern Railways - the GWR, SR, LMS and LNER) under the 1921 Railways Act. Then, just as the railways were becoming adjusted to the new structural landscape and other conditions of the 1920s, the world trade recession of the 1930s developed, which hit the railways' staple traffics of coal and steel very hard indeed.

Almost immediately upon the outbreak of war in 1914 - in fact as rapidly as the second day - the Government took control of the railways in Britain and did not relinquish that control until August 31 1919. The three years after 1919 were then spent preparing for what today would be described as a 'Big Bang' - the Grouping, which came into effect on January 1 1923 and produced the 'Big Four.'

The LMS was by far the largest (indeed, at the time it was one of the biggest joint stock companies on the planet) and whilst the three other groups were reasonably logical it is interesting to speculate on other possible permutations - such as a fifth group composed of the Midland, the Great Central and the Glasgow & South Western, which would have resulted in five groups of more equal size.

Above: A detail view of the picture at the top of page 53. The horrific fires have been extinguished and the breakdown cranes are at work moving wreckage at Quintinshill, after the three-train collision of the early morning of May 22 1915. Throughout this book, the two leading causes of death and disaster on the railway were mistakes by drivers or errors by signalmen. In this instance, the drivers were blameless and the signalmen were doubly at fault: they not only forgot about a train blocking the main line but were also guilty of a fairly common but serious breach of signing-on rules, to which railway companies across the country had previously tended to turn a blind eye. *Getty Images.*

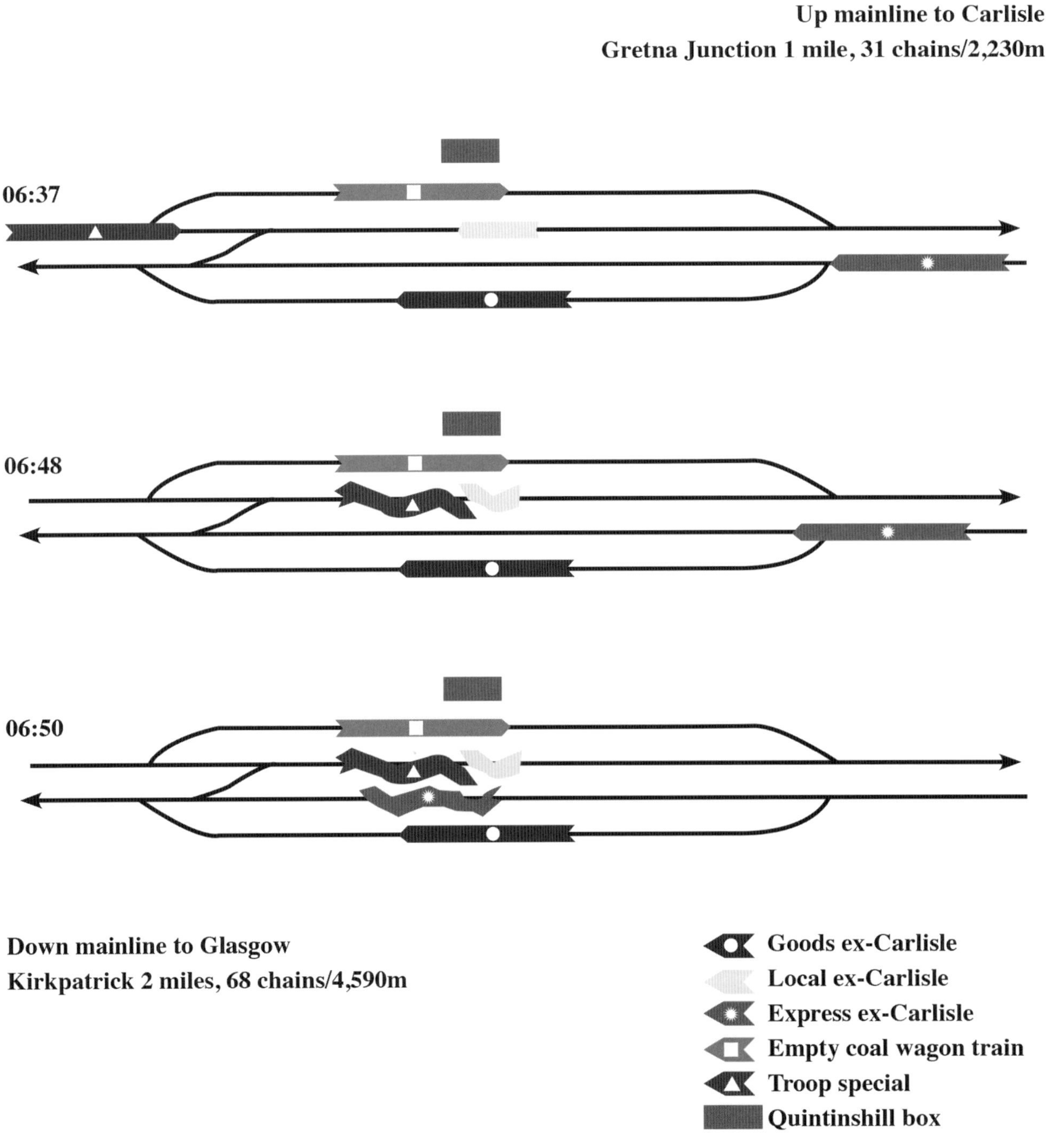

Above: A graphic which explains the sequence of events in this three-train collision.

Above: Quintinshill, recovery under way. The troop train consisted of 15 ageing Great Central wooden carriages, 11 of which were six-wheelers. The dreadful human toll is put in to sharp focus by the almost incidental detail here of the two men on the left, walking in step across the field, a coffin on their shoulders... a task carried out a further 223 times. This was one area in which the railway companies dragged their feet heavily in implementing RI recommendations to replace highly inflammable acetylene gas with electricity for lighting. This was doubtless explained, but not excused by, the very large numbers of gas lit carriages in service and the high cost of dealing with them all. ***Getty Images***

At the end of 1922, railway capital amounted to £1,174m. Net income was £54.5m and the average dividend for the year on ordinary shares was 4.62%. The results of the largest four pre-Grouping companies for 1922 were:

	Ordinary Authorised Share Capital	Dividend	Passenger Receipts	Freight Receipts
LNWR	£202m	8½%	£19.1m	£22.8m
MR	£205m	6%	£9.1m	£16.2
GWR	£149m	8%	£14.7m	£18.8m
NER	£101m	7½%	£6.8m	£12.7m

The Big Four inherited 24,319 steam and electric locomotives, 51,570 passenger-carrying vehicles, 722,639 goods vehicles and 678,105 staff (including 71,440 drivers and firemen and 24,074 guards). There were also approximately 630,000 privately-owned wagons.

Finally, in this statistical survey, the results of the Big Four for their first year were:

	Total Capital	Passenger Receipts	Freight Receipts
LMS	£415m	£32.6m	£46.2m
LNER	£318m	£22.0m	£36.2m
GWR	£161m	£13.8m	£18.1m
SR	£144m	£17.3m	£6.1m

Within the Inspectorate there was also some change. Lt-Col von Donop retired in 1916, after 17 years service, and Lt-Col Druitt in 1918, after 18 years, to be replaced by Maj (later Lt-Col) Hall 1919-1927 and Maj Mount later Lt-Col Sir Alan Mount 1919-1949. The father of the Inspectorate during this period was Col Sir John Pringle (knighted in 1925), who had joined the service at the turn of the century, became Chief Inspecting Officer in 1916 and remained until 1929. The Inspectorate was transferred from the Board of Trade in 1919 upon the formation of the Ministry of Transport but its duties, rights and responsibilities were unchanged.

Lt-Col Sir Alan Mount CB, CBE
Chief Inspecting Officer: 1929-49

Alan Mount was commissioned in the Royal Engineers at the age of 20, and after training he was sent to India and appointed Assistant Engineer on the North Western Railway. In 1911, he was in charge of the construction of the Delhi Durbar light railway system and on the outbreak of war in 1914 he went to France, becoming finally Deputy Chief Engineer Railways, for which service he was awarded the Legion of Honour in 1917.

In 1919 he accepted an appointment as an Inspecting Officer of Railways, becoming chief in 1929, a post which he held for a further 20 years until his retirement in 1949.

In 1938, he went to India accompanied by W. A, Stanier, Chief Mechanical Engineer of the LMS. At the request of the Indian Railway Board, Mount went to serve as Chairman of a special committee to investigate the unexplained serious derailments of some new 'Pacific' locomotives. He was made a Commander of the British Empire in 1919, Companion of the Order of Bath in 1931, and received a Knighthood in 1941.

During the Second World War, the Inspectorate, under Sir Alan's guidance, was responsible for sanctioning and supervising the expenditure of some £100m by the railways on additional works needed to meet the very heavy wartime commitments. These works included arrangements for closing central London tubes in emergency to prevent flooding from bomb damage.

A strong advocate of Automatic Train Control (ATC), he persuaded the Railway Executive on its formation to plan for its extension to all main line routes, though the system finally adopted was the inductive type instead of the mechanical contact type in use on the GWR.
At the same time, largely as a result of his advocacy, the Railway Executive decided to embark on an extensive programme for the installation of safety devices to assist signalmen, such as track circuits

Below: A similar panorama from the other side of the line to the picture above, during recovery at Quintinshill. The signals all stand at danger while three breakdown crane jibs break the skyline amidst the wreckage. The force of the collision was so great that the 213-yard train was reduced in length to just 67 yards. Soldiers who survived convalesced at Liverpool and were then sent to fight in the Gallipoli landings. ***Getty Images.***

Above: In the immediate aftermath of the Quintinshill disaster of 1915, an army of railwaymen, white-uniformed nurses and other recovery staff tend to the injured on mattresses in an adjacent field. Note the man in a flat cap in the right foreground, kneeling alongside and comforting one of the injured, his hand gently resting on a heavily bandaged head. In addition to 224 deaths, there were 191 serious injuries. *Getty Images.*

to control signals and block instruments.

During the Second World War and in its aftermath, the workload and responsibilities of the Chief Inspecting Officer were very heavy and shortly after retirement his health broke down, due mainly to continual overwork. He died in 1955 and is remembered as a man of great charm.

What were the major preoccupations of the Inspectorate and the Big Four in 1923, so far as safety was concerned? The three main issues continued to be:

- The need to do more to help the driver, especially during fog and darkness.
- The need to do more, by the increased use of technical equipment, to prevent errors by signalmen.
- The need for stronger coaches and the elimination of gas lighting.

Although wartime conditions and their aftermath, were not representative in many respects and will not be considered in this history, there were two accidents which must be mentioned because they illustrate so clearly the typical dangers of the times.

The first was at Quintinshill, near Gretna, on Saturday May 22 1915. Quintinshill is 10 miles north of Carlisle, on the Caledonian Railway main line to Glasgow, between the signalboxes at Gretna Junction (1m 31ch to the south) and Kirkpatrick (2m 68ch to the north). There were up and down passenger loops.

The 6.10am local passenger train from Carlisle, consisting of 4-6-0 No. 907 and four vehicles, had to be shunted at Quintinshill out of the way of the midnight express from Euston to Glasgow, which was close behind. As the down passenger loop was occupied, the signalman decided to reverse the train through the crossover to stand on the up main line.

Obviously, the local would have been in a very vulnerable position standing exposed on the main line and a number of safeguards had been devised to meet such an eventuality.

Right: A Topical Press Agency picture of witnesses arriving at the official inquiry into the Quintinshill disaster. The RI investigation made clear that track circuiting would have prevented the multiple collisions and urged the provision of more emergency tools and equipment, plus fire extinguishers, on all passenger carriages. A positive aspect of the Quintinshill disaster is that track circuiting was widely adopted thereafter on main lines. *Getty Images.*

Firsty there was Rule 55. It was the fireman's duty to go to the signalbox to remind the signalman of the presence of his train and to stay there as a continuing reminder unless the signalman gave an assurance that he had taken protective measures. As required, the fireman went to the signalbox - but he then made a fateful mistake by leaving without checking that a collar had been placed on the lever controlling the signal his train was standing at. This was a not uncommon occurrence.

The signalman did not give that vital assurance because in fact he had not taken - and did not take - any protective measures at all. He failed to place a lever collar over the up home signal lever even though collars were provided at Quintinshill - but the signalmen only bothered to use them when the loops were blocked with stabled wagons. This breach thereby confirmed the views of those companies which had resisted the use of lever collars on the grounds that

they could be counter-productive unless they were *always* used. Companies feared that the provision of lever collars might cause signalmen to be less vigilant and in any event the use of lever collars by signalmen has always been somewhat sporadic.

Secondly the signalman should also have sent the 'Blocking Back' bell signal to Kirkpatrick and placed his up main block indicator to 'Train on Line'. This would have told the Kirkpatrick signalman not to offer another train to Quintinshill where the signalman would thereby have been reminded not to accept one. Unfortunately, at the time, the block indicator was already at 'Train on Line' for an empty wagon train which was making its way into the up loop. When it was clear inside, one of the signalmen gave 'Train out of Section' to Kirkpatrick but failed to follow it up with the 'Blocking Back' signal to warn about the presence of the standing local on the main line, which was now entirely unprotected. All was now set for the tragedy that followed. Kirkpatrick offered another train - a troop special - which was immediately - and wrongly - accepted by Quintinshill, in contravention of the Block Regulations, because the local train was standing on the same line right outside the signalbox. The signalman had simply forgotten about it.

Disaster now became inevitable. All the signals were cleared for the heavy and packed troop special of 15 coaches and six vans, conveying the 1/7 Royal Scots. This doomed train was now approaching fast, down the favourable gradient. At the same time, approaching from the south, was the Scotch express on the down main, double-headed and with 13 coaches on the drawbar.

As the last fateful seconds ticked away, the two signalmen carried on, completely oblivious to the imminent catastrophe. The night shift man was reading the newspaper while the early turn man was busy completing the train register book (TRB). The signalmen should have changed over at 6.00am but by 'local arrangement' the early turn man travelled to Quintinshill on the local train and so did not arrive until 6.30am. To avoid being 'found out' - this was strictly against the Rules - the night man wrote all the TRB entries after 6.00am on a piece of paper, to be copied later into the TRB by the early turn signalman, in his own handwriting. It was not an uncommon practice throughout the railways and the authorities knew all about it, but turned a blind eye. Both manager and front line workers quietly colluded in one of those elaborate charades that were part and parcel of the everyday employee/supervisor relationship on the railway. It was always an unnecessary charade - but on this occasion it distracted

CONTINUED ON PAGE 58

Above: Significant media interest in major rail disasters is not new and the newspapers of the day reported extensively on the Quintinshill catastrophe. This was a news picture of Signalman James Tinsley, a key witness at the accident inquiry. He was the Quintinshill day signalman, who took over from night turn Signalman Meakin. The pair connived to falsify train register paperwork to enable Tinsley to start his shift late, whilst giving the false impression in the Train Register that he had started on time. Both faced criminal charges - Tinsley was sentenced to three years penal servitude while George Meakin was jailed for 18 months. Both were released in December 1916. *Getty Images.*

Above: The terrible business of transporting 224 bodies away from the Quintinshill crash site was a significant task in itself. A local trader's lorry is discreetly parked behind a barn as this harrowing work continues. Once again, the RI strongly urged both the abolition of gas lighting and the adoption of steel for carriage construction but progress was slow: incredibly, 10% of passenger coaches were still gas lit as late as nationalisation, 33 years later, in 1948. *Getty Images.*

Above: Locomotive boiler explosions were not uncommon in the early/middle 19th century, especially with locomotives fitted with primitive Salter-type safety valves, which could be manually 'screwed down' (thereby increasing boiler pressure beyond safe limits) by enginemen seeking more power. Subsequent Ramsbottom and the even more modern Ross 'pop' safety valves were sealed and eliminated tampering - but other risks nevertheless remained. The last boiler explosion amongst pre-Grouping companies occurred at Buxton 12.45am on November 11 1921, when the boiler of an LNWR 0-8-0 goods tender engine failed at a pressure later estimated at 600 pounds per square inch - *three times* its safe maximum working pressure! The boiler was completely destroyed. Both enginemen were killed in the explosion, which occurred as the engine started away with a 34-wagon goods train for Oldham. Some ruptured plate work landed more than over 220 yards away. *HMRI/ORR.*

Above: Root cause of the Buxton explosion of 1921 was a private contractor in Glasgow, which had overhauled the locomotive for the LNWR. Glasgow machinists left very little 'play' in the components, which then jammed because of differential expansion of brass, gunmetal and cast iron components in very cold weather. This effectively sealed the safety valve in the closed position. Incredibly, various enginemen had repeatedly reported faults with the locomotive's pressure gauge, which was said to have reached 300psi! The gauge was changed several times - including the day before the explosion - but it occurred to no-one that the gauges had all been working properly and that the real problem lay with the jammed safety valves, leading to massively increased boiler pressure. LNWR cab and boiler design precluded the temporary fitting of a second, calibrated test gauge whilst the locomotive was in steam, to compare readings with the locomotive's own gauge. This was the last UK barrel explosion, future boiler failures being limited to collapsed fireboxes caused by lack of water on the firebox crown. *HMRI/ORR.*

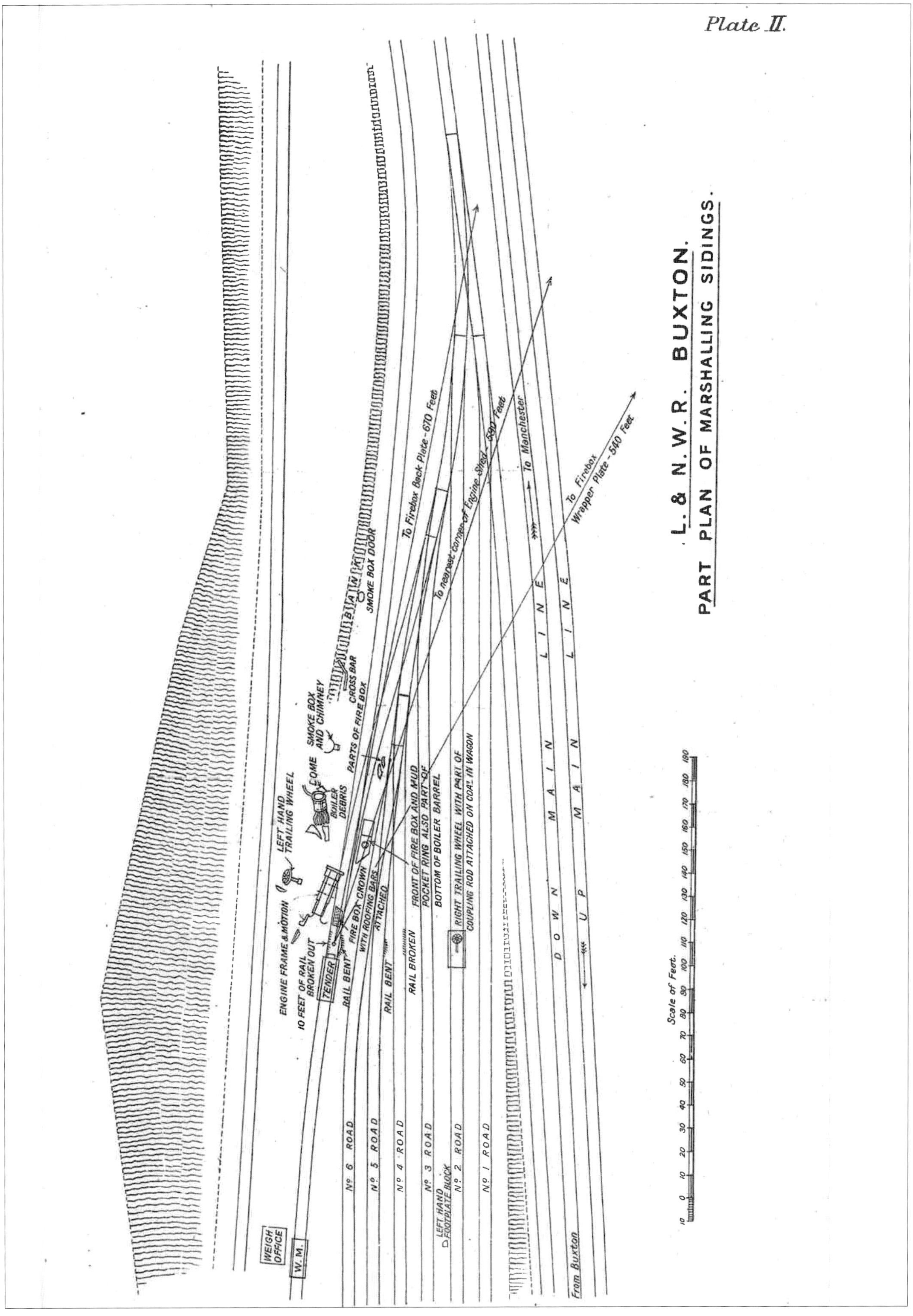

Above: A diagram from the RI report into the Buxton boiler explosion of 1921, showing how the locomotive was destroyed. At least one driving wheel was torn from its axle while some heavy boiler platework - the firebox wrapper plate - landed 540 feet away. *HMRI/ORR*.

Right: A major issue in the year of the Grouping was the sheer number, diversity of ownership and varied condition of 10-foot wheelbase four-wheeled good vehicles, many of which were very old, unbraked and running on primitive grease axle boxes. In 1923, there were 722,000 goods wagons, plus a further 630,000 which were privately owned, many in poor condition. *Getty Images.*

CONTINUED FROM PAGE 55

the early turn signalman at a critical moment. At 6.40am, the troop train crashed head-on at high speed into the engine of the local train with great force. Moments later the Scotch express ploughed into the wreckage, also at high speed from the opposite direction. The old wooden coaches in the troop train were smashed to pieces and fire immediately broke out, the flames fed and intensified by gas escaping from ruptured tanks and pipes beneath the coaches. In the terrible collision and fire, 215 troops aboard the special were killed, while seven passengers in the express died, plus two in the local train. It was Britain's worst rail disaster and was caused, concluded Lt-Col Druitt (who conducted the public inquiry) by the inexcusable carelessness and inattention to duty of the two signalmen. He did not blame the Caledonian Railway for not installing track circuits there, although they would have prevented the accident. Perhaps there was not as much recognition in those days of the need to guard against human error or carelessness. As a direct result of Quintinshill, track

Above: The RI was also responsible for monitoring and investigating accidents on the London Underground, whose safety record was nowhere near as good as it is today. This is the aftermath of a December 1922 mishap involving a 'Central London' train. *Getty Images.*

circuits were subsequently installed on a very wide scale and have done a very considerable amount since to improve safety.

Once again, the Inspector condemned the use of coal gas for lighting carriages and urged the use of steel in their construction, both for greater strength and to reduce fire risk. He considered that the fire was started by live coals in the wooden wreckage and was then intensified by the escaping gas. He was also of the opinion that the wreckage would have been destroyed by fire even if the carriages had been electrically lit.

Sad and tragic beyond words is that the soldiers lucky enough to escape with their lives, were then sent to serve in the ill-fated Gallipoli landings, where many more of them were killed.

Later the same year, at St Bede's junction NER, there was a serious collision between the 7.50am passenger train from South Shields to Newcastle and a light engine. The first two coaches, both gas-lit, were telescoped and caught fire. Eighteen passengers were killed. Lt-Col von Donop, in one of his last inquiries, found that the cause of the accident was an error by the signalman, compounded by a delay by the fireman in carrying out Rule 55.

These two accidents aside, the safety record during the remainder of the war and its aftermath was not as bad as you might expect. A total of 55 passengers were killed in train accidents between 1916 and 1922, an average of eight per year - but the new era of the Big Four started ominously. At 5.00am on February 13 1923, the up Aberdeen sleeping car train passed all signals at danger at Retford and collided with a goods train at 60mph, killing the driver, fireman and a locomotive inspector. The express was headed by Atlantic No. 298 and consisted of 11 vehicles, all electrically lit. Lt-Col Pringle considered that the absence of passenger fatalities was due to the use of buckeye couplings and Pullman-type gangways, which helped keep the train upright and in line. There were no detonator-placers in the signalbox and they might have prevented the collision. Pringle recommended that they should be provided 'pending ATC', from which remark it seems clear that he expected ATC to be installed on the East Coast Main Line within the next few years. Little did he know that it was to be nearly 40 years before that happened.

Above: Steam locomotive wheels were not solid - they were fitted with a flanged, rolled steel tyre, which was heated in a large gas ring on a workshop floor and then shrunk on to the spoked wheel centres as they cooled. The complete wheels were then pressed onto axles. As the tyres wore and the flange profile sharpened in use, they were put on large lathes and tyres reprofiled not merely to lengthen life but to avoid derailments. A poor wheel profile with a 'sharp' flange and the radius between wheel tread and flange worn into a near right angle could easily derail, especially on check-railed points and crossings. After several 'cuts' the tyre would become too thin (with the risk it could break up) and would be cut off, scrapped and replaced. Occasionally a worn or defectively-manufactured tyre would break-up and disintegrate in service. This happened to the 4.40pm Liverpool-Blackpool express, at Lytham, between Preston and Blackpool, on November 3 1924, causing this disaster. The locomotive was Lancashire & Yorkshire Railway 4-4-0 No. 1105, still in LYR livery. *Getty Images.*

It is odd that the railway companies were so slow to provide useful and effective yet cheap equipment - such as lever collars - to enhance safety. It is very difficult to understand why this was so. Equally puzzling is the failure of the Inspectorate to press the issue as hard as it might have done and one cannot escape the feeling that both Inspectorate and the railway companies were perhaps in a state of some complacency over the perceived good safety record. This false sense of security would have been bolstered by the excellent result in 1925, when not a single passenger was killed in a train accident on the main line railways (although one was killed at Baker Street station on the Metropolitan Railway). Indeed, Sir John Pringle, knighted that year, was sufficiently moved to remark - somewhat rashly in view of later events - that the case for the adoption of ATC was less urgent

CONTINUED ON PAGE 62

Above: The 1924 LYR 4-4-0's (see previous page) leading left driving wheel tyre fractured and disintegrated at about 50mph and the locomotive and first two carriages derailed, the wreckage first hitting a bridge and then demolishing Warton signalbox. Coals from the engine yet again ignited leaking gas from carriage lighting tanks and 14 passengers died in the subsequent fire. The tyre broke up because of a large unknown 'blow hole' in the steel, which failed as the tyre wore. It had been manufactured in 1920 and had run more than 100,000 miles. The original caption reports that amongst the dead was Commander Charles Graeme of the White Star ocean liner *Bardin. Getty Images.*

Above: The devastation left when an LMS express from Manchester was in a head-on collision with a goods train at Hope station, in the Peak District, on September 5 1925. *Getty Images.*

Above: Runaways and shunting incidents in goods yards and private sidings always created a spectacle for local media and onlookers alike and at Tunstall, Staffordshire, a large crowd of 'gawpers' has gathered to see the goods wagon pile-up at Newfield Pottery. In June 1925, a 20-wagon train, including nine loaded wagons, were being shunted towards a buffer stop when Driver Alfred Hill, of Stoke, discovered the hard way that his engine brakes were insufficient to control the train and it ran away and ploughed through the stop block, leaving this mess for the breakdown crew to disentangle. *Getty Images.*

Above: Congested and complex track layouts around stations were always risky areas, where a misread signal could easily result in derailment, front or rear impacts, or - as seems to be the case here - a flank collision. It's May 13 1925 and a Southern Railway Drummond Class M7 0-4-4T pilot engine has seemingly come to grief during empty stock movements between Cannon Street and London Bridge stations. The carriages are vintage wooden short bogie vehicles and even include a 'birdcage' roofed brake carriage. *Getty Images.*

CONTINUED FROM PAGE 59

and that the expenditure which would be incurred could not be justified at the present moment.

In 1997, HMRI did precisely the same thing, reporting that the case for Automatic Train Protection was likewise not justified in terms of the benefits in relation to costs.

Back to the 1920s. Level crossings had always been a source of concern, with many deaths of pedestrians and road users each year, but because fatalities were mainly the result of the user's own actions, little was done to make crossings safer. There had been a few derailments and some passenger deaths, but as long as a big heavy locomotive could generally be expected to brush aside a light road vehicle, the railways were satisfied to leave things as they were.

One of the more serious accidents in which the train fared the better occurred at Naworth, between Low Row and Brampton, on the Newcastle to Carlisle line, on August 30 1926. The minor road level crossing was protected by distant and stop signals, but these were not interlocked with the gates, which were thus free to be opened at any time. The gatekeeper, who was also the porter at the station, was provided with repeater indicators of the block instruments for the section, so that he could be made aware when a train was in the section. Just after lunch, an open 26hp charabanc, with five transverse seats, approached the level crossing. The porter, fatally, did not look at the block indicators nor did he put the signals to danger, but straight away opened the gates. The vehicle moved on to the level crossing at no more than walking pace just as the 1.18pm express from Newcastle to Carlisle swept through the station at 50mph. The locomotive, 4-4-0 No. 1029, demolished the charabanc, killing eight of its passengers. The porter himself was also killed. It transpired that the signals were not always put back to 'danger' when the gates were opened and Lt-Col Mount recommended that they should be interlocked with the gates. Naworth was a quiet little station, handling no more than 15 passengers and eight milk cans a day.

The year 1928 dispelled whatever complacency had taken root. No fewer than 48 passengers lost their lives that year in six separate accidents, whilst a further 275 were injured. It was the the worst peacetime year since 1906. Two accidents are worthy of note.

Wamphray was a small signalbox between Dinwoodie and Beattock, at the end of the 35 miles of easy gradients on the West Coast Main Line north of Carlisle. The signalman had received 'Train entering Section' for a down freight train - then he dozed off. Waking with a start he jumped to the conclusion that the freight train must have passed whilst he was asleep, so he gave 'Train out of Section' signal to the signalman at Dinwoodie and was immediately offered the 7.30pm 'Royal Highlander' from Euston to Aberdeen and Inverness, double-headed by 4-4-0s No. 14435 and Standard Compound No. 1176, and 12 coaches. He accepted the express and shortly afterwards received the 'Train entering Section' signal. It was just before 3.00am on October 25 1928. The express was running easily at over 60mph when the pilot engine driver suddenly glimpsed the tail lights of the goods train ahead. It had not passed clear of the section after all but had failed with an engine defect. In the ensuing collision all four enginemen were killed when their engines overturned and rolled down an embankment. Thankfully, partly because their train was lightly loaded there were no passenger deaths.

Lt-Col Mount criticised the guard of the freight train for not carrying out protection duties to the rear of his train quickly enough - the goods train had been standing for 15 minutes - and he resurrected the old idea of the flare or Very light, which might have given more timely warning to the unfortunate crews on the express. He was, however, surprisingly silent about the absence of 'lock and block', which would have prevented the accident on this main line.

A more serious collision, in terms of its consequences, had happened less than a fortnight earlier, on October 13 at Charfield, a small wayside station on the Midland Railway's Birmingham to Bristol line. It was Col Sir John Pringle's final public inquiry and its particular characteristics must have seemed very familiar to him. The signalman at Charfield was between Berkeley Road Junction signalbox to the north (6 miles) and Wickwar to the south (2 miles). He had accepted the 9.15pm GWR fitted goods train from Oxley Sidings (Wolverhampton) to Bristol and had decided to shunt it clear of the main line to allow a following train to pass, by setting it back into the down lie bye. The goods, consisting of 49 loaded wagons and headed by 2-6-0 No. 6381, arrived at 5.15am and was slowly propelling into

Left: In the days of timber-bodied carriage bodies on steel under frames with conventional buffers and coupled using screw shackles over draw hooks, telescoping in crashes was an almost inevitable and usually fatal outcome. This is an especially graphic example: the body of the right hand vehicle has remained secured to its under frame, but it has detached from its bogie and ridden over the buffers of the clerestory carriage, the steel under frame slicing into the adjacent carriage body destroying the end compartments of both vehicles. Central 'knuckle'-type buckeye couplings, widely introduced with the BR Mk. 1s in the 1950s, largely prevented telescoping and also helped to keep coaches upright and in line in collisions. The original news agency captions tell us: 'Railway collision at Old Oak Common, North Acton. Steam Rail motor train runs into back of empty train.' That isn't strictly true: No. 137 was actually a 70ft auto-trailer, converted from a previously self-powered steam rail motor No. 47 and returned to traffic as a trailer in October 1922. Driver and guard were both injured and the picture makes clear the terrible risks to the occupants of telescoped carriages - especially if they were gas lit and then caught fire, as was the case at Hawes Junction (1910), Ditton (1912), Ais Gill (1913), Lytham (1924) and Charfield (1928). ***Getty Images.***

the trailing lie by. A minute later the signalman accepted the 10.00pm Leeds-Bristol down mail and passenger train from Berkeley Road Junction; he received 'Train entering Section' for it at 5.16am. He was quite in order in accepting the Mail because he had an outer home signal 440yd in rear of his inner home, which had been specially provided to allow him to accept trains when the line beyond the inner home signal was still occupied.

Meanwhile, he had accepted an empty wagon train on the Up Main Line from Wickwar and had received the 'Train entering Section' signal for it at 5.13am. The signalman was anxiously watching the progress of the GWR freight train setting back because he knew that the Mail was closely approaching and he feared that it might be delayed if it had to stop whilst the shunt was completed. The thought that the Mail might run past his signals at danger never entered his head. Why should it have done?

The train was not one of the LMS's crack expresses and was mainly run for the conveyance of mails. The passenger coaches were between 19 and 29 years old and three out of the four were gas-lit. There were about 60 passengers on the train.

The signalman saw the track circuit indicator at the outer home signal change

Right: Poor quality Southern Railway main line track - for which the RI's Col Sir John Pringle had strong words in his investigation report - led to the derailment of 'River' class 2-6-4T No. 800 ***River Cray*****, at Sevenoaks on August 24 1927, whilst working the 5pm express from Cannon Street. The 'River' class engines had a reputation for instability and lateral rolling at speed and this was the result when poor track and poor riding converged. No. 800 derailed at 60mph but ran upright and in line for some distance before a set of catch points and a collision with a bridge caused the locomotive to slew and roll onto its left side on the cutting side. The carriages then piled up around it, 13 passengers losing their lives in the wreckage.** ***Getty Images.***

Right: On the right, the wrecked No. 800 is glimpsed leaning on the steep cutting side through the smashed wreckage of its eight-coach train, which included a Pullman car. A bizarre aspect of this accident was that several uninjured passengers had their shoes torn off, which they recovered - with the laces still tied - from the debris. Subsequent test running on the Great Northern Main Line north of Kings Cross (between St Neots and Huntingdon) revealed that the 'River' class engines ran without problem at high speed on good quality GN metals, hence the RI focus on poor SR track quality. As a result of the Sevenoaks crash, the entire class was rebuilt as 2-6-0 tender engines and the SR set about an upgrading of its main line track. *Getty Images.*

Above: 1928 was a bad year: 48 passengers died on trains, 16 of them at Charfield on October 13, a small wayside station on the MR's Birmingham-Bristol line. A terrible pile-up and fatal fire followed after a passenger train driver passed adverse signals and then collided with a goods train setting back into a lie by in front of his train. The debris was then in immediate collision with a goods train coming the other way. Yet again, Col Sir John Pringle had to report on a fatal fire in gas lit wooden coaches, a decade and a half after the Hawes Junction catastrophe of 1915. The incinerated underframe here bears witness to the severity of the blaze. *Getty Images.*

from 'Clear' to 'Occupied', which told him that the Mail had arrived, but then he was somewhat taken aback to see it return to 'Clear'. Was it possible, he thought to himself, that the Mail had run past his signal? No, surely not? It must be the indicator playing up. He glanced again to see whether the GW freight had got clear inside. The engine was still on the main line but he reckoned that within a few moments it would be inside and he would be able to restore his points and clear his signals for the Mail. Whilst idly musing on this he suddenly glimpsed a flash of light through the over-bridge by the points - and he heard the terrible and unmistakeable sound of a collision. The goods train engine was still on the main line when the Mail engine hit it and then bounced off into the empty wagon train which was just passing in the opposite direction on the up main line. The two engines and some wrecked wagons virtually blocked the way beyond the bridge. The Mail's coaches had nowhere to go and so they piled themselves up on each side of, and under, the bridge in an inextricable mass of steel and smashed timber.

Fire broke out in the wreckage and rapidly became furnace-like with the result that the first seven vehicles of the Mail were completely burnt out.

Sixteen passengers were killed and 24 were injured; more than half the complement. Thirteen GPO sorters and four train crew members were also injured. There was one very curious, tragic and ultimately very mysterious aspect to this crash, which remains unexplained. Among the dead were the bodies of two small children who have never been identified. There is a memorial in Charfield Church to them and the others who lost their lives.

Sir John Pringle set to work to investigate the cause of the accident amid intense public interest and speculation. The position of Charfield's Down distant was the key question. Was it at caution or clear? According to the signalling equipment and interlocking it must have been at caution. The driver of the GWR goods train had clearly seen it showing a full red light only a few minutes earlier. The Mail driver had also seen it clearly and claimed that it was showing a green light. The fireman said that he also saw it at clear. 'He's got it off, mate', he had said to the driver. He confirmed that it was showing a full green light. Half an hour after the accident the Mail driver went to the signalbox and said to the signalman 'The down distant was off when I passed it'.

'Impossible', replied the signalman.

Sir John was faced with contradictory evidence but he came to the only possible conclusion based on the evidence - that the Mail train driver had passed the down distant signal in the caution position,

Above: Termini always demanded great care from approaching drivers - and this applied especially to the LNWR's Euston, at the curving foot of the steep gradient from Camden. This was collision damage photographed on April 30 1928, when 20 passengers were injured in No. 13 platform. The accident happened at about 1.50pm when an inbound empty stock train (for the 2.35pm Euston-Liverpool) intended for Platform 12 was wrongly signalled into Platform 13. This was already occupied by the partly-occupied 2.20pm Euston-Wolverhampton, which was hit by the ECS train and propelled 23 yards onto three carriages standing at the bufferstops. In the Wolverhampton train, 18 passengers, two members of dining car staff and two non-passengers suffered minor injuries and shock. Two women were detained in hospital. There was no derailment and the engine was undamaged, but the eight leading vehicles of the Liverpool train suffered damaged gangways, headstocks and buffing gear. In the standing train, all headstocks were bent. The accident was caused by a misunderstanding between Euston No. 2 box Signalmen Andrews and Chapman, who had 70 years experience between them. *Getty Images.*

and thereafter passed the down outer and inner home signals at danger. The jury at the coroner's inquest were unanimously of the opinion that the collision was caused by the negligence of the driver in passing his signals at danger. The Coroner interpreted the verdict as one of manslaughter and committed the driver for trial on that charge. However, the magistrates found that there was not a *prima facie* case and he was discharged. At the Gloucester Assizes, the jury returned a formal verdict of 'not guilty'.

Sir John now had to reconsider his words a few years earlier about the desirability or otherwise of installing ATC. He recommended rather guardedly that ATC should eventually be adopted. His words deserved the serious consideration of the four main line companies, but did not lead to any action on their part (except for the Great Western). Pringle had been chairman of the Automatic Train Control Committee which had sat from 1920 to 1922, and he had also been Chairman of a second committee on the same subject, which commenced its work in 1927 and had still not completed its task by the time of the Charfield collision.

By now, Col Sir John Pringle was an expert on Automatic Train Control, and his committee made a positive recommendation in favour of a fixed warning system of the Great Western type at distant signals, but very little came of it. Yet another opportunity to give drivers crucial assistance when approaching distant signals was missed.

Left: Even relatively low speed collisions can cause considerable damage and injury - sometimes even with fatalities. On August 27 1928, 30 passengers were injured when this LNWR engine, according to the original news agency caption, "crashed through the buffer stop, coming to rest against a ladies waiting room at Euston." The 9.45am 'Mancunian' express from Manchester London Road (now Piccadilly) failed to stop in the No. 2 arrival platform and collided heavily with the bufferstops resulting in injuries to 55 passengers, 19 dining car staff and two non-passengers. Two ladies were detained in hospital. This was a significant impact. The 4in diameter buffer plungers had a travel of 2ft, and were destroyed, after which the engine shattered the stopblock's supporting timbers before ploughing 9ft into the platform behind the buffers, coming to rest 3ft 6in from the adjacent waiting room wall. The original caption was, therefore, a slight exaggeration! Only the engine's leading bogie derailed, as it left the end of the track. The first three coaches (of 13) were forced together by the violent compression of the impact and their gangways, communication, buffing gear and other fittings were heavily damaged. The engine was reboilered 'Claughton' 4-6-0 No. 6017, driven by H.H. Simpson, who at 67 years of age had 51 years service, 42 years as a driver and with 18 years under his belt driving passenger trains into Euston - a man of very good record. The RI concluded that he had entered the platform at around 25mph (it should have been 10mph) and then misjudged his braking. Fireman Armstong (who stepped off the engine just before the 10mph estimated collision) was exonerated but Guard G.B. Rhodes, a man of 37 years experience, was criticised for not paying sufficient attention and an error of judgement in failing to apply the train brake during the over-rapid entry into the platform. ***Getty Images.***

The conflicting evidence about the position of the arm of the down distant signal illustrates clearly how difficult it is in such circumstances for the driver to prove his case. We shall never know the truth in the Charfield disaster. Did the driver really see a green light at the distant signal? Did he genuinely but mistakenly think that he had seen a green light? Or did he 'make up' the story as an excuse? It is difficult to see how, in the circumstances, a green light could have been displayed. There may have been malicious interference but it seems highly unlikely, especially at that time in the morning. However, as part of their armoury of protective devices in the signalling system, the railway companies devised an additional safeguard, known as 'distant signal arm-proving'. The position of the distant signal arm was generally repeated in the signalbox by an electrical indicator, and this was subsequently used to provide a control on the block instruments in such a manner that a 'Line Clear' could not be given to the signalbox in rear unless the distant signal arm indicator was showing 'On'. It was a simple but effective additional safeguard and not expensive, and the Inspectorate should have pressed the railway companies to adopt it more quickly, if only to reassure drivers.

The Inspectorate's concern about fire was quite naturally intensified by the Charfield accident, and Sir John Pringle was sufficiently moved to remark that progress in phasing out the use of gas as an illuminant had not in all cases been so rapid as was desirable. It is interesting to speculate on what the outspoken Col Yolland would have had to say about it! The returns for November 1928 showed that the percentages of gas-lit carriages still in use were as follows:

- **LMS**: 50%
- **LNER**: 54%
- **GWR**: 67%
- **SR**: 30%

Many of these carriages were in use on branch lines, or were spare stock used on only a few occasions a year.

Less than three months later, whilst speculation on the Charfield disaster was still raging, there was another serious mail train accident not many miles away on the same line at Ashchurch. By a strange coincidence, many of the same factors applied.

Three of the train's 45 passengers were killed and many people were injured, including Post Office staff. The driver of the mail was also killed.

It fell to Lt-Col Mount, now Chief Inspecting Officer following Sir John Pringle's retirement, to investigate this accident. He remarked: "This is another instance similar to that of Charfield, which confirms the utility of Automatic Train Control as affording, under modern conditions, desirable assistance to the driver, particularly when running in fog. A system like that which is installed at the distant signal on some sections of the GWR would assuredly have prevented this accident." However, again the railway companies turned a deaf ear and again the Inspectorate did not press the point. The LMS was putting its faith in colour-light distant signals, which were admittedly much easier to observe in fog, but that was only part of the answer. Accidents continued to occur, both in clear weather and in fog, even with colour-light distants. Fog was, and continued to be, the great enemy.

Left: To bring this chapter to a close, here are two parting powerful reminders of the destructive power of a high energy collision on timber built rolling stock. The timber bodies of the carriages of the day were not at all crashworthy, as this destruction makes horribly clear. It's August 25 1927 at Sevenoaks and this is the splintered wreck of the carriage in which most of the 13 fatalities lost their lives. A further 132 were injured. *Getty Images.*

Below: As a passenger, your chances of surviving a collision like this, at Ashchurch, near Tewkesbury, on January 8 1929, were negligible. Four people (including express driver, F.W. Crabtree) were all killed instantly and 21 were injured when the 14-coach LMS 7.20pm up express mail hauled by 'Compound' 4-4-0 No. 1060 collided at 50-55mph at just after 9pm, with a goods train, in heavy fog. The 23-wagon goods was being shunted in the opposite direction over a trailing crossover between the up and down main lines at the north end of the station. The original Topical Press Agency typewritten caption pasted on the back of the print says: "...the carriages were crushed like eggshells and torn strips of cardboard. The wreckage was piled as high as a two-storey house." In his official report for the Ministry of Transport, Lt Col Mount concluded: "The resulting wreck was exceptional and it is remarkable that fatalities were not more numerous...From the first point of contact with the wagons, the engine came to rest on its left side in 91 yards. It was evidently derailed at once and ploughed its way deeply beneath the rails and sleepers of the adjacent siding...The leading nine vehicles, with the exception of the fifth, an all-steel brake van, were destroyed..." Mount commented that a GWR style distant signal approach control system (ATC) "would assuredly have prevented this accident." *Getty Images.*

CHAPTER 5

A TOO BRIEF RENAISSANCE 1930-1947

Above: A picture which captures beautifully the impression of glamour and cutting-edge modernity which the LMS and the LNER sought to convey during the mid-late 1930s. Express locomotive streamlining dovetailed perfectly with the art-deco fashion and styling of the time, which inspired the design of everything from hotel architecture to dining table chairs, electric lights and teapots. A group of at least 13 trainspotters are waiting at Harringay in 1937 for Gresley 'A4' 4-6-2 No. 4489 (later BR No. 60010) *Dominion of Canada*, hauling the down 'Coronation.' The Railway Inspectorate was supervising a railway where even larger independent companies than those in 1895 were again 'racing to the north,' with all its attendant risks. This was still a railway where there was no Automatic Train Control and safety depended entirely on vigilant drivers peering down boiler sides, often in grey and foggy weather, looking for filthy semaphore signal arms by day and dimly oil-lit red, green and yellow spectacles by night.
D. T. Greenwood/Rail Archive Stephenson.

The 1930s began with a new team of Inspecting Officers under the Chief, Lt-Col Sir Alan Mount and they were to serve right through the period covered by this chapter. Col A. C. Trench had entered the Inspectorate in 1927 and he was joined by Lt Col E. Woodhouse in 1930. Maj G. R. S. Wilson came on the scene in 1935. These four officers were responsible for the Railway Inspectorate's policy and views on railway safety until Nationalisation in 1948.

Lt Col G. R. S. Wilson CBE
Chief Inspecting Officer: 1949-58

George Wilson (Bob) was commissioned in the Royal Engineers in 1914 at the age of 18 and saw service in field companies in France and Macedonia during the First World War after which he completed a course on the Longmoor Military Railway in Hampshire. After serving in the Transportation Branch of the War Office he was appointed an Assistant Inspecting Officer of Railways in 1935.

He returned to the army in 1939 as Assistant Director of Railways with the British Expeditionary Force in France until the evacuation from Dunkirk in June 1940, when he resumed his inspection job, being appointed an Inspecting Officer in 1941.

Bob Wilson was something of a railway 'buff'. In his schooldays, he contrived to frequent a favourite Wiltshire signal box - possibly Devizes - and he continued throughout his life to correspond with the signalman who first taught him the rudiments of railway operation. His remarkable aptitude for mechanical engineering found expression in his delighted study of locomotives (of which he was a connoisseur) and he was completely at home on the footplate. One story told about him concerns the engine of the 'Sud Express' behind which he and his family were once travelling to the Basque country on holiday. It developed a fault and the train came to a stand, whereupon Bob Wilson went to the front of the train and helped the driver to locate and rectify the problem! A good railway inspector, like a policeman, is never 'off duty!'

He conducted the inquiry into the double collision at Harrow in 1952, the worst peacetime disaster in the history of Britain's railways (the 1915 crash at Quintinshill was the worst). The initial Harrow collision might have been prevented by ATC and Col Wilson gave an interesting historical review of the development of the equipment from 1912 when the GWR system was coming into use on that railway, up to the time of the Harrow accident in 1952. Col Wilson pointed out that 28% of all fatalities in train accidents during that period (1,093 passengers killed between 1912 and 1952) might have been prevented had ATC been installed. That would have been approximately 300 lives saved. A sobering thought.

He spent much time checking the working of the new form of ATC and in pressing the Railway Executive to accelerate its tests. Finally, in 1956, he at last had the satisfaction of recommending the adoption

Left: Another picture which illustrates the way that timber built passenger carriages disintegrated in accidents. At least two separated roofs lie in the ballast, having been lifted clear of the wreckage by the steam breakdown crane. This crash occurred on November 3 1931, when a goods train hauled by LMS Hughes-Fowler 'Crab' 2-6-0 No. 13153 collided with an empty stock passenger train near Tring. Possibly as a result of very strong wind, drizzle and drifting steam and smoke, the driver of the goods train failed to observe the outer and inner home signals at danger. The train was travelling at about 40-45mph when the driver realised his error and applied the brakes. Colonel Mount had no recommendations but pointed out yet again that ATC would have undoubtedly prevented the collision. (see also overleaf) *Getty Images.*

Above: Whilst some crack express passenger services were styled in the modern art-deco feel of the times, the goods railway of the 1930s remained pretty much as it had been since the late 19th century. In c1932, North Staffordshire Railway 'L' class '3F' 0-6-0T No. 2241 passes Longport, with an up goods. Most of the vehicles are 10ft wheelbase, unbraked wooden wagons, many of which would have been privately owned by collieries. It would appear that an allotment-style vegetable patch has been planted between the cess and the fence in the foreground, possibly by the signalman? *F.R. Hebron/Rail Archive Stephenson.*

Above: A detail view of the aftermath of the West Coast Main Line rear end collision near Tring, (see also page 69) between a goods train hauled by 'Crab' 2-6-0 No. 13153 and an empty stock passenger train on November 3 1931. Impact with the rear carriage has flattened the 'Crab's' convex smokebox door and pushed it deep inside the smokebox. The destruction of the rear carriage bogie is horribly apparent. *Getty Images.*

of the new equipment for installation on all the major main lines in the country.

Lt Col Wilson initiated the investigation into level crossing protection which led to the introduction of lifting barriers worked manually or automatically by the approaching train.

At the time of his death in 1958, he had nearly completed his investigation into the collision earlier that year at St Johns, Lewisham, the third worst railway disaster in Britain with 90 fatalities. A Cannon Street to Ramsgate steam hauled express collided with the rear of a ten coach electric unit after passing a signal at danger. There is little doubt that the strain and distress caused by this last investigation contributed to his untimely death. Lt Col Wilson was the archetypal Inspecting Officer, who clearly loved, and was devoted to, his job, and unsparing of his energies.

The big concerns remained unchanged - the eradication of dangerous errors by drivers and signalmen and improvements in the fire and crashworthiness of carriages. Whilst the Inspectorate was keen to reduce the number of accidents, it was equally anxious to cushion passengers against the effects of collisions and derailments.

The 1930s started well. Only a single passenger was killed in 1930 in a train accident and a total of 17 lost their lives in the next three years. Whilst the causes were depressingly familiar and nearly all the fatal accidents could have been prevented by the application of existing technology. The problem, ironically, was that such a perceived good safety record did not encourage a heavy programme of capital investment in safety measures, at a time when the railways were increasingly suffering from the effects of unbridled road competition and a world slump in trade.

However, it would be wrong to give the impression that the railways were doing nothing during the 1930s to increase safety. Quite the reverse. They were quietly installing track circuits and block signalling controls on a large scale and replacing semaphore distant signals with colour lights to ease the driver's heavy burden during darkness and fog. Such weather conditions had been, and continued to be, common contributory causes of accidents. In suburban areas, multiple-aspect colour-light signals were being very widely introduced. Whilst these various measures also helped the signalman by providing safeguards against errors on his part, it was thought that colour-light signals would be of great assistance to drivers. This was certainly the case during fog and darkness, but colour light signals were not 100% effective in isolation, as we shall see: they needed the assistance of ATC. Paradoxically, the Great Western put its faith in semaphore distants with ATC until virtually the end of its independent existence and its splendid safety record speaks for itself. From 1923 to 1947, excluding the war years, there were only two fatal GWR train accidents, with a single passenger killed in each, an unparalleled record.

The year 1931 was notable for two fatal high speed derailments, reminiscent of the early years of the century. Lt Col Mount investigated both. The first took place on January 3 at Carlisle Canal when the 12.00 noon Edinburgh Waverley-St Pancras was derailed at 45-50mph on the sharp 15mph curve between Carlisle No. 1 and 3 signal boxes. The train consisted of seven coaches, headed by 'Shire' Class 4-4-0 No. 2758 *Northumberland;* the first four coaches were wrecked. Fortunately, the train was lightly loaded, but three of

Facing page: The crash at Leighton Buzzard, on the West Coast Main Line, on March 22 1931 was almost a repetition of the LNWR Ditton disaster of 1912 (see pages 46-47). This 14-coach train derailed at 55mph after its driver failed to slow to the required 20mph for a crossover from the down fast to down slow line. He had passed the home signal at danger. The accident happened in clear, sunny weather, but the driver's forward view was obscured by exhaust smoke and steam hanging around the front end of parallel boiler 'Royal Scot' 4-6-0 No. 6114 *Coldstream Guardsman* - a fault for which the class was notorious. The 'Scot' rolled onto its right side after the derailment, the first few coaches telescoping behind it, as shown here on March 23. Again, note the large crowd of onlookers lining the fences on both sides of the line. *Getty Images.*

the 35-40 passengers were killed. The Coroner's Inquest returned a verdict of manslaughter against the driver but he was acquitted at Carlisle Assizes.

Lt Col Mount considered what could be done to help drivers in such circumstances. With considerable foresight he suggested that ATC warning apparatus fixed on the approach to permanent speed restrictions would ensure that drivers did not overlook them, but it was to take several more serious derailments before the railway authorities implemented this, more than 40 years later. He also mentioned the advisability of keeping distant signals at caution to ensure that drivers slowed down; a simple enough measure but one which could have led to an increase in signals passed at danger. In purist terms, the purpose of the distant signal is to give the driver advance information about the home signal. Thus, if the distant is always at caution this valuable function is lost. Lt Col Mount also recommended the provision of speed indicators or boards at the lineside and the LNER subsequently adopted their well-known cut-out signs.

Whilst Lt Col Mount was turning these ideas over in his mind, there came news of the second derailment. This occurred at Leighton Buzzard on the LMS West Coast Main Line at 12.20pm on Sunday March 22 1931. The 11.30am express from Euston to Glasgow and Edinburgh was to be diverted from the down fast line to the down slow, owing to engineering work. The signalman had set the route accordingly, but he had not cleared his signals. The train approached at 55mph, ran past the home signal at danger and became derailed on the sharply-curved crossover. There were 183 passengers on the train, together with 20 dining car and other railway staff. Three passengers and three railwaymen were killed in the resulting wreck.

In this accident, there was no question of the driver having been misled or confused by junction signals. It was a straightforward case of a signal being wrongly passed at danger and Lt Col Mount said that it would have been prevented by ATC. The question of the signalling arrangements at facing junctions has always been a contentious issue, both in respect of regular timetabled movements and those which are made without the driver's having been advised beforehand. It had long been the custom to provide directing distant

Above: A huge crowd of onlookers lines the boundary fence on March 23 1931, the day after the March 22 WCML crash at Leighton Buzzard. Unsurprisingly, the driver and fireman were among the six dead, which included three passengers and a restaurant car cook. It is striking how often the death toll in rail accidents of the early 20th century included dining car staff, maybe because they were either standing at the time of the crash, or were working in dangerous environments such as kitchens. Unlike the very similar Ditton Junction derailment of 1912, there was no fire. Trains were being diverted onto the slow line because of engineering works and whilst this was an indirect cause of this disaster, AWS would almost certainly have prevented this accident. ***Getty Images.***

Above & Right: As it ploughed along at speed on its left side at Leighton Buzzard on March 24 1931, No. 6114's boiler cladding was pierced by a rail which passed through the space occupied by asbestos insulation, and emerged just in front of the cab. The very tight 'S' bend forced into the rail alongside the smokebox illustrates the power of the high-energy forces unleashed in a high speed rail crash. The rail has torn the mechanical lubricator from its seating on the running board and then slotted behind the nameplate before piercing the boiler cladding plates. The regulator handle is in the fully closed position and the driver's brake application valve in the fully released position - although they could have been moved during or after the crash. *Getty Images.*

signals so that the driver would know positively which way his train was being routed at a junction and giving him the opportunity to match the speed of his train to the speed required at the turnout. There were directing distant signals at Leighton Buzzard, but it subsequently became the practice to provide only one distant signal, which could not be cleared for the lower-speed route. Drivers would thus know instantly which route they were taking according to the aspect displayed.

1937 was one of those bad years that occasionally afflict the railways, with 49 passengers being killed in four separate accidents. The worst one was at Castlecary on the North British line of the LNER. At 4.37pm on December 10 the 4.03pm express from Edinburgh to Glasgow ran past Castlecary's home signal at danger at 65-70mph and crashed into the 2.00pm passenger train from Dundee to Glasgow, which was standing in rear of the starting signal. At that speed there was inevitably a great deal of wreckage and of the 110 passengers in the Dundee train, 22 were killed. Thirteen of the Edinburgh train's 198 passengers met the same fate, in the worst peacetime railway disaster ever up to that time on the British mainland (excluding the Tay Bridge collapse). There was some dispute about the position of the distant signal arm at Castlecary. It was not repeated in the signalbox (there was no indicator to show the signalman whether the signal was at caution or not) nor

Above: On March 13 1935, there was a four-train goods collision at King's Langley, on the West Coast Main Line, which shows how busy the railway was at this time. It was the most heavily worked section of four-track main line in the country and had the latest interlocking block equipment. A broken vacuum brake pipe caused the 4.55pm up express meat train, from Alexandra Dock to Broad Street, to come to a stand on the up fast line. It was a 42-wagon fitted freight, with brake van, and the pipe failure applied the train brakes, as designed. The driver quickly repaired the fault and was moving slowly away six minutes later when his train was run into at the rear, three-quarters of a mile south of Nash Mills box, by the 5.50pm Stafford to Euston milk train consisting of 22 tanks and vans, which was running under clear signals, at about 25mph. Colonel Mount reported that the signalmen were preoccupied and distracted by non-railway business and that this caused this horrific multiple crash. Wreckage fouling the down fast and slow lines was then run into violently at about 40mph by the 45-wagon 10.30pm Camden-Holyhead partially fitted freight, running under clear signals on the down slow. A few seconds later, a coal train of 70 wagons running at about 25mph ran into the wreckage to complete the carnage. No. 5511, which was hauling the Camden to Holyhead freight train, is surrounded by wreckage, which piled up to 30ft. Note the upturned wagon visible above the 4-6-0's firebox. Once again, there is the full range of cloth caps, trilbies and bowlers, denoting 'pecking order' rank and position amongst the railway front line staff and managers of the day. ***Getty Images.***

did it have a control on the block instrument which would have prevented the signalman from giving 'line clear' if the signal arm had been in any position other than horizontal (caution). Despite both drivers protesting that the signal had been at 'clear', the driver of the Edinburgh train was charged with culpable homicide in the Edinburgh High Court on March 30 the following year. The next day the Lord Advocate withdrew the charge and the jury was directed to return a verdict of not guilty. Lt Col Mount reported that certain aspects of the evidence were unsatisfactory and he doubted whether all the facts would ever be fully established. He recommended the installation of a system of ATC and the appropriate signalling controls as a means of avoiding such accidents in the future. 'Distant arm-proving', as it became known, with a control on the block instrument, was already installed on 31% of the signals on the Edinburgh-Glasgow line and on 67% on the Edinburgh-Berwick line.

These last few years before the Second World War were the streamlined era and marked a period of welcome renaissance for the railway companies. They had overcome the upheavals of Grouping, the years of depression were receding and the companies were getting to grips with road competition. It is a matter of great regret that just as the railways were really getting their act together, war should have come along and put a stop to it all. It was a cruel act of fate and, as in 1914, things would never be the same again for the railways. Nevertheless, those war years were to see a rich flowering stemming from that renaissance. As had happened in the First World War, the railways' customary high safety standards were well maintained. The six years of war saw traffic levels 50% higher than pre-war and many experienced staff were called to serve in the forces. Despite all the problems of bombing and the blackout, the suprisingly low number of 140 passengers were killed in train accidents during the whole of the war, compared with 93 in the previous six years of peace and 220 in the first six postwar years. Lt Col Sir Alan Mount had been knighted in 1941 and his comments in his Annual Report for 1944, written in July 1945, must have brought a glow of pride to all railwaymen. They are worth repeating:

"There can be no doubt that the services rendered by the railways contributed in no small measure to the success of the country's war effort. Besides normal transport activities connected with industry, vast movements of men and materials for the services were involved both before and during the build-up after the landing of the Allied Forces in France on 6th June. Compared with prewar, passenger miles increased by 68% and freight ton-miles by 47%. These unprecedented demands on the railways were met with depleted staffs and impaired equipment; their record is an eloquent tribute to their efficiency, standard of maintenance and the high factor of safety attained, all of which reflect the greatest credit on every railway man and woman for the part they played in this historic year."

During the war years, the work of the Inspectorate had naturally been on a reduced scale, with fewer public inquiries and inspections of major new works. After the war, it was time to look again at safety standards and to see where attention needed to be concentrated. Fog was still the railwayman's enemy and whilst the spread of colour-light signalling was of some assistance, the lack of ATC on all railways except the GWR was a serious handicap - about which the three other companies seemed inclined to do little. Lt Col Mount concluded his 1947 Annual Report by saying that there were substantial grounds for the extension of ATC and that it

CONTINUED ON PAGE 79

Above: A more general view of the aftermath of the King's Langley four freight train crash of March 1935. Once again, the picture is a graphic illustration of the energy and forces which are violently released or contained in a crash involving heavy trains. The driver of the milk train left his cab and started back on the left hand side, to try and stop the approaching 12.25pm Toton-Willesden coal train - which he had passed shortly before the crash on the up slow line. He was killed when the 10.30am fitted freight ran into the wreckage with considerable force at around 40mph. His body was buried under the towering wreckage and was not recovered until the next day. LMS 4-4-0 No. 5310 was not involved in the crash - it was part of the clear-up fleet despatched to the scene by the LMS. *Getty Images.*

Above: The year 1937 was not a good one for rail safety: no fewer than 49 passengers were killed in four separate accidents. Today's safety record is a superb contrast: as this book went to press, the railway was about to complete 12 passenger fatality-free years, since the single lost life in the Virgin West Coast 'Pendolino' high speed derailment of February 2007. In addition to the four fatal passenger accidents of 1937 there was the then usual tally of goods train mishaps. This was the fate of an express freight hauled by LMS Hughes-Fowler 'Crab' 2-6-0 No. 2765, at West Hampstead, on February 23 1937. *Getty Images.*

Below: The same compression forces created when a locomotive stops suddenly and caused wooden passenger carriages behind to telescope and concertina likewise led to significant pile ups when short 10ft wheelbase timber goods wagons were involved, as here at West Hampstead in February 1937. The wagons behind the tender were all-but destroyed as the heavy train crushed them against the rapidly slowing locomotive while subsequent vehicles reared up in dangerously unstable pile-ups which represented a major risk for the breakdown crews. ***Getty Images.***

Above: A shipper's, valuable bagged consignment is exposed in the wreckage of a box van being recovered from the West Hampstead express freight crash of February 1937. The destruction is all too clear. ***Getty Images.***

Below: The 'bacon slicer' effect which can occur in longitudinal flank collisions is a horrific - and probably fatal if you were in the vehicle - consequence of some rail mishaps. This shows the remains of one such incident at London Bridge on January 3 1938. ***Getty Images.***

Above: As if operating a busy railway at night with no control, in bad weather wasn't enough, the Air Raid Precautions (ARP) introduced after the outbreak of war on September 3 1939 made matters even worse - and led directly to this disaster at Bletchley on October 14. The night's Euston-Inverness express was standing in the down platform as an LNWR 0-8-0 eased up to attach an extra van at the rear. As the 0-8-0 carried out this shunt, it was hit at about 40mph by LMS 4-6-0 Stanier 'Black 5' No. 5025, piloting 'Royal Scot' 4-6-0 No. 6130 *The West Yorkshire Regiment*, which were double-heading the Euston-Stranraer express. The massive impact propelled the 0-8-0 violently backwards, killing its driver and destroying not only the van it was shunting, but also the two beyond. The LNWR engine was propelled forcibly onto the platform where it demolished the refreshment and waiting rooms. There were four deaths and 35 other injuries. *Getty Images*.

Right: No. 5025's driver had failed to observe and act upon the Bletchley distant at caution and danger indications of the outer and inner home signals. He was running at around 70mph - 10mph faster than the wartime speed limit imposed in September by the Railway Executive Committee. But in pitch darkness, heavy rain and with no speedometer this is understandable - but the crew should certainly have kept a sharper look-out. Once again the RI recommended Automatic Train Control but there was no chance in the war. Interestingly, No. 5025 was quickly repaired and returned to work. The carriage wheel jammed between the 5MT's rear driving wheel and the platform. *Getty Images.*

Above: Violent accidents in stations visited fatal risk on innocent bystanders on platforms and in waiting rooms. Considering this, the death toll of four at Bletchley in October 1939 was mercifully light: in addition to the 0-8-0 driver there was a postman, a porter and an RAF serviceman passenger. The horror of being on a station when stationary vehicles are hit by a double headed train travelling at 40mph out of the rain and darkness can scarcely be imagined. *Getty Images.*

Above: In September 1945 there was another fatal crash on the West Coast Main Line which illustrated yet again the increasingly urgent need for some kind of Automatic Train Control on the distant signal. On September 30, up trains were being diverted from the up fast to the up slow line at Bourne End, virtually in front of the signal box. This fast-slow transfer was protected by a colour light distant (1¼ miles in rear) which showed an automatic double yellow when the crossing movement was signalled, followed by an outer home semaphore and then, a quarter mile after that, a splitting pair of inner home semaphores signalling the diversion. It was never explained why Driver Swaby, on unrebuilt 'Royal Scot' 4-6-0 No. 6157 *The Royal Artilleryman*, hauling the 8.20pm Perth-Euston sleeping car express from Crewe to Euston ignored all the warning signals and took the 20mph crossover at 50mph, with the disastrous results shown here. *Getty Images.*

Above: On July 2 1941, No. 8293 (one of 25 Stanier Class 8F 2-8-0 goods engines loaned to the Great Western Railway to ease a power shortage) collided head-on with the up Plymouth-Paddington night train, hauled by a 'Castle' 4-6-0, on the Dolphin Junction diamond crossing, near Slough. Formal Railway Inspectorate reporting was suspended during the war and only a brief summary was provided to Ministers. Five persons were killed and the driver of the freight train was seriously injured. As was the case for most of the war, traffic was running out of course and the signalman misjudged the routing of the previous train and in his haste to minimise delay to the Plymouth-Paddington passenger train made a fatal error of reversing the cleared signal for the freight train and setting the crossover for the passenger train when the freight train was almost at the signal. The brief report noted that the loaned LMS '8F' was not fitted with GWR ATC equipment. This engine was the last of the 25 loaned Stanier '8Fs' to be returned to the LMS, doubtless after a spell in Swindon for repairs. *Getty Images.*

CONTINUED FROM PAGE 74

deserved high priority in relation to other operating and signalling improvements. He also mentioned that in October 1947 the GWR had demonstrated a modified form of ATC equipment designed to give three indications, green, double yellow and single yellow, so as to suit multiple-aspect colour-light signalling. The Nationalised railway, formed in 1948, unfortunately did not develop the idea, the lack of differentiation between single and double yellow being a major factor in several accidents in later years. There is a brief, but fascinating Pathé film news item about this crash available on the *Britishpathé.com* website.

The proportion of accidents attributable to signalmen was gradually declining, thanks to the continuing installation of such safety devices as track circuits, interlocked block ('Line Clear' release), Welwyn control, and other block control equipment.

Welwyn control (see also page 89) prevents the signalman turning to 'line clear' whilst a train is in section. A train is proved as having passed right through the section. An emergency time release is provided to override the Welwyn control in the event that a 'line clear' has been given but the train does not require to enter the section. The time delay gives the signalman time to consider his actions. Welwyn control was a recommendation of the report following a fatal rear end collision at Welwyn Garden City on June 15 1935 when the signalman forgot there was a train already in section.

Two accidents in 1944/45 indicated clearly that colour light signals alone were not the complete answer to the perennial problem of drivers passing signals at danger, either in clear weather or in fog, and that only ATC could provide this. A wartime accident at Ilford, on the Liverpool Street to Ipswich line, on Sunday January 16 1944, provided one of the first illustrations of the fallibility of colour-light

CONTINUED ON PAGE 82

Above: The points of the 20mph crossover are still set from the up fast to the up slow at Bourne End, which Driver Swaby and Fireman (who were both killed) took at 50mph on September 30 1945. It must have been a truly horrific spectacle for the signalman, helpless, opposite, who had done all the right things. Driver Swaby had many years experience on the route, and knew of the diversion. The weather was fine and clear with only a little haze - but other drivers that day had remarked about the sun being in their eyes and finding the colour lights hard to see, many saying they preferred semaphores. This 'swamping' was a problem which was said to play a significant part in the Ladbroke Grove disaster of October 5 1999 (see pages 151-153). However, Swaby was well aware of the diversion and given his long years of route knowledge it is hard to believe he could have mistaken his position in such good weather. *C.R.L. Coles/Rail Archive Stephenson.*

Above: The violent swerving at 50mph on the 20mph main line crossover at Bourne End on September 30 1945 caused the 137-ton 'Royal Scot' 4-6-0 to roll onto its left side, whereupon it careered down the 9ft embankment, coming to rest in a field. The six leading coaches were completely wrecked and piled up around the 4-6-0. Only the last three coaches of the 15-coach train remained on the rails. Of the passengers, 38 (including the engine crew) lost their lives immediately and five more died subsequently from their injuries. There were a further 64 serious injuries. The destruction of the carriages is horribly apparent. *C.R.L. Coles/Rail Archive Stephenson.*

Above: The wrecked carriages have been removed at Bourne End on September 30 1945, together with the locomotive's tender and all the loose plating on the 4-6-0, including cab, boiler cladding, smoke deflectors and all pipework. The lifting chains are in place and it appears that the breakdown crew is ready to attempt to set the wrecked engine on its wheels before lifting it back onto the track. It was subsequently repaired and returned to work. This was the third similar disaster in ten years - very similar crashes had taken place at Leighton Buzzard (1931) and Great Bridgeford 1932. Some kind of ATC would in all likelihood have prevented all three catastophes. Progress was very slow: as late as 1952, the dreadful multiple fatal collision at Harrow & Wealdstone was another appalling illustration of the urgent need for GWR-style Automatic Train Control (ATC). *C.R.L. Coles/Rail Archive Stephenson.*

Above: A picture which says a very great deal about how differently such incidents are handled today, not least in terms of appropriate clothing and equipment for the railwaymen and emergency services staff. Workmen at Bourne End on September 30 1945 are in dungarees, jackets and cloth caps whilst managers are neatly 'suited and booted' and wearing trilby or bowler hats according to status and grade. Nurses appear to be wearing the same uniforms they would wear in a hospital ward. Prominent in the right foreground is a tea mug! *C.R.L. Coles/Rail Archive Stephenson.*

Above: These pictures convey an almost comic feel to this incident but it was very serious and could have been catastrophic - a higher speed could have had the express plunging from the viaduct at Docker, Grayrigg, in the Lake District. Single line working was in force on the down line, forward from Lambrigg signalbox. All trains were being stopped and then being assisted (if required) by this 4-4-0 to set their trains back up the 1 in 106 gradient and over a crossing to the down line after which they ran forward in the up direction. The driver of No. 46235 *City of Birmingham*, with the 10am express from Glasgow to Euston, missed the Lambrigg distant at caution and by the time he saw the home at danger it was too late to stop. He reduced his train speed from 60mph to 25-30mph, at which he collided head-on with the 4-4-0, whose driver saw what was happening and had actually got his engine moving away from the approaching 'Princess Cornation' and this significantly reduced the force of the impact. *Getty Images*.

CONTINUED FROM PAGE 79

signals during fog. The 2.40pm express from Norwich to Liverpool Street, composed of 12 coaches hauled by 'Bl2' 4-6-0 No 8564, ran past several colour-light and semaphore danger signals and collided at 20-25mph with the 2.38pm express from Yarmouth to Liverpool Street. Nine passengers were killed. There were no fog signalmen on duty and double block-section working was in force, which is a method of keeping a clear section between two trains, as a partial safeguard against a driver's missing the signals at one signalbox. The line was equipped with Sykes 'lock and block' signalling equipment. Lt Col Sir Alan Mount and Maj Wilson both had a hand in the Inquiry and could do no other but point out that ATC would have prevented the accident.

The following year there occurred what at the time was Britain's worst-ever peacetime rail disaster after Tay Bridge, and concerned a special use of double-yellow colour-light distants. This method of signalling facing junctions had been in dispute for many years.

Originally most junctions were provided with a separate distant arm for each route, and this gave a positive message to drivers. If no arm was lowered, the home signal was at danger. On the other hand if either arm was lowered the driver could then tell for which route the facing points were set and, if a speed reduction was necessary through a diverging junction, the driver could brake accordingly. However, if for any reason the driver omitted to reduce speed there was a risk of derailment and, to overcome this danger, some railway companies had decided to have only a single arm at the distant signal, to be cleared only for the straight route. This caused little or no delay where the driver had a good long view of the home signal and where the points were immediately beyond the signal, but in other circumstances it could lead to some delay if the driver had to reduce speed prematurely, especially where an outer home signal was provided and this could be an unacceptable situation on a busy four-track main line. Following an accident at Great Bridgeford in June 1932, the LMS had introduced a new signalling definition in connection with distant signals. At certain places they replaced semaphore splitting distants with a double-yellow colour-light distant, and drivers were told that two yellow lights meant:

'Pass the next signal at restricted speed, and if applicable to a junction may denote that the points are set for a diverging route...'

On Sunday September 30 1945, the 8.20pm Perth to Euston Sleeper approached Bourne End on the up fast line at about 65mph. The signalman had set his route from up fast to up slow, because engineers were working on the up fast line in Watford Tunnel, and he had cleared his up fast outer home and his up fast to up slow inner home junction signal. His up fast distant showed two yellows. The train came on at full speed and started to go through the 20mph crossover at almost 60mph. It was too much to hope that the train could hold the rails at such a speed. The engine, 'Royal Scot' class 4-6-0 No. 6157 *The Royal Artilleryman,* rolled over into a field, killing both enginemen. Six of the seven leading coaches piled up and were destroyed. Of the 398 passengers on board, 41 were killed and 64 were seriously injured.

Sir Alan Mount investigated this accident. His observations regarding the signalling are masterly and repay the closest study for anyone wishing to go into the subject in more detail. He also had quite a lot to say about ATC and suggested that the accident would not have happened if there had been warning control at the distant signal. Inspecting Officers' reports on serious accidents are valuable not only for the logical and lucid manner in which they proceed to conclusions about the cause, but also for the observations on the history of the particular type of accident and the possible safeguards. Following this incident LMS abandoned the special use of two yellow lights in connection with junction working.

Sir Alan Mount also investigated an odd triple collision which occurred at Potters Bar on the LNER East Coast Main Line just after

Above: The impact destroyed the front framing of both engines, whose smokebox doors came close to touching. The light engine had been driven forward 77 yards and although its bogie wheels were derailed there was no impact with the stone parapet of Docker Viaduct, which is 130 yards long and 77ft high. About 120 yards of up main line had to be replaced. There were no serious injuries although three passengers were hospitalised. The 'Duchess' was hauling a 13-coach train of more than 370 tons. Driver Stubbs accepted full responsibility for the crash and expressed regret: he had missed the distant because he had been rummaging in the locker behind him for his handkerchief, leaving him running too fast when he saw the danger signal, by which time it was too late to stop. He openly admitted he 'forgot' the Lambrigg distant, which did not impress Inspector Lt-Colonel G.R.S. Wilson, who also criticised the guard for failing to be alert and watchful when he knew the single line working was ahead. Although he further commented that ATC would have prevented this incident, he also made clear that a driver's job was to be watchful and vigilant and that Stubbs had no excuse for his lapse. *Getty Images.*

10.00pm on Sunday February 10 1946. At that time the up slow line from Hatfield terminated just north of the station and there were only two lines through the platforms. The 9.32pm local train from Hatfield to King's Cross was approaching Potters Bar on the up slow line, with the signals at danger, whilst on the main lines all signals were cleared for the 9.45pm express from King's Cross to Edinburgh and the 5.00pm express from Bradford to King's Cross. The signalman at Potters Bar saw the local train run past his inner home signal at danger at about 20mph and to prevent it from crashing into the buffer stops at the end of the up slow line he threw his up main line signals to danger and reversed the crossover to take the local train on to the up main line. He was just too late and moved the points under the first coach, which caused a derailment, fouling the down main line. Within a minute the down express had crashed into the derailed coaches at about 45mph, then a minute later the up express also ploughed into the wreckage. Fortunately its driver was on the alert and had seen the signals go back to danger, thus he was able to reduce his speed to about 10mph. Although there were 595 passengers in the down express and 450 in the up express, the only fatalities were two passengers in the lightly-loaded local train. Sir Alan Mount suggested that the LNER should press on with its plans for widening the line through Potters Bar so that there were four tracks instead of two. This was finally achieved eight years later, in 1954. 1947, the last year of existence of the 'Big Four' private railway companies, was one of the worst ever for passenger fatalities - in fact it was the worst peacetime year in the whole history of railways up to that point. On the Southern Railway 36 passengers were killed in four separate collisions (South Croydon, October 24, 31 killed; Motspur Park, November 6, 3 killed; Herne Hill, also November 6, 1 killed; Farnborough, November 26, 1 killed), which spoiled its very fine safety record - because from 1923 to 1946 only 15 passengers had been killed in four collisions. The LNER fared no better, 52 passengers being killed in 1947 in three accidents. In contrast, the Great Western ended its independent existence in triumph, with its fifth consecutive year free from fatal train accidents.

Errors by drivers and signalmen were among the causes but that demon, fog, was present on several occasions. Viewed from today's standpoint, with colour-light signals, diesel and electric traction, and AWS and TPWS, we are in awe that drivers managed to run their trains at all during fog in years gone by, with oil-lit semaphore signals, steam locomotives and no ATC, yet run them they did and with only very occasional lapses.

The Southern Railway's worst accident occurred on October 24 1947 near South Croydon Junction on the main line from Brighton to London Victoria. Again, there was dense fog. 31 passengers and a driver were killed.

There were two more fatal accidents a few days later in November, on the Southern Railway. This spate of four fatal accidents in two weeks would have created an almighty furore had it happened today, with calls for the resignation of the Secretary of State for Transport and demands that a formal public inquiry be set up, but all this happened before the days of mass television. Besides, the public, having recently survived far worse horrors, took things in its stride, as did the Inspectorate. And so, on December 31 1947 the 'Big Four' passed into history, with many a nostalgic backwards glance. No doubt, as they switched off the lights in their offices on that New Year's Eve, the quartet of long-serving Inspecting Officers, Lt-Col Sir Alan Mount, Col Trench, Lt-Col Woodhouse and Lt-Col Wilson looked back to some of the more significant accidents and inquiries of the previous quarter of a century and wondered what changes were to come under the British Railways regime. They need not have worried. For several years it was going to be a case of *Plus ca change, plus c'est la meme chose.*

Chapter 6

Great Changes, New Problems 1948-1968

Nationalisation on January 1 1948 brought comprehensive changes to the political and financial control and organisation of Britain's railways. As they now came under public ownership and as the making of profits was no longer the ultimate aim (or so it was rather naively thought at first) more attention and more money could perhaps be devoted to safety? The newly-formed Railway Executive might have been expected to behave in such a responsible manner that the existence of an independent watchdog on safety such as the Railway Inspectorate could in future be considered superfluous. And indeed, the new men at Railway HQ quickly threw aside a half-century or so of prevarication and announced almost at once that they would embark on a programme to extend ATC (now called Warning Control) on main line routes. However, it very quickly became clear that finance for safety was not unlimited, when the Executive tempered their statement with an ominous remark that 'it should be initiated as soon as circumstances would allow'. Any lingering doubts that the Railway Inspectorate had become redundant were quickly dispelled. The new railway authority was faced with the same difficult decisions about investment in safety measures that had plagued previous railway managers and a separate independent body, able to make judgements free from political, financial, and indeed any other pressures, was essential if the safety of the travelling public was to be properly taken into account. The duties and responsibilities of the Inspectorate therefore remained unchanged and even its *modus operandi* was largely the same. Its routine and regular contacts were however with the new Regional headquarters as successors to the main line companies, rather than with the Railway Executive.

For at least the next 10 years, the main safety problems confronting the railways were the very familiar issues of collisions caused by drivers' and signalmen's errors. Then, as the application of modern signalling controls and ATC began to take effect, new perils arose from the introduction of new technologies, a process which became particularly marked in the 1960s.

An example of one of the familiar accidents in a familiar location took place at Winsford, on the West Coast Main Line, about eight miles north of Crewe, shortly after midnight on April 17 1948. The 5.40pm express Glasgow to Euston was halted in mid-section between Winsford Junction and Winsford Station signalboxes when a soldier who wanted to get home quickly (he lived nearby) pulled the communication cord. The signalman at Winsford Station signalbox then made a fatal error. Although he had not seen the train go past,

Above: The new BR 'cycling lion' heraldic device is applied via transfer to a newly painted tender carrying the pre-Grouping LNWR lined black livery adopted by the new BR regime, for mixed traffic locomotives after 1948. It was at first thought that safety investment would flow much more freely in the brave new world of public ownership: it didn't and the RI's role in leading the charge for rail safety improvements remained as important as ever. Fully 38 years after the terrible train fire fuelled by gas lighting at Hawes Junction in 1910, one in ten carriages were still gas lit. Automatic Train Control to assist drivers in the sighting and response to crucial distance signals was still the exception rather the rule on main lines other than the old Great Western, with its own system - and would remain so. *CC Collection.*

Above: The 'Big Four' (Great Western, Southern, London Midland & Scottish and London & North Eastern Railways) created in the Grouping of 1923 had been literally worn out by the heavy traffic demands of the Second World War. The so-called 'golden era' of the 1930s was a distant memory in the post-1945 era and the railways were even more desperately in need of investment than they had been after the Great War of 1914-18. The Labour Government which unexpectedly ousted Churchill's Conservatives to win the General Election of July 1945 set about its socialist agenda of nationalising the country's means of 'production, distribution and exchange.' British Railways was born on January 1 1948. This shows the nationalised East Coast Main Line over which the RI presided: timber-framed bogie rolling stock, semaphore signals, patchy main line track circuiting (indicated by the horizontal diamonds on the signal dolls), all still presided over by Sir Nigel Gresley's famous 'Pacifics'. 'A4' No. 60028 *Walter K. Whigham* engages York from the south with the down 'Flying Scotsman' on August 8 1950. The 'BRITISH RAILWAYS' brand is evident not only on the 'Streak's' tender, but also on the tanks of the station pilot, one of whose crew relaxes in the summer sunshine. His engine carries the number 8310, prefixed by a small 'E'. *Donald T. Greenwood/Rail Archive Stephenson.*

he assumed that it must have done so and he sent 'Train out of Section' to Winsford Junction signalbox. It is a circumstance that had been seen so many times before. The Junction signalman immediately offered forward a following express, the 6.25pm Postal, Glasgow to Euston, of 13 bogie vans drawn by 'Pacific' No. 6251 *City of Nottingham*, and, upon having it accepted, cleared all his signals. The Postal entered the obstructed section at full speed but then the driver saw a red light ahead. It was the guard of the first train carrying out his protection duties, but he had only covered about 400yds. The driver made an emergency brake application and had managed to reduce speed to 40-45mph when the collision occurred. The impact severely damaged the last two coaches of the standing train, killing or fatally injuring 24 of their occupants. Matters might have become worse still, as the down Postal was closely approaching, but before the accident happened the

Above, right: A superb image of later 1950s BR: the steel-bodied Mk 1 carriage has arrived, but the opportunity provided by modernisation to standardise on air brakes was missed. Vacuum brakes were retained both for passenger trains and also goods, the majority of which continued to be carried in short, 10ft wheelbase four-wheeled wagons and vans, many of which remained unbraked and which ran loose-coupled. This wonderful panoramic westbound view of Stoke Gifford Yards encapsulates the greatest safety risks which worried the Railway Inspectorate - driver/signalman error as a result of no nationwide Automatic Train Control leading to catastrophe, or derailments at speed of four-wheeled goods wagons. This train of at least nine carriages is being hauled by an unidentified Riddles BR 'Britannia' 4-6-2; it is thought to be a Paddington-South Wales express. At least 220 goods wagons are visible in sidings shown in this picture. *The late George Heiron.*

Left: Shunting accidents on the very busy newly-nationalised railway were frequent - and buffer stop over runs could lead to precarious outcomes. On June 1 1948, a carriage precariously overhangs Stroud Green Road, Islington, about 10ft above a lovely gas lamp and one of the once-common white-glazed brick walls. *Getty Images.*

Winsford Station signalman began to have doubts about his actions and he put his down main line signals to danger, thus bringing the down Postal safely to a stand.

Lt Col Wilson, who investigated the accident, had no particular recommendations to make, although 'Welwyn Control' would have prevented the accident. He did, however, raise yet again the question of the provision of flares, to be used by the guard in just such an emergency to warn an approaching driver of an obstruction ahead. He records in his report that the idea was still under consideration by the railway authorities but they would probably have imported more risk than they were supposed to mitigate and were rightly dismissed by the safety experts in BR.

Another type of accident which was to become increasingly familiar for the next 30 years - until BR took action to prevent it - occurred on November 18 1948 at Woolwich Arsenal on the Southern Region. The driver of the 12.28pm electric multiple-unit (EMU) train started from Woolwich Dockyard station on receipt of the guard's 'Right away' hand signal - and then ran past the platform starting signal at danger into the section ahead, where it collided with the 12.17pm Cannon Street-Gravesend EMU, at not less than 15mph. Two people were killed. Col Trench attributed the accident to a lack of concentration on the driver's part, which led him to react to the guard's handsignal and fail to observe the platform starting signal. This type of accident became known as a 'Ding-ding and away', taking its name from the two rings given by the guard on the bell communication to the driver. A similar accident occurred at Newcastle Central on August 17 1951, when three people were killed. Lt Col Wilson remarked in his report that there had been seven collisions of this nature in the last three years, but a solution to the problem continued to elude both BR and the Inspectorate.

1949 was a landmark for the Inspectorate. The Chief Inspecting Officer, Lt Col Sir Alan Mount, retired on July

Above: This is yet another serious rail accident which happened because London Midland West Coast Main Line drivers were not assisted by any kind of automatic warning system for distant signals. Safe operation in any weather depended entirely on the driver's vigilance. On November 18 1951, the 10.30pm up sleeping car express from Glasgow to Euston was signalled to be crossed over from fast to slow line at Polesworth. The driver of the 12-coach train missed the distant and so failed to brake until he saw the home signal at danger: he took the 15mph crossover at 55mph, leading to the derailment of his locomotive and its first eight coaches. Unstreamlined Stanier 'Princess Coronation' 4-6-2 No. 46252 *City of Leicester* rolled to the left but was prevented from falling onto its side until it reached the end of the platform. Note the neat railwaymen's vegetable patches inside the boundary fence on the right, to the right of the policeman! *HMRI-ORR*.

Above: The 1951 Polesworth derailment must have been a highly alarming spectacle for the signalman, watching the derailment play out from his box just beyond the footbridge. The platform helped keep the derailed coaches generally upright and in line. Of the 174 passengers, just two were injured - and only slightly. One received first aid at the scene, the other was taken to hospital but discharged the same day after treatment. As an incidental, note the manicured ballast and immaculately maintained cess on the right. *HMRI-ORR*.

31, after 30 years' service, including 20 years as Chief, the longest tenure in that post in the history of the Inspectorate. Even so, he did not divorce himself entirely from railway safety, as he became a consultant to the Railway Executive on matters concerned with safety measures. However, that was not to last for long. He had continually overworked himself since the outbreak of war and his health broke down to such an extent that he was practically an invalid until he died in 1955. Like so many Inspecting Officers, he was utterly devoted to his job and he worked relentlessly hard. Col Trench said of him afterwards that he had great charm of manner and took pride in the fact that ever since a Government Railway Inspectorate had been set up more than 100 years ago, its technical staff had been provided by officers of the Corps of Royal Engineers, pointing out that an adequate degree of Government supervision was exercised with the minimum of statutory powers and with an economy of staff unequalled in any other country.

Col Trench, who himself retired in 1949, went on to say that it was in the daily routine of approval and inspection of new works and discussion of safety measures, that Sir Alan Mount showed his talent for persuasion, and, most important, for maintaining and improving friendly co-operation with the railway companies' staff in the pursuit of the common aim of safety. He was justifiably proud of the outstanding record of the British railway companies in this respect and of the share of the Inspecting Officers in contributing thereto.

Lt Col Woodhouse also retired the same year, leaving Lt-Col Wilson, who now became the Chief, as the only link with the pre-war railway. His colleagues were Brig C. A. Langley (1946-1963) and Col D. McMullen (1948-1968), both of whom became the Chief in their turn. They were later joined by Col W. P. Reed (1953-1968).

Brig C. A. Langley CB, CBE, MC

Chief Inspecting Officer: 1958-63

Charles Langley was born in Cork in 1897, the son of the Under-Secretary of State to the Egyptian Government. He was commissioned into the Royal Engineers in 1915, and served in France, being awarded the Military Cross twice.

He spent most of the inter-war years at the Longmoor Military Railway, becoming Chief Instructor, apart from a six-year spell, 1927-33, when he worked on the electrification of the Bombay-Poona line. During the war he held important posts in transportation in the Middle East, in India, and in South East Asia, for which he received the CBE (Commander of the British Empire).

In 1946, he retired from the army and became an Inspecting Officer, being promoted to Chief Inspecting Officer in 1958. Although he retired from the Inspectorate in 1963 he continued to be actively involved in rail transport affairs until he was in his 80s. He died in 1987.

Col D. McMullen

Chief Inspecting Officer: 1963-68

Dennis McMullen joined the Inspectorate in 1948. He succeeded Brig Langley as Chief Inspecting Officer in 1963, and retired in 1968. Some of the greatest changes on the railways - and challenges for the Inspectorate - occurred during his five year tenure as CIO. Steam locomotives were replaced by diesels. The West Coast route became Britain's first main line to be electrified at 25kV ac and there was large-scale modernisation of signalling. Under McMullen, the Inspectorate also had to deal with the freight train derailment problem of the 1960s.

Accidents caused by the faulty maintenance of locomotives gave the Inspectorate further great concern in the post-war years, one of the most serious being at Weedon, on the West Coast Main Line, on September 21 1951. 'Pacific' No. 46207 *Princess Arthur of Connaught*, hauling the 8.20am express Liverpool to Euston, left the rails at 60-65mph owing to a bogie defect, resulting in the deaths of 14 passengers and a dining car attendant. The following year a tender brake rod came adrift and caused the derailment of the 9.15am 'Thames-Clyde Express' Glasgow to St Pancras at Blea Moor on April 18 1952. The ten-coach train was double-headed by Midland 'Compound' 4-4-0 No. 1040 and 'Royal Scot' Class 4-6-0 No. 6117

Right: A detail view of the two derailed coaches beneath the Polesworth station footbridge seen on page 87. The gangways have been crushed but there is only a few inches of telescoping, compared with the catastrophic destruction which followed similar previous mishaps, when one coach first over-rode and then ripped into the body of the next. Polesworth's semaphore distants had already been replaced by colour lights to make them more visible to drivers but they nevertheless failed to prevent this non-fatal mishap. AWS was essential - but still it did not come. *HMRI-ORR.*

Below: The Weedon derailment of September 21 1951 was caused by a mechanical defect - believed to be a tight locomotive axlebox. While running at around 65mph, the leading bogie of Stanier 'Princess Royal' 4-6-2 No. 46207 *Princess Arthur of Connaught* derailed to the right, but on straight flat bottom track the derailed wheels continued over the sleepers for around three-quarters of a mile - incredibly, the crew didn't notice. Just outside Stowe Tunnel (in the background), the train emerged onto bullhead track whereupon the derailing wheels began smashing the cast rail chairs, knocking the rails out of gauge derailing all but the last two coaches. The 4-6-2 rolled to the left and slid down the 12ft embankment, off to the bottom right of this view, decelerating rapidly as it dug into soft ground. The leading derailed coaches compressed as a result into a concertina behind and alongside the locomotive, killing outright seven passengers and a dining car attendant. A further seven passengers died in hospital. Both lines were blocked. The driver, driving on the left side onto which his engine rolled, was very lucky to escape with injuries after being buried in an avalanche of coal from the tender. His fireman clung to the right hand side of the cab and miraculously escaped uninjured. The signalman at Heyford, 950 yards ahead, heard the crash and acted very quickly to avert further tragedy by stopping the approaching 'Royal Scot' express near his box. *Getty Images.*

Above: The Midland Railway's 'Long Drag' spectacular 72-mile Settle - Carlisle main line over the Pennines is completely blocked at Blea Moor on April 18 1952 after the high speed derailment of the double-headed up 'Thames Clyde Express' at 1.23pm. Hauled by 'Compound' 4-4-0 No. 41040 (pilot) and Class 7P 'Royal Scot' 4-6-0 No. 46117 *Welsh Guardsman* (train engine), the 9.15pm Glasgow-St Pancras left the track as it passed over facing points at Blea Moor at around 55mph. Poor locomotive maintenance led to the leading end of a brake rod on the 4-4-0 becoming detached north of Blea Moor Tunnel. The crew were unaware of the flailing loose brake rod end bouncing on the sleepers all through the 2,629-yard tunnel: it then struck the lock stretcher bar of the up facing points at Blea Moor. It buckled the stretcher by 6¾ inches, thereby shortening it by 1⅞ inches and pulling the left hand switch rail away from the stock rail by 9/16 of an inch - it effectively opened the points in front the 'Scot' and derailment was inevitable. There were, incredibly, no fatalities amongst the 200 passengers, 29 of whom (plus five railway staff) were injured. Inspector Col D McMullen was critical of maintenance standards at Leeds Holbeck Motive Power Depot which he said was responsible for "bad maintenance of the engine". Not for the first time, RI reports spoke of the sloppy fitting and inspection of the humble split pin, which caused this accident. "...a well fitting split pin, with its legs properly splayed, will not fall out of its own accord," said Col McMullen. He also praised the welded underframes of the Mk 1s and their steel bodies, which had ensured none of the telescoping which we would have undoubtedly seen in earlier years in a mishap like this. *Getty Images.*

Welsh Guardsman. The 'Compound's' loose brake rod struck and damaged a facing point lock stretcher bar, causing one of the switch blades to be opened sufficiently to cause derailment of the train, which was running at 65mph. Fortunately there was no loss of life, but there were many injuries.

The Western Region's fine record of freedom from fatal train accidents at last came to an end after 13 years on Sunday November 20 1955, but only because a 'foreign' (in other words, a BR Standard!) engine was involved, 'Britannia' class 4-6-2 No. 70026 *Polar Star*. The engine was hauling an excursion from Treherbert to Paddington and was being diverted from the up main line to the up goods loop at Milton, near Didcot, because of engineering works. The engine took the turnout at excessive speed and became derailed, resulting in the deaths of 11 passengers. The driver was at fault and had failed to react to the ATC warning at the distant signal and the automatic brake application had been over-ridden either by the driver or by the fireman. 'Britannia' class 'Pacifics' differed from GWR locomotives in several respects and the driver was not really familiar with the changes. The assertion made by the driver was that the handrails on the smoke deflectors obscured his view and as a result the deflectors on the Western Region Britannia Pacifics were modified to have six cut out hand holds in place of the traditional handrails. It is extremely improbable that the original handrails could really have obstructed a clear view.

A few days later, on December 2 1955, there was another serious accident, this time at Barnes, on the Southern Region, which has some familiar features. Eleven passengers and two train crew were killed when the 11.12pm EMU Waterloo to Windsor and Chertsey was irregularly admitted to the section between Barnes East and Barnes Junction signalboxes and collided with the 10.55pm freight train from Battersea to Brent, which was slowly moving forward. The line was equipped with Sykes' lock and block apparatus, and, as had happened on a number of previous occasions, the signalman had momentarily forgotten about the freight train and had used his release key to reset his block instrument to allow the signalman at the box in rear to clear his signals for the passenger train. The ability to reset without sufficient thought was the Achilles heel of the Sykes system. Neither the Midland rotary block system nor the Welwyn control system suffered from this defect. To release rotary block from the 'Train on Line' (or 'Train in Section') position requires the signalman to press a button which is recessed behind a piece of glass. To operate the button, the signalman has to break the glass, which is not undertaken lightly because it entails sending for a technician to replace the glass. A report giving the reason for using the release had also to be sent to the stationmaster.

To release the block indicator under the Welwyn control system requires an indicator to be turned through 360°. The turning movement is generated by a small handle, which itself has to be turned about a hundred times, a laborious process which gives plenty of time for reflection.

The Welwyn control system was devised following a serious accident at Welwyn Garden City in 1935. There was another accident near that station on Monday January 7 1957. The 6.18am six-coach local from Baldock to King's Cross, headed by 2-6-4T No. 67741, had left the up slow platform and was then turned out on to the up main line as booked. The 7.10pm Aberdeen to King's Cross express was already closely approaching, having been accepted by the signalman up to his outer home signal, which was at danger; but it failed to

General View of Wreckage from North (paras. 6, 7 and 8)

Above: An annotated official photograph of carnage caused - yet again - by the lack of Automatic Warning System on the West Coast Main Line, this time at Harrow & Wealdstone, on the autumn morning of October 8 1952. In patchy fog, the 11-coach 8.15pm Perth-London express, hauled by Stanier Class 8P 'Duchess' 4-6-2 No. 46242 *City of Glasgow*, over-ran a colour light distant and then two stop signals at danger before ploughing at 55-60mph into the rear of an up nine-coach commuter train standing in Harrow & Wealdstone station. The shocked signalman immediately threw all his signals to danger: it was too late - within seconds, a London-Liverpool/Manchester express hauled by Stanier 'Jubilee' 4-6-0 No. 45637 *Windward Islands* and 'Princess Elizabeth' class 'Pacific' No. 46202 *Princess Anne*, crashed at speed into the wreckage. The 'Duchess' had torn into the rear of the commuter train with such force that its last standing three coaches were telescoped and piled up into the length of a single vehicle. *CC Collection.*

Above: Three rear coaches of the Harrow & Wealdstone commuter train, three leading vehicles of the Perth express and seven coaches of the Liverpool express - which would normally have occupied a length of 238 yards - were piled up and telescoped into a compressed mass just one fifth of this length. The wreckage was just 45 yards long, 18 yards wide and 30 feet high - all of it crushed, with their occupants, between the platforms. Note the empty stretchers, awaiting occupants, on the carriage roof. A total of 108 passengers and four enginemen were killed. This included the Perth crew, whose engine was buried under this wreckage - and we still do not know why the driver passed the distant and two stop signals at danger. Because the fog was patchy, regulations did not require fogmen to be called out. *Getty Images.*

Above: A Cowans Sheldon steam breakdown crane undertakes a frighteningly perilous and clearly unstable carriage roof lift which would never be attempted today - especially with so many unprotected rescue workers standing calmly beneath! On the extreme right, a tube train stands out of harms way. The crash tore up the conductor rails and so tripped the Underground's circuit breakers, meaning approaching Tube trains were safely stopped. There were many serious injuries amongst the 157 passengers hurt. This remains our worst peacetime British railway disaster. *Getty Images.*

stop there and continued past both that signal and the inner home. The signalman operated his emergency detonator-placer and heard the explosion, whilst the signalbox lad rushed to the window and held out a red lamp. Both were ignored by the driver and the train roared through the station at 65mph. It quickly caught up with the local train, which had accelerated to 30-35mph and smashed into it, wrecking the last coach and killing one of the passengers. The express engine, Class A2/3 'Pacific' No. 60520 *Owen Tudor*, rolled over onto its side.

Lt Col Wilson investigated this accident, and was faced by a claim by the express driver that the up distant had been at 'clear', although he admitted that he missed the outer home and said that the inner home was blotted out by smoke and steam. The distant signal was a power-worked semaphore, located below the Welwyn North signals, and the arm had to be proved to be horizontal before 'Line Clear' could be given. After a very thorough investigation Lt-Col Wilson reached the conclusion that the signal had been at caution when the driver passed it.

There was some disappointment that the express driver had failed to react to the explosion of the twin detonators and it was recommended that larger detonators should be used. ATC equipment had already been installed at the distant signal but No. 60520 had not yet been equipped. There was great faith that ATC would eventually eliminate such accidents, but there had been another warning only a few months previously that ATC was not 100% infallible.

On September 6 1956, at Ludlow, the driver of the 2.00pm parcels train Penzance to Crewe, headed by a GWR 2-6-0 No. 9306, failed to react positively to an adverse distant signal, cancelled the automatic brake application and continued forward at speed. He then passed two signals at danger and crashed into the 4.45pm express Penzance to Manchester at about 45mph. The express was stationary at the time. Fortunately there were no fatalities. There was some suggestion that the warning siren on the engine had become muffled by cotton waste, but this did not affect the automatic brake application, which must have been cancelled subconsciously by the driver. This accident and the 'Britannia' incident at Milton a year earlier, were warnings that ATC was not completely foolproof, but there is no doubt that its benefits far outweighed any shortcomings. This was emphasised by two of the worst collisions in railway history, at Harrow & Wealdstone in 1952 when 108 passengers and four staff were killed and subsequently at Lewisham St Johns in 1957, when 89 passengers and a guard were killed. Both these accidents have been fully described elsewhere and it is almost certain they would have been prevented if ATC had been in use.

However, as the installation of ATC proceeded (now known as the Automatic Warning System - AWS) coupled with the extension of multiple-aspect colour-light signalling, there was a corresponding reduction in the number of serious accidents caused by drivers' and signalmen's errors. But new concerns arose, particularly in the 1960s, such as buckled track, broken rails and freight train derailments. It would, perhaps, be wrong to describe these as new perils, but they were certainly intensified by the application of new technologies, such as continuously welded rails (CWR) and diesel locomotives. The automation of level crossings was also to be a matter which occupied a great deal of the Inspectorate's time and thoughts.

The operation of public level crossings had changed little in the previous 100 years and the railway was still protected by very heavy timber gates which had to be swung across to block either road or railway by signalmen or crossing keepers. The legal requirement to maintain attendance at public level crossings, imposed by the Railways Clauses Consolidation Act 1845, was not only a heavy financial burden on BR, but caused other problems. In the post war labour market it was often difficult to recruit and retain staff for the responsible but poorly paid and often boring job of crossing keeper and the staff recruited were not always of the right calibre. The signalling and safety arrangements at many crossings were quite

Above, left: Herbert Eccles, Director of Rescue Operations at Harrow & Wealdstone, after the catastrophic double collision of October 8 1952. Normally he was the District Goods Superintendent at Broad Street, London. *Getty Images.*

Above, right: Clearing up after a major accident was a traumatic as well as extremely difficult job for the railwaymen involved. Today, a full range of counselling would be available for staff. In 1952, there was just a vicor. Picture Post photographer Raymond Kleboe has captured a moment of decision making amidst the wreckage at Harrow. This was also long before high-vis was ever thought of! *Getty Images.*

Above, left: A very sad spectacle: tattered clothes and battered documentation: Harrow police detectives sift personal possessions strewn around the wreckage, to try and identify victims, whose relatives would receive a terrible visit from a police officer. *Getty Images.*

Above, right: Eight people and just four telephones - one of which is truly ancient - in Harrow & Wealdstone's cramped third class waiting room, commandeered as the control room. These men and women did everything from arrange the laying of new track to distributing cash to ease immediate hardship. Herbert Eccles is seated at the top left of the picture. *Getty Images.*

Above: The strained expressions say it all - grief and sadness is etched into the face of the lady holding blankets on the right as an overcoated police sergeant leads the removal of just one of the 108 people killed that terrible morning. Note the railwayman just left of centre, putting a gentle, steadying hand on the stretcher's occupant as they make their way carefully along the platform edge. *Getty Images.*

primitive and whilst they were perhaps adequate for the horse and cart era, their shortcomings were increasingly exposed as the volume of motorised road traffic continued to grow. Furthermore, the need at many crossings to close the gates across the road several minutes before a train was due, in order to give time for the signalman to clear his distant signal before it came within the engine driver's sight, led to heavy delays for road traffic. There was therefore an urgent need to take action to improve the situation on three counts: to improve safety; to reduce or eliminate manning costs; and to reduce delays to road traffic.

In order to make progress, the Chief Inspecting Officer asked Cols McMullen and Reed to visit Continental railways, accompanied by officers of BR and the Ministry of Transport, to study automatic level crossing installations and make recommendations. The visit took place from October 4-13 1956 and the main recommendation which emerged was for a form of automation that became known as the automatic half-barrier (AHB) installation, with the barriers being lowered automatically, triggered by the approach of a train, usually using a treadle on the track. The Inspectorate permitted the introduction of such level crossing equipment without attendants, but development work was undertaken very cautiously and there was often considerable public opposition to what became known, somewhat disparagingly, as 'Continental level crossings'.

The Inspectorate recognised that the education of the public and the changing of public opinion, would be major and time-consuming tasks and so they have turned out to be. The first automatic half-barrier (AHB) level crossing was brought into use at Spath, near Uttoxeter on February 5 1961 and during the 1960s they were introduced in increasing numbers, so that by the end of 1967 some 200 had been installed. Plans to accelerate the programme were drawn up and were being implemented – but then came a terrible accident.

On January 6 1968, a massive road transporter lorry carrying a 120-ton English Electric transformer was proceeding very cautiously over an AHB crossing on the West Coast Main Line at Hixon, Staffordshire, when the red lights started to flash and the barriers descended. The lorry was moving so slowly that it was unable to get clear of the crossing before the train, a Manchester to Euston express - whose approach had triggered the barriers and red lights - arrived at the level crossing, still travelling at almost full line speed (75mph). The AL1 electric locomotive struck the transformer and hurled it aside, becoming derailed itself in the impact. Several coaches were also derailed and 11 passengers were killed. BR should have been informed beforehand of the movement of the transporter lorry over the level crossing so that signallers could have taken special precautions, but no such prior notice was received from the haulier. (See also page 8-9)

The British public had always been suspicious of these new-fangled AHB level crossings and loved the sturdy, old-fashioned white gates, with their big red bullseyes. The Hixon accident served only to reinforce and confirm their mistrust, despite widespread evidence from the rest of Europe about the safety of AHB crossings. Conversely, in Britain we had been reminded plenty of times about the dangers of manned, gated crossings. By this time German Federal Railways had more than 800 AHBs and the French Railways more than 2,000. Nevertheless, the spectacular nature of the accident inevitably attracted tremendous public attention and the Government decided that a more formal inquiry should be held under the provisions of Section 7 of the 1871 Regulation of Railways Act. They appointed Mr E. B. Gibbens, QC to hold the inquiry, rather than one of the Inspecting Officers, because it was felt that as the Inspectorate had been so closely involved in formulating proposals for AHBs they could hardly be considered independent. In the circumstances it has to be considered a correct decision, even though it was the first time it had been done since the Tay Bridge disaster of 1879. The outcome was a confirmation of the policy of automating level crossings, but with additional, and in some cases unnecessary and irrelevant, safeguards which had the effect of defeating the policy of automation because the extra costs of the complex control systems, four lay-bys, road widening and regarding, lighting and presence detectors made it uneconomic for BR to do so. The automation programme therefore came to a sudden stop and there was to be little or no progress for the next ten years or so, during which time thousands of level crossings were automated on the West European railways.

Lt Col Wilson died very suddenly on March 20 1958 at the age of only 61 and, as in the case of Sir Alan Mount, the demands of the job had taken their toll. Lt Col Wilson had to undertake the inquiries into two of Britain's worst rail disasters, both of which occurred in the 1950s - Harrow in 1952 and Lewisham in 1957. Few people realised

Above: An evocative and extremely moving picture by *Picture Post* photographer Raymond Kleboe, during the Harrow & Wealdstone rescue and clear-up. Salvation Army ladies are hard at work with their tea urns and biscuit tins, ministering to the needs of the rescue teams. In the left foreground, a vicar is there to minister to emotional and spiritual needs. Maybe one of those needing support was the signalman, hauntingly glimpsed in the open end window of Harrow No. 1 signalbox, overlooking the extensive death and devastation. *Getty Images.*

the great strain that the Harrow disaster imposed upon him, or appreciated the depth of his sympathy with all who suffered so terribly in that tragedy. His health was impaired by this traumatic investigation, but he resumed work after some weeks' rest. Sadly, he did not live to complete his investigation into the Lewisham accident. Lt Col Wilson was succeeded by Brig C. A. Langley, who completed the Lewisham Inquiry and retired in his turn in 1963 at the age of 65. He then began a third career as a transport consultant, being involved in the electrification of the Pakistan Western Railways. As Managing Director of the UK Railway Advisory Service, a consultancy service set up by the Ministry of Transport, he travelled all over the world. He finally died at the age of 90, in 1987.

Col. J. R. H. Robertson CBE
Chief Inspecting Officer: 1969-73

John Robertson was commissioned into the Royal Engineers in 1932 at the age of 20 and spent his pre-war years at the Railway Training Centre, Longmoor. Wartime duties took him to France, Norway, India and South East Asia. His army career continued until 1958, when Lt Col Wilson's untimely death gave him the unexpected opportunity of becoming an Inspecting Officer of Railways.

He suffered increasingly from arthritis and retired in 1973, having been Chief Inspecting Officer for five years, and died in 1977. He is remembered by many for the courageous way he overcame his physical disability, insisting on playing a full part in sometimes onerous inspections and accident investigations. This is epitomised by his inspections of the West Coast Main Line electrification, during which, in the depths of winter, he had himself strapped into a chair bolted to the flat roof of a wiring train so that he could view the clearances at bridges.

Lt-Col I. K. A. McNaughton BSc, CEng, FIMechE, FCIT, FIRSE
Chief Inspecting Officer: 1973-82

The Angel of Platform 6 – USAF Nursing Lieutenant Abbie Sweetwine.

A remarkable legacy of the Harrow & Wealdstone disaster was the modern 'paramedic' – thanks to the US Air Force's Abbie Sweetwine, dubbed 'The Angel of Platform 6.'

Harrow's emergency services were struggling to cope on October 8 1952. Several USAF men from the 494th Medical Group, stationed nearby at South Ruislip, happened to be on one of the trains. They immediately went to work but, overwhelmed, asked police for permission to send for help. A phone call placed the '494th' on full alert and a team of seven doctors and a nurse, led by Lieut Colonel Weiderman USAF, arrived.

Lieut Col Weiderman and other commanders realised a mistake had been made in sending 'walking wounded' to hospital by ambulance, leaving severely wounded people behind, urgently needing life-saving treatment. Experienced in wartime operations, the USAF team launched a battlefield-style response. Plasma transfusions via IV kit were started on the station, with the most badly wounded treated on site. This saved many lives.

Enabling doctors to prioritise, Abbie Sweetwine calmly started triage, identifying the most severely injured, marking them out for priority treatment. Crucially, she put a lipstick 'X' on the foreheads of treated patients and an 'M' on those who had received morphine. She told ambulancemen to explain these marks to hospital doctors, enabling them to optimise treatment and avoid morphine overdoses. More lives saved.

These battlefield techniques were used at Harrow for the first time in a major civilian disaster. The NHS – then just four years old – realised that getting injured patients to hospital was not always the best option. The USAF had shown how a major incident should be handled – while Abbie Sweetwine virtually invented today's paramedic. This reponse template spread around the world.

Born in May 2015, Sweetwine served the USAF for 20 years, retiring in 1969. She died on March 7 2009 at the age of 87 and is buried at the US National Cemetery in Arlington, Virginia.

Above: This derailment at Goswick station a few miles south of Berwick up on Tweed, on the East Coast Main Line, happened on Wednesday October 28 1953. Class A2/1 'Pacific' No. 60509 *Waverley* was working the 9.15pm up express from Glasgow to Colchester, comprised of four bogie coaches, four bogie vans and a four-wheeled fish van, all weighing 158 tons. Somewhere north of Goswick, two valve gear nuts on the top bolt holding together the two halves of an eccentric strap worked loose, came unscrewed and fell off. The eccentric rod then became detached at its rear end, with part of the broken strap still secured to it. This flailed and bounced over the sleepers for 115 yards until the lug on the bottom half of the eccentric strap still secured to the rod caught the stretcher bar of a set of facing points, which it bent and broke. This opened the facing points, derailing the locomotive and its train. The locomotive ploughed into the ballast and came to rest, 270 yards from the point of derailment. Its train remained upright and in line. None of the train crew were injured and only one of the 58 passengers required first aid. The locomotive was remarkably undamaged, there was virtually no bodywork damage to the coaches, which retained all their bogies despite the 55mph speed of the derailment. The railwayman sitting on the cab roof looks remarkably nonchalant! *HMRI/ORR*.

Above: The aftermath of the East Coast Main Line mishap at Goswick in October 1953. This little wayside station had staggered platforms, either side of a public road level crossing. It closed from September 15 1958. This view is looking north, with the signalbox on the up side, near the locomotive; the up platform was beyond the crossing. Trains normally passed at 60-70mph and the track had been good condition, said Col W. P. Reed in his report. So prompt was Relief Signalman G. Richardson, on hearing a noise "like something catching and bumping on the sleepers" as the train passed his box, he had sent 'Stop and examine' to the next box even before the derailment. He quickly followed up with 'obstruction danger' and was commended by Col Reed on his promptness of action. *HMRI/ORR.*

Born in 1920, Ian McNaughton was commissioned as a Second Lieutenant in the Royal Engineers and his war service took him to Northwest Europe, for which he was mentioned in despatches. His military career also took him to the Middle East in 1949 (General Headquarters, Middle East Land Forces), and to Cyprus in 1955, after which he returned to Germany in 1960 to join the British Army of the Rhine.

He retired from the army and joined the Railway Inspectorate in 1962, becoming Chief Inspecting Officer in 1973, a post he held for nine years. During those nine years he saw a steady improvement in safety on BR, thanks to the extension of the Automatic Warning System, continuing modernisation of signalling, 25kV electrification, installation of continuous welded rails and improved braking systems.

In 1977, recognising that the automation of level crossing protection had almost come to a full stop, he arranged for a joint Department of Transport/British Rail Working Party, headed by Lt Col A. G. Townsend Rose and Fred Walmsley (BR), to visit railways in Belgium, Holland and France to study their practices. The Working Party's report led to many changes such as the replacement of gates with lightweight lifting barriers and allowed the progress of automation to be resumed.

Lt Col Wilson and Brig Langley were succeeded by Col R. H. Robertson (1958-73) and Lt Col I. K. A. McNaughton (1962-82). The Inspectorate was increased to five to cope with the increased workload: Maj Peter M. Olver arrived in 1965 and he remained in the Inspectorate until 1989, having the distinction of being the longest-serving Inspector since Lt Col Sir Alan Mount, who had retired 40 years earlier. The workload of the Inspectorate became much heavier during the 1960s owing to the large number of inspections of new works that were required, such as level crossing modernisation, station rebuilding, track remodelling, electrification and signalling modernisation, much of which arose from implementation of the BR Modernisation Plan of 1955. Furthermore, the railway system was becoming much more technically complex and the

Above: A sobering reminder of passenger vulnerability when timber-bodied carriages were involved in high energy collisions - and this mishap took place at just 20mph. The LNER coach has literally been torn in half. Incredibly, only four passengers were in the coach and they escaped with only minor injuries. No-one else was hurt when the 2.21pm Liverpool Street-Ipswich express of September 4 1953 derailed at Bethnal Green. Running under green signals, the express derailed on the facing points of a crossover leading to the down platform. The locomotive remained in line with the down main line but the derailed rear bogie of the first coach was deflected to the left. The vehicle slewed broadside and was then smashed in two when it hit the OLE mast on the platform. *ORR/HMRI.*

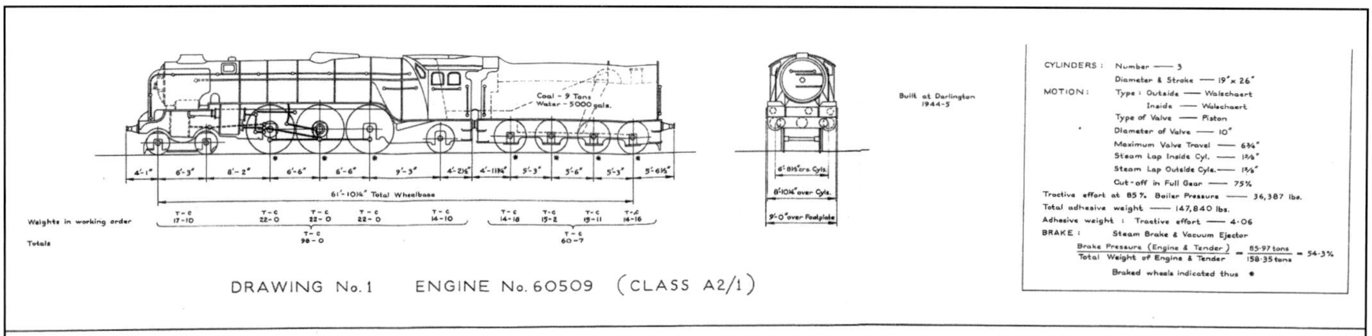

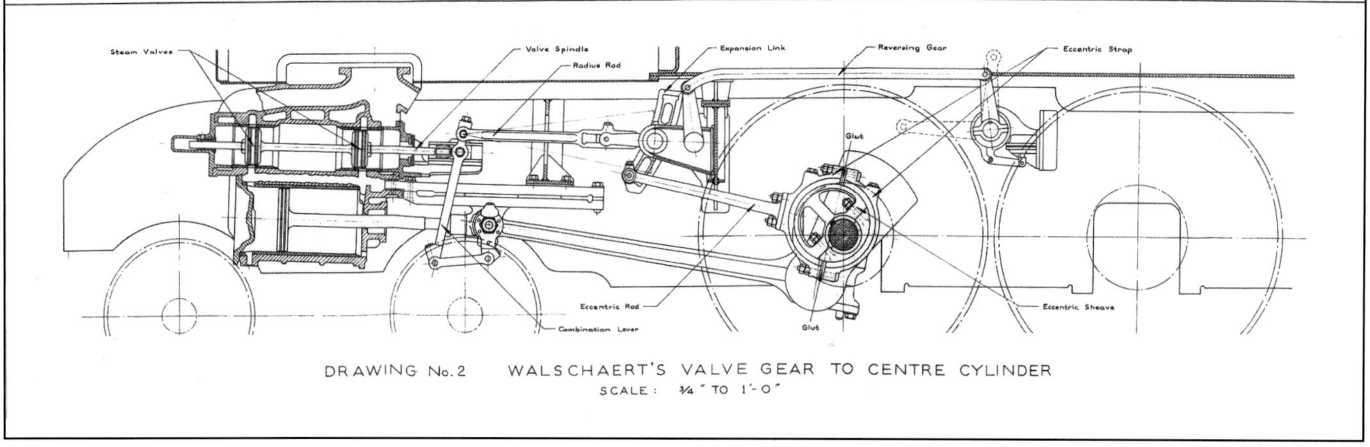

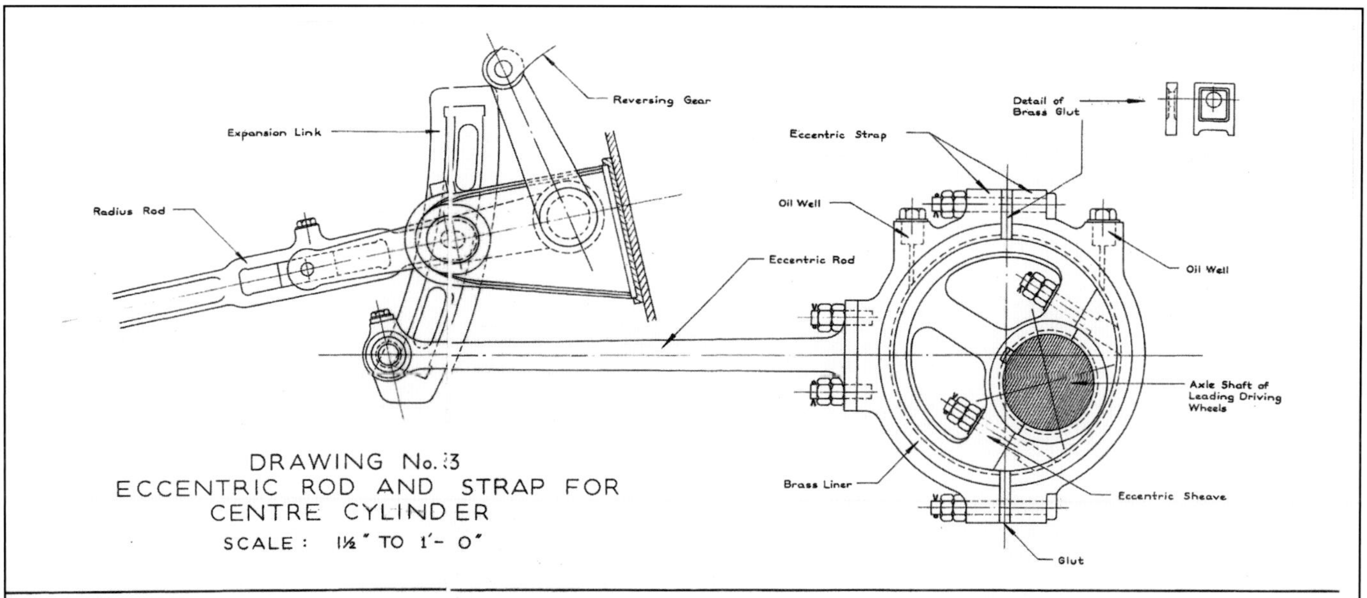

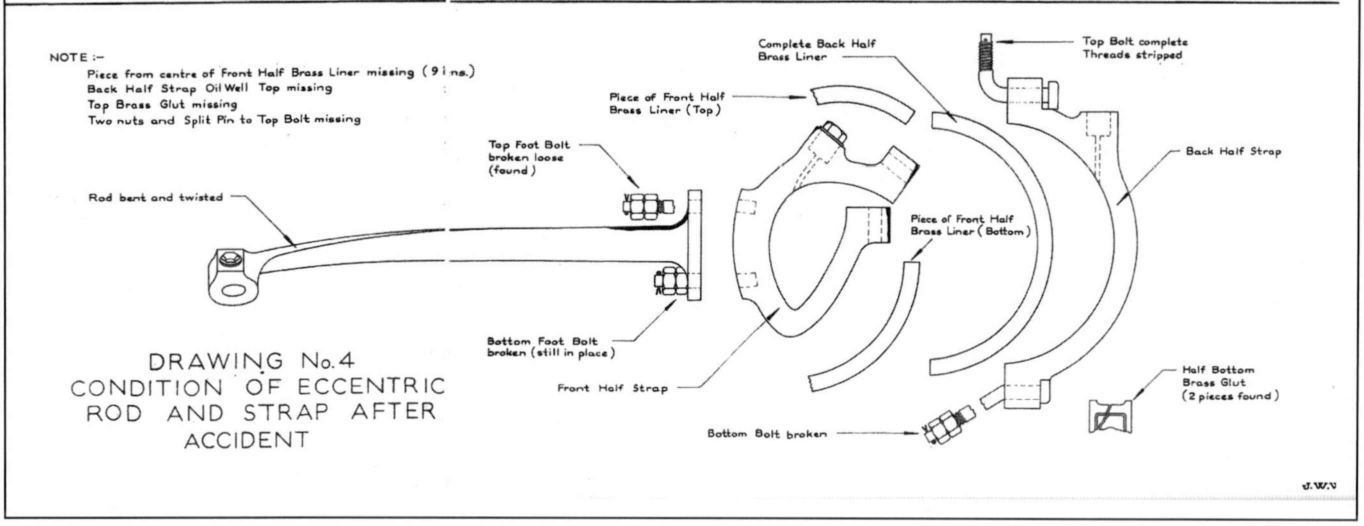

Above: Drawings prepared for the RI Goswick report, showing the design and layout of the Waschaerts valve gear fitted to No. 60509 and how the eccentric bolts came loose, leading to the strap parting company with the sheave and allowing the loose rear end to bounce along the track and open a set of facing points at Goswick. Col Reed was critical of "far from meticulous" standards by fitters with regard to the correct fitting of appropriate split pins to secure nuts on critical bolts. He pointed out "...carelessness in the fitting of split pins was reponsible for three accidents on British Railways in 1952" and that "inattention to detail in fitting and examining work at the sheds may have very serious consequences." *HMRI/ORR.*

Above: An express was derailed by a broken rail (top) in Watford Tunnel on February 3 1954. The last three carriages became divided as the train entered the station and one vehicle mounted the platform; 15 people were injured. An express passing on an adjacent line grazed the wreckage, leading to minor damage to the steel-built BR Mk 1 stock. The rail end had broken through the fishplate bolt holes (top, left), causing the triangular section of railhead about 8in long (top, right) to break away. *ORR/HMRI.*

Inspectorate had to keep abreast of such developments.

The 1960s are remembered in the Inspectorate as the era of the freight train derailment problem, or to put it more precisely, the derailment of short wheelbase four-wheeled freight vehicles running at speed on plain track. For no apparent reason a wagon would suddenly become derailed whilst the train was proceeding normally and the derailed vehicle would continue along, bouncing over the sleepers until it either fell to pieces or hit an area of points and crossings. In either case the train would break in two, and the rear portion would pile up into a heap of derailed and damaged wagons, spilling their contents far and wide and blocking the railway. From BR's point of view, it was an expensive episode and its customers were not very pleased at the loss, damage and delay which their goods suffered. From the Inspectorate's point of view, there was always the danger that a passenger train on the next line would be too close to the accident to be stopped and would plough into the wreckage. Col Robertson commented that the number of derailments had been causing concern for some time and BR accordingly had imposed a speed limit of 50mph from April 16 1963 on all trains conveying short wheelbase vehicles.

Following the derailment of an empty banana van near Steventon, on the Western Region between Didcot and Swindon on January 21 1966, BR took what Lt Col McNaughton referred to as a highly restrictive step of reducing the maximum permitted speed of all trains conveying 10ft wheelbase wagons to 45mph, even though it was known that this would have a most serious effect on traffic

Above: September 1 1955. The 3.50pm King's Cross-Leeds express had reached about 20mph, accelerating away from Peterborough, when it derailed at Westwood Junction, a half mile north of the station. The low speed contributed to a low count of four injured passengers who were detained only overnight in hospital. This is a northern view, from the city's Westwood Road bridge. *Peterborough Advertiser/Peter Waszak.*

movement. However, despite this action the number of freight train derailments continued to increase apace, from 259 in 1966 to a peak of 383 in 1969, after which the figure fell back rapidly to 230 in 1972 and 146 in 1976. The problem was never satisfactorily resolved. It was eased by improved wagon maintenance and other steps but it gradually ceased to be a major problem with the rapid rundown in the number of short wheelbase wagons in the 1970s.

The cause of the phenomenon has subsequently become clear, but even if it had been known at the time, the knowledge would not have helped to provide a solution. Short wheelbase wagons had run for many years at speeds well in excess of 60mph and without derailment, but they were wooden wagons running on conventional track, with bullhead rails on wooden sleepers. Both wagon and track were therefore flexible and could easily absorb any bumps or imperfections without causing oscillation or 'hunting' to be set up. However, newer wagons had steel frames and continuous welded rail on concrete sleepers is far more rigid. This lack of flexibility in track and wagon, combined with the rapid acceleration and sustained high speeds achieved by diesel locomotives plus the higher speeds of freight trains in general due to the increased availability of brake-fitted wagons, were the roots of the problem. It was clear there was no answer other than a new wagon suspension system such as was installed on the emerging fleet of modern, long wheelbase air braked vehicles.

The other major area of worry in the 1960s concerned broken rails. After the number of cases had hovered around the 200-250 mark annually throughout the late 1950s-early 1960s, there was a sudden and dramatic increase from 1965 onwards to such an extent that the annual rate had doubled by 1969. The incidence of broken rails continued to increase throughout the 1970s. Broken rails only occasionally led to a derailment but the most serious accident was caused by a broken rail at Hither Green on the Southern Region

Right: The Peterborough signalman in the box shown in the previous picture must have had a terrible moment as derailed unique Gresley 'W1' 4-6-4 No. 60700 ploughed towards him. This engine was built in 1929 as Gresley's famous and unconventional 'Hush Hush', fitted with a Yarrow marine type boiler. Disappointingly poor performance led to its rebuilding in 1936 at Doncaster in this 'A4' outline; it was repaired after this mishap but was withdrawn and scrapped in 1959. The broken side frame plate is clearly visible in front of the rear bogie wheel. *Peterborough Advertiser/Peter Waszak.*

Right: No. 60700's derailment was caused by breakage of the trailing right side bogie frame plate - failure was traced back to defective workshop repairs some years earlier. The broken frame plate is shown in this RI picture, shot on September 3 1955, just two days after the mishap. *HMRI/ORR.*

on November 5 1967, when the 12-coach 7.43pm diesel-electric multiple-unit train Hastings to Charing Cross was derailed at 70mph, killing 49 passengers. The 1968 total of 436 broken rails in plain line was made up as follows:

- Breaks at rail ends 200
- Breaks away from rail ends 109
- Breaks at welded joints 127
- There were also 205 breaks in points and crossings

Many of the trends in railway safety went the wrong way in the 1960s. It was a very worrying period, because although the number of serious accidents caused by errors of drivers and signalmen was declining, the new technical problems of goods train derailments and broken rails were not only getting worse year by year but there seemed to be no readily available solution. Cols McMullen and Reed, who retired in 1968, must have been very disappointed at the situation they left behind. Col Robertson became the new CIO and he was joined by two new Inspecting Officers, Lt Col A. G. Townsend-Rose and Maj C. F. Rose, who was the last Chief Inspecting Officer to have been an officer of the Royal Engineers.

Major C.F. Rose; Chief Inspecting Officer, 1982-88

Major Charles (Freddie) Rose was born in 1926 and started his railway career in 1942 as a trainee civil engineer with the Southern Railway. He was commissioned in the Royal Engineers in 1947 and for the next four years was engaged in railway construction, maintenance and operation in Palestine, Egypt and Libya. After this, he divided his time between railway work, including a year's secondment to British Railways in the late 1950s and more general soldiering and military engineering. His military service took him to Germany, Korea, Kuwait and Thailand, where he was the engineer for a major road construction project close to the Laos border at the height of the Vietnam war.

He was selected for promotion to Lieutenant Colonel in 1968 but elected to leave the Army and join the Railway Inspectorate as an Inspecting Officer. He was appointed Chief Inspecting Officer in 1982 and from 1986 combined this with Chairmanship of the Channel Tunnel Safety Authority. He retired in 1988 but continued to work with the Channel Tunnel until 1990. Freddie was a very friendly, enthusiastic and pragmatic Inspector who dedicated his life to railway safety.

Right: The scene on the Cannon Street station throat on March 20 1961 after the 8.33am Addiscombe-Cannon Street (nearest the camera) collided with a down empty coaching stock ECS from the terminus, bound for Grove Park depot. The crash was caused by driver error - the loaded up train passed two stop signals at danger and then ran into the 9.14am 12-coach ECS train, which was crossing its path under clear signals from Platform 6. A pair of Sulzer Type 2 diesels are in the distance with six of the ECS diesel-electric train's carriages, which have been shunted clear. *HMRI/ORR.*

Below: A detail view alongside the two coaches on their sides shown in the picture on page 102 (lower), showing the results of the sidelong flank impact on the outbound ECS train by the inbound loaded commuter train. Of the 650 passengers - who were walked to safety on Cannon Street station - just 11 suffered minor injuries. The accident happened at 10-15mph and as late as 1961, there was still no Automatic Warning System (AWS) protection, even on this very busy route into this City of London commuter terminus. *HMRI/ORR.*

Left: The aftermath of the East Coast Main Line accident at Welwyn, in mist at 7.12am on January 7 1957 when the 7.10pm sleeping car express from Aberdeen to King's Cross, collided with the rear of the 6.18am local train from Baldock to King's Cross. At the point of collision, the express was running at around 65mph whilst the local train was travelling at around 35mph. There was some contradictory evidence but the RI decided that all signals at Welwyn had been against the express and that the driver passed them regardless. He also failed to respond to detonators near the signal box. The express was hauled by Class A2/3 4-6-2 No. 60520 *Owen Tudor*, with 11 carriages; the six-coach Baldock train was hauled by Thomspon 'L1' 2-6-4T No. 67741. The rear coach of the local train was wrecked, killing one passenger. The penultimate coach also overturned. After this accident, the outer distant signals were replaced by colour lights and RI recommended louder detonators. (see also pages 89,91) *Getty Images.*

CHAPTER 7
THE NEW RAILWAY 1969-1990

Above: Whilst locomotive-hauled carriages of BR Mk 1, 2 and 3 outline remained the mainstay of long distance services through the 1970s - notwithstanding the introduction of the InterCity 125 HST from 1975 - local and some inter-urban services remained dominated by Mk 1 diesel multiple units (DMUs). This is the north end Newcastle upon Tyne on May 14 1977. Class 47/4 No. 47549 is getting away over the famous diamond crossings with the 11.00am King's Cross-Edinburgh, amidst a mixture of DMUs on local services, including units from Metropolitan Cammell and Craven. This view is still available to enjoy from the top of the Keep Tower but the bay platforms and tracks to the right are all long gone: it's all car parking today. The neatness and tidiness of the track is striking: there's not a single weed to be seen. *Gavin Morrison.*

Above: The freight railway on the pre-electrification 1980s East Coast Main line. On September 7 1983, surrounded by loaded merry-go-round coal wagons, Class 56 No. 56118 is ready to leave Black Carr Yard, south of Doncaster. King Coal still reigned supreme. They are bigger, steel framed and air braked - but MGR wagons were effectively a modern version of the timber chauldron which had given birth to railway coal carrying in north east England in the early 19th century. (see also pages 116-117) Today, coal traffic is in deep decline. *Gavin Morrison.*

The year 1969 can confidently be said to be the start of the new railway era. The last steam engines had been phased out in the north west the previous year. Modernisation of signalling was proceeding apace - Trent, Derby and Saltley power signal boxes were opened in 1969 and the Transport Act of 1968 had brought local authorities very substantially into the whole field of suburban passenger transport planning and financing. From here on, our railways were not only technically more complex, but also much more politically involved.

Keeping abreast of these major changes, and their effect upon safety, was the Railway Inspectorate, which in 1969 consisted of the Chief Inspecting Officer, Col J. R. H. Robertson (who retired in 1973), Lt Col I. K. A. McNaughton (who succeeded Col Robertson and retired in 1982), Lt Col A. G. Townsend Rose (retired in 1986), and Maj C. F. Rose, who became Chief Inspecting Officer in 1982 and retired in 1988. Finally, the longest serving Inspecting Officer since Lt Col Sir Alan Mount (who retired in 1949) was Maj P.M. Olver, who joined the Inspectorate in 1965 and retired only in 1989. Col Robertson was replaced in 1973 by Maj A. G. B. King, and the Inspectorate was strengthened in 1977 to cater for the increasing

Right: On May 7 1969, the 1940 King's Cross-Aberdeen express (hauled by Class 55 'Deltic' No. 9011 *The Royal Northumberland Fusiliers*) derailed on the sharp curve at Morpeth, on the ECML north of Newcastle, after the driver's concentration lapsed and he entered the sharp 40mph curve at 80mph. Five passengers and a Travelling Ticket Inspector were killed and 121 passengers were injured, 19 seriously. Only the locomotive remained on the track, coming to a stand in the station, 508 yards from the point the first carriage left the rails when it tilted to the point of overturning. The 11-coach train was completely derailed, heavily damaged and came to rest in five portions. A Freightliner train following under caution on the down main line thankfully stopped just short of the point at which the track had been destroyed by the derailing carriages. *Alamy*

workload, by Major C. B. Holden.

The problems that faced the late 1960s Inspectorate in its never-ending quest to improve safety standards on the railways were very much a mixture of old and new. The spread of AWS and power signalling with multiple-aspect colour-light signals accompanied by continuous track circuiting had certainly reduced the number of serious collisions caused either by signalmen's errors or by drivers passing signals at danger. Indeed, of the 29 fatal train accidents on BR in the 21 years from 1969 to 1989, signaller errors were involved in only three - a remarkable change from the record in earlier days. However, drivers were still responsible, wholly or partly, in 15 cases and it had become very clear that not enough attention had been paid to, and not enough money invested in, measures to assist the driver, especially at distant signals.

It may perhaps be helpful to compare the decade 1980-89 with earlier decades, to see to what extent the causes of accidents had changed. In comparing the number of fatalities and the number of fatal accidents, regard must be paid to the very great improvement in safety which had been achieved in the design and construction of modern coaches. In earlier years, many passengers were killed in accidents who today might - and probably would - have survived, in instances when coaches simply disintegrated, or where coach bodies became detached from their underframes; or, most terrible of all, when one coach was telescoped into the next, destroying compartments and killing their occupants.

	1900-09	1930-39	1980-89
Number of fatal train accidents	31	23	12
Number of passengers killed	169	117	75
Number of passenger journeys	1,199m	1,249m	750m

It might be misleading to attempt to draw firm conclusions from a small number of accidents - but nevertheless, if the 1980-89 traffic levels are equated to those of 1930-39, there would appear to have been very little improvement over that 50-year period, either in the number of fatal train accidents or in the number of passengers killed. This is despite the very considerable investment in equipment to safeguard against errors made by drivers and signalmen, the effect of which is clearly demonstrated by the figures. The fact is that whilst the old, familiar dangers had been largely overcome, new dangers had arisen consequent upon the introduction of new technology; also trains ran faster, on lines of higher density.

1969 was a particularly bad year for derailments caused by buckles in continuously-welded rails. During June and July of that year there

Above: Recovery under way at Morpeth after the 80mph derailment of a King's Cross-Aberdeen express on May 7 1969. Driver Byers was distracted and entered the 40mph curve at twice the approved speed - he was preoccupied by a management request that he explain four lost minutes he was responsible for whilst driving a similar train the previous day. He had been handed the formal request for an explanation during the earlier Newcastle station stop and he was worrying about it as he drove north. Secondman Graham did notice the over-speed but was unwilling to be perceived as 'interfering' - so said nothing. By the time he decided to act and crossed the cab to alert the driver it was too late and he was thrown to the floor, he thought, by the locomotive entering the curve. As he struggled to his feet, he heard Byers say something like: "I lost my bearings....I should not have been thinking about that report." Col. J.R.H Robertson said that whilst being "very seriously at fault" he was "much impressed by Driver Byers, who never sought to make excuses and who was open, frank and co-operative, freely admitting he had entered the 40mph curve at 80mph. "I got the impression that a Notice of this kind (requiring an explanation for the four minutes list on the previous run) tended to unsettle him and that he attached more importance to it than it really warranted although he agreed that it was in fact of a routine nature." Byers admitted that he had been reliving that previous journey and was only brought to his senses when Graham crossed the cab; he then realised where he was and at once made a full brake application. It was, however, too late to avert disaster. "Driver Byers alone was responsible for this derailment," concluded Col Robertson. After this, procedures were changed so that 'Form 1' 'please explain' requests like this were only presented to drivers at the end of their shift, when their driving duties are over. *Alamy.*

Above: This remains the greatest single incident loss of life on the London Underground - 43 deaths - but the cause of the Moorgate disaster of February 28 1975 remains a mystery. A six-car train of 1938 stock ran at speed through terminal Platform 9 at Moorgate and smashed into the solid end wall at the end of a short 66ft 9in dead-end over-run tunnel. Two and half Tube cars were compressed into half their normal length by the 35-40mph impact, creating a rescue and recovery task of "unprecedented difficulty", according to RI accident investigator Lt. Col Ian McNaughton. This picture makes the difficulty of the rescue and recovery task very clear. Of the 300 passengers aboard, a further 74 needed hospital treatment. It took four days to reach and retrieve Motorman Newson's body, which by this time, in the high temperatures of the tunnels, was significantly decomposed, thereby hampering investigations. Newson was described as a conscientious, cautious driver whose approach to stations was "usually slow." He was reported by several witnesses on the platform who saw his train speed through the platform, to be sitting upright with his hands on the controls, impassively looking ahead as his train approached the dead end at up to 40mph. McNaughton concluded: "... that Newson was conscious up to the point of of collision and that he made no effort of any kind to stop the train." He raised the possibility of what now might be described as 'suicide by train' when he said: "...there must remain the possibility, which cannot be disproved, that the actions of Motorman Newson were deliberate." This notion remains deeply disturbing and it resurfaced again a quarter-century later after the Ladbroke Grove disaster of October 5 1999 (see pages 149-154) regarding the actions of Thames Trains driver Michael Hodder, whose behaviour - which resulted in 31 deaths - also remains unexplained. In 2015, the co-pilot of a German Wings Airbus A320, locked his captain out of the flight deck and deliverately crashed his airliner into the Alps, killing all 144 people on board, so the principle is not unknown. *Alamy*.

were no fewer than four, although fortunately they were all without fatality. The derailments took place as follows:

June 10: Lichfield LMR, Electrically-hauled carflats.
June 13: Somerton WR, Paignton to Paddington express.
June 15: Lamington SCR, Freightliner.
July 23: Sandy ER, Down Tees-Tyne Pullman.

This problem was the subject of a very lengthy and thorough investigation by Maj Rose, resulting in both an interim and a final report (the latter not appearing until 1974), which explained in detail this technically complex matter of how the significant forces within the rails have to be controlled to prevent movement and buckles. BR took prompt action to deal with the problem and whilst buckles still occur today they have been considerably reduced in number, although not completely eradicated, as the derailment of a freight train at Langworth, near Lincoln on June 30 2015 demonstrated.

Broken rails, however, proved a much more difficult problem, as these figures show:

	1969	1978	1988
Number of breaks at rail ends	225	185	135
Number of broken welds	177	368	242
Number of breaks away from rail ends	105	210	177

Broken rails were responsible for two fatal train accidents in the 1980s, at Ulleskelf (Eastern Region) in 1981 and at Elgin (Scottish Region) in 1983 (see page 107). A broken weld caused the derailment of the 8.25pm Euston to Manchester express at Bushey on February 16 1980; the train was travelling at almost 100mph and the accident resulted in 19 passengers being seriously injured. However, the number of broken welds shown in the table below has to be set against a considerable increase in the number of such welds and the rate of breaks per 1,000 miles had been halved since the early 1970s.

One of the most remarkable features of railway operating history has been the apparent reluctance of railway managements to take ongoing and progressive action to help the driver in the three main fundamentals of his job:

- To keep to the timetable.
- To keep within the speed limit of track and train.
- To stop when signals tell him to do so.

Perhaps it sounds too easy when boiled down to just three simple bullet points - but it is a fact that generations of railway managers have either failed to acquire an effective understanding of the demands placed upon drivers - or been too slow in helping a driver meet those demands. Consider how little the railways have done to help drivers run their ever-faster, heavier trains more safely until circumstances have left them absolutely no choice and compelled them to do so.

With the noteable exception of the Great Western, none of the railways were prepared to adopt automatic train control unprompted and it was not until 1948, in the euphoria of the early days of nationalisation, that the decision was taken to equip main lines with ATC (later known as AWS). Even then, progress was hardly

Right: At 1.23pm on Saturday January 16 1982, the 12.22am Three Bridges-New Cross Gate Civil Engineers Departmental goods train collided at around 30mph with the 11.18pm mail and parcels train from Brighton to London Bridge, which was standing in the platform at East Croydon, on BR's Southern Region. The rear three vans of the mail/parcels train were deflected to the left and severely damaged by the very heavy collision. The driver of the engineers train was trapped in his crushed cab and was not released until 8.45pm when, despite the best efforts of the emergency teams, part of one leg had to be amputated to release him. A member of the platform staff and six Post Office staff were slightly injured. *ORR/HMRI.*

Below: The rear end of Class 73 electro-diesel No. 73115, which was hauling the Croydon engineers train. The guard, riding in the drivers assistant's seat in this rear cab, miraculously escaped injury. He heard the noise of the impact and as the locomotive lurched and he heard the sound of escaping air he instinctively twisted out of the seat to go forward in case the following wagons crushed the cab - which is precisely what happened. He was trapped only by his coat, therefore, when the rails on the following bogie wagon slid forward and smashed through the cab front. He heard no brake application before the crash and subsequent tests proved the signalling to be in working order as were the brakes. It seemed likely that the locomotive was under power at the time of the impact and Inspecting Officer Major A. G. B. King concluded that "it seems probable that he (Driver Walton) was distracted in some way or fell asleep."..."I feel that if AWS had been fitted to the signals he would almost certainly have been alert to the restrictive aspects displayed," he added. *HMRI/ORR.*

Above: Derailments - sometimes fatal - could be caused by track failures, including buckles in hot weather, weld failures and breaks at rail ends. Between 1969 and 1988, rail end breaks declined from 225 to 135 but in the 1980s such failures nevertheless twice led to fatalities - at Ulleskelf (Eastern Region) in 1981 and Elgin (Scottish Region) in 1983. This was the fatal aftermath of the broken rail-end derailment at Elgin in the late afternoon of Thursday February 3 1983 at Llanbryde, about two miles east of Elgin station. Class 27 No. 27007 was hauling the five-coach (240 tons) 1.50pm stopping train from Aberdeen to Inverness when a broken rail end derailed the leading end of the third coach. The fourth coach was also derailed. The coaches divided from each other but remained upright. The fifth coach also derailed, shed its bogies, rolled onto its side and whilst still attached to the fourth coach, slid for around 100m before coming to rest. One passenger was killed, three were seriously injured and nine more suffered minor injuries. Several hundred metres of the single line were destroyed. *HMRI/ORR.*

dramatic. It was to be 10 years before installation commenced and another 30 before the programme was complete, by which time about two-thirds of BR's track mileage had been dealt with. Long before then, the weakness and vulnerability of the BR Automatic Warning System in failing to differentiate between single and double-yellow signals had become horribly apparent. Drivers would cancel the AWS on single yellows believing the warning to be for a double yellow or forgetting what aspect was displayed as they continued at speed towards a red signal. Even the horrific Harrow & Wealdstone multiple collision of October 8 1952 (112 fatalities) failed to galvanise BR into significantly accelerating the AWS installation programme. Contrast this laggardly progress with the way in which the high speed Ladbroke Grove fatal head-on collision (death toll 31) of October 5 1999 prompted the very rapid deployment of Train Protection Warning System in just three years, between 2001 and 2004.

The GWR had already devised a means of advising drivers what signal aspect he was approaching with its ATC (incredibly, first used in 1906 on the Henley branch.) but BR not only failed to incorporate this crucial facility in its own system - despite considerable pressure from the Southern Region to do so - but, worse, failed to promptly modify its system when this flaw became clearly apparent.

Yet again, railway authorities failed to act until they were given no choice and were forced to do so by the weight of public pressure following the Purley accident on March 4 1989, when the 8-car 12.17pm EMU from Littlehampton to London Victoria ran past a danger signal at high speed and collided with the 4-car 12.50pm EMU from Horsham to Victoria, killing five passengers and seriously injuring a further 32 (see pages 118-121). There had been a similar accident at Wembley in 1984, when an evening commuter train collided with a freightliner train, killing three passengers. There had been several other non-fatal collisions but the implications were not acted upon.

The problem with the BR AWS system lay not just in its failure to differentiate between single and double yellow signals but also in the absence of any check that the driver has actually responded to the warnings that he had received. This, of course, is the ultimate safeguard and it is incorporated in all modern systems. It would have prevented not only the accidents mentioned, but also others in which drivers for one reason or another failed to respond to an AWS warning. For example, there was an accident at Shields Junction near Glasgow Central in 1973 when the 9.35pm EMU from Wemyss Bay ran into the back of the 9.10pm DMU from Ayr, the driver having failed to react, first to caution and then to danger signals. It transpired that the driver was suffering from severe arterial disease and may have been taken ill suddenly when approaching Shields Junction, to such an extent that whilst he was sufficiently conscious to cancel the AWS warnings he could neither apply the brake nor release the Driver's Safety Device (DSD) which itself would have applied the brake. We can never be certain precisely what happened, because the driver was killed in the crash. The important fact is that the Automatic Warning System was ineffective, for the simple reason that it was not designed to cater for such a situation. BR always maintained that its AWS was only an advisory system, which is perfectly correct - but it simply left too many loopholes and vulnerabilities for fate to exploit. And that's exactly what happened.

In his report into the 1984 Wembley collision, Maj Rose said that the fact that AWS had been unable to prevent the accident had important implications for safety. He made clear that it had been apparent for some time that whilst AWS had proved a most important

Left: An official photograph of the Elgin broken rail joint: the railhead strike marks are clear. Class 27 Driver Masson braked after he felt a very severe jolt as he passed over the broken rail end. His locomotive and first two carriages negotiated the damaged joint safely, but the right hand wheels of the third and fourth carriages derailed into the four-foot at the joint, bursting the rail outwards and becoming divided because of the heavy vertical oscillation while running derailed. As the fifth coach slid on its side, all the windows were broken, ballast was forced inside and internal fixtures and seats broke free. The fatality and all injuries happened in the fifth coach. *HMRI-ORR*

aid to drivers and had undoubtedly helped to reduce the number of collisions, it did not guard against incorrect cancellation of the kind that can arise when drivers are running under a sequence of cautionary signals - still less the 'unconscious' cancellation of the kind that apparently happened at Wembley. He also mentioned that the Inspectorate was already discussing with the British Railways Board, before the Wembley accident, the question of AWS and other aids to drivers and that these discussions were continuing. This was clearly a cause of some frustration to the

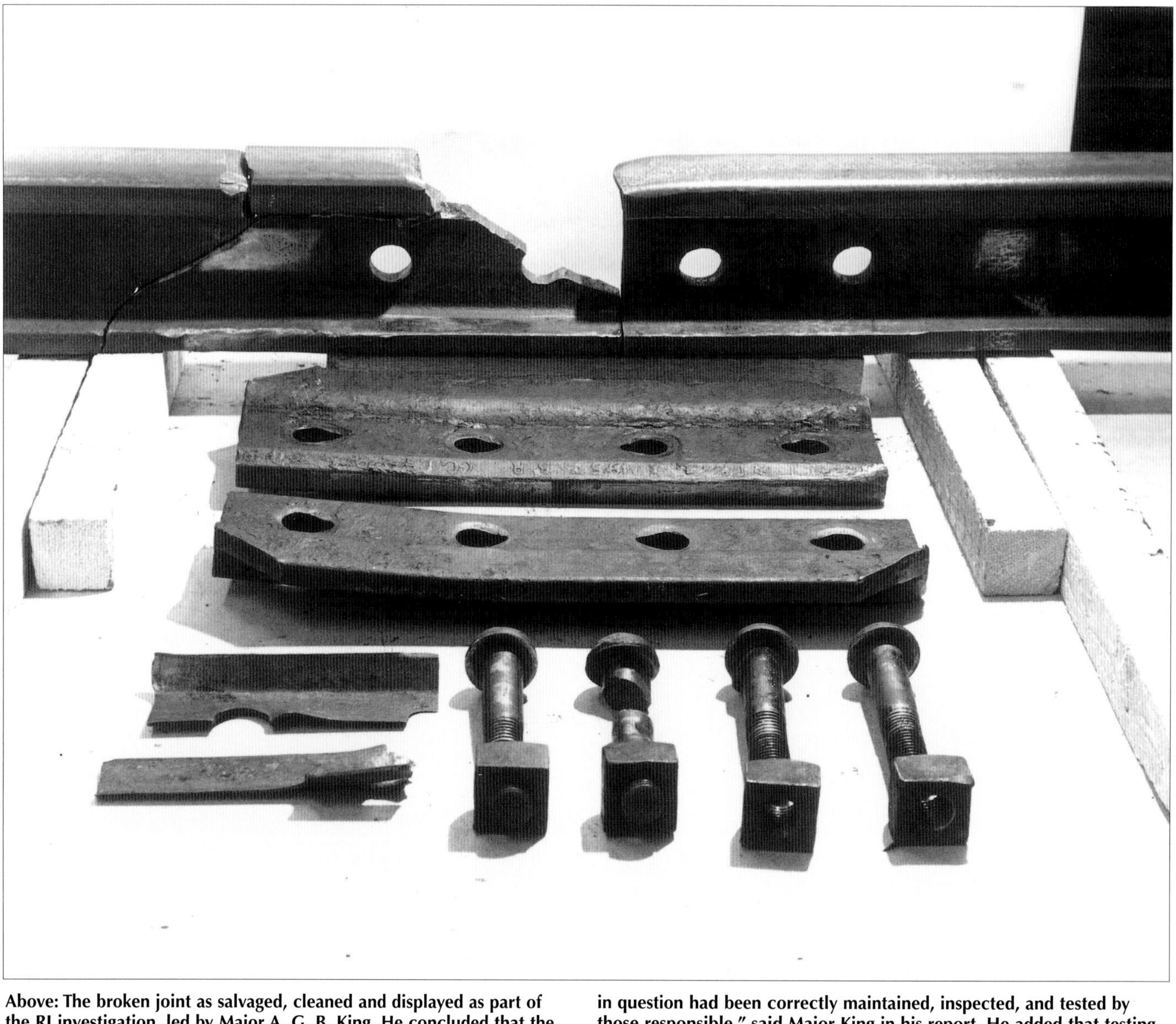

Above: The broken joint as salvaged, cleaned and displayed as part of the RI investigation, led by Major A. G. B. King. He concluded that the track had been maintained correctly and testing of the rail, fishplates and bolts all confirmed they were of correct specification and that the rail was not worn beyond any limits which would have demanded its replacement. "There is no doubt in my mind that the track and joint in question had been correctly maintained, inspected, and tested by those responsible," said Major King in his report. He added that testing for fatigue cracks had been carried out at nearly double the required frequency. "It is clear from the evidence that the cracks and fractures could have grown from the limits of detection up to failure size, since the previous inspections and tests." *HMRI-ORR*.

Above: The severe ECML curve at Morpeth station was responsible for a third high speed derailment (the others had been in 1926 and 1969) on Sunday June 24 1984 - although this time, the protection afforded by Mk 3 rolling stock ensured no deaths. A total of 29 passengers and six train crew were injured. The nine coach Aberdeen-King's Cross sleeping car train entered the 50mph station curve at between 85 and 90mph. It derailed and overturned and came to rest as shown. The Class 47 hauling the train is glimpsed on its side in the trees immediately right of the badly damaged house at the bottom of the picture. It had crossed over the down line, it's train careering into the domestic gardens on the left - the house in the centre had a very lucky escape. This was long before zero tolerance to alcohol on the railway, and Driver Allan admitted immediately after the accident to having "taken drink" before joining his train at Edinburgh Waverley. Incredible though it seems today, Allan had consumed a fifth-gill of whisky and a pint of Foster's lager in a pub en route to work, followed by two cans of Tennants lager (one extra strong) between signing-on at Haymarket and joining his train at Waverley. Allan therefore drank before and actually on duty, which even then was against the rules. He told the inquiry that he did not regularly drink before work and was not a heavy drinker. He admitted his driving ability "...could have been impaired." His maximum blood-alcohol reading would have been around 120mg/100ml at around midnight and between 74mg and 90mg/100ml at the time of the accident. The legal limit for driving a road vehicle is 80mg alcohol/100mg of blood. The driver also said he suffered from coughing fits. Allan was charged under three counts of 'damaging property with intent' and endangering the safety of passengers but was tried only on the latter count. He was found not guilty by a jury. Lt. Col Townsend-Rose seemed inclined to dismiss Allan's claims that incapacitating coughing caused the accident: "I must say I am strongly inclined to the possibility that he fell fully or nearly asleep as the most likely [cause]." (see also page 130). ***HMRI-ORR***

Above: There had been no recorded incident of a death being caused by a train hitting an animal since at least 1948 - until Monday July 30 1984 at Polmont, between Glasgow and Edinburgh. Incredible though it may seem, this wreckage was the catastrophic consequence of a low axle weight Driving Brake Second Open (DBSO) carriage hitting a cow in the four-foot whilst leading a seven-coach, 315½-tons express shuttle, propelled by a Class 47/7 diesel-electric, at around 85mph. No fewer than 13 passengers died whilst a further 14 and three railway staff were seriously injured. The wrecked coach on the right is the DBSO. The train was running towards the photographer and after derailing, the DBSO veered left, careered up the embankment and demolished the wall, after which the leading end struck a tree. The force of the train behind swept the back end of the DBSO round until it came to rest as shown, facing the way it had come, without its bogies. The second coach was also spun end-for-end by the force of the following train and is out of sight beyond this wreckage. The coach on the left was the third in the formation and with first and second vehicles spun end-over-end and forced to both left and right, the remaining five coaches forced their way between them, to come to rest as shown, with the leading end of the DBSO buried in the side of the train's third carriage. *The Scotsman Publications Ltd. (TSPL)*

RI because Maj Rose drew attention emphatically to this question in his 1986 Annual Report, when he said:

"Whilst the overall state of railway safety during 1986 was not unsatisfactory I have to draw attention once again to the rising trend in the proportion of accidents caused by staff error. More than half of the serious or potentially serious collisions and derailments that did occur during 1986 were attributed to this cause and the number of signals passed at danger (including those where no accident resulted) continues to rise. British Rail are well aware of this and are currently analysing the figures in detail, with the help of outside consultants, to try to establish the underlying reasons. These studies should help the Board to decide on its future policy in respect of train control and operation. Should it follow the trend already established on many other European railways and go for some form of automatic train protection, or is the cost of such measures not worth the benefits they would bring? The question is a difficult one, and not only on grounds of cost, since much of BR is now equipped with a standard form of multiple-aspect signalling and associated advance warning system, much of it with years of service left before it needs renewal ... Nevertheless I believe the time has come when the Board must face the questions and seek answers that will enable it to establish a clear policy for the future. I have made clear in previous reports the Inspectorate's view that more needs to be done to assist the driver in the cab."

The Wembley report is dated February 21 1986 and it was not to be long before another AWS loophole of the kind the RI had repeatedly warned about was horrifically demonstrated. On Friday September 19 1986 the 5.00pm express from Euston to Manchester, hauled by electric locomotive No. 86429, ran past a danger signal at Colwich and came to a stand with the locomotive partly across the junction to Stoke. It blocked the path of the 5.20pm express from Liverpool to Euston, also electrically-hauled by locomotive No 86211, approaching at almost 100mph. The unfortunate driver of the Liverpool train had no time to react and lost his life in the very high energy impact crash, which flung the carriages of his train in a jumbled heap (see also page 114). Looking at photographs of the crash one would have expected a high death toll, especially as there were almost 900 passengers in the two trains, but miraculously there were no fatalities at all among the passengers and there can be no more testimony to the life-preserving qualities of modern coaching stock than that. However, it was inevitable that there would be many injuries and 32 passengers were detained in hospital.

It appears that the driver of the Manchester train had been confused by a new junction signalling system of flashing yellow lights which had only recently been installed. He assumed that the road was set for him to proceed on to the Stoke line, but he was mistaken: the flashing signals only allowed him to proceed as far as - but not actually onto - the junction. Here again, the precise details of the cause are of no real consequence. What really matters is that AWS yet again did not prevent the accident because it was not designed to do so. After the Colwich accident no-one could argue that the existing BR AWS was no longer adequate and that a system was needed that would ensure that a train stopped at a danger signal irrespective of anything the driver did, or did not do. Sadly, prompt action did not follow and it was not until the Purley accident (another three years) that BR finally decided to take action.

The driver's duty to keep within the speed limits of track and train has already been stressed and the history of railways is marked with instances where drivers have failed to fulfil this basic, crucial responsibility. It is not at all surprising that this is the case, however, because until BR days, few locomotives were even provided with speedometers. Further, until the late 20th century, drivers received little or no advance warning that they were approaching sharp curves. Change here came about following a major derailment at Morpeth on May 7 1969, when the 7.40pm sleeping car train from King's Cross to Edinburgh attempted to take the station's still-notorious and restrictive very sharp 40mph curve at 80mph. Five passengers and a travelling ticket inspector were killed in the high

Above: Polmont says a very great deal about the devastating uncontrolled forces unleashed in a high energy crash where the train leaves the rails which define its linear movement. The DBSO, having spun end-over-end, slid for 105m on its side before coming to rest at the top of the cutting side. Driver H. Kilpatrick, approaching the crash site on the 5.30pm Glasgow-Edinburgh express, was leaving Polmont at about 65mph when he saw a tremendous cloud of dust and a coach which he described as "somersaulting in the air with a twisting movement." This was the DBSO. He stopped and after finding a signal post telephone not to be working, sent a passenger to use a telephone in a nearby housing estate to call the emergency services - this was the pre-mobile phone era. Major A.G.B. King concluded that push-pull operations were "acceptably safe" but said they should be made safer through rule book changes, better fences (and their maintenance), cab radio for better and faster emergency and safety warnings and the fitting of object deflectors to low axle weight leading vehicles. *The Scotsman Publications Ltd (TSPL).*

speed derailment and there were many injuries.

Col Robertson held the public inquiry into the Morpeth derailment and took the view that on a high speed line the driver of an express train should receive a special warning that he was approaching a severe speed restriction on the open line, which he suggested ought to be provided where a reduction of speed of one-third or more was required on lines where speeds of 75mph and above were permitted. He further suggested that this warning should take the form of an illuminated advance warning board, which should be installed at braking distance from the speed restriction and that a permanent AWS-type magnet should be placed between the rails 200yd before the warning board, to draw the driver's attention to this crucial warning.

BR adopted the Inspectorate's proposals - but regrettably they did not go far enough. A speed of 75mph was just too high for the dividing line between the provision and non-provision of warning equipment. Several derailments had occurred on lower speed lines and lines with a maximum speed of 60mph were subsequently embraced in the arrangement. However, there was a special situation in the up (southbound) direction at Morpeth. The sharp curve was approached by a series of descending speed restrictions, firstly to 80mph, then to 70mph and therefore it did not fall within the parameters laid down. Consequently, no warning equipment was provided in the up direction, leaving a safety loophole which was cruelly exploited on the night of June 23-24 1984 (see page 109). The intoxicated driver of the 7.50pm sleeping car express from Aberdeen to King's Cross, the 'Night Aberdonian', failed to reduce speed and passed through Morpeth station at between 85 and 90mph. The train hit the 50mph curve through, and south of the station and shot off at a tangent, directly towards residential bungalows, which were damaged. As the pictures show, some of the damaged houses only narrowly avoided complete demolition by the high speed derailed carriages. Astonishingly, not a single passenger was killed. Action was subsequently taken to deal with such situations involving a descending 'cascade' of speed restrictions.

Drivers are expected to be aware of all permanent speed limits but when temporary speed restrictions speed were imposed, usually on track either awaiting or undergoing repair, the driver was informed beforehand in a weekly booklet containing all the temporary speed restrictions on the lines he had to work over. In addition, a warning sign would be erected at the side of the line, sufficiently far back to enable the driver to brake in time, while the actual site of the speed restriction would be marked by further temporary lineside signs. These signs are illuminated at night, originally by paraffin oil, then later by bottled gas and now by electric batteries.

On the night of June 5-6 1975, the 11.30pm sleeping car train from Euston to Glasgow approached Nuneaton at 80mph, where it became derailed on a 20mph temporary speed restriction. The lights at the warning board had gone out and the driver - who did know about the TSR from the printed notices - concluded that the restriction must therefore have been removed. This was a classic case of 'the light that failed', so beloved by 19th century dramatists.

The TSR warning board lights had gone out because all the gas had been used, vindication of the fact that for some time the Inspectorate had been pressing BR for improvements in the method of illumination and general appearance of warning boards. It is surprising that there had not already been similar accidents. An examination was made of continental practice and it was found that several railway administrations there made use of the automatic warning device employed in the signalling system in order to alert drivers to the fact that they were approaching a temporary speed restriction. After some hesitation - and worries about possible side-effects - BR decided to place a permanent magnet of the AWS type between the rails 200yd before the warning board, a simple, elegant and effective solution and one which drivers welcomed.

After the high speed collision between an express train and a electrical transformer which became stuck on Hixon level crossing in 1968 (see pages 8-9), the ongoing automation of Britain's 2,000 or so public level crossings came to an abrupt halt. Despite the crash, the necessity for automation not only remained, but had become increasingly urgent. Not surprisingly following the report of the Hixon Inquiry, held by Mr E. B. Gibbens QC, the principles to be

Above: Eight passengers and a road vehicle passenger died on July 26 1986, when the 9.33am Bridlington-Hull four-car Class 105 DMU, running at 50mph, struck a Ford Escort van on the level crossing at Lockington. The Automatic Open Crossing (AOCR) non-barrier crossing was protected by an audible 'Yodalarm' and flashing red lights, giving 24 seconds warning of a 70mph train. Investigating Officer Major A.G.B King concluded that the crossing was operating properly and that the Escort van was driven slowly onto the crossing giving the DMU driver no time to react. The leading coach derailed to the left and progressively brought all four vehicles off the track, leaving the leading car skewed round on its side facing the direction in which it had come and the second car slewed across the other track. A second collision with the wreckage was averted by the prompt action of Guard P. Sturdy, who climbed out of the wrecked train and ran ahead in time to give an 'emergency stop' signal to an approaching train, which passed him braking heavily and managed to stop before reaching the derailed DMU. Major King concluded that the van had been driven onto the crossing possibly because a cursory glance at the lights, which being against the sun, was not enough for the driver to register they were flashing red, or, more likely, that the driver was distracted by his passenger (his son, who died) or his dog, both of whom were in the van. Major King also expressed his alarm at the "casual and thoughtless attitude among some road users of the crossing." Again, the RI was implicitly critical of police actions, which were seen as compromising safety investigations. "Because the police sealed off the relay room at the crossing for several hours after the accident, the BR technicians were unable during that period to ascertain whether there was a defect in any of the equipment which might affect safety elsewhere." Tension between those whose job it was to discover cause and those whose job it was to consider criminal action was growing. *HMRI/ORR.*

Above: This 1984 fatal accident at Eccles, in Manchester, happened on a section of absolute block, semaphore-signalled main line with no AWS protection. More than three decades after the 1952 catastrophe at Harrow & Wealdstone, safe operation still relied on driver vigilance alone. No fewer than 32 years after 112 lives were lost at Harrow because the driver had no assistance, BR had still not fitted AWS to the world's first and oldest passenger railway between Liverpool and Manchester. The eight-coach 10.05am Liverpool Lime Street-Scarborough of December 4, hauled by Class 45 No. 45147, collided at 10.37am with the rear of a slow, gas oil tank train: it had passed the Eccles distant at caution and subsequent home signal at danger. The 'Peak'-hauled passenger train collided with the tank train, which was travelling at 10mph, 1,305m beyond the stop signal, at 60mph. The rear three loaded bogie tankers derailed, the rearmost coming to rest lying across the 'Peak', where hot engine exhaust ignited gas oil leaking from the punctured tanker. Fire rapidly engulfed the three derailed tankers, the locomotive and its leading carriage. The leading half of the second carriage was also badly burned. The 'Peak' driver died in his crushed cab and two passengers also lost their lives (one immediately and one later in hospital) with a further 68 people injured, who were taken to three local hospitals. The non-AWS signals to which No. 45147's driver failed to respond were also found to be very poorly-sited, oddly and inconsistently spaced, and with confusing and distracting backgrounds. The accident happened alongside the M602 road, which at least gave easy access for the emergency services. *Alamy.*

adopted in the installation of automatic level crossings were greatly complicated by the addition of an approach layby, telephones and complex controls. This made them so expensive to install that it was no longer cost-effective for BR to do so. There followed 10 years of stalemate, during which the number of automatic half-barrier (AHB) installations increased only marginally from 201 in 1968 to just 234 in 1978. It was clear to everyone that something had to be done to find a solution and accordingly, in 1977 Lt Col McNaughton (now the Chief Inspecting Officer) arranged with BR to set up a joint working party with the following aim:

"To consider ways in which methods of level crossing protection can be further developed in Great Britain, taking into account the cost and the need to maintain an adequate and publicly acceptable standard of safety - and to make recommendations."

Lt Col Townsend-Rose was appointed joint chairman with a BR representative, and the working party visited a number of Continental railways. Its report, issued in 1978, not only recommended some easement of the onerous conditions in regard to AHBs (thus allowing a further 100 gated crossings to be converted to AHB in the next few years) but also suggested that a new type of level crossing automation system should be introduced. This was similar to an AHB installation but without barriers, and with reliance being placed entirely upon the road user's obedience to the flashing red road traffic signals at the level crossing. These new crossings were called Automatic Open Crossings (AOCR) and 44 were in use by 1986. However, that very year, the doubtful wisdom of relying upon road users to responsibly obey red traffic lights was demonstrated by a very serious accident at Lockington (see page 112), on the Hull to Bridlington line. A DMU became derailed after a small van drove onto the level crossing in front of it: eight passengers and an occupant of the van were killed.

There was often a strong - and to some extent illogical - local feeling against the automation of level crossings and this was exacerbated by serious public disquiet following the Lockington accident. Secretary of State for Transport the Rt. Hon. Paul Channon therefore felt impelled to have yet another independent inquiry into the safety of level crossings and appointed Professor P. F. Stott, "to review the safety record of automatic open level crossings, to consider the lessons gained from the experience so far and to make recommendations ..."

His subsequent report of July 17 1987, generally recommended some tightening of the conditions applicable to automatic open crossings, which had the result of requiring conversion of some of the existing AOCR installations as AHBs.

Both of the major accidents at public level crossings were followed by a review carried out by neither BR nor the Railway Inspectorate, but by The Rt Hon Sally Oppenheim. This had been done in the name of independence, undoubtedly with some justification, as both road and rail sections of the Department of Transport were deeply involved in drawing up the principles to be applied to the automation of level crossings. It simply would not have been appropriate for the Department to have been seen as both judge and defendant. The 1871 Regulation of Railways Act had made provision for this more formal type of inquiry, either held by an Inspecting Officer assisted by a QC or similar person, or vice versa. The procedure had been invoked several times in the 1870s but the practice was abandoned as it was found to be cumbersome, time-wasting and less effective than the usual form of inquiry held by an Inspecting Officer

CONTINUED ON PAGE 118

Above: On Friday September 19 1986, the driver of the 5.00pm express Euston-Manchester failed to stop at the red signal protecting a diamond crossover ahead of him at Colwich Junction, where his Manchester line turned right to cross the up main line from Liverpool. Despite an emergency brake application, his locomotive came to rest on the diamond crossing where he was almost immediately struck by the 5.20pm Liverpool-Euston, which was running at 95-100mph, under clear signals. The Manchester train driver had misunderstood then-new flashing yellow signals, which he thought meant his route across the junction was clear. By the time he realised his catastrophic mistake, he could not stop in time, leading to this wreck. The driver of the Liverpool train was killed and 32 passengers seriously injured. The Manchester locomotive and first two coaches were thrown on their sides while the Liverpool locomotive and its first coach likewise overturned. Three Liverpool coaches slewed sideways and came to rest on top of the second coach of the Manchester train. *ORR/ Alamy*.

Above & Opposite Page Lower: At around 7.30pm on the evening of November 18 1987, a fire started in the hidden runners of a wooden escalator at King's Cross Underground station, after a passenger dropped a lit match after lighting a cigarette whilst leaving the station. The match fell through gaps in the side of the stair tread, where 30% of the 'fire cleats' were missing. A fire quickly took hold, unseen, beneath the escalator and at 7.45pm it erupted in a violent 'flashover' into the ticket hall/concourse at the top of the escalator, causing 31 deaths and many horrific injuries. A couple of policeman happened to be on site but because their radios didn't work underground, one ran to the surface to call the London Fire Brigade. They arrived just two minutes before the flashover which killed 31 people. Desmond Fennell OBE QC, who reported on the fire for the Department of Transport, said that not one drop of water was put on the fire between 7.30pm and 7.45pm. Complacency, confusion and unclear responsibilities were identified not only within London Underground but also within the Railway Inspectorate, which was said to have misunderstood its inspection responsibilities with regard to the Underground. Further, said Fennell, the relationship between RI and the Underground was described as too informal - cosy, even - and that more stringent use of existing powers by RI could have ensured the tension required to ensure safety. These were grim lessons for everyone, which were very painfully learned. *HMRI/ORR.*

Below: On March 6 1989, at 12.45pm, a Class 303 three-car EMU train on the double track branch from Glasgow Springburn was correctly approaching the main line junction at Bellgrove, just over a mile east from Glasgow Queen Street on the Helensburgh-Airdrie suburban line, under clear signals. The connection at Bellgrove was via a single lead junction over its last few yards onto the double track main line. A short distance from the branch end of the single track section, the train collided head on with a main line train which had turned onto the branch. It had started against a signal at danger in Bellgrove station, forced its way through trailing points on the main line correctly set for the branch train, ran over the single lead and then turned onto the wrong line on the branch, to collide with the approaching train. At the last minute the main line driver who had passed the signal at danger realised the branch track he should have been on was to his left and braked: too late. The driver of the branch train running under clear signals died when the main line train rode over his cab, crushing it; a passenger also died. The guard of the train heading for the branch failed to check the starting signal aspect at Bellgrove before giving the driver the two bells indicating that train duties were complete. The driver, believing he had seen the signal go 'from red to green' didn't look at it again and set off when he heard the guard's signal: the classic so-called 'ding-ding-and-away' error. It was fatal for the driver of the approaching train. The RI highlighted the lack of clarity in the rule that said guards should check signal aspects "where practicable" before advising drivers via the bell that train duties were complete. The report by Principal Railway Employment Inspector A. Williams said that single lead junctions were safe when signalling was in good order and drivers obeyed their aspects, which in this case did not occur. *Alamy.*

The watershed three-train collision at Clapham, December 12 1988

Above: Looking west at Clapham. The stationary train from Basingstoke is in the right foreground, it's rear carriages thrown up the cutting side by the square-on rear impact of the Poole train. Its rear carriages stretch off into the distance. It's leading carriages were forced to their right by the impact, into a flank collision with the ECS train which happened to be passing in the opposite direction on the adjacent line. This is the train on the left. The leading carriage of Driver Rolls' Poole train was caught between them and the leading third of this vehicle was destroyed. It's remains are in the middle, being lifted by the crane. *Alamy*.

Just after 8.00am on Monday December 12 1988, three Mk 1 electric multiple units (EMUs) were converging on the cutting just south of Watford Junction station. Two heavily loaded passenger commuter trains were heading into Waterloo, one, the 12-coach 7.18am from Basingstoke, the second, running close behind, was the 12-coach 06.14am from Poole. The third train was the 8-coach 8,03am Waterloo- Haslemere, running empty stock in the opposite direction on the adjoining down line.

Approaching Clapham, Driver McClymont in charge of the two 4VEP units forming the Basingstoke- Waterloo train saw multiple aspect colour light signal WF138 turn directly from green to red (which should never happen) and following rule book procedures, which stated:

If a Driver or Guard observes anything which may endanger the train, he must stop his train immediately but should avoid stopping where it may be difficult to deal with the emergency.

He stopped at the next signal, WF47, to telephone the signalman, in the utter faith of a railwayman that the signal behind him, WF138, had to be at red, thereby protecting his train at the rear. It was not showing danger. The signalling system was malfunctioning and had not automatically detected, as it should have done, the arrival on its track circuits of Driver McClymont's following train, from Poole and showing a red aspect. WF138 was actually displaying a green aspect allowing the following Poole train to proceed towards signal WF47 - and towards the rear of the stationary Basingstoke train which was concealed behind a left-hand curve.

Driver John Rolls, on the Poole train, ran into the cutting having passed clear signals in his favour but as he cleared the visual obstruction of the steep bank on the left-hand curve he suddenly came upon what was normally unthinkable – and impossible - immediately ahead of him was the Basingstoke train on the same line, stationary and within a short distance in which his train could not possibly be stopped.

Despite Rolls' full emergency braking, the leading coach of his train collided square-on with the rear of the Basingstoke train at around 35mph. That major collision forced the Poole train out to its off-side, where it struck the third carriage of the ECS train which was passing in the opposite direction on the adjacent line, towards Haslemere. This second impact was more of a glancing blow, which, while it derailed part of the Haslemere train, probably kept the Poole train from running yet further to its off-side, where it would have blocked other tracks.

The 35 people, train crew and passengers, who died as a result of the collisions had all been in the first two coaches of the Poole train, which were ripped open on their left-hand sides. The first third of the leading coach of Rolls' train suffered total disintegration. Driver Rolls was killed in the impact.

During recent modernisation and upgrading of the signalling system, a crucial single wire, which should have been cut back and removed, was left in place, loose, with its core exposed. It was still 'live' and was making an electrical contact with its former circuit. This single wire was therefore able to feed current into the new circuit when that circuit should have been dead: the presence of this current prevented signal WF138 from turning to red, as it properly should have done, to protect the rear of Driver McClymont's stationary train.

Two weeks before the collision, the signalling system had been renewed to provide four-aspect signals, and this had involved many wiring changes in the Clapham relay room. A new wire had been installed for signal WF138 and the old wire should have been disconnected and electrically isolated at both ends - at its fuse end and also at the signal relay.

The reality was that no disconnection had been made at the fuse end so the wire remained live and although the redundant wire was properly disconnected at the other end, it was not cut back as it should have been, neither was it either 'taped up' to insulate it, or secured well clear of its previous contact. Although it had been 'pushed off to one side' the wire was left long enough, loose enough - and close enough - to its previous terminal for it to be physically possible for it return to its old position if the wrong circumstances arose.

Those circumstances did arise two weeks later on the day before the accident when the old wire between the fuse and the relay was disturbed. The consequences were disastrous because the redundant but live wire sprang back into its old position. It made contact its former terminal, the electrical current flowed into the system and sent a false demand to the signal for a proceed aspect, which was displayed to Driver Rolls. Disaster was now inevitable. Owing to the horrific loss of life, Conservative Secretary of Transport Paul Channon initiated a public enquiry and appointed Anthony Hidden QC to chair the inquiry and produce a report, rather than a more conventional HMRI report.

Anthony Hidden exposed multiple systemic failings in BR management, training and supervision of safety critical staff engaged in signalling installation, commissioning and testing. He produced a report that was highly critical of BR which highlighted now fewer than 16 root causes behind the three-train fatal collision:

- Working practices were permitted to slip to unacceptable and dangerous standards.
- The quality of supervision was permitted to slip to an equivalent degree, so that those unacceptable and dangerous working practices were allowed to continue.
- The quality of testing did not meet standards set by BR and testers were allowed to believe that their role was limited to functional testing only.
- There was no proper system of training of installation and testing staff, nor was there any proper system of refresher training.
- There was no proper system of allocating meaningful job descriptions to particular staff, so that they were clear as to their duties and as to what was expected of them.
- There was no effective system of communicating to the workforce the proper standards required of installation and testing work.
- There was no vetting of the weekend workforce in order to prevent individuals working excessive overtime.
- There was no review of the Waterloo Area Re-signalling System (WARS) timetable to ensure that the constant pressure of weekend work was not blunting the edge of the skills of the workforce.
- There was no effective planning of the weekend work to ensure sufficient numbers of appropriately qualified staff were available to match that particular weekend's workload.
- In fact, there was no effective project control of WARS at all, so that no overall view of the WARS workload and timetable was taken.
- There was no effective control over the Design Office to ensure that the workforce were supplied with drawings which accurately reflected the work to be done.
- There was no proper realisation of the potential danger of unprotected wrong-side failures, and as a result there was no effective monitoring of such wrong-side failures.
- There was total failure to ensure that lessons were learnt from such failures and taught to the relevant staff.
- The reorganisation of 1988 was under-resourced and therefore badly implemented.
- There was a total failure to consider and deal with the effects that that reorganisation might have on WARS Stage 7B;
- Finally, there was a total failure to communicate effectively both up and down the lines of management.

In addition to his many recommendations relating to safety culture, management issues and the hours of work for safety critical staff Anthony Hidden also made a number of far-reaching recommendations on the rolling stock involved, which literally disintegrated. He recommended that:

- BR should carry out research into structural integrity and expand its involvement in European studies.
- BR should agree with the Inspectorate structural changes to all rolling stock with a life span of over eight years.
- Rolling stock should be brought within the Railway Inspectorate's approval regime.
- The government should ensure the Railway Inspectorate was adequately staffed to match the recommendations in his report.

These recommendations quickly led to the recruitment of more Railway Inspectors and the implementation of new regulations enabling the Inspectorate to approve new rolling stock in addition to infrastructure, This was the Railways & Other Transport Systems Approval of Works, Plant and Equipment Regulations 1994, colloquially known as ROTS.

Below: A detail view of the crushed leading carriage of the Poole train. The Basingstoke train is on the right with the ECS train on the left. ***Alamy.***

CONTINUED FROM PAGE 113

without interference from the legal profession. It was therefore of interest to see this otherwise obsolete process reinvented with some justification over a century later.

It had been over 100 years since the formal public inquiry mechanism was last invoked in the case of a collision between trains but public demands for a 'full independent inquiry' following the serious multiple train fatal collision at Clapham Junction in December 1988 were so great that Secretary of State for Transport the Rt. Hon Paul Channon could not resist and a formal inquiry was established under Anthony Hidden QC. Public opinion is not always a good guide, especially in complex matters such as railway safety and it would have been entirely appropriate for an Inspecting Officer to have held the inquiry into the Clapham accident. There was no precedent for the Secretary of State's decision, as every inquiry into a railway accident in the whole 150 years of the Inspectorate's existence (excepting the two special cases of the Tay Bridge collapse and the Hixon level crossing accident) had been held by an Inspecting Officer. But the modern media age was dawning and the appalling scenes being broadcast on news bulletins and printed in newspapers created a febrile public mood to which a public inquiry was the inevitable response.

The Inspectorate was also in a period of change after almost a century and a half of remarkable stability. When Maj Rose retired as Chief Inspecting Officer in 1988 he was replaced by Mr Robin J. Seymour, who had previously been employed by the Health & Safety Executive. This was an unprecedented and very big development for two reasons:

- No previous chief had been appointed, who had not already had considerable experience as an Inspecting Officer.
- Every previous chief had been an officer of the Corps of Royal Engineers.

Robin J. Seymour joined the Railway Inspectorate as Chief Inspecting Officer in 1988, having previously been with the Health & Safety Executive working as Her Majesty's Deputy Chief Inspector of Factories in the Hazardous Substances Division.

For reasons already given, it was of course inevitable that the source of Inspecting Officers would change and the process had indeed already started in 1982 with the appointment as an Assistant Inspecting Officer of Alan Cooksey, who had previously been a Principal Railway Employment Inspector. The Railway Employment Inspectors were concerned with the safety of staff employed on the railways and were established in 1900 following the passing of the Railway Employment (Prevention of Accidents) Act that year. This is not the place to document the history and activities of the Employment Inspectors, who rather deserve a book of their own, because they were important and the migration of one of their number into the RI actually made sense in the modern era. They were originally established owing to the high death rate and the number of injuries among railway staff. For example, in 1900, 24 railwaymen were killed in train accidents while a further 559 - a truly horrifying number - died from other causes. This was indeed a terrible record. There has been since then a steady and continuous improvement. Alan Cooksey was promoted to the new post of Deputy Chief Inspecting Officer in 1988 and retired as something of an elder statesman of the railway in 2005, having assisted in the formation of the Rail Accident Investigation Branch. By pure coincidence, he was travelling in the train following the HST wrecked at Southall on September 19 1997 and acted quickly to take signalling records into evidence within minutes of the fatal crash.

Above: All fatal rail accidents are appalling - but some are so horrific that they become branded into the public consciousness. The fatal crash at Purley on Saturday March 4 1989 was just such a watershed accident. This relatively undramatic picture (with the station behind the photographer) shows its least visually dramatic aftermath. At 1.39pm, the 12.50pm Horsham-Victoria had correctly left the station on the track in front of the lens, before crossing to the line on the left. This train is in the distance, derailed and leaning to the right. The non-stop 12.17pm Littlehampton-Victoria ran past a red signal, overhauled it on the track on the left and struck the Horsham train a glancing blow at around 40mph, derailing and deflecting its first six carriages (of eight) to the left. The all-AWS signalling had been installed only five years earlier, in 1984. However, this fatal accident brought AWS's flaws into very sharp focus: specifically that it failed to differentiate between single or double yellow cautionary signals which meant that resetting AWS whilst running under yellow signals could become an automatic reaction, leading to drivers being suddenly taken aback by a red at too fast a speed to stop. Deputy Chief Inspector Alan Cooksey investigated this accident and came to precisely this conclusion in his report. *HMRI/ORR.*

Above: The rear of the Horsham train at Purley, showing damage from the glancing impact of the Littlehampton train, which was deflected down a 20m embankment. Deputy Chief Inspector Alan Cooksey praised railwaymen in his investigation for how rapidly and effectively they reacted to the crash, not least in leading passengers to safety despite worries that the 750 volt DC traction current in the third rail could not be shut off. Crash site clearance was much quicker in 1989: the accident happened on Saturday March 4 causing, said the RI report "considerable disruption" - yet the up/down slow lines reopened at 0517 on Monday March 6, with the up/down fast lines going back into service that afternoon, at 1543. *HMRI/ORR.*

One development which had a significant (and often controversial) impact on the Inspectorate was the Health & Safety at Work Act of 1974, which was passed "to make further provision for securing the health, safety and welfare of persons at work, for protecting others against risks to health or safety in connection with the activities of persons at work ... "

Whilst the Act was not specifically intended to be applied to railway employment, it does so along with the generality of other employment. To avoid duplication, the Department of Transport concluded an Agency Agreement with the Health & Safety Commission in respect of the application of the Act to railway workers and under this agreement the Railway Inspectorate carried out those functions relating to "the health, safety and welfare of persons at work engaged in the operation, inspection or maintenance of any statutory railway, and protecting people other than those at work against risks to health or safety arising out of or in connection with these activities." This situation still applies today.

The 1974 Act contains the phrase "...and protecting people other than those at work" - which means passengers. The previous legislation under which the Railway Inspectorate operated, had no such enforcement provisions in this respect. The Inspectorate could previously only make recommendations, but the 1974 Act provided a battery of sanctions. This powerful piece of legislation has stood the test of time. If implemented earlier, it would have made it so much easier for Inspectors of the past to have driven changes in urgent matters such as Automatic Train Control and gas lighting. Many lives would have been saved.

Reductions in the railway network, the widespread introduction of the automatic warning system, the elimination of steam and the modernisation of signalling have all played a part in the improvement in the figures, but these were all largely achieved by 1980, when the question was: what more can be done to improve the record still further? Do the causes of the fatal accidents in the 1980s give us any clue?

Let us briefly list them:

1981 Ulleskelf - Broken weld in rail.
Seer Green - Signalman's error. Excessive speed by driver after having been cautioned.
1983 Elgin - Broken rail at fishbolt hole.
Wrawby - Signalman's error.
1984 Polmont - Animals straying on the line.
Wembley Central - Driver passed a signal at danger. AWS ineffective.
Eccles - Driver passed a signal at danger. No AWS.
1986 Lockington - Van driver failed to obey the flashing red lights at an automatic open level crossing.
1987 Glanrhyd - Bridge collapse.
1988 Clapham Junction - Error by signal engineering technician.
1989 Purley - Driver passed a signal at Danger, AWS ineffective.
Glasgow Bellgrove - Driver passed a signal at danger. Guard failed to observe the signal before giving 'Train ready to start' bell ring to driver.

Of these 12 cases, four - Wembley, Eccles, Purley and Bellgrove - would have been prevented by the new Automatic Train Protection system which BR was by then developing and is, although effectively obsolete and increasingly difficult to maintain, still fitted on sections of the Chiltern and Great Western Main lines.

POLICE

Above: All four carriages of the leading unit of the eight-coach Littlehampton train, and the first two carriages of the second unit, were strewn along the embankment. The high-energy plunge down the steep bank flattened mature trees of up to 20m in height. Survivors endured a horrific experience. Mrs F. Donnelly was travelling in a Standard class open compartment at the trailing end of the first coach of the Littlehampton train. Deputy Chief Inspector Cooksey said: "She closed her eyes and attempted to hold on to a seat. She felt she was being "beaten with baseball bats" and tumbled around. She believes she was thrown through a window because when the train came to rest she was lying in a tree with her feet through the remains of a window. She could see the compartment that she had been sitting in had been completely destroyed and it was unrecognisable as a railway coach." *HMRI/ORR.*

Facing Page, upper: This view lays bare the full horror of Purley, not only for rail staff and passengers, but also for lineside residents, whose property had a narrow escape. Five passengers died and 88 people (including three rail staff) were injured. Driver Morgan was travelling at around 80mph when he sighted the red signal and despite an emergency brake application was still running at around 40mph at the point of impact. Investigations revealed that Signal T168 had been passed at danger no fewer than four times in recent years, including one incident in which a second train was crossing in front of the train which failed to stop at T168 - although in that incident there had been no collision. The accident report also covers some arcane detail: it revealed that Driver Morgan ate a pre-shift breakfast in a cafe, where he bought two take-away sausage rolls which he subsequently ate during a signal check at Worthing! *HMRI/ORR*

Facing page, lower: This starkly illustrates the terrible consequences of a high-energy collision - even if, as at Purley, one train is the victim of only a glancing impact. The Horsham train (on the track) received just such an impact, but although derailed, remained coupled and upright. However, six coaches of the Littlehampton train were deflected at speed down the embankment in precisely the same way that the GNER express was deflected to its left and down the embankment into the lineside field at Heck, on February 28 2001. The two wrecked coaches on the right are the leading Mk 1s of the four-car second EMU set of the Littlehampton train - which makes the destruction of the front four coaches all the more horrifically apparent. Note how nearly half of the driving coach has been reduced to matchwood after its leading end 'dug in' as it crashed through the trees and down the bank and the momentum and energy of the following seven coaches forced it round in an anti-clockwise direction, destroying nearly half the carriage. The second coach is furthest away and has breached a garden, narrowly missing its shed. After pushing the second/third coaches out of alignment, the energy of the derailing train behind had reduced enough for the fourth coach to remain in line, despite rolling partially onto its roof. The driving car in the Grayrigg 'Pendolino' of February 2007 suffered a very similar fate - but note the massive improvement in crashworthiness, as shown by the picture on 171. *HMRI/ORR.*

Chapter 8

A watershed year for HMRI 1990

It is important to recognise that 1990 was truly a watershed year for HMRI and so justifies a chapter of its own. It was a very significant - and indeed pivotal - moment in the history of the Railway Inspectorate. This is because of three momentous events.

The first was that 1990 marked the 150th anniversary of the Inspectorate. It is therefore valuable and instructive to compare where railway safety and the Inspectorate and its activities were at that point, compared with today. Times have changed a great deal and this comparison provides a fascinating contrast. It is remarkable to see how many issues the Inspectorate faced back then that have either improved on the one hand, or, on the other, are still with us - but in a different form. It is also a cause of considerable pride within the Office of Rail & Road to see the Inspectorate today having an outward-facing respected presence on the global stage. This presence and respectability continues to grow. Today, the Inspectorate is seen as a world-leading railway health & safety authority, actively supporting similar bodies across the globe. In 2016 alone, the Inspectorate gave assistance to the USA's National Transportation Safety Board , the Roads & Transport Authority of Dubai and Hong Kong rail operator MTRC. HMRI also provided advice to new railway construction projects in Abu Dhabi.

The second very important milestone occurred on December 3 1990, when it was announced by Sir John Cullen, Chairman of the Health & Safety Commission, that HM the Queen had graciously granted permission for the Inspectorate to be re-named: 'Her Majesty's Railway Inspectorate'. This will surprise some readers, for there is a mistaken, but very widely - held belief, that the 'HM' bit of the HMRI title has been in place since Victorian days - but this is not the case. The title was bestowed only in 1990, before which its title had simply been 'the Railway Inspectorate'.

Above: The Great Western Main Line scene of 1989 remained pretty much unchanged for another quarter century, after which a controversially expensive electrification scheme gathered momentum. Original indicative cost estimates of around £800m more than tripled to £2.8bn, causing major political controversy and much turbulence in the rail industry, with knock-on impact to other route modernisations and train cascades right across the country. Carrying InterCity 'swallow' livery and in lovely sunny weather on May 6 1989, IC125 power car No. 43175 leads its 2+8 High Speed Train (HST) past Southall, bound for Paddington. Who would have thought the HSTs would reach more than 40 years in service, with a further 'refurb' ahead of them, not least for the express front line service in Scotland? ***Gavin Morrison.***

Above: Semaphore sunset on December 19 1988, at Wrawby Junction, Barnetby, with a Class 56 diesel electric, running light. At the time this picture was taken, these impressive and very attractive bracketed upper quadrant semaphore signals had a further 27 years of service ahead. They were decommissioned and felled in 2016. Signals like this controlled trains from the days of Stephenson and whilst the GWR's Automatic Train Control (ATC) system dated from 1906, giving drivers crucial assistance in responding to signals, all other companies dragged their feet. As late as December 4 1984, at Eccles, in Manchester, a fatal accident happened because driver vigilance in observing signals like this was the sole safeguard: there was no AWS. (see page 113) *Gavin Morrison.*

Above: Sir John Cullen, Chairman of the Health and Safety Commission, watches while David Eves, Deputy Director General of the Health and Safety Executive (right), hands Robin Seymour, Chief Inspecting Officer of Railways, a framed copy of the letter creating the title 'Her Majesty's Railway Inspectorate'.

The third milestone event was one of the most far-reaching in the Inspectorate's history. This was its ultimately very controversial transfer (reversed in April 2006, when HMRI moved to the ORR) from the Department of Transport to the Health & Safety Executive. This transfer to the HSE also involved a physical move for the Inspectorate's HQ, from Westminster to the HSE headquarters in Bayswater, London. Around the country, HMRI regional inspectors were likewise moved and co-located in the HSE's various area offices.

This move had been under discussion for some years, and it was finally decided by Ministers that the balance of advantage was for the Inspectorate to be closer to a centre of occupational safety management expertise. At the time, HSE was Britain's leading authority in occupational safety, so if only in theory, there was some logic behind the move. Formal transfer occurred on December 1 1990. It will be for you to judge for yourselves as you read the remainder of this book if this transfer to the HSE, in the fullness of time - and, of course, with the benefit of hindsight - was the best decision.

HMRI's status as part of the HSE was certainly very hotly-debated in the late 1990s/2000s. As we describe in Chapter 11, less than 16 years later HMRI would move again, leaving HSE to become part of the newly-created Office of Rail Regulation. This did indeed make sense, as the two organisations had already been working closely before the transfer, to ensure that any financial settlement awarded to the main line network operator - Railtrack until 2002 and subsequently Network Rail - to fund its operation did not compromise health and safety. Today, to ensure that health and safety is regulated effectively, ORR is currently responsible for health and safety on the operational railway, including asset renewals and maintenance, HSE has much more limited responsibility for rail safety, only for the construction of new-build railway, such as Crossrail and HS2, through their construction phase and strictly only to the point where the railway becomes operational. Thereafter, HMRI is quite properly the safety regulator. The importance of developing a robust safety management system approach to railway regulation was recognised at that time and has developed significantly since; this is covered in later chapters.

Staffing in the Inspectorate

The years before 1990 had seen an upward trend in headcount at the Inspectorate and this continued through 1990, driven by recognition of the potential catastrophic impact of railway incidents, as painfully made clear in the devastating and fatal King's Cross station fire in 1987 (31 deaths) and Clapham Junction train collision of 1988, in which 35 people died. Both had occurred in London and both had inevitably - and quite rightly - generated substantial broadcast and print media coverage, much of it critical.

This relentless media focus developed significantly (and very rapidly) with the expansion of 24-hour rolling news through the 1990s. No longer did a rail incident command only a couple of minutes on isolated and relatively brief news bulletins which had previously covered global events. The day of the brief news summary of a railway disaster was long gone. A railway incident in the late 20th century media era would run for hour after hour on 24/7 news

Above: This Bournemouth-bound Class 442 EMU was a sleek BR design, introduced in 1988 and was a modern train when this picture was taken on April 28 1989, leaving Waterloo. This is the classic station throat view from a lineside block of flats, familiar since steam days. In the background, on the left is a 'large logo' Class 47, hauling traditional coaches. But also visible are three MK 1-based slam-door EMUs, which were withdrawn from the network in the early 2000s when new trains swept through the Southern commuter network. These older Mk 1-based trains had a very poor record of crashworthiness in collisions, because of the separate body-and-chassis design, compared with the very strong Mk 3-style monocoque construction of the newer Bournemouth train. The Colwich crash of September 19 1986 (see page 114) had proved how passengers had a much better chance of survival in a crash in this type of coach. Despite the very high energy crash at Colwich, there were no fatalities. It's shocking to see today in films of the time, but as they approached the buffer stops, inbound train drivers at all London termini were routinely overtaken by their own passengers after commuters opened slam-doors at maybe 10mph and rode on the narrow solebar steps until they judged the train was travelling slowly enough to safely leap off and save precious seconds as they ran towards the ticket barrier *en route* to their offices. Note that this was taken before the Eurostar terminal was built on Waterloo's northern flank. *Gavin Morrison.*

channels and the RI had to face and meet this challenge too. The Inspectorate's staffing compliment in 1990 increased to 46 staff (one was part-time). Within that complement, an additional four were added to the 23 professionally-qualified staff following concerns expressed by Ministers that the Inspectorate was lacking sufficient numbers, especially following the Kings Cross fire and what seemed to be an increasing number of incidents..

In 2019, there is a standing inspectorate of more than 110 full-time staff plus part-time and professionally-qualified staff. The proportion of HMRI's professionally qualified staff has increased over the years; today the Inspectorate shares a proportion of ORR's 18 specialist engineering and analytical resource. Today it is a more highly-skilled and flexible organisation, despite being considerably smaller than when HMRI reached its peak after the series of fatal incidents in the late nineties and early part of the 21st century, which will be discussed in a later chapter.

Some important changes were made to staff grade titles in 1990, as part of a move towards a unified professional inspector grading structure. This structure remains in place today:

FORMER TITLE	NEW ROLE TITLES IN 1990 WHICH REMAIN IN PLACE TODAY
Inspecting Officer of Railways	HM Assistant Chief Inspecting Officer of Railways
Assistant Inspecting Officer of Railways/ Principal Railway Employment Inspector	HM Principal Inspecting Officer of Railways
Railway Employment Inspector	HM Inspecting Officer of Railways

Then, as now, the posts of HM Chief and Deputy Chief Inspector of Railways remain in place. In 2019 those posts were held by Ian Prosser (appointed 2008) and Paul Appleton (appointed 2018)

Safety on the railway in 1990

As at the start of each chapter in this book, we have included a visual and descriptive 'snapshot' of the railway safety landscape in 1990. It is only a quarter century or so ago and safety had been improving on a continuous basis in the years up to this watershed year of 1990. Even so, the contrast with today is quite stark, particularly when you consider the growth of main line passenger journeys from 762 million in 1990 to 1.6 billion in 2017. No-one saw that explosive growth coming! Quite the reverse was forecast, because in the early 1990s the railways were seen as being of fading relevance but increasing cost, with falling passenger numbers. The Railways Act was conceived by the Government and Treasury of the day to effectively manage the iron road's anticipated continuing decline. They could not have been more wrong.

In 1990, there were 84 fatalities (other than suicides and trespassers) on Britain's railways, roughly comparable with the 84.6 average for the previous five years (1984 -1989). Of those 84 deaths, 39 were passengers, of which 37 involved train movement incidents. This compares starkly to the 15 fatalities in 2016-17 of which seven were passengers involved in the Croydon tram derailment at Sandilands. These tramway deaths were the first time in ten years that rail-borne passengers were killed, all the other fatalities occurred at the platform/train interface. In 1990, 22 members of staff and contractors lost their lives doing their duties, which compares with 1 in 2016/17, again a very significant improvement. This was seven passengers and one member of staff/contractors too many and so the vision since 2008 has been for zero industry-caused fatalities to the workforce, public and passengers.

Much can also be said about how London Underground has improved its safety performance since the tragic events of the King's Cross fire in 1987. In 1990, there were two fatal incidents involving infrastructure workers. On May 17 at Chorleywood, four men were killed when a permanent-way engineers wagon ran away in a track possession and struck them; on October 23 a painter fell approximately 13 metres to his death from a working platform erected under the roof at LU's Hainault depot .

Winding the clock forward to today, London Underground (LU) has not had a train movement workforce fatality since 1998-21 very impressive safe years. This demonstrates that hazardous maintenance work, of which there is much on LU's infrastructure, can be delivered safely on a busy network with often challenging infrastructure, with zero fatalities. All this proves how safety management in the rail sector has been utterly transformed since 1990, to the extent that LU is now regarded globally as one of the safest high-capacity urban railways in the world. It is seen as having become an exemplar of progressive health and safety management, since the appalling fire at King's Cross station in 1987, where 31 people died.

Comparisons between collisions and derailments on the main line railway in 1990 and 2019 are also indicative of wider operational improvements. No passengers were killed in a collision or derailment on the railways in Britain in 2017; the last passenger fatality had been in the derailment at Grayrigg on February 23 2007.

In 1990, things were a little different, there were 102 derailments, of which 26 involved passenger trains, whereas in 2016-17 there were just six derailments in total, further demonstrating the significant transformation we have seen in the intervening years. This is all excellent news which is too often not fully appreciated, not least by a wider general media.

Similarly, while there were 59 significant train collisions in 1990, there were none in 2016/17. So, we have not only seen a significant reduction in harm over the years but also the virtual elimination of precursor events that can cause major consequent harm to both public and workforce.

Level Crossings

As in 1990, level crossing safety still unfortunately features heavily today in terms of safety incidents and fatalities to members of public. However, safety has improved significantly since 1990 and especially since 2009. In 1990, there were 9,231 public crossings on the main line railway - this is 3,000 more than we have today. Since 2009, through the encouragement of the Inspectorate and an active programme from Network Rail, more than 1,000 crossings have been closed. We are very unlikely to be able to eradicate crossings altogether but continuing to close them is important to help reduce risk further. In 1990, there were 23 level crossing fatalities, of which 19 involved pedestrians - a predominant characteristic of crossing fatalities. In 2016-17, there were two fatalities at level crossings - a record low - testament to hard work by both HMRI and the industry. In 1990, there were 412 automatic half-barrier crossings, which were seen as an effective way of reducing crossing operating costs. However, in some cases they increased risk posed by a crossing because they provided opportunities for abuse by irresponsible crossing users who zig-zag around the barriers, when lowered to allow a train to pass. The Inspectorate is now working with the industry to eliminate half-barrier crossings in the longer-term, particularly near stations and public areas, such as schools.

Locally monitored Automatic Open Crossings (AOCL), of which there were 206 in 1990, have now virtually been eliminated because of their history of accidents.

Just as in 1990, level crossings remain a key element of the Inspectorate's activity because of the inherent risk they will always pose. When trains cross public footpaths and roads on the level, there is a very high level of potential risk which must always be carefully managed and borne down on. In 2019, level crossings are a historical anachronism from the days of horses and carts and they have no place amidst millions of cars, lorries and buses.

Train command and control

As in 1990, the future direction and development of command and control technology remains at the forefront of our thinking and activities.

During 1989, the first of a new generation of signal boxes, known

Above: The very grubby freight scene in which HMRI operated in 1990. This is the north end of Doncaster on February 13 1986, as an unidentified and filthy Class 56 diesel electric makes a smoky departure north, snaking through the station with a merry-go-round (MGR) train of pulverised power station coal. The works yard in the background is remarkably untidy. ***Gavin Morrison.***

Above: This was almost the end for the once very common annual summer Saturday 'extras', which ran from industrial areas to seaside resorts, in the days when a family would travel out from home, clutching much smaller suitcases than you see today, on one Saturday and then returning back home the next weekend after a hopefully sunny week relaxing on the beaches. On August 25 1990, Class 47 No. 47973 heads a seven coach rake of mixed slam-door Mk 1 and Mk 2 carriages on the seafront approaching Dawlish, with a Summer Saturday 'extra' from Rose Grove (Burnley) to Paignton. The penultimate vehicle still carries BR corporate blue and grey livery. *Gavin Morrison*

as Integrated Electronic Control Centres (IECC), was installed at London's Liverpool Street terminus. At the time, the IECC combined what were then modern display screens with computer networking techniques and HMRI approved the display screen system adopted at the time by British Rail. The screens show track diagrams, provide train information and enable signallers to visualise and control traffic movements. A computer local area network economically integrates the signallers control desk with the signal interlocking system and with systems for providing passenger and management information.

An automatic route setting computer (ARS) was provided which automatically set routes for all timetabled trains; it routinely optimises train movement capacity, but the signaller can still intervene at any time and take manual control of all or part of the system.

In 1990, further projects were underway for railway control centres at York, Glasgow and Newcastle. Interestingly, at the suggestion of the Inspectorate, HSE was engaged to analyse control room displays using its occupational human factor disciplines, to look at workloads and prioritising alarms. Today, we have our own in-house human factors capability and control room operations remain a key focus of their activity. Progress marches on and as is always the case, the once cutting-edge IECCs themselves are now becoming obselete. Network Rail is steadily implementing both its new Operating Strategy to rationalise national signalling control to just 12 Regional Operating Centres (ROCs). It is also starting to implement the European Train Control System, which together will radically change how the future railway operates. The success of the implementation of European Train Control System (ETCS) and Automatic Train Operation (ATO) in the Thameslink core in 2018 allowed 24 trains per hour (TPH) operation – a prelude to a the digital future.

Assisting other agencies

In 1990, the Inspectorate was already highly regarded worldwide and had given advice to other Inspectorates and railway systems around the world. This included Hong Kong, Singapore and Sweden. Today, this recognition and credibility has grown yet further and in recent years Inspectors have shared their expertise and experience in countries including South Korea, Dubai, Abu Dhabi, Sweden and Hong Kong.

HMRI has also worked closely with our European counterparts and provided a strong input in the work of the European Rail Agency (ERA). These examples show that although the Inspectorate has undoubtedly lived through some troubled times at home in the last couple of decades, the underlying strength of its approach and the enduring qualities of professionalism and technical expertise have continued to grow and been felt around the world.

Above & Below: HMRI exercised authority over a whole spectrum of safety issues quite apart from the operational matters which featured in the headlines. It's very different today, but scenes like this at the time tended not to feature in the news agenda of the day, probably because of the limited time available in the much shorter bulletin-based nature of broadcast news back then, on both TV and radio. Operating cranes safely has always been a tricky business and the crews need to be acutely aware of - and respect - the safe maximum load lifting radius of any crane, which decreases rapidly as the jib radius extends. Get it wrong and this is what happens - the whole crane tips over. This is what happened at Longwood & Milnsbridge on April 29 1979 (below) and York Yard (above) in early 1988. The signalman at York and his box had a very narrow escape! *David Sykes/HMRI.*

CHAPTER 9

A DECADE OF CHANGE 1990-2000

Above: In the early 1990s, the Southern commuter network was characterised by slam-door EMU trains of up to 40 years old, based on the Mk 1. On the right, a ten-car train made up of two four-car/two-car mixed Class 414 2-HAP/Class 423 4-VEP units dating from 1956-63 (2-HAP) and 1967-74 (4-VEP) is alongside a 1982-vintage Class 455 unit, just west of Clapham Junction, near the site of the 1989 fatal accident on December 12 1988. By 2005, all Mk 1 slam-door trains had gone from our main lines (although South West Trains retained two units, strictly limited to the Lymington branch until 2010) other than the derogated charter fleet of locomotive-hauled Mk 1s, fitted with internal manual door bolts, operated individually by stewards. *Gavin Morrison.*

The 1980s closed with the publication of the Clapham Public Inquiry findings (the Hidden Report) amidst a period of unprecedented change for the Inspectorate, with its move from the Department for Transport. The Inspectorate had been granted the title 'Her Majesty's Railway Inspectorate' on its 150th anniversary in 1990 but it was subsequently transferred to the Department of Employment, where HMRI was subsumed as a division of the Health & Safety Executive (HSE) in 1990. Given HMRI had always been a very proud standalone department, this absorption by HSE was by no means universally welcomed.

The wider railway was also plunged into the most fundamental changes the industry had experienced since Nationalisation by the post-war Labour Government, in 1948. This was a direct consequence of the Conservative Government's policy of privatising British Rail (BR). Privatisation in the 1990s did not turn back the clock to the structure of the 'Big Four' (WR, SR, LMS and LNER) although Prime Minister John Major was known to favour this option. Instead, the new Railways Act created a completely new world. Although the pre-Nationalised (1948) and pre-Grouping (1923) railway had seen a large number of separate private companies, they were generally vertically integrated responsible for both infrastructure and train operations (and much more besides, including hotels, docks, road services and shipping). More than 120 of them were 'grouped' on January 1 1923 to establish the 'Big Four' - the Great Western (GWR), Southern (SR), London Midland & Scottish (LMS) and London & North Eastern (LNER) Railways.

The 1990s Conservative privatisation did not follow this course of vertical integration; instead its liberalisation of access to the railways launched the greatest restructuring of the British railway industry ever attempted. Although EU Directive 91/440 only mandated separation of infrastructure and operations in accountancy terms (in order to make real costs transparent), Prime Minister John Major's Conservative Government chose to interpret this directive in more fundamental and extremely radical terms, by creating completely separate entities to own and operate track and trains. This 'fragmentation' of the industry at the wheel-rail interface has been the subject of intense disagreement and debate ever since.

The decade was punctuated by intense media and political interest in the effects of privatisation as framed by The Railways Act of 1993. This placed the Inspectorate in a pivotal role as the independent voice of safety performance in the new era of private train operations on a network now owned not by the state, but by a private limited company, owned by shareholders - Railtrack - which sought to pay dividends to its shareholders.

The Labour opposition had promised to renationalise Railtrack immediately on taking office, should it win the 1997 General Election and this (as intended by Labour) made sale of Railtrack much more difficult, because would-be investors were deterred by the prospect of losing those investments in the event of the Labour victory which did indeed follow in the 1997 'Things can only get better' General Election. This election, which swept Tony Blair's New Labour to power, was the first of an unprecedented three General Election victories for Blair.

Not for the first time, a pre-election political promise/threat proved to be empty: renationalisation of Railtrack failed to be implemented over the life of two successive Labour administrations between 1997 and 2010, when the Conservatives were returned to power under David Cameron. Indeed, in its 13 years in power, Labour failed to reverse any of the Conservative privatisations.

Far from rolling back the new private sector, Tony Blair and Gordon Brown's Labour Governments further entrenched and significantly developed the model put in place by the Conservative Railways Act of 1993. Major had personally been in favour of recreating the 'Big Four'

(LMS, LNER, GWR and SR) of the pre-1948 era but was unable to win the day because of the requirement of 91/440 to separate infrstaructure and operations, at the very least in accounting terms. The Treasury triumphed and imposed the structure which was still largely in place in 2019 as this book went to press - although the Williams Review launched by Secretary of State Chris Grayling in September 2018 was looking likely to make significant changes.

The seismic change made by John Major's Government in selling Railtrack triggered frequent and damaging 'profits before safety' rows which continued for years, with regard to the train operators in particular. Network Rail was effectively renationalised on September 1 2014 - although ironically by Conservatives and not Labour - and so no longer suffers from these criticisms.

HMRI also found itself no stranger to controversy. It made decisions - not least about Automatic Train Protection - which in the light of subsequent events, returned to haunt it. In 1997, HMRI concluded that the statistical safety benefits of Automatic Train Protection (ATP) in terms of the very small number of lives it would save, did not justify its very high cost. In strict risk assessment terms, this was undeniably true and was perfectly in line with thinking and decisions routinely made without fuss in other modes of transport - but in the febrile media mood of the later 1990s, as shaped by what was too often described as 'a spate' of fatal accidents (especially Ladbroke Grove on October 5 1999) it made it easy for critics to claim that HMRI was either out of touch, or in thrall to, and under the control of, its political masters. The public, media and political mood around rail safety became incredibly volatile and sensitive: this created an atmosphere in which rational debate became impossible. When NR Commercial Director Richard Middleton commented in the aftermath of the Hatfield accident that the 'hysteria around rail safety needed to calm down' it became a thunderingly criticial front page story for next day's newspapers and TV news.

The mood around rail safety was febrile because the 1990s approached their close with a trio of very high profile, fatal accidents: Southall (September 19 1997), Ladbroke Grove (October 5 1999) and Hatfield (October 17 2000). The industry and its too-often hapless spokesmen were firstly overwhelmed and then engulfed by a highly sensitized and often angry level of public, media and political scrutiny never previously experienced. Neither industry nor HSE/HMRI were prepared in any sense for this sustained onslaught and the result was a tendency to 'hunker down' and say as little as possible. This led to lasting damage for the railway's public reputation and did nothing to encourage public understanding of its difficulties. By association, the Inspectorate also entered the new millennium subjected to similar intense and sustained scrutiny, not to mention controversy. There was considerable uncertainty as to whether HMRI would even survive this battering to its reputation and credibility.

It was all made much more difficult by the Labour Government of the day's stubborn refusal (largely in the shape of Deputy Prime Minister John Prescott) to give the political 'air cover' required to ensure the public mood did not 'go critical' and boil over. This demanded a degree of political courage which was simply not forthcoming and the railway was left entirely undefended to 'swing in the wind' as a public and media punchbag.

Public opinion was not in the mood to understand the complexities whilst a hostile media was unwilling to engage with, let alone explain, the detail; this inflamed understandable public anger still further. What made matters especially difficult for HMRI was what fortnightly *RAIL* magazine frequently condemned as 'backside covering' and self-serving 'grandstanding' by the HMRI's masters at both HSE and its Health & Safety Commission parent. Far from the tough but supportive approach that HMRI had developed post-2006, the HSE's attitude to rail was hostile and overly critical. This served only to inflame the public, media and political mood yet further. The HSE's approach led to a very difficult time for HMRI.

Critics repeatedly condemned both HSE and HSC for what they saw as their joint failure - refusal, even - to be the responsible voice of reason. Rather than seek to calm entirely understandable nerves, it seemed the HSE's approach simply inflamed public anger further. Bluntly, HSC and HSE routinely poured petrol on the flames of public concern and with no political air cover, the unprotected rail industry was left to largely fend for itself - a task for which it was both unprepared and ill-equipped. Reputational damage was immense.

Critics perceived that HSE was 'playing to the crowd', when they believed it should have been framing a considered, supporting context for its hard-pressed and often harangued officers. This increasing

Above: As recently as 1998, there was a brisk traffic in steel coil from Ebbw Vale: but no more, even though the line was reopened to passengers in 2008, steel is long gone and this yard has been cleared. On September 17 1998, a quartet of Class 37s are awaiting their trains in the busy yard. On the left are Nos 37212 and 37274, whilst on the right are 37901 and 37903. *Gavin Morrison.*

tension eventually led to Secretary of State for Transport Alistair Darling setting aside intense HSE/HSC lobbying when he took the decision to remove HMRI from HSE and place it within ORR, in 2006.

Transferring the newly-created HMRI to HSE in December 1990 had partly been in response to Anthony Hidden's recommendation in the Clapham Inquiry that the Inspectorate should be properly resourced and staffed. It is certainly true that this at least had been successful: transfer to HSE had indeed allowed easier access to technical and other expertise: this heralded a period of steady expansion. External candidates were expected to have considerable experience of the rail industry but the Division was also supplemented by internal transfers and secondments from within HSE. Not surprisingly, this injection of non-railway personnel did not find universal approval, not only in the industry, but also within the Inspectorate. Critics complained that specialist railway responsibilities were inappropriately being put in the hands of 'factory inspectors' more accustomed to manufacturing. These were unsettled times at HMRI.

Historically, the Inspectorate had certainly found it difficult to recruit staff, with candidates often citing pay constraints as a barrier to joining, so it did indeed benefit from the transfer of skills in areas such as health and safety management systems, risk assessment and the wider pool of HSE technical expertise. On the other hand, HSE believed that HMRI had little experience of using enforcement powers under the Health & Safety at Work Act and other safety legislation. HSE was surprised to discover that BR had never been subject to formal enforcement action, despite a number of significant incidents. Of course, HMRI still had Inspecting Officers (who dealt with British Railways Board senior managers on approvals, and inspecting level crossings, for example) and Railway Employment Inspectors who were supposed to look at employee safety. In fact, they were expected to refer to RIHQ if they were considering serving enforcement notices on British Railways Board. The HSE enforcement policy (which HMRI as a Division of HSE was now required to follow) was noticeably in contrast to the more collaborative and less formal approach RI had previously pursued with the industry. HSE inspectors were accustomed to serving enforcement notices 'on the spot' and so internal tensions were inevitable - and sometimes unhelpful.

1991

Operationally, single lead junctions became a major bone of contention. This is where a double track railway converges into a single bi-directional line immediately before joining the nearest track on a double track railway, with the other line then being rapidly accessed by a crossover between the main lines. These replaced the classic double turnout junction, thereby eliminating diamond crossings. Single lead junctions were introduced as a cheaper (both to install and maintain) alternative to a conventional double turnout, with its requirement for a diamond crossing in one of the two main lines.

This concern was brought into sharp focus after a fatal accident in Newton, Scotland on July 21 1991 where four people died. This followed a similar accident on March 6 1989 at Glasgow (Bellgrove, pages 115) and the Inquiry into this Scottish accident examined the further problem of a train starting away in error from a station against a danger signal - a long-known risk. Single lead junction installations were all subject to HMRI approval and whilst this was examined as part of the Bellgrove Fatal Accident Inquiry, the issue of approvals would be a recurring topic through the 1990s.

This was a major source of concern to HSE, because at a time when the industry was debating improved train protection, the significant risk profile of single lead junctions was a major worry. This applied especially when these incidents were associated with station signals - the so-called 'ding-ding-and-away' phenomenon, where a guard gave the rightaway despite the train 'not having the road' and the driver

Above: The very sharp ECML curve south of Morpeth station caused derailments in 1877, 1969 and 1984 - and in 1994 claimed its fourth victim. On June 27 1994, Class 47 No. 47783, hauling 1S04, the 4.33pm King's Cross-Glasgow parcels (two BGs/five GUV vans) derailed at 80mph at Milepost 16¼ at 9.49pm, despite the permanent 50mph speed restriction. The Driver-Only train was running under clear signals and a hot axlebox detector at Dam Dykes (eight miles before derailment) recorded speed as 92mph. The locomotive and first, third and fourth vans overturned on the outside of the 50mph curve whilst the second vehicle came to rest on the up main line adjacent to the front of the locomotive. The fifth, sixth and seventh vehicles remained upright but derailed, other than the trailing bogie of the seventh van. All wheels, bogies, running gear and track were subsequently found to be in good order. Investigations revealed nothing to suggest a defective speedometer. Calculations suggested GUVs had a minimum overturning speed of 75mph on a curve radius of 350 metres. The 1877 Morpeth derailment had not been caused by excessive speed - the 10.30pm Edinburgh-London King's Cross was travelling at only 25mph when it derailed on defective track. Interestingly, the RI's Captain Henry Tyler had commented in 1877: "It would obviously be better if a deviation line could be constructed, to avoid the use of so sharp a curve on a main line." A century and a half later, that same sharp curve, with the same 50mph permanent speed restriction still applies, notwithstanding no fewer than three subsequent excessive speed collisions, one of which (in 1984) claimed six lives. (see also page 109). *HMRI/ORR*

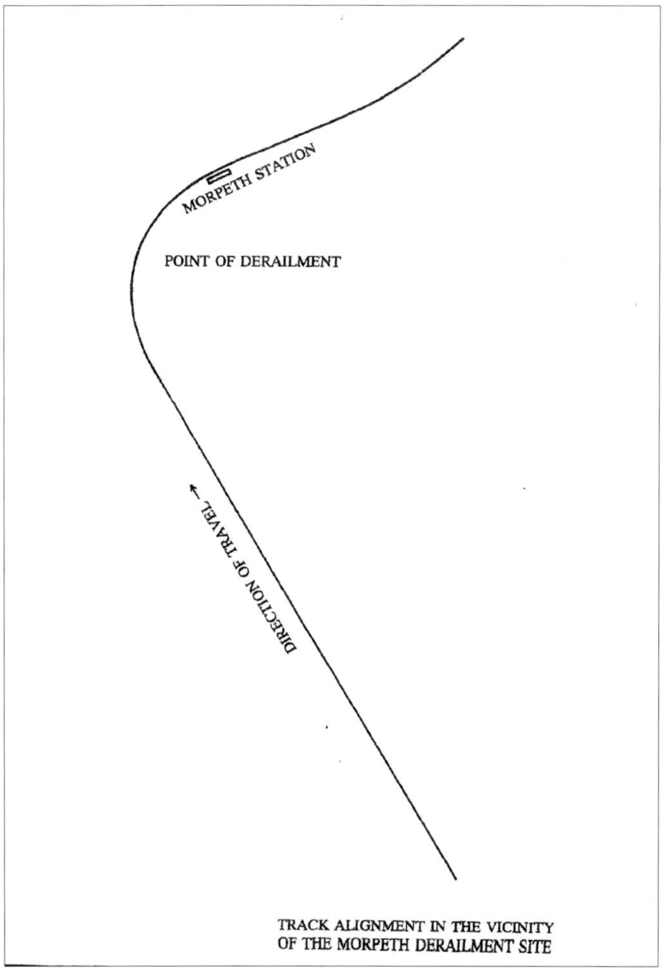

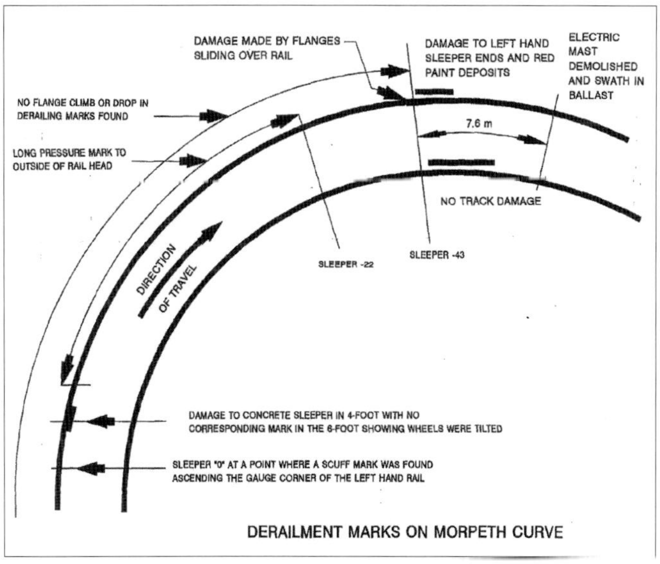

Above: The Morpeth route outline, showing the severity of the curve south of the station, together with a diagram showing progression of the derailment as revealed in the investigation (by the British Rail Research Dynamics Group, at Derby) by marks on rails and damage to sleepers. *HMRI/ORR*

departing in error against a red stop signal. These worries resulted in a reassessment of these layouts. As a consequence, a number of single lead junctions were restored to conventional double track configuration.

HMRI had also been concerned by the number of injuries arising from passengers falling from open doors on moving trains of Mk 1 carriages and had previously commissioned the Health & Safety Laboratories (HSL) to undertake a study. There was a strongly-held industry belief that these incidents were mainly self-inflicted by passengers, with alcohol thought to be playing a part in most fatalities. There was little concrete evidence, however, for this widely-held view. The HSL report made a series of recommendations about the maintenance standards of slam-door stock as well as suggesting engineering improvements to door locking arrangements. HMRI made a series of spot-check visits to depots to monitor the robustness of maintenance arrangements and was mandated to investigate all instances where passengers had fallen from open doors on moving trains.

Chief Inspector Robin Seymour, who had overseen HMRI's transfer to HSE, retired in 1991. He was credited with prompting BRB to look more closely at improving the arrangements for track worker safety. His successor was Stan Robertson, an imposing figure who was an engineer and had also been the Deputy Chief Engineer in the HSE Technical unit.

1992-93

Preparation for liberalisation of access to the railways continued apace and the HSC launched a study into the safety implications of privatisation. HMRI and HSE were significant contributors to this work. The industry was also focussed on implementing the recommendations of key public inquiries, including the Fennell and Hidden reports which followed the King's Cross fire (November 18 1987) and the Clapham collisions (December 12 1988).

HMRI's reporting year was realigned to the fiscal year end (April) adopted by HSE, although interestingly the industry still worked on a calendar year. During 1992-93 the HSC report into the liberalisation of the railways, 'Ensuring safety on Britain's Railways' was published and well received. This resulted in a number of key work streams, not least the need for primary legislation, such as the Transport & Works Act 1992 as well as the provision of regulations including the Railways (Safety Case) Regulations 1994 which introduced safety cases to the rail industry for the first time, together with a cascade of acceptance arrangements.

Railtrack and LUL, as Infrastructure Controllers, needed an accepted safety case before they could commence operations and a cascade of safety case acceptance required all operators to have an accepted safety case prior to operating trains on any railway infrastructure. Supporters of the new regime would say that safety cases ensured that safety arrangements were properly assessed and formally captured and expressed in a series of documents. Critics refuted this and claimed that the regime leaned too heavily on arrangements in other high hazard industries more suited to a single location facility, such as an oil platform or petro-chemical site, but which were not suitable for 11,000 route miles of railway infrastructure covering the length and breadth of Britain. On reflection, the critics were probably right. That said, the subsequent move to the regulator approving dutyholder safety management systems has been more successful.

This was genuinely a time of rapid change and activity in the industry with many significant work streams proceeding in the run-up to privatisation, which took effect on February 4 1996. As well as contributing to the liberalisation agenda, there was still the 'day job' of ensuring that the rail network was managed safely. It is well known and understood that change presents new safety risks, not least because individuals can become preoccupied and distracted as to the security of their own employment. This period undoubtedly put additional strain on the industry and it is testament to the dedication of all rail staff that safety standards did not deteriorate in the run-up to privatisation.

HMRI played its full part in maintaining safety performance and senior railway managers often commented that during a time of great change and uncertainty the Inspectorate represented the only force for continuity and stability in safety that the industry would know for the next few years. The Inspectorate was also having to find resource for numerous additional activities surrounding privatisation, whilst staff were also seconded onto various project teams to implement the recommendations of the HSC report. Transport & Works Act requirements also brought new rolling stock into the approvals process for the first time, a loophole that had been highlighted in the Clapham Report. The Inspectorate also had to look at a number of emerging mega-projects, including the Channel Tunnel, Crossrail, Jubilee Line Extension, Heathrow Express Link and Docklands Light Railway.

The Inspectorate's resources were consequently becoming severely and increasingly stretched and new works schemes were taking longer than was ideal to receive approval. There were several reasons - but there were clearly errors on both sides and the use of so-called 'comfort letters' which gave a no-objection-in-principle, *in lieu* of inspection, became necessary to allow this rapidly expanding programme to continue.

The Inspectorate clearly needed further resources both to deal with the increase in new works but also to address the additional requirements to accept the new safety cases and also to deal effectively with the dozens of new duty holders created in the new structure. No longer would it be possible to speak to BRB alone and receive a commitment that a given matter would be addressed across all parts of the railway. The Inspectorate had now to deal with a huge increase in the number of duty holders and a sizeable influx of new key players who did not have specialist knowledge of our railway. Thus, HSE embarked on a major recruitment campaign and HMRI began to grow

Above: The appalling crashworthiness of steel-bodied multi-door BR Mk 1s, demonstrated so horrifically at Clapham on December 12 1988 (35 deaths) was exposed yet again at Cowden, on the single line branch to Uckfield, in thick fog on October 15 1994. Two passenger trains collided head-on at 8.27am, killing five people and injuring a further 12. Both drivers died, together with the up train Guard. This was the impact point, on the north side of the embankment. The trains were the 8.00am Uckfield-Oxted and the 8.04am Oxted-Uckfield. The accident was caused by the up Oxted train passing the danger signal protecting entry to the single line from Ashurst to Hever. AWS was working but the signal had a degraded visual performance, made worse by thick fog. Investigations revealed that Guard Brett-Andrews of the Up train from Uckfield was 'riding irregularly' in the driving cab and there were unproven suggestions that he was at the controls - which did not change the finding that Up train Driver Barton was 'wholly responsible.' This picture shows the down train in the foreground, with the up train beyond. The leading carriage of the down train was forced to the left by the impact, wreckage cascading down the embankment. *ORR/HMRI.*

significantly with further transferees from HSE joining HMRI, alongside industry recruits.

Track worker fatalities had blighted the industry for many years, with an average of 20 avoidable deaths each year in the late 1980s and early 1990s - which we rightly find shocking today. There were 11 track worker fatalities in 1990. With the emphasis placed on this area by the previous Chief Inspector and the increase in Employment Inspector numbers, there was now scope to devote more time to this tragic subject, where there was clearly considerable scope for improvement.

BRB had already been looking at this very serious issue and in the early part of the decade had proposed a major new initiative that would allow better protection of staff working on or near the line. This was the precursor to the current philosophy of line blockages and separation of trains and staff. Less activity now takes place in red zones where work is conducted on live tracks and innovation has seen the introduction of new engineering trains where track workers operate within the safety of a 'bottomless' vehicle spanning the track, which is fully protected, both from adjacent lines and bad weather.

The effects of the HSL report into passengers falling from train doors seemingly also had a positive impact on safety standards with fatal accidents reducing from 19 to three in 1996 - a figure that fell further through the 1990s. With the eventual withdrawal by 2005 of most slam door stock (or the introduction of secondary locking) fatal falls from train doors has virtually been eliminated. That said, where slam doors survived in 2019 (classic, unmodified HSTs on national services) there were still occasional incidents of doors found 'on catches' (partly closed, but not properly secured) or indeed actually open in traffic, on the few remaining charter trains which use 1950s vintage BR Mk 1 rolling stock.

1993-1994

Railtrack was incorporated and its safety case accepted by HMRI in time for its launch on April 1 1994. There was also a programme of authorising train operating companies (passenger and freight) which all had to have their own bespoke safety cases. New infrastructure maintenance contracting arrangements also came into being, with the BR Infrastructure Services maintenance companies set up to carry out maintenance activities alongside other new companies who were also tackling infrastructure renewals. Safety case submissions were extremely time-consuming, both in terms of their production and assessment. Unfortunately, in too many instances, Inspectors reported that these documents were being regarded merely as a passport to access and that, once accepted, the documents were seen as some kind of bureaucratic 'box' which had been successfully ticked and could thereafter be left to gather dust, rather than be properly implemented on the front line. This was clearly not the intended - or required - outcome and was one of the root causes that led to some tragic incidents and, ultimately, the collapse of Railtrack after the fatal Hatfield derailment of October 17 2000. A northbound Great North Eastern Railway express derailed at speed after a rail beneath it shattered into more than 300 pieces as a result of what is known as either 'gauge corner cracking' or, more scientifically, rolling contact fatigue. The rails were severely overdue for renewal but the job had not been done (see also pages 157-159).

As the Inspectorate expanded, it reorganised into three units, RI1 dealing with new works, mega-projects and level crossings; RI2 was a new strategy/policy unit while RI3 consisted of the field teams carrying out inspections and investigations. RI3 was becoming increasingly focussed on passenger safety and catastrophic risk areas. The distinction between Inspecting Officers and Employment Inspectors had been removed in 1990, to the great satisfaction of the field teams. The Inspectorate was still increasing in size at this time and stood at 71 Inspectorial staff in 1994.

There was clearly an urgent need to train inspectors to deal with all these new responsibilities. New legislation affected all of HMRI and there

Above: The impact point at Cowden, from south of the embankment, showing the devastating damage to the Mk 1s, whose bodies detached and were destroyed in the high energy collision. Both trains were Class 205 DEMUs, from BR's South Central Train Operating Unit (TOU), before privatisation, after which TOUs became Train Operating Companies (TOCs). Modern colour light signals and AWS on the Uckfield branch were controlled from Oxted, from 1990. Cab Secure Radio (CSR) was not fitted and other radio coverage was patchy, so staff were supplied with unreliable commercial mobile phones, which had fallen into disuse. After the SPAD by the Oxted train, the signaller, who could see from his panel what was about to happen, could not warn either driver of the fatal catastrophe about to engulf their trains. *HMRI/ORR.*

Above & Below: Cowden wreckage at the point of impact, looking west, showing the catastrophic destruction of the Mk 1s. Railtrack South Signaller Webb at Oxted had set the route for the down train, crewed by Driver Rees and Guard Boyd, as far as signal OD59 in Ashurst Loop, while clearing the Up train to signal OD58, so they could cross in the loop. The Up train ran past OD58 at danger, ran through the trailing points at Blackham Junction (which were set for the down train) in the reverse direction, triggering an alarm. Signaller Webb realised instantly a collision was inevitable but with no stop signals ahead of either train, and no radio, he had no way to warn either driver. All he could do was make an emergency call to Railtrack Control at Croydon to call out emergency services, before the accident had even happened. CSR could have stopped the crash, because when the alarm sounded the trains were still a mile and a half apart - a running time of two minutes. Signals and AWS were all found to have been working properly. *HMRI/ORR*

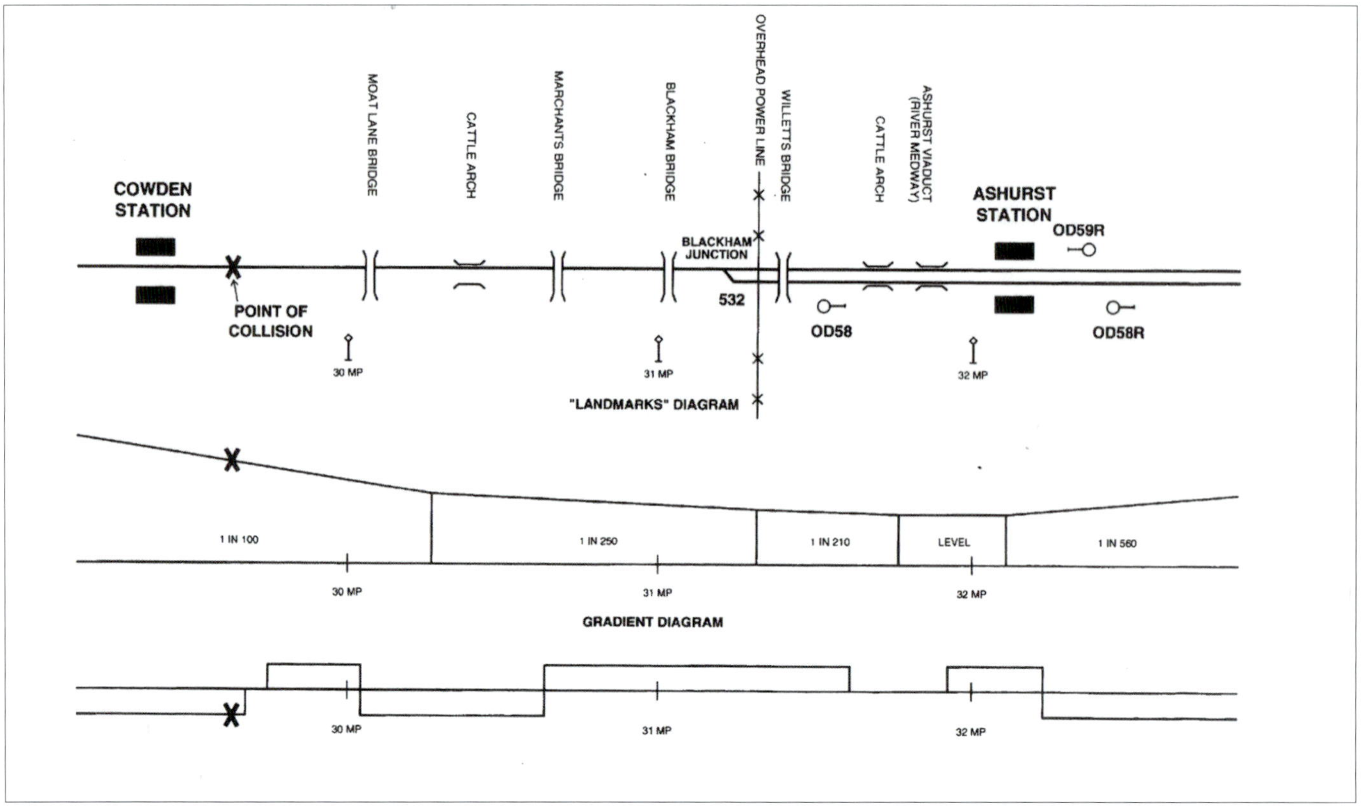

was a major training load to be addressed. In subsequent years, another staff anomaly arose whereby inspectors transferring from HSE were generally on lower pay than inspectors recruited externally and there was a scheme to enable HSE inspectors transferring-in to demonstrate their competency via an assessment panel and therefore upgrade to higher pay. Nonetheless, there was a continuing undercurrent of ill-will, criticism and some adverse press comment about inspectors who did not have sufficient specialist knowledge - the old 'chip shop inspectors' allegation. Despite these internal changes in the Inspectorate, it continued to be seen as a rare fixed point in a rapidly-changing and volatile railway landscape.

Within the rail companies, there was similar internal criticism of incoming private company personnel who were not deemed to have sufficient rail knowledge. This criticism is perhaps understandable in an industry that had a very long tradition of employing maybe several generations of the same family, accompanied by a strong tradition of promoting internally. This tradition had created very effective railway 'DNA' which critics said was being diluted.

Some commentators claimed that Railtrack was not a sufficiently informed client and lacked the expertise necessary to adequately monitor its contractors. This argument found much validation at Hatfield. Inspectors were continually commenting that Railtrack did not have an adequate asset database and was unable to confirm the condition of the assets within its portfolio. This was a criticism made repeatedly and strenuously in subsequent years by Rail Regulator Tom Winsor (1999-2004). In the light of subsequent developments - not least the fatal Hatfield derailment - it's clear he was on the right track.

1994-1995

The Inspectorate had been warning of the dangers of vandalism for some time and train drivers had been increasingly subject to missile throwing, both from the lineside and overbridges, for many years. It was clear that such events were increasing - in one reported incident, a sack of ballast had been suspended by rope from an overbridge, at cab windscreen height. Some notorious railways became known as 'Bomb Alley' by train crews. In this respect, this issue was as much a societal matter as a problem specifically for Railtrack and its contractors, who had duties to keep scrap and materials secure, so as to deprive vandals of lineside ammunition which could potentially derail a train. Sadly, a double fatality occurred at Branchton, Scotland in June 1994, after trespassing youths placed concrete troughing lids on the line. A Scotrail train derailed and hit a bridge abutment, fatally injuring the driver and a passenger. The youths responsible were caught and convicted with 15-year custodial sentences: this was the first time an act of vandalism which had caused passenger and staff fatalities had resulted in a prison sentence.

This incident also highlighted other problems. The youths had trespassed on the railway adjacent to a school and the whole issue of unauthorised access to poorly-protected tracksides therefore became a major issue for the new cohort of inspectors. Historically, railways had been delineated (you can hardly say 'protected') from neighbouring land either by rather flimsy wire fences with timber or concrete posts, or timber post-and-rail fences, neither of which were more than waist height. Many of these fences, over hundreds, if not thousands of miles, were in very poor condition (in many places, only the posts survived) meaning that many hundreds, if not thousands of miles of main line railway, were effectively unprotected against the determined (or even casual) trespasser.

Several enforcement notices were served, requiring improvements to railway fencing and this resulted in thousands of miles of rather ugly, spiked galvanised steel palisade and other fencing being rapidly erected around the network. Those who criticise the cost of railways in the modern era often overlook such significant costs as this, which BR simply never had to meet to anything like a comparable degree.

Those were very different times culturally in other ways too, regarding access. Today, entrances to railway sites such as depots,

Above: Another west facing view at Cowden of the point of impact, showing the remains of the up train, whose passenger accommodation was smashed to matchwood. It was never definitively established who was driving the up train when it passed OD58 at danger - but Guard Brett-Andrews was known to have aspirations to be a driver and had first received a verbal warning in mid-1992, for riding with the driver. He was later found riding in the driving cab again and was given a more severe second warning, but which still fell short of formal disciplinary action. Brett-Andrews was found riding in the driver's cab yet again on January 8 1994: he was formally disciplined and given a final warning on February 4 1994. Major CB. Holden concluded that Guard Brett-Andrews' presence in the cab was a distraction and that insufficient disciplinary action had been taken against him, despite repeated instances of him being found travelling with drivers. Evidence as to who was driving at the time of the collision was inconclusive. *HMRI/ORR*

Above: Bufferstop collisions caused concern in 1995, including two on July 11. The more spectacular was at Largs, on the Ayrshire coast, where the six-car Class 318 EMU forming the 6.15am from Glasgow Central collided heavily with the bufferstop. It mounted the platform, careered across the concourse, demolished two shops and part of the 1885 station, finally coming to rest in the street. The driver, guard and three others were injured, but there was no loss of life. Investigations concluded that the driver - who was inexperienced driving on greasy rails - had approached at too high a speed and failed to brake early enough. The other accident that day was at Liverpool, where eight passengers from the 200 commuters aboard a two-car Class 142 from Wigan hit the buffers at low speed at Lime Street, which is at the foot of a 1-in-88 falling gradient. *HMRI/ORR.*

works, goods depots and other facilities are routinely (and expensively) gated and locked with security of access. Back then, you could often simply just walk in off a public road, unchallenged, at just about any railway premises. Such gates as there were were often routinely left wide open, if they existed at all - or were even capable of being closed. These access points are also very costly for the railway to make secure - but there are clear safety benefits from doing so which under the new arrangements the Inspectorate pursued and for which it demanded compliance.

It will remain a talking point in hindsight that with the advent of infrastructure maintenance contracts, issues such as cess walkways, boundary fencing and even the unchecked growth of invasive buddleia in the brickwork of bridges and retaining walls, were perhaps not as clearly specified as track patrolling and maintenance requirements. The Inspectorate heard many traditional contracting dispute arguments, where the client was expecting the contractor to maintain fencing in a condition that prevented unauthorised access, while the contractor believed he was only required to maintain the asset in the condition it had been in at the start of the contract. In BR days, such conversations would not have needed to take place, although funding would still have been a challenge.

The first major industrial dispute during the privatised era occurred at this time when Railtrack signallers launched industrial action in 1994. The company attempted to run a limited service by rostering managers in signal boxes to keep passenger services running. This was in the era of the Citizen's Charter, then newly-created by John Major's Conservative government - and HSE's policy was to respond to all complaints. The RMT Union submitted a large number of complaints (more than 100) alleging that these managers were not competent to undertake such duties or were working excessive hours. The industry still used the Hidden Report requirements to manage fatigue at this time and HMRI was compelled to formally follow-up all these allegations in order to be satisfied that the network was being operated safely. This was an example where HMRI was clearly in the glare of an unremitting and merciless media spotlight: if anyone was still in doubt that the privatised railway was of rapidly increasing interest to the wider broadcast and print media, this dispelled any lingering doubts. New rolling TV news broadcasts had an insatiable need for content and if visually and emotionally dramatic, so much the better. The railway was a rich source of such content.

The number of Signals Passed at Danger (SPADs) remained a concern for the industry. This had been highlighted by HMRI, but evolving effective action was painfully slow. Signal engineers instinctively tended to claim that if only the drivers did what they were paid to do, then SPADs would not occur. Operators, on the other hand, believed that signal engineers should eliminate potential SPAD traps through new design solutions. Both were correct, of course! To put the situation into perspective, there had been 944 reported SPADs in 1991/92 compared with 313 in 2018/19. Even where signals had seen multiple run-by incidents (known as multi-spad signals) there was little evidence that the industry was taking prompt and effective action to tackle the problem. Rail industry understanding of human factors such as distraction or fatigue which can lead to human error was also not well developed at this time.

Whilst these stand-off views weren't universal, it is easy to see how infrastructure controllers and train operators developed entrenched and opposing views that hindered progress. Although the Clapham Inquiry had recommended Automatic Train Protection (ATP) the industry had been slow to implement engineering solutions to avoid SPADs and this would be a matter that would need to be addressed in legislation at a later date. And of course, HMRI had concluded in 1997 that ATP did not justify the very significant expense in terms of lives saved.

The impression - certainly so far as independent observers were concerned - was that railway companies were prepared to 'live with' numerous SPADs as a matter of routine. There wasn't even a requirement to report individual SPADs to the regulator. Therefore, it is only fair to say that the same independent observer would also conclude that HMRI also did not put enough emphasis on this area either. The analysis on Automatic Train Protection was completed and HSC was asked to comment on the report. It agreed with the industry view that it was not reasonably practicable to install ATP across the network due to the significant cost which according to the analysis far outweighed the safety benefit in terms of the very small number of lives likely to be saved, although ATP would be installed on new high speed lines, such as the 300kph Channel Tunnel Rail Link.

Notwithstanding this setback, HMRI and certain parts of the industry were still keen to look at solutions, and Train Protection Warning System (TPWS, also known as AWS-Plus at the time) was seen as a short term solution until the emerging European Train Control System (ETCS) was fully developed and installed.

Regrettably, accountants were neverthess firmly in charge and several perverse decisions were made by Railtrack, such as scrapping its only ultrasonic rail testing train, leaving only hand-held or push-along ultrasonic testers for this crucial work on its 11,000 route mile network. Investment in important machines such as rail grinders was also blocked. This risky thinking could not continue and indeed, looking back from today, it seems inconceivable that these things really happened.

1995-1996

A revision to the Inspectorate's Requirements ('the blue book') - which was badly in need of updating - was finally published with a suite of documents entitled 'Railway Safety Principles & Guidance (RSPG)'. These documents were written more in a spirit of goal-setting rather than being prescriptive but it did nevertheless provide key specific requirements for new works, such as infrastructure clearances.

RSPG had been a major resourcing exercise for RI2 and the documents were well received by industry. They greatly assisted in the approvals process since submissions could be clearly and objectively assessed against published criteria rather than using the former subjective assessement. Although they were subsequently withdrawn with the advent of the ROGS legislation in 2006 (see pages 166-168) because of their prescriptive nature, some guidance documents for the industry have been published in topics where the Inspectorate believe 'lines in the sand' are needed.

RI3 engaged in a major audit of Railtrack's management of its contractors. There was concern that Railtrack did not have a sufficiently robust asset database which was capable of providing a reliable indication of the condition of all infrastructure assets. This had been a frequently expressed concern for many years, by Rail Regulator Tom Winsor, who served from July 1999 to July 2004, when his post was abolished and its duties and responsibilities passed to the Board of the reconfigured Office of Rail Regulation.

There was serious concern about Railtrack's ability to properly monitor the activities and performance of its contractors. Infrastructure Maintenance Companies (IMCs) were primarily focussed on keeping trains running, so what were too often regarded as peripheral, less important issues - including fencing, cesses and other walkways - were often neglected, with unwelcome outcomes seen in terms of trespass and track worker injuries and even fatalities. This audit was probably the most resource-intensive project the Inspectorate had undertaken, amounting to more than 2,500 man hours. This was seen as a key risk area and resulted in formal enforcement action against Railtrack to remedy legal non-compliances regarding fencing and walkways.

The view that key assets were being allowed to deteriorate was clearly demonstrated when the condition of Railtrack's most iconic structure - the mighty Forth Bridge, (opened on March 4 1890 after eight years of construction) became the focus of constant (and it, has to be said, jusitifed) scathing media criticism. It was also the subject of an adjournment debate in the House of Commons. Such is its historical and global importance, the Forth Bridge was in 2015 designated as Scotland's sixth UNESCO World Heritage Site.

It was seemingly obvious to everyone but Railtrack that the mighty bridge had been allowed to deteriorate and it was obvious that this early massive example of steel construction in a coastal, salty-air environment was suffering badly. Major areas of paint were peeling away from the steel and flaking off, accompanied by sizeable clods of rust, all of which were thudding with increasing frequency into the gardens of Queensferry residents living beneath the structure. They were understandably unhappy about this cascade of rusty lumps of paint and complained vociferously to a steady stream of journalists who were only too ready to beat Railtrack with these clumps of rust and paint.

Strictly speaking, what was thumping into the Queensferry vegetable patches was generally clods of many layers of built-up red oxide paint which had become detached, rather than critical elements of the bridge. That didn't matter of course - perceptions are important and there was a real risk of injury and property damage. In media terms it was embarrassing to see Railtrack seeking to turning a Nelsonian blind eye to this problem. And longer term, there was clearly going to be an obvious structural issue if this problem was not properly dealt with - soon.

Although this deterioration had been happening for several years (BR was alleged to have declared a "maintenance holiday" some years before) the fact that the structure was now in private hands meant it became - and remained - a very highly-charged political media story - and not only in Scotland. None of this was 'going away' any time soon.

Recalls *RAIL* Managing Editor Nigel Harris: "I had asked Deputy Editor Philip Haigh, to follow up the story about 'lumps of rust and great clods of ancient paint' falling into Queensferry gardens. He came back, mightily amused, to tell of an irritated Railtrack press spokesperson's response: "It is not rust!" were the angry words fired his way, "It is merely superficial surface corrosion!"

Unsurprisingly the words 'laughing stock' echoed way beyond the specialist press when a similar reply was given to merciless Scottish broadcast and print journalists.

HSE Director General John Rimmington had been lobbied by firebrand local MP Tam Dalyell about the deteriorating condition of the bridge, concerns over the falling debris and the implications of its sustainability as a long term strategic role as the primary main line rail route to the Kingdom of Fife and beyond, to North East Scotland and thence the Far North, in Caithness. Although HSE agreed to undertake an assessment of the bridge's structural integrity, this was somewhat

Above: One of six Royal Mail postal staff working on a mail train was killed at Rickerscote, 1¼ miles south of Stafford, at 11.08pm on Friday March 8 1996 when a northbound nine-coach Travelling Post Office, hauled by Class 86 No. 86239 and four of its postal vehicles were derailed (five remained on the track). It collided with a double-headed (Class 37s 37071/37207) southbound Transrail freight train, one of whose four-wheel tank wagons became derailed and fouled the down main line after one of its axles broke. The freight was running up from the bottom of this picture - the '37s' and first eight wagons remained on the rails and ran ahead, coming to a stand off the top of this field of view. The TPO, running down from the top of this image, hit the derailed 4W tank in its path. No. 86239 derailed, jack-knifed and its rear end pushed the derailed tanks backwards (towards the bottom of the picture), its mail vans coming to rest in concertina formation. The fatality occurred in the destroyed gangway between the first two vehicles, alongside the '86.' The other postal workers were mainly in the fifth and sixth coaches; houses on the right had a very narrow escape. *HMRI/ORR.*

Above: The derailed tank at Rickerscote was owned by CAIB UK and a key aspect of the investigation looked into any safety impact of privatisation/fragmentation. The very rare wheelset fracture was thought to have been caused by a crack, but damage sustained to the axle ends in the crash destroyed corroborative evidence. The 23-wagon train had left Glasgow that day at 2.40pm and had been inspected at Warrington, bound for Willesden. It included 13 46-tonne carbon dioxide tank wagons, pressurised at 350 pounds per square inch (PSI) some of which were pierced in the collision and started leaking; they had to be safely vented by the emergency services. The train had passed a hot axlebox detector north of Stafford at 10.55pm - less than ten minutes before the crash - but no warnings had been triggered. The freight train came to a stand because the derailing tank wagon had fractured its air brake pipes and it had only just stopped when the Travelling Post Office hit it. *Jeremy Caldecoat.*

outside the usual remit of a safety regulator. It is for a duty holder to ensure the safety of its assets but it is perhaps a telling demonstration of the level of public concern and critical media focus on the railways that the DG felt he had no option but to surrender to the growing clamour for HSE to intervene. However, HSE was at pains to stress that it was not the role of the regulator to check the structural integrity of bridges - as had been importantly determined more than a century before, during the Board of Trade Tay Bridge Disaster Inquiry of 1879.

A team of HMRI/HSE experts advised by external consultants (who were understandably seizing the opportunities offered by privatisation) was established and their report was published the following year. It concluded that the bridge was indeed capable of carrying current loads but that Railtrack needed to better understand the condition of its structure and to put in place a proper plan to monitor all key components. This especially applied to thermal movements within the bridge as well as starting a maintenance plan to rectify defects. Enforcement action was also taken to ensure this happened.

The need for action on the Forth Bridge was a concern to the regulator and this resulted in closer scrutiny of the other key strategic bridge in Scotland where disaster had already struck in 1879. The Tay Bridge, north of the Forth Bridge on the route to Dundee and Aberdeen was a less complex structure, constructed of multi-span decks and access was much easier, but sadly failings were found with the condition of the Tay Bridge too - and so enforcement action followed there also.

An HMRI Improvement Notice was served on Railtrack to assess and maintain its bridges. These episodes were not only revealing but also alarming. The fact that Railtrack had to be instructed by its safety regulator to properly care for such high-profile, high risk bridges played a part in significantly eroding its reputation - which then completely broke down after the Hatfield fatal derailment of October 17 2000. (see also pages 157-159)

This catastrophe happened when a running rail - known to be long overdue for replacement - shattered into more than 300 pieces beneath a Great North Eastern Railway (GNER) express running at linespeed. Four passengers were killed in the GNER buffet car, which rolled onto its side and its roof was sliced off by the sharp edge of a lineside catenary stanchion.

Railtrack responded by placing operating restrictions on the Forth Bridge by banning freight trains and stopping all traffic when wind speed reached critical levels, until the structure was assessed. Following engineering assessment, both the Forth and Tay bridges underwent extensive refurbishment. The Forth Bridge was subjected to a £130m refurbishment which took ten years to complete. All paint was shot blasted back to bare steel, repairs carried out as required and then all steelwork was recoated using a high-tech paint containing glass particles that settled into a layer intended to provide 25-year protection. After well over 100 years, the famous expression: "It's like painting the Forth Bridge" to represent a never-ending task, finally became redundant. It is a testament to the bridge designers of the 19th century that such structures are expected to be carrying rail traffic safely for many decades to come.

The Inspectorate also turned its attention to the replacement of 1950s design Mk 1 rolling stock, which had featured in the Clapham accident (December 12 1988) report, as well as many other incidents. These coaches were known to be a key risk in collisions. Mk 1s perform poorly in crashes because the separately constructed body and chassis can become separated. Subsequent coaches - especially the incredibly successful Mk 3 and Mk 4 stock, as found in HSTs and East Coast Main Line (ECML) Class 91-hauled trains, featured very strong tube-like moncocque construction which contain and protect passengers in crashes to a much greater extent.

Given the slow pace of progress over earlier decades in eliminating gas lighting (that took many years and repeated calls from the RI) and in the adoption of train protection systems, it was maybe unsurprising that the regulator felt that it was likely that legislation would be necessary to ensure the industry made acceptably rapid progress to withdraw Mk1 rolling stock, along with requirements to introduce On Train Data Recorders and train protection.

The work on passengers falling through open doors from moving trains seemed to be having the desired effect with only three deaths occurring 1995-96.

1996-1997

By 1996, questions were being raised about whether privatisation had brought a positive or negative impact on safety. It wasn't an easy question to answer because reporting arrangements for safety incidents had been changed in recent years and this made meaningful like-for-like comparison difficult. Furthermore, most key performance indicators (KPIs) in the railway industry were either reactive or lagging. This was an issue HMRI would keep coming back to in subsequent years, because this is not a reliable approach to safety performance in any industry. There is always an element of chance, for example, as to whether an injury or death results in an accident. HMRI Chief Inspector Stan Robertson referred to this in his annual report in 1997 and whilst injuries to staff had risen, other statistics had fallen. In particular, the total number of fatalities was at an all-time low of 25, so he felt there wasn't enough data to reach a satisfactory conclusion and no changes to the regulatory structure were therefore considered. The Chief Inspector's principal concern was vandalism and the increase in the numbers of young trespassers being killed. Vandalism had caused 887 train accidents and 171 train fires, a staggering statistic.

The year also coincided with the final transfer of safety responsibilities from the British Railways Board (BRB) to the new rail companies. There was also the drafting of a Railway Group Standard on the installation of a Driver Reminder Appliance (DRA) in the cab of most passenger trains. This was designed to assist drivers by reminding them they had received a cautionary signal aspect - especially at stations - and preventing the train leaving by blocking traction power. This was designed to put an end to the notorious 'Ding Ding and away' problems where a Guard wrongly gave the rightaway whilst a red signal was showing and the driver made the mistake of setting off. Some drivers had also inappropriately been using the DRA 'on the move'

At the same time, design and planning for Train Protection Warning System (TPWS) was progressing: this remains one of the most important (and ultimately successful) initiatives undertaken by the post-1993 Railways Act rail industry acting together to mitigate the outcome of a SPAD. TPWS enhances the older AWS considerably but it does not provide continuous speed supervision over an entire journey, such as that provided by more advanced Automatic Train protection (ATP) systems. This perceived weakness led to very extensive (if not especially well-informed) public and media debate following the Ladbroke Grove fatal accident in particular (October 5 1999; 31 deaths). Critics claimed TPWS was a 'cheapskate solution' by an industry seeking to avoid the costs of what was frequently described as 'full ATP.' History has proved these critics comprehensively wrong: TPWS has effectively eliminated train collisions and accidents arising from SPADs - significantly, risk is less than 10% today compared with 1999.

Changes in the use of Mk 1 rolling stock - which Hidden had concluded post-Clapham was not practical to withdraw and was not inherently unsafe - took place, as modern stock came increasingly on stream. It was powerfully clear that Mk 1 carriages did not afford anywhere near the same level of safety as new trains, especially in high energy collisions, where the carriage body could separate from its chassis, as happened so horrifically at Purley and Cowden. Southern stock was also weak longitudinally because of the large number of bodyside doors giving passenger access to multiple compartments. HSE was rightly anxious to see rapid action in this regard.

The use of quantified risk assessment (QRA) was also becoming more prevalent in the rail industry at this time. QRA provides quantitative figures for the level of risk but relies on accurate and comprehensive data: this essentially calculates the probability of a fatality or serious injury, using known figures for SPADs, broken rails and embankment failures, for example. However, QRA is a guide, not an accurate prediction.

QRA clearly had its place in the decision on proposals to fit ATP/ TPWS - but HMRI was finding that QRA was also being used by the industry in a whole range of other areas to justify not carrying out improvements instead of using a proper risk assessment. This was not acceptable. The Inspectorate was finding it occasionally needed to consider serving formal notices to ensure that duty holders carried out suitable and sufficient risk assessments. There was a need to warn the industry against over-reliance on QRA, which HSE insisted should only be a component part of a much more comprehensive safety assessment and not a tool in its own right.

1997-1998

The last quarter of the decade was perhaps the darkest period the Inspectorate had ever had to deal with - and it was all conducted in the relentless 24/7 glare of media, public and political scrutiny, much of it hostile. This was not helped by the tensions within HMRI over

Above: The surreal spectacle of wrecked Rail Express Systems (RES) vans, tightly surrounded by houses, during recovery. This fatal crash was especially sensitive because Railtrack was about to be sold; Ed Burkhardt's Wisconsin Central had already bought BR's goods business and the Rail Express Systems mail operation. Signalling, track and driving techniques were all excluded as causes. Some confusion was caused by private company staff liaising directly with emergency services rather than through Railtrack's Incident Officer and this was criticised in the official report. This revealed that wagon maintenance standards were not consistent between those formerly employed by BR and those leased by specialist companies such as CAIB. A key recommendation was that these standards should be harmonised. ***Jeremy Caldecoat.***

its home within HSE. This period saw the industry suffer a number of catastrophic fatal accidents (Southall,1997; Ladbroke Grove,1999; Hatfield, 2000) which resulted in significant changes to the way the industry was structured. Indeed, it eventually led to the collapse and extinction of Railtrack as a private company, with far-reaching further implications and outcomes, not only for the wider industry, but also for HMRI itself.

The Southall collision on September 19 1997 was the worst railway accident since Clapham (December 12 1988) with seven deaths and 139 injuries. (see also pages 147-150) A Great Western Trains (GWT) HST failed to stop at a red danger signal and collided with a stone train crossing its path in the opposite direction. The ATP in use (unique to the GWR main line) installed on the GWT train had been switched off before its departure from Swansea, but what made the disaster much more likely was that the AWS in the leading HST driving cab was also faulty. The driver therefore had no assistance whatsoever and had to rely on line of sight and vigilance alone, whilst working a 125mph express. AWS was working correctly in the rear cab of the HST but there had been pressure not to turn the train on the triangle at Swansea prior to departure (in order to put AWS at the front of the train, to assist the driver) to avoid any possible poor performance financial penalties which were routinely imposed by the new regime for late running. This was a very controversial aspect of the debate which followed Southall: were railwaymen (albeit maybe unwittingly) putting performance before safety for financial reasons?

The practice of allowing trains to enter passenger service with defective safety equipment was immediately banned after Southall, unless other mitigations were in place. However, in terms of operating culture, this accident highlights that there was a level of complacency over on-train safety equipment, which was, in the operating culture of the time, obviously perceived to have limited benefit. It also called into question the effectiveness of risk assessments that duty holders undertook as part of their control arrangements.

The industry had made some progress in improving track worker safety and falls from train doors but the Inspectorate remained concerned over track condition and the management and monitoring of maintenance contractors by Railtrack.

Chief Inspector Stan Robertson retired in 1998 and was credited with having taken the industry forward in a number of key areas, such as worker safety as well as removing the distinction between field inspectors and Inspecting officers based in HQ.

1998-1999

Vic Coleman became HMRI's Chief Inspector in 1998. He had joined the Inspectorate in 1990 as a Principal Inspector and was pivotal in the report entitled 'Ensuring the safety of Britain's railways'. Coleman also led RI3 from 1995, was well known to the Inspectors and was a popular appointment amongst other staff. He also worked hard to engage positively with the media - especially the specialist rail media - with whom he was friendly and popular, whilst always maintaining an appropriate professional distance.

HMRI continued to highlight continuing concerns over SPADs and an apparent lack of action by the industry. Indeed RI3 undertook a key inspection looking at driver management arrangements in every TOC. This report was published only a few weeks before the Ladbroke Grove collision and recommended that the need for enforcement action would be reviewed if momentum in achieving improvements was not maintained. The number of serious SPADs that if repeated could cause a high speed collision, increased from 42 in 1997/98 to an alarming 52 in 1998/99.

Track condition also remained an area of concern for HMRI, with the Office of the Rail Regulator also frequently raising concerns about the numbers of rail defects. Broken rails are clearly a safety concern and cause performance to deteriorate. Broken rails, for example, were exceeding a thousand a year at this time, compared with around 100 today. A good example of significant improvement in a key safety metric.

Fortunately, most rail breaks are normally detected immediately by track circuit failures (the break in the rail breaches the circuit and raises the alarm) - but not always - as the fatal derailment at Hatfield (when the rail shattered actually beneath the train) made horribly clear. HMRI highlighted that other track quality issues were of similar concern and that there had been a number of derailments caused by poor track condition such as gauge spread caused by the deterioration of sleepers and their fixings.

Vandalism and staff assaults were also on HMRI's radar. These were, of course, reflective of wider societal problems, but they seemed to be escalating and the railways seemed to be bearing a heavy burden in terms of problems caused. Non-violent abuse of staff was also a problem which continued to worsen and from 2005 so-called 'spit kits' were in routine use on the railway, to help identify abusers and provide British Transport Police with conclusive DNA evidence for criminal prosecutions.

1999-2000

The last year of the decade saw, in the words of Chief Inspector Vic Coleman "….everyone's worst nightmare realised". The high speed head-on collision at Ladbroke Grove on October 5 1999 and the resulting intense Coach H buffet car fire (caused by the ignition of atomised diesel sprayed from the ruptured HST power car fuel tank) saw 31 passengers lose their lives with a further 520 injured - and it remains the worst incident on the Great Western Railway. The accident was caused by a catalogue of failures, including inadequate driver training, the robustness of safety consideration for new works and the ability of the industry to work together to address long-standing known weaknesses.

Although the Inspectorate had been highlighting the issue of SPADs for several years, changes to signalling at Ladbroke Grove had actually been formally approved by HMRI. The layout had been designed for the subsequent retro-fitting of ATP. As part of this design, the practice of flank protection, where a train passing a signal at danger is not placed in head-on conflict with trains on another line, had been abandoned. Thus when the Thames Trains Turbo driven by Michael Hodder passed SN109 at danger, he was directed to his left at the next set of facing points - directly into the path of the inbound HST. Under previous practice, he would have been diverted to the right on those facing points, towards a trailing junction into the down slow, where he would have run the risk of a flank impact with a train running alongside, but in the same direction. Given that the left-hand path into the route of the HST was much longer, maybe the view taken was that a half-mile SPAD at speed was not likely - and in any event, it was expected that ATP would soon be fitted.

Chief Inspector Vic Coleman reflected that the industry had not been sufficiently "self-challenging" - and he rightly included the Inspectorate in that clearly critical analysis.

HSE Director General Jenny Bacon submitted evidence to Lord Cullen's Ladbroke Grove Inquiry conceding that the Inspectorate had taken too long to approve the signalling scheme; that progress to resolve issues had not been effective and that risk analysis had not been rigorous enough. She concluded her evidence with a damning conclusion on her own Division: while she admitted that HMRI had suffered from a lack of resources (an issue that had plagued the Inspectorate for many years) she also conceded that it had not pursued issues with sufficient vigour, whilst placing too much trust in promises by duty holders.

In order to satisfy a public and media clamour to 'get tough', there was a knee-jerk reaction within HSE, where Inspectors were told that there was now an expectation that improvement notices should be served without hesitation or discussion, to ensure railway companies complied with actions that previously would have been subject to written agreement. This placed very considerable stress on crucially important working relationships between HMRI and the industry and served only to foster an unhealthy, less-open and increasingly fraught relationship in which trust suffered. This is not an atmosphere in which safety management can thrive and deliver the improvements intended and required.

These were, without doubt, some of HMRI's most difficult times. It was under the most intense level of public, media and political scrutiny it had ever known - and which has not been repeated since, thankfully. The Head of RI3 served enforcement notices on Railtrack; a situation no inspector in HMRI could remember had ever occurred before with such a senior officer being the signatory to Improvement Notices.

HSE further reacted to the accident by proposing to 'brigade' HMRI with another, much larger division within HSE - the Field Operations Division (FOD) - which had evolved from the former Factories Inspectorate. The Inspectorate's very survival hung in the balance and a significant number of inspectors were so alarmed that they co-signed a letter to Chief Inspector Vic Coleman, objecting to this brigading, seeing it as a first step in what they (and others) feared was the creeping abolition of HMRI.

Although Ladbroke Grove dominated the landscape in the final year of the decade there was also other significant work in hand which should not be overshadowed or overlooked. This included the introduction of new legislation for train protection, leading to the installation of TPWS; this was perhaps the most significant initiative to reduce the catastrophic risks of SPADs. Changes were also being worked through to revise safety case regulations such that HSE accepted all safety cases of train operators rather than only the Railtrack safety case.

HMRI also remained very concerned over the condition of track, not least broken rails. It was interesting to note that Lord Cullen (and also the specialist press, *RAIL* magazine in particular) commented on the different penalties levied by the Rail Regulator, and explored the idea that maybe subliminal, but nonetheless powerful messages, were being sent to those who operated trains, as a consequence of this discrepancy. There were, for example, multi-million pound financial

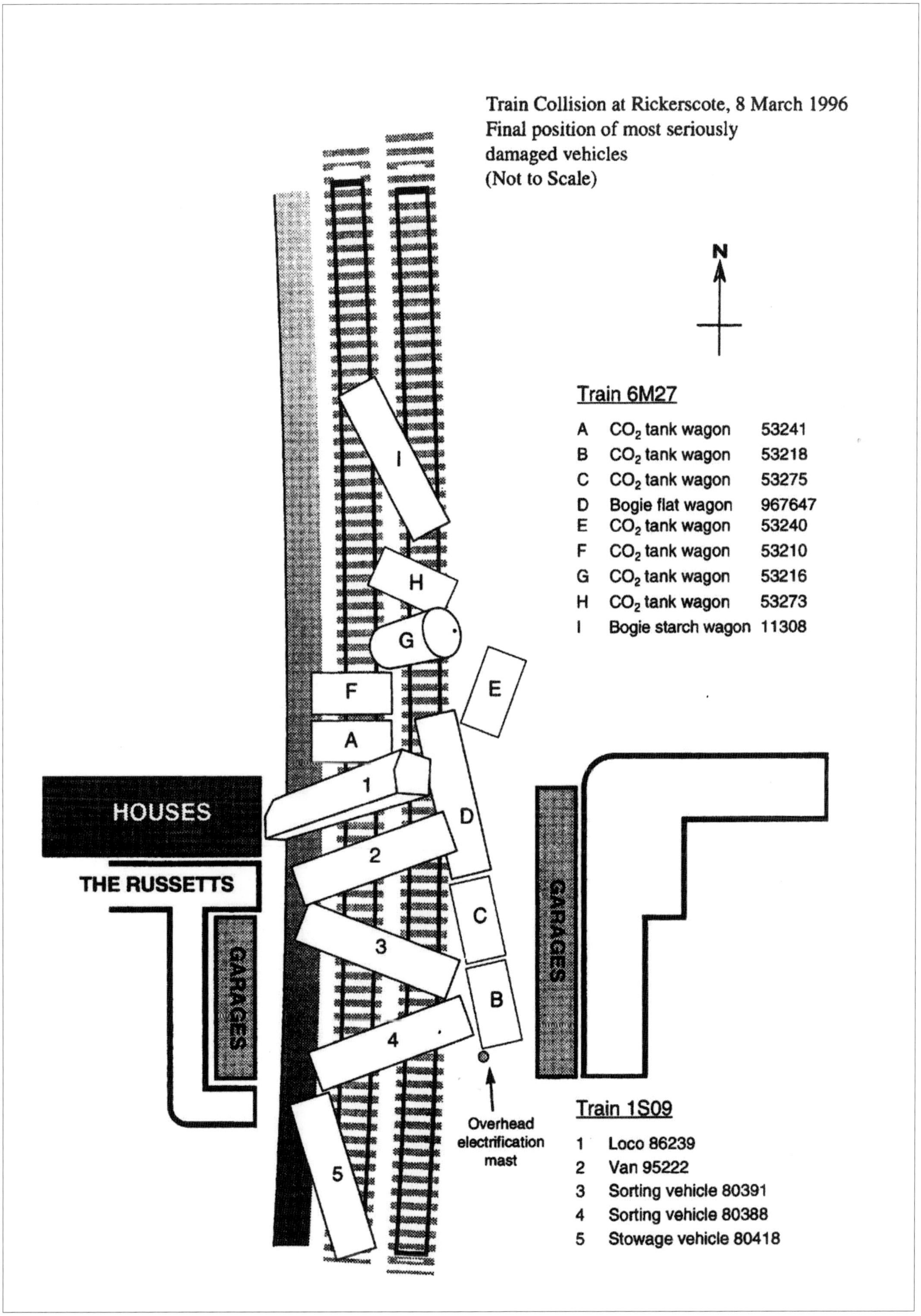

Above: The investigator's diagram showing where the northbound Travelling Post Office and its vans came to rest amidst the derailed tank wagons from the southbound freight. ***HMRI/ORR***

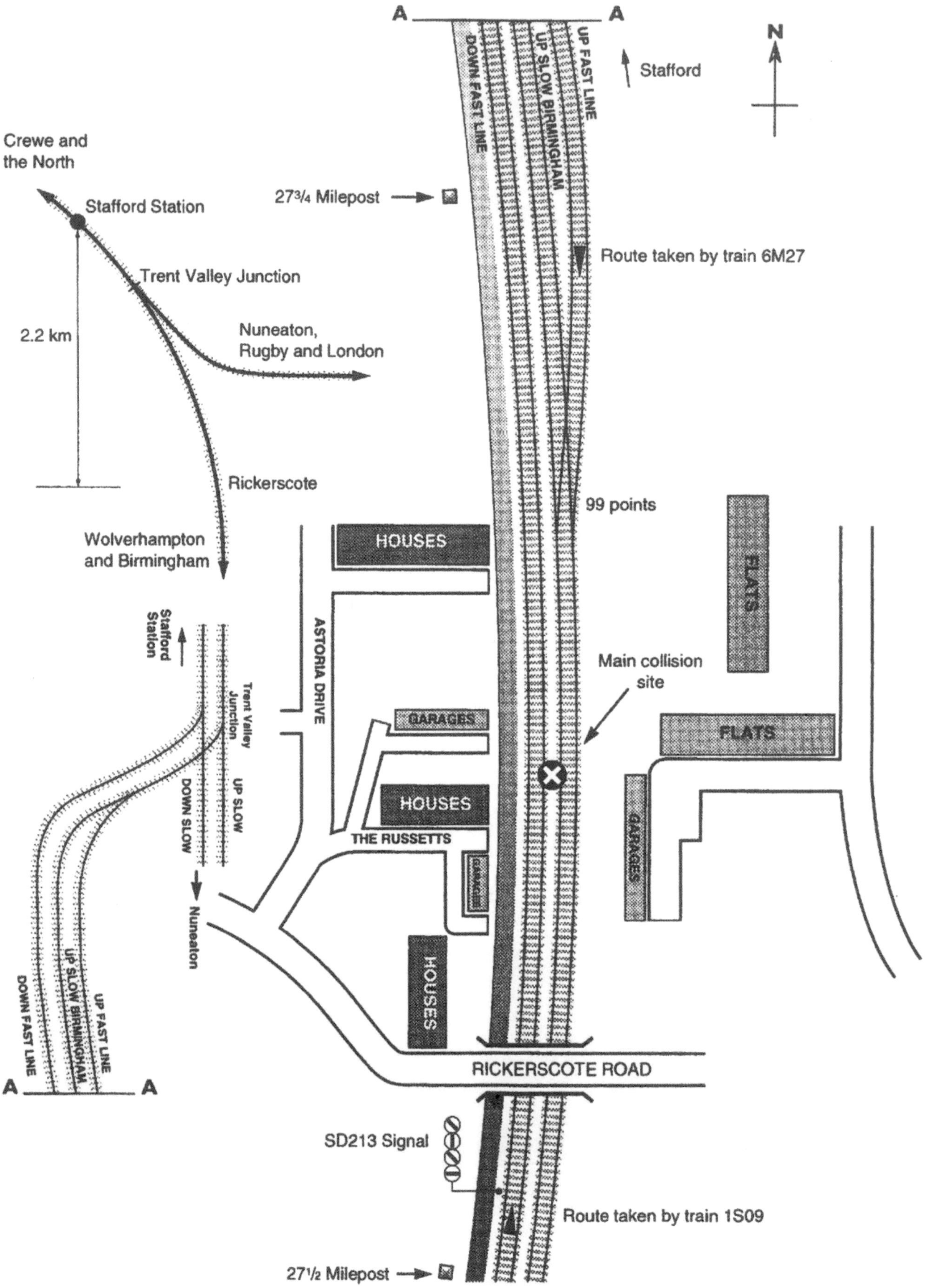

Location Plan of Train
Collision at Rickerscote,
8 March 1996
(Not to Scale)

Above & Right: This is one of the more surreal outcomes of a railway mishap: On November 1 2000, English Welsh & Scottish Railway Class 67 No. 67002 precariously came to rest thus after a 50mph rear end collision with a train of four-wheel HAA merry-go-round coal hoppers at Lawrence Hill station, Bristol. The Royal Mail train hauled by the Class 67 had run away for three miles and passed two red signals before colliding violently with the slower-moving coal train at 3.40am. No. 67002 was on a short five-miles trip from the Bristol Parkway mail terminal to Barton Green depot, to refuel. The impact launched the Class 67 40m through the air to land on this MGR wagon at the rear end of the 45-wagon train, with 67002's roof hard against the road overbridge. The EWS driver suffered a broken arm, fractured chin and shattered shoulder. The accident was caused by the incorrect setting of an air brake pipe cock on the locomotive, which isolated the train brakes.

penalities for punctuality delays whereas serious health and safety breaches received much smaller financial punishment. On July 27 1999, Railtrack was fined £1.5m after the seven deaths at Southall whereas penalties for passenger train delays that year amounted to some £8m. The whole debate over safety and performance came to a head when Rail Regulator Tom Winsor explained that his multi-million pound penalties on Railtrack for broken rails should be seen as "incentives". This became a matter of intense discussion and controversy, with HMRI at its centre on many occasions.

The Cullen Inquiry into Ladbroke Grove, as well as the events at Hatfield in 2000, where a shattered rail derailed a GNER service and resulted in four passengers being killed, would further shape the direction of the industry and the Inspectorate as it entered the new millennium.

1990-2000 was also a time of intense activity on the development of light rail as the second generation of UK tramways came along. DfT had, over time, gradually and understandably removed tramcar and trolleybus provisions from the Road Traffic and Road Traffic Regulation Acts. London had seen its last tram run as long ago as 1952 and the last city tramway in the UK had been in Glasgow, where 'the caurs' ran for the last time in 1962. Only Blackpool's promenade tramway (the resort's so-called 'inland routes" had all closed and been replaced by buses) had survived as something of an isolated and unique tourism curiosity, until the late 20th century light rail revolution of the 1980s/90s. When HMRI looked into this during the approval of Manchester Metrolink, it realised that it had rendered the operation of the tramway at Blackpool potentially illegal, as the tramcar exemptions had been removed. Furthermore, the system then actually under construction at Manchester could also not be brought into use! Fortunately, HMRI was still part of DfT when the approving inspector, Major Holden and Geoffrey Claydon from DfT's legal department (who also had knowledge of tramways, set about drafting the "Tramcars and Trolley Vehicles (Modification of Enactments) Regulations" which came into force on July 1 1992. The timing meant that in the strict legal sense Manchester Metrolink had operated unlawfully for about one week!

Following the introduction of short sections of street tramway in Manchester, the next tramway construction in Sheffield was mainly a street-running operation. Putting a tramway through Sheffield's suburban streets, given the road traffic conditions of the 1990s, was a major (and costly) challenge and the Inspectorate had to engage heavily with the highway authority, police traffic division and DfT to ensure safe integration of the new trams. It was a question of relearning, a half century later, the long-forgotten lessons of new tramway operation, because the last new tramway overseen by the Inspectorate had been the Belle Isle extension of the Leeds tramway, as long ago as 1949!

Chapter 10

Crashes of the late 1990s & early 2000s

The second half of the decade following UK rail privatisation of the 1990s, shaped primarily by the 1993 Railways Act, was regrettably also marked by a series of serious and tragically fatal train accidents. These produced a combined total of 42 fatalities (Southall, seven; Ladbroke Grove, 31; Hatfield, four) and they had a highly significant effect on the future, culture and even the eventual home of the Railway Inspectorate created in 1840, with George Stephenson's encouragement.

In 1990, following public inquiries held into the King's Cross Tube station fire (November 18 1987) and the Clapham fatal multiple collision (December 12 1988) the Railway Inspectorate's 27 inspectors had been transferred from the Department of Transport to the Health & Safety Executive (HSE). This transfer was intended to lead to greater emphasis on risk assessment and the implementation of a modern safety case regime. The idea was that these rail safety cases would be comparable with those in which HSE was already widely experienced in the country's major hazard industries (oil, gas and chemicals) although despite this intent it was not for another four years that the RI would become responsible for railway safety case acceptance.

It was anticipated that being part of HSE would give HMRI's railway inspectors greater ease of access to the wide range of technical disciplines and resources necessary for this fundamental shift of approach. HSE was seen as a safety regulator with a clear and proven record of enforcement and the move to HSE was underpinned by a ministerial determination that HMRI (which had not previously followed this approach) should in future behave in a similar, much more assertive and legalistic fashion.

While traditional approvals work continued, early Railway Inspectorate work within HSE brought modern risk assessment into play for the first time on the railway, to address some long-standing issues. The highest profile safety issue of the day was the uninitiated and unexpected opening of slam doors on moving trains, which had led to a number of fatalities when passengers fell out onto the track. Following this investigation, rolling stock was progressively fitted with central door locking (CDL) and these door-opening accidents gradually ceased as a direct consequence. There had, incidentally, been some peculiar press coverage around these incidents, with hints that some inexplicable 'X Files' type strange forces might be at work! The truth out there, was discovered to be much more prosaic and practical and the problem was controlled and then eliminated.

Relatively soon after the move to HSE, the 1993 Railways Act set the scene and 'rolled the pitch' for rail privatisation, which came into law on

Above: Railways developed rapidly in the early 19th century, principally in north east England, for transporting minerals hewn from the earth. This was first by horse, from mine to staithe and then, from the mid-1820s, by steam locomotives developed by Timothy Hackworth and then father and son George and Robert Stephenson. The great leaps forward were George's *Locomotion* for the Stockton & Darlington Railway, in 1825, and more particularly with son Robert's *Rocket*, for the Liverpool & Manchester Railway, in 1830. After this, railways covered the entire country within 20 years, leading to establishment of the Railway Inspectorate, at George Stephenson's instigation, in 1840. Coal carrying is now largely a traffic of the past - but aggregates continue to thrive and there's a direct line of descent from the unbraked four-wheel wooden chaldrons of the early days (see page 16) to these 100-ton capacity, air-braked bogie hoppers carrying limestone quarried in the Peak District. This was the very busy scene at Peak Forest on September 8 2006, with an English Welsh & Scottish Railway Class 60 centre stage. *Gavin Morrison.*

Above: Shortly before 8.45am on Wednesday June 23 1999, the driver of the 8.44am First North Western Crewe-Manchester empty coaching stock (ECS) train ran past four-aspect signal WD12 at danger, on the West Coast Main Line, near Winsford in Cheshire. This is where the four-track main line converges into two running lines. The driver was well aware of his mistake because he had over-run the 294 yards beyond Winsford South Junction, where the down slow line he was running on curved right to trail into the down fast main line. He then 'ran through' the trailing point (set against him) and came to rest blocking the down fast. The FNW driver immediately made an emergency radio call to stop all traffic. The emergency message was promptly made and in any case, the 'run through' would have turned signal WD13, red on the down fast - but it was already too late. The 6.30am Virgin Trains Euston-Glasgow express, led by Class 87 electric No. 87027, hauling eight Mk 3 carriages and a Driving Van Trailer (DVT) had already passed WD13 - it suddenly turned red as Driver Eccles approached it on the 110mph line - and despite an immediate emergency brake application his express rapidly closed on the stationary pair of two-car Class 142 'Pacers' blocking his line, with their brakes on hard. He collided with them at around 50mph at 8.45am. The high energy impact severely damaged the rear of the '142' and the force was sufficient to break the four 'wire straps' securing the body to the underframe. The body was then propelled forward as the Class 87 over-rode the frame. *Alan Sherratt.*

April 1 1994. At that point, a new company - Railtrack - became both owner and manager of Britain's main line rail infrastructure. British Rail (BR), passed into history after 48 years - and the nationalised railway born on January 1 1948, was no more.

There followed very significant fragmentation of the rail industry, with commercial contracts awarded to a wide spectrum of private companies for track maintenance, combined with the award of passenger franchises for the operation of passenger trains and stations, also the leasing and maintenance of passenger rolling stock. The freight businesses were sold outright.

Nineteen months later, Great Western Trains (GWT) acquired its train operating franchise on April 1 1996, having already become a separate operating 'train operating unit' (TOU) within BR, when Railtrack was established. The fatal Southall accident on the Great Western Main Line (GWML) occurred barely 18 months later, on September 19 1997. Seven people were killed in the very high speed collision between a London-bound InterCity 125 HST and a westbound loaded stone train crossing its path. Just over two years later, on October 5 1999, the Ladbroke Grove collision - also on the GWML - caused the deaths of 31 passengers (many in a very severe buffet car fire) after a 140mph closing speed head-on collision between an IC125 and a Thames Trains DMU, which had passed a signal at danger, leaving Paddington. These terrible incidents triggered an enormous and understandable media, political and public outcry from which emerged a fundamental review of the role and resourcing of HMRI.

Southall: September 18 1997

At about 1.15pm on September 19 1997, the 10.32am Great Western Trains Swansea to Paddington High Speed Train (commonly known as an Intercity 125) collided at speed with a stone train crossing its path at Southall. The high energy collision and derailment killed seven passengers and caused many injuries.

The English Welsh & Scottish Railway (EWS) freight train should have been protected, as it crossed the up and down main lines (from Acton yard), by colour light signal (SN254) which was correctly displaying a red 'stop' aspect, properly showing to Driver Larry Harrison on the London-bound HST. Thus, signal SN254 was at red, SN270, 1,530m before it was at a cautionary yellow, to warn Harrison that the next signal was at red and that he must prepare to stop, whilst SN280, 1,056m before this, had in turn been properly at double-yellow to indicate that SN270 ahead was a single yellow aspect. Driver Harrison failed to react to both cautionary and the subsequent red signal - with the terrible consequence that his HST crashed into the EWS freight across his path, at a speed of around 80mph.

Professor John Uff's QC's inquiry into this fatal Southall collision laid bare a shocking catalogue of rail industry failures.

For example, Uff revealed a lack of coherent thinking about the GW Automatic Train Protection (ATP) system. This was a unique pilot scheme which, if it had been working, would have automatically 'supervised' Harrison's train speed as it approached the red stop signal protecting the freight train movement, thereby preventing it reaching a conflict point. It would have progressively reduced his speed at the two cautionary yellow signals and then stopped his train at the red. Should ATP have been regarded by GWT as an absolute requirement for running trains on the route, or was it simply a drivers' aid which was therefore optional?

The HST involved in the accident had been scheduled to run with functioning ATP protection - but it was not switched on because

Above: At around 1.15pm on September 19 1997, the 10.32am Great Western Trains HST from Swansea, passed signal SN254 at danger, approaching Southall, running at 125mph. Driver Larry Harrison had disregarded two previous caution signals (SN280/70) and collided at around 80mph with a train of 20 empty stone hoppers strung across his path, running in the opposite direction, at 15-20mph. He was due at Paddington five minutes later. Seven passengers died and there were 139 injuries. This is the leading power car (in which neither AWS nor ATP was operational) pictured from towards the top left corner of the diagram opposite. There was much controversy as to crossing a freight train in front of an approaching 125mph express. The truth was that, even before privatisation, with 12 such movements every day, BR had used the introduction of faster freight trains and the introduction of Automatic Route Setting (ARS) to regulate these conflicting movements so as to minimise overall delay, in preference to always giving priority to expresses, which had led to freights sometimes waiting for hours for clear routes. In answer to another controversy of the day, Sir John Uff's Public Inquiry Report also concluded that there was no evidence of signallers putting commercial considerations ahead of safety. *RAIL*.

Left: There were 24 passenger injuries at Winsford (four of them serious) and three railway staff were hurt aboard the express. After the crash, Virgin Driver Roy Eccles, 56, picked himself up from the cab floor and jumped 11ft from his cab to the ground, severely injuring his ankle, but he nevertheless 'went back' to help passengers and secure the line. Eccles was as a result the winner of the first Outstanding Personal Contribution Award at the inaugural National Rail Awards, in 2000. He impressed judges with his simply expressed courage: "I made that emergency brake application and then lay down on the cab floor and waited to die," he told them.

Driver Harrison - in common with others working for GWT - was not qualified and certified to drive with ATP in operation. This would be inconceivable and unacceptable today but it's an illustration of the operating culture in force in the late 20th century on a high speed main line.

The Railway Inspectorate itself (HM Railway Inspectorate, as it had become within HSE since 1990) was also the subject of some stinging criticism in Professor Uff's report (together with other players) for this lack of clarity about what ATP was actually for and whether it should function on all trains. BR had also fitted a second pilot ATP system on the GW main line from 1989. The Chiltern lines also had a non-standard pilot ATP system installed in 1990, based on the German LZB technology and this was still operational in 2019.

Said Uff: "The delay which occurred [in introducing ATP] can be explained but not excused. GWT bear a major responsibility for the delays, but the actions of BR, Railtrack and HMRI all played their part ... and the absence of any co-ordinating system or authority was pivotal. It can now be seen with clarity that the effect of privatisation was to leave no-one in the driving seat. In retrospect, it was inevitable that the ATP pilot project should be brought into full service. It is a matter of the greatest regret that the Southall collision had to be the catalyst that finally brought this about".

More damning still for GWT was the relatively common accepted operating practice in 1997 of running GW expresses at 125mph with the Automatic Warning System (AWS) isolated and not working. AWS alerts drivers by sounding a horn and displaying a visual warning to the driver on the approach to a cautionary (yellow) signal or a signal at danger (red). This warning must be acknowledged by the driver, who must quickly press the reset button. If the driver fails to acknowledge this warning within three seconds then the train brakes are automatically applied. If the approaching signal is clear, a bell rings to give the driver audible confirmation of the clear road ahead past the next signal. To set the importance of AWS in context, on a high speed main line there is usually a signal every 1,500m so at 125mph, so the warning horns (or 'all clear' bells) come in rapid succession... about every 30 seconds. Operational AWS is crucial to not merely to assist but to actually ensure, a driver's concentration. But on that day in 1997, Larry Harrison had neither AWS nor ATP to help him. He had not been trained on ATP and the AWS had failed. It's inconceivable now, but the safe working of his 125mph express relied on his vigilance and eyesight alone.

AWS on the Southall HST had been isolated because of a fault and was not operating, either on arrival or departure from Swansea, and also at the time of the accident. Yet Driver Tunnock's report earlier in the day to the GWT Control Centre that the AWS was unserviceable had resulted in no action being taken to mitigate the risk of the driver 'missing' a cautionary or danger signal whilst in charge of this 125mph express.

As a result of Southall, on September 30 1997, HM Deputy Chief Inspector of Railways, Vic Coleman, wrote to all Train Operating Companies (TOCs) and also Railtrack, highlighting rules that were already in existence covering AWS isolation. These rules - which had not been enforced that day - made clear HMRI's interpretation that trains should not commence their journey without operational AWS and that every effort should be made to replace a train which was defective in this respect, should a fault develop during the journey.

Professor Uff did not, however, share HMRI's view that the meaning of these rules was clear. At the inquiry, Coleman, by then Chief Inspector of Railways, had given oral evidence in support of HMRI's actions following the Southall accident. His conclusions were not accepted by Uff's inquiry.

"It was suggested to Mr Coleman that the ambiguity in the Rules was apparent to all parties, yet neither HMRI nor Railtrack had thought it appropriate to change or clarify the Rules"

Uff's report also pointed out that the inquiry inspector in the fatal Cowden rail collision (three years before) of October 15 1994 (see pages 132-134) had recommended strengthening AWS fault-reporting procedures for drivers. It was also suggested that although the rules had been known and understood for some time to be ambiguous, HMRI had reacted and addressed this ambiguity only in the aftermath of the fatal Southall collision.

Professor Uff noted that AWS was not classed as being essential to the continued running of trains by the rail industry's own inquiry into the Southall collision and he pointed out that neither did that inquiry lead the rail industry to produce any "clear and generally accepted interpretation" of the Rules. It was damning all round for the railway.

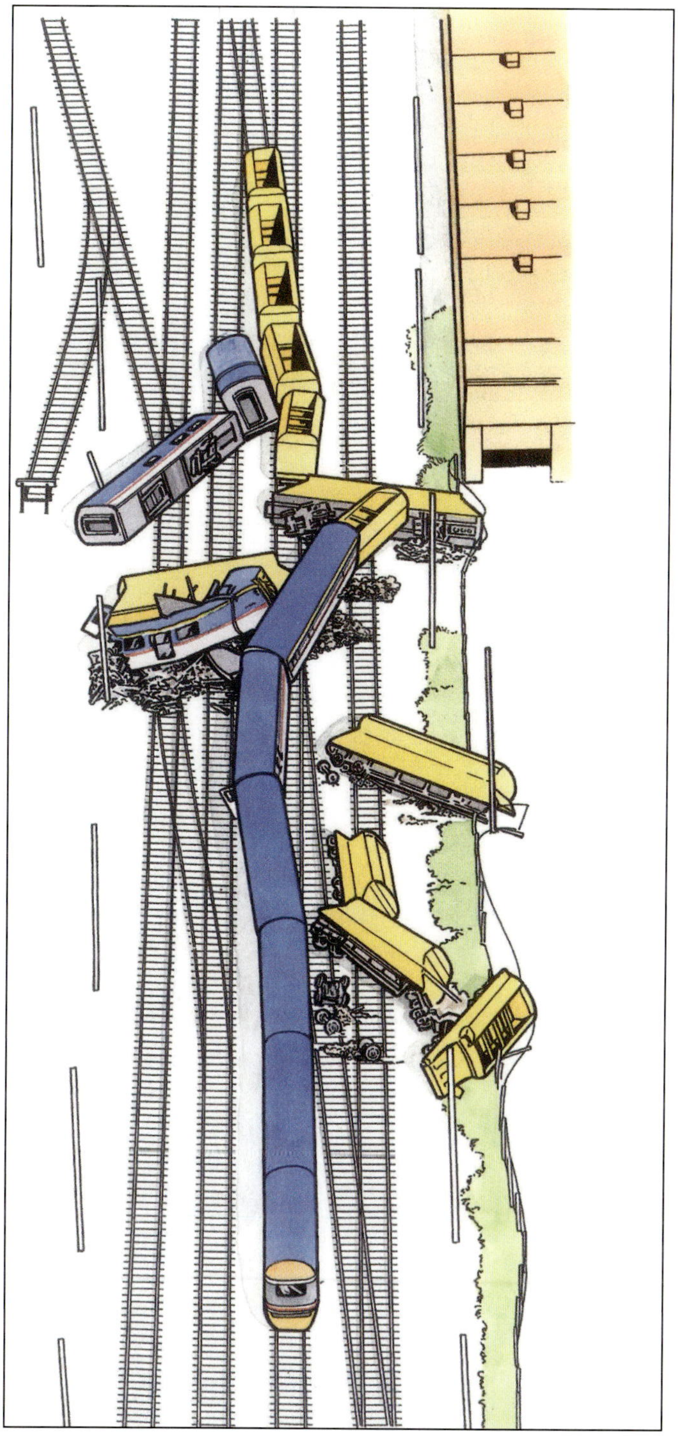

Above: The graphic produced by *RAIL* magazine at the time as part of its news reporting of the Southall crash. Leading power car No. 43173 (alongside the fourth yellow hopper) made glancing contact first with the seventh hopper and progressively with those following, which quickly derailed as the HST impacted at high speed. Class 59 No. 59101 freight driver Bricker, heading for Southall yard, knew instantly that a collision with his train was inevitable when Harrison's HST tore towards him, dust flying from its wheels under full braking. Instinctively, he applied power to try and clear his train from Harrison's path and whilst this was both professional and commendable, it was futile. Harrison had passed signal SN254 at red at 125mph, barely a mile from impact. He therefore needed well over a mile to stop: his fate - and that of the seven passengers who died after the 80mph collision - was sealed in that moment. *RAIL*

While Coleman had reiterated to the Uff inquiry that AWS was an extremely important safety system, Professor Uff retorted in his report that:

"No risk assessment had ever been carried out on the consequences of running with AWS isolated. After the Southall crash, no-one was to be heard justifying the decision to allow service 1A47 to run normally between Swansea and Paddington with its AWS isolated. Yet with very few exceptions, such concerns were not being expressed before the

Above: Air pipes on the derailing stone hoppers at Southall were severed, applying the brakes and bringing the English Welsh & Scottish Railway train to a rapid halt - which made matters even worse for the HST. The third Mk 3 (Coach G) became detached and lost much of its right side in its high speed sidelong impact with the hoppers. Reconstruction indicated that hopper No. 19891 collided with an overhead line stanchion and reared up, trapping the leading end of Coach G, which then wedged beneath it. Still travelling at speed, the Mk 3's monocoque structural strength had been destroyed when its right side had been largely torn away and it thereafter suffered this horrific distortion, when it was virtually bent double into a U shape after being struck from the rear by Coach F. *RAIL*.

accident. This demonstrates both the spread of opinion that existed and the ambiguity within the Rules"

At the end of the second week of the Southall Inquiry, on September 30 1999, proceedings were adjourned at the request of passenger groups who required more reading time.

Ladbroke Grove

Within a week of this adjournment being granted, the very high speed head-on passenger train collision at Ladbroke Grove occurred, on October 5, in West London - not only on the very same main line as the Southall collision, but also relatively close by. (see also page 140) The two crash sites were just seven miles apart. Tragically, 30 people died in the accident itself, with 160 more injured, some critically. Another person died shortly afterwards, bringing the death toll to 31.

The October 5 1999 collision at Ladbroke Grove was caused when a Class 165 Thames Trains 'Turbo' DMU passed signal SN109 at danger after leaving Paddington station. The train continued to accelerate for about 700m past the red gantry signal before colliding head-on with an inbound High Speed Train operated by First Great Western, the successor to Great Western Trains, running at line speed. Closing speed in the horrific head-on impact was estimated at around 140mph. The IC125 was driven by veteran footplateman Brian Cooper, 56, whilst the 'Turbo' was driven by a very new driver Michael Hodder, who had been qualified for just 13 days. This was only his tenth turn of duty.

It rapidly emerged that Signal SN109 was a multi-SPAD signal, having been passed at danger no fewer than seven times in the preceding five years. In particular, there was an almost identical incident on February 4 1998 when Driver Bunney of FGW driving an eight-coach HST passed SN109 at danger at 60mph. He saw six red signals on a gantry across the tracks ahead of him - including SN109 - but he had mistakenly concluded that the flashing yellows at the preceding signal meant he had a clear route. Driver Bunney managed to stop his HST just before the fouling point and thereby avoided a certain collision with a Heathrow Express train. The industry inquiry into this SPAD concluded that the signalling was confusing and effectively a driver's SPAD trap. Established procedures to respond to such incidents and introduce improvements were not followed quickly enough by Railtrack and follow-up by HMRI was equally slow and ineffective.

The Ladbroke Grove head-on collision happened between the then-Eurostar (now Hitachi) North Pole train depot on the south side of the main line and a brick retaining wall to the north, next to a Sainsbury's supermarket. The store car park and its elevated position combined with the West London location close to TV studios to ensure there was round-the-clock, very dramatic media coverage which became febrile in tone - public alarm was understandably intense. Mistakes were made by police, who cranked up the public and media alarm even more at one point by estimating deaths in the hundreds - based on nothing more than a finger-in-the-air guess, solely looking at the numbers of cars parked at stations down the line towards Bristol. This pushed public anxiety, political sensitivity and damning media coverage to yet higher levels of anger and emotional rawness. The railway - and Railtrack in particular - were very much 'in the dock'.

Inevitably, fuelled by political panic, media furore and public anger, a public Inquiry into this disaster was immediately announced by the Health & Safety Commission. This was to be chaired by Lord Cullen with a separate technical report on railway safety systems to be prepared by Sir David Davies, President of the Royal Academy of Engineering. Cullen was chosen as an experienced and steadying pair of hands. He had previously chaired the public inquiry into the horrific explosion and destruction by fire of the Piper Alpha oil production platform in the North Sea, on July 6 1988, when 167 of the 229 people on board the rig at the time died, in just 22 minutes.

In 1996, Cullen had also led the inquiry into the school massacre at Dunblane Primary School on March 13 1996, when gunman Thomas

Hamilton shot dead 16 children and one teacher, before killing himself. Now Cullen was charged with inquiring into the 31 deaths in buffet car H, on the stricken GW IC125 at Ladbroke Grove

Although the terms of reference for Cullen's Inquiry were focused on SPAD prevention and protection, the role and function of the railway inspectorate itself was once again inevitably very much under scrutiny. Part 2 of Lord Cullen's Inquiry report was to focus on the management of safety and the railway's safety regulatory regime.

Deputy Prime Minister John Prescott became personally involved and convened a 'rail summit', in London, to discuss the Ladbroke Grove collision and actions being taken as a consequence. Naturally, this led to continued high profile media coverage and more highly critical headlines. Clearly, political involvement at this level reflected the understandably very high levels of public concern. Prescott pressed for a monthly analysis of Signals Passed at Danger, which was implemented and published from November 1999. The railway acronym 'SPAD' entered the wider public and media vocabulary.

On October 29 1999, HSE issued its second interim report into the accident, listing actions to be taken or which were in hand following the Ladbroke Grove collision, including enforcement by HMRI and other initiatives to bear down on SPAD risk.

HMRI served improvement notices in respect of safety briefing procedures on two Train Operating Companies. HMRI also expressed concern at the poor standard of briefing offered to safety-critical staff, including drivers, and was "urgently considering" whether further notices should be served on other TOCs. HMRI therefore served three enforcement notices on Railtrack on October 8 1999, relating to specific hazards identified in the accident investigation. These were:

(i) An Improvement Notice requiring Railtrack to install additional controls at the 22 signals which Railtrack's own analyses identified as leading to the greatest number of SPADs (because they had been responsible for five or more SPADs), or that Railtrack devise another, agreed means of securing an equivalent or higher standard of safety;

(ii) An Improvement Notice requiring Railtrack to produce a timebound plan for developing a means to reduce the risk to all remaining signals with a recent history of repeated SPADs;

(iii) A notice prohibiting the use of signal SN109, which Thames Turbo Driver Michael Hodder had accelerated past at danger, until Railtrack provided effective means for preventing further SPADs at this multi-SPAD signal.

Railtrack formally appealed against all three Improvement Notices. The appeal against the Prohibition Notice was heard on November 30 and December 13/14 1999. Hugh Carlisle QC represented HSE, while Roger Henderson spoke for Railtrack.

Railtrack's appeal against the first Improvement Notice relating to 22 multiple-SPAD signals (including SN109), was heard on March 20 2000. Railtrack's appeal was dismissed although the Tribunal modified the Notice and extended the date for compliance to May 22 2000. Railtrack

CONTINUED ON PAGE 152

Above: The glancing but severe initial impact of the GWT HST with the seventh hopper neatly sliced the entire side from Larry Harrison's power car, No. 43173. The junction occupied by the stone hoppers had been properly protected by three successive signals: SN280 at double yellow when Harrison (who took the train over at Cardiff) passed it; SN270 at yellow and finally SN254 at red. All were adequately visible in good light and working perfectly; no faults were found. The ATP, although operable, was isolated because Harrison was not certified to use it; the faulty AWS was also isolated. When Harrison, who had never driven without AWS, saw that a high speed crash was just seconds away, he retreated into the engine room corridor - on the far side of the leading end of this power car. He emerged severely shaken and shocked, but substantially uninjured. At 125mph, the HST covered the distance between signals SN280 (double yellow) and SN270 (single yellow) in around 18 seconds: "The matter which stands out from the available evidence is Driver Harrison's inability to offer any proper explanation for his failure to respond to signals SN280 or SN270," said Uff. "His account of putting things into his bag could not have accounted for more than a few seconds. It is possible this could have been the reason for missing one of the signals, but not both." *RAIL.*

EXTRACT FROM RECORDING OF DRIVER LARRY HARRISON'S CONVERSATION WITH THE SIGNALMAN AFTER THE SOUTHALL CRASH, ON SEPTEMBER 19 1997

SIGNALLER: What train were you driving?
LH: The HST.
SIGNALLER: You were driving the HST?
LH: Yeah, I've got the head code. Hang on, I've got to go in my pocket, hang on, hang on - that's One Alpha Forty Seven.
SIGNALLER: One Alpha Forty Seven. Right, and you're at a stand and you're ringing from SN51. Driver, are you okay?
LH: I'm okay, yeah, I was just putting me stuff away in the bag... the A... the A... the AWS has been isolated because some... some brake problem I believe, so I had no AWS so, I put me stuff in the bag and the next thing I knew, I was coming up against red, up, such coming through... through.
SIGNALLER: Through Southall station?
LH: Through Southall, yeah.
SIGNALLER: Right, I see Driver, can you bear with us one moment? That's the driver of the train, have a word with him. Yeah, S251 is the nearest signal he could get to ... Hello driver?
LH: Hello.
SIGNALLER: Hello Driver
LH: Hello there.
SIGNALLER: Hello mate. Are you...were you the driver on One A Forty Seven?
LH: One Alpha Forty Seven, yes.
SIGNALLER: Right. Er....
LH: AWS is isolated.
SIGNALLER: Right.
LH: And I was just putting me stuff away in the bag, like I would normally do, you see.
SIGNALLER: Right.
LH: And, er, all of a sudden I was whizzing through Hayes with a red at Southall.

Driver Larry Harrison confessed to packing his bag but claimed this was only for a few seconds and Uff regarded suggestions that he had used his bag to weigh down the Driver Vigilance Device as impossible to prove. "I conclude that there is no credible evidence to support the suggestion that Driver Harrison was misusing his bag in a manner that might have contributed to the accident. The allegation is of such a damaging nature that in the absence of clear evidence it should be firmly rejected." Uff also said: "As for Driver Harrison, he showed somewhat grudging remorse in the witness box. I put this down to having borne, for more than 18 months, the burden of criminal charges with the possibility of imprisonment, if convicted. I prefer to recall Driver Harrison's more frank and open expressions of grief and shock at the time, as a more fitting response to the terrible accident he had caused." Harrison was charged with seven counts of manslaughter on April 17 1998 and released on bail: these charges were all dropped on July 2 1999 and the judge directed that he be found not guilty. The final hearing against GWT went ahead on July 27 1999 and resulted in a fine of £1.5m.

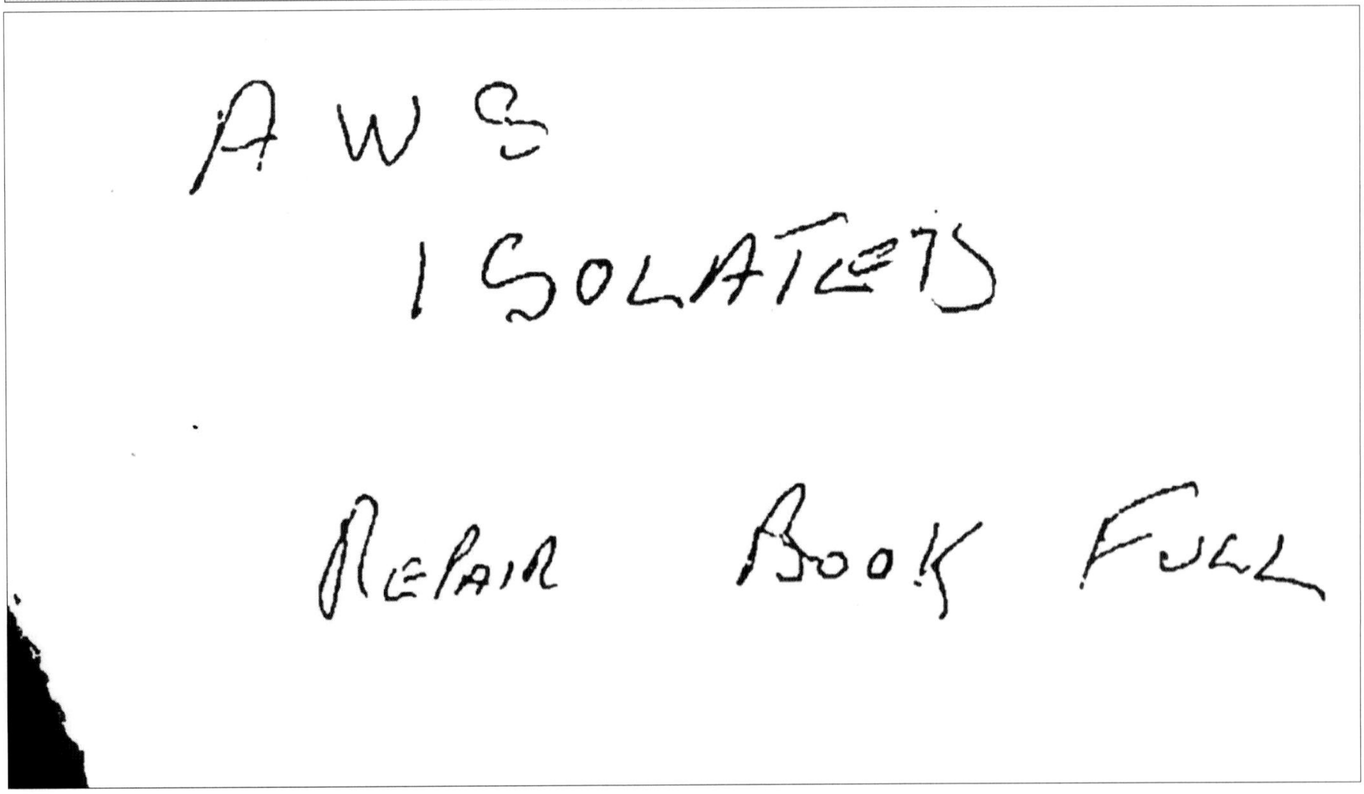

Above: Driver Tunnock, who earlier in the day had repeatedly tried to get 43173's faulty AWS attended to by fitters from the moment he discovered the failure at Paddington that morning, was at pains to ensure that Larry Harrison was aware of the problem, when he took over at Cardiff. The fault reporting book was full and so Tunnock left this handwritten note prominently on the control desk. Uff was extremely critical of not only GWT's fault reporting, but also its maintenance practices at Old Oak Common depot, engineering resources and communications. Driver James Tunnock had reported the faulty AWS repeatedly since taking the HST over at Paddington that morning but his messages were either lost or not passed on by GWT Controllers at Swindon. This was the first major rail accident to occur on the national network following privatisation, which was formally launched with the transfer of all infrastructure to Railtrack on April 1 1994. GWT won its franchise on February 1 1996 and had been operating as a private TOC for just 19 months when this accident happened. Professor John Uff QC FREng, who chaired the Public Inquiry, made clear his view that it would be "wrong to see the Inquiry and this report as an inquiry into privatisation."

Above: Looking west over the Ladbroke Grove crash site, two miles from Paddington, alongside the North Pole depot (left), then the home of Eurostar - as indicated by the two spare cabs at the top of the picture. The FGW HST, driven by the highly experienced Brian Cooper was running towards the camera at 81-84mph while the three-car Thames Turbo DMU, driven by newly passed-out Driver Michael Hodder - who qualified just 13 days before the accident - was running towards the top of the picture at around 50mph. The burned out Buffet Coach H is lower left on the trackside. The compression and then catastrophic failure of the leading HST power car fuel tank released an 'aerosol' of six tonnes of atomised diesel spray which ignited the fireball which destroyed Coach H. The crash happened at 8.11am on October 5 1999, after Hodder's Class 165, bound for Bedwyn, passed SN109 at danger, just three minutes after leaving Paddington, 700m before the impact, which was virtually head-on. There were 31 deaths, including Drivers Cooper and Hodder. Seven died on the HST and 24 from the '165', with a further 227 taken to hospital. 296 were treated on site for minor injuries. The bodyside panel on the HST Mk 3 roof is virtually all that remained of the Turbo leading car. *RAIL.*

Above: One of the '165' coaches was so comprehensively destroyed in the 130mph closing speed impact that a torn-off body side fragment was left draped over the roof of the seventh of the HSTs Mk 3 carriages. This view is from Eurostar's North Pole depot. The aluminium-bodied '165' suffered far greater damage than the monocoque-bodied steel Mk IIIs in the HST in this very high energy crash. The point of impact was around 3,173m from Paddington and the leading HST power car travelled approximately 90m from the point of impact. Hodder had been recruited by Thames Trains on February 1 1999 and had made 111 departures from Paddington and had successfully stopped at red signals on 109 occasions. He had been passed out on September 22 and had completed just nine shifts as a qualified driver by the day of the crash. *RAIL*

Above: FGW Driver Brian Cooper, 56, who was in charge of the inbound HST involved in the Ladbroke Grove collision. Cooper was a veteran footplateman who had driven this train only from Reading that day, which was unusual - it would normally have been a Bristol driver, from Cheltenham. There was disruption that day however, and as a Paddington driver, Brian Cooper was sent to Reading to work the HST into London.

CONTINUED FROM PAGE 149

Railtrack immediately requested the Tribunal to review its decision but the Tribunal dismissed Railtrack's application.

HMRI reported that SN109 was one of many signals that should be fitted with a protection system, such as Train Protection Warning System (TPWS), by December 31 2003, by virtue of the Railway Safety Regulations 1999. Furthermore, HSE concluded that the accident would in all likelihood have been prevented by TPWS.

Ultimately, the HSE investigation formally concluded that SN109 was one of the 22 signals most frequently passed at danger on the entire Railtrack network. Signal sighting of SN109 by drivers (who had to spot it under a low road bridge, tucked amidst the OLE) was found to present "an exceptionally difficult signal reading task" and further that the signalling in the Paddington area did not comply with relevant industry standards.

Because of the constraints of low overbridges on the approaches to Paddington, the recently installed 25kV overhead lines were very low and their support structures had consequently compromised signal sighting. As a result, SN109 in particular was of a rather strange non-standard design with one aspect positioned off to one side of the other three, in an odd reverse L-shaped configuration. There were also concerns about visual 'swamping' of the signal's aspects by very bright sunlight, making them difficult to discern clearly by drivers of approaching trains. With TPWS, of course, this is much less of a problem.

Deputy Prime Minister John Prescott commissioned HSE to review safety management in Railtrack and this commenced on October 21 1999, being completed on November 18 the same year.

Tellingly, the review team was made up of 14 inspectors from across HSE, plus one from the Civil Aviation Authority. HSE staff came from a variety of disciplines and sectors including nuclear, offshore, chemicals, manufacturing, railways and HSE's Operations Unit. This marked a significant move toward the involvement of a wide variety of non-railway inspectors in railway safety auditing. It seemed to anticipate the shift that was to follow, with increasing safety regulation of the railway by inspectors from diverse backgrounds, many of whom had no prior railway career or relevant experience. Although understandable in the highly sensitized

Above: Thames Turbo Class 165 Driver Michael Hodder, who passed SN109 at danger on the day of the accident, causing the 140mph closing speed head-on collision barely a half-mile later. He had undergone a 27-week driver training programme, during which he completed 250 hours of practical accompanied train handling and was assessed as competent on September 22. This was after a formal route knowledge assessment during which, the investigation revealed, he was not asked any questions about the Paddington-Ladbroke Grove section. Hodder's demeanour on the day of the accident had not been considered unusual or abnormal by witnesses and post mortem tests confirmed the absence of both drugs and alcohol. What precisely happened in his cab that morning remains unexplained.

context of the time, this development was ultimately controversial and the subject of criticism because of the perceived lack of a deep understanding of railway operations amongst these non-railway inspectors. To set this in context, after an air crash, it would seem very odd to suggest that the experts of the Civil Aviation Authority and the specialists of the Air Accident Investigation Branch should be supplemented by factory, railway and oil refinery inspectors. Yet this is what was done put as a strategic move, to try and calm the media, political and public furore. These were actually important safety recommendations that set the scene for safety going forward.

Recommendations from this HSE multi-disciplinary audit of Railtrack included items relating to the increased use of risk assessment, incident investigation, monitoring and auditing that could be seen to come straight from HSE's general guidance on safety management in other industries HS(G)65.

HSE further recommended that Railtrack undertake "external benchmarking with other high hazard industries on safety management system documentation, processes and safety culture as an aid to learning and continuous improvement in safety management practice."

Driven by increasing political, public and media pressure, it became clear that the HSE was increasingly seeking to draw parallels with techniques used in high hazard industries, such as chemicals manufacture. As we shall see, this stance caused something of an industry backlash - some of it ill-informed - but driven essentially by concern about so-called 'gold-plating'. This ultimately was to have major implications not only politically, but also specifically for the inspectorate. There's an argument that this was the point at which the campaign to have HMRI moved out of HSE really got under way.

Hatfield

On October 17 2000, even before the conclusion of Part 2 of Lord Cullen's inquiry into safety management and regulation following the Ladbroke Grove disaster, a down Great North Eastern Railway express formed of Class 91 electric No. 91023, hauling a rake of Mk 4 carriages with a Driving Van Trailer (DVT) at its rear, derailed at 115mph on the Welham Curve, just south of Hatfield station in Hertfordshire. The derailment was caused by a rail shattering into more than 300 pieces beneath the train, as a result of rolling contact fatigue (RCF) in the steel - more commonly known as as gauge corner cracking. Four passengers died. Railtrack and maintenance contractor Balfour Beatty had known about these rail defects but successive attempts to replace the rails were not effectively scheduled and they remained in use, until failing catastrophically beneath the wheels of the 12.10pm London King's Cross-Leeds Intercity 225 service.

HSE/HMRI closed the East Coast Main Line for three weeks whilst conducting a highly detailed 'fingertip' investigation on site that critics insisted added precious little to what had been observed and learned in the first few hours of investigation, following the derailment. The evidence of the shattered rail could not, after all, be missed.

The aftermath of Hatfield was as damaging reputationally for the railway as the crash itself had been; it came to be described by the late Sir Alastair Morton, then chairman of the Strategic Rail Authority, as 'an institutional nervous breakdown'. It was a perfect summary, which captured not only the detail of what happened but also the 'feel' of the experience and its impact on the wider industry.

The knock-on effects on the 11,000-mile network were as far-reaching as they were crippling of both train performance and reputation, with hundreds of speed restrictions as low as 20mph in place for many months. This was because 20mph is judged to be the fastest a train is safe to run without it rolling over if it derailed - and those 20mph speeds continued until such time as confidence in the rails could be justified. On one night, very critical national news headlines erupted about the closure of the Anglo-Scottish West Coast Main Line between Gretna Junction, Carlisle and Glasgow, after Railtrack Scotland Director Janette Anderson revealed that ultrasonic rail tests had pinpointed:

Above: A *RAIL* magazine graphic showing the normal sequence of colour light signals (left) and the accompanying Automatic Warning System alerts (right). They are:

GREEN (clear): Continuous bell for several seconds; black screen on AWS instrument.

DOUBLE YELLOW: (caution, next signal single yellow)) - Warning horn; black AWS screen changes to black and yellow 'sunflower'

SINGLE YELLOW: (caution, next signal is at red/danger: Warning horn; black AWS screen changes to black and yellow 'sunflower'

RED: (danger, stop) Warning horn; black AWS screen changes to black and yellow 'sunflower'

For the caution signals, the driver must cancel the audible and visual warnings within two seconds, otherwise the train brakes are applied.

Above: Gantry No. 8, carrying colour light signal SN109 - it is the third from the left and has been photographed on a sunny morning at the same time of day as Hodder passed it at danger. There was much discussion of how bright light from the low rising sun from behind the driver might have 'swamped' the aspect, making it difficult to discern. The gantry was immediately west of the road bridge just off the top of the picture, so the signal heads were of a non-standard 'reverse L' shaped design to assist sighting from a distance, by drivers, beneath the bridge span. SN109 was one of the top 22 signals most frequently 'run by' on the Railtrack network at the time of the crash; it had been passed at danger seven times since February 1995.

"20 locations which require remedial work, including re-railing." This crucial link was closed from Wednesday October 25 until Thursday October 26. This was an especially high profile example, but day after day, news bulletins brimmed with stories about our national network running at a crawl.

The media was full of noisy demands - especially from survivors (and their lawyers) of both the Ladbroke Grove and Southall disasters - for root and branch reform of Railtrack, which was utterly demonised. By implication and association, HMRI as safety regulator was also inevitably heavily criticised.

The Guardian of October 30 2006 reported that outspoken lawyer Louise Christian, of the Southall & Ladbroke Grove Survivors Group, said Railtrack could no longer be trusted after the latest disaster.

She called for a "new, totally independent watchdog to supervise all elements of rail safety."

Christian claimed that prior to the Southall, Ladbroke Grove and Hatfield crashes "the public were not told about the wholly unacceptable risk on the railways"

About Ladbroke Grove, she said: "Railtrack knew that Signal 109 had been passed at danger [the cause of the Paddington crash] and they had meetings to discuss it for over five years.

"They were warned before the Paddington crash that the last thing they should do was to do nothing. There was nothing wrong with the technical expertise given to Railtrack. They simply did nothing.

"We believe that the same failure to act is what caused Hatfield to crash (sic). Railtrack knew of the danger to the travelling public.

"They had meetings about it and were

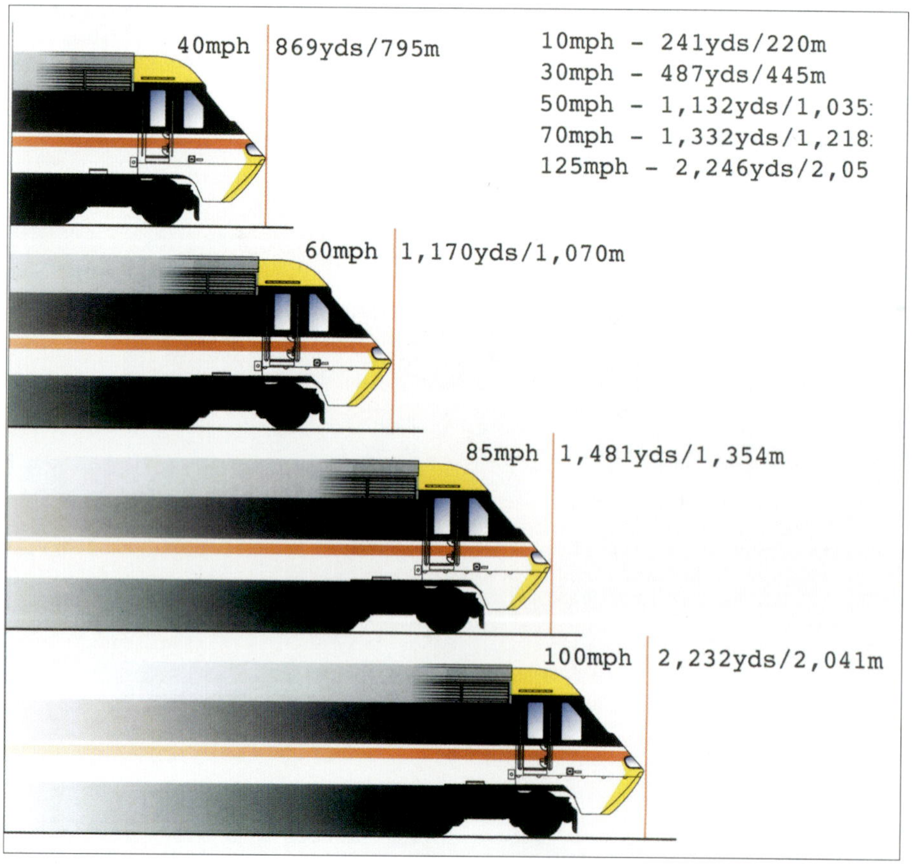

Above: A sobering graphic showing stopping distances for an HST running at various speeds. At the 81-84mph estimated speed of his train, Brian Cooper would have needed roughly three quarters of a mile to stop. From the point of the 130mph impact, his power car travelled just 90 yards. *RAIL*.

Left: The Public Inquiry into the Ladbroke Grove crash was chaired by Lord Cullen, who had previously chaired public inquiries into both the Clapham rail crash of December 1988 (35 deaths) and the horrific Piper Alpha North Sea oil platform explosion and inferno, which killed 167. Cullen was appointed three days after the crash, on October 8 1999 and his first preliminary hearing was on December 21 1999. Part 1 inquiry hearings began at Central Hall, Westminster on May 10 2000 and ended on September 28. Cullen made 89 recommendations covering support for the bereaved and injured, track and signalling changes, driver management and training, safety auditing, signal sighting, SPAD investigation, signallers instructions, training, briefing and working conditions, radio communications, preservation of data, crashworthiness, fire mitigation and passenger protection, evacuation and escape.

advised about it but they did not act.

"There has been complete secrecy and it's not good enough for them to blame the structure of the industry."

On September 20 2001, the Health & Safety Commission published Part 2 of Lord Cullen's Inquiry into the management of safety and the regulatory regime of the railway industry. Two weeks after its publication, Railtrack was, without warning, put into administration by Secretary of State for Transport Stephen Byers. A last-minute attempt by Rail Regulator Tom Winsor to throw Railtrack a procedural lifeline curiously went ungrasped - and the company was dissolved in October. A single short letter to Winsor requesting a review could have forestalled the process, but the Railtrack Board effectively gave up and allowed itself to be defenestrated.

Cullen was highly critical of the industry and the impact of fragmentation brought about by privatisation. He highlighted:

Above, Left: Back in 1999, the practice of establishing floral tribute shrines at the sites of human tragedies was far less common (or developed in extent) than it is today and so these floral tributes attracted a great deal of media attention at the time. These bouquets were from members of the public and local organisations and were placed against the wall overlooking the railway in the Sainsbury's car park, on the opposite side of the line to the North Pole Eurostar depot. *Nigel Harris.*

Above, Right: Reading the labels on these flowers is always a deeply moving experience. They don't come simpler or more heartbreaking than this. *Nigel Harris.*

- A perceived emphasis on train performance ahead of safety;
- Defensive and insular attitudes hindering the proper identification of underlying causes of accidents or the learning of lessons from them;
- Compartmentalised skills and working, insufficient properly trained and competent personnel;
- Inadequate processes in the award of railway contracts and inadequate controls for contractor management.

He also highlighted a management-by-rules culture with a lack of effective safety leadership and a lack of worker involvement in decision-making. By implication and inference, this was directly critical of HMRI, albeit that Cullen acknowledged that it was not HMRI's duty to manage the railway. Cullen cited HSE's General Issues Report which considered the HMRI's general approach to regulating the rail industry. That report stated:

"HMRI has followed a consensus-seeking approach to dealing with duty holders, with a reluctance to use formal enforcement powers. The 'light touch' approach was derived during a political climate of deregulation and at a time when the true nature of the reorganised industry was still emerging. Such an approach is less appropriate for an industry which is more driven by commercial imperatives and in which levels of co-operation and trust appear to be declining".

Cullen continued:

"There is no doubt that there have been significant deficiencies in the HMRI's performance, as described in their own Internal Inquiry Report and General Issues Report. It is clear that one of the factors has been the shortage of resources. However, there are other deeper causes. There has been a failure to adapt to the changing conditions brought about by the disaggregation of the rail industry and the barriers created by competing commercial interests. The evidence also gave me a strong impression of a difficult relationship with Railtrack, largely due, in my view, to the latter's dominant position."

However, he went on "The deficiencies in the past performance of the HMRI, while significant, do not seem to me to reveal a question of principle as to whether the HSE are the appropriate body to be the safety regulator. Nor do they show that the HMRI are not capable, given adequate resources and effective leadership, of adequately discharging that function as part of the HSE. They have shown a capacity for self-appraisal, and are applying the lessons of past failures. They are reviewing the extent to which they should recommend that a more intrusive and interventionist approach should be taken and, in the light of that, the extent to which they require additional resources and personnel with relevant experience and expertise in regard to the railways. As regards leadership, there is a need for the HMRI to be placed under the direction of a new post, to be filled by a person of outstanding managerial ability, not necessarily with a railway background."

HMRI was presented and therefore perceived as having been on its back foot in dealing with the newly-configured industry - being reactive rather than proactive. It was also exposed as being under-resourced to deal with the weight of extra work presented by the plethora of bodies of which the industry was now constituted and the increased responsibilities of the safety case regime. There had been no coherent response to the numerous SPADs in the Paddington throat in previous years and HMRI had neither approved the signals nor followed up on promises of risk assessment.

Potters Bar

Some six months after the publication of Part 2 of the Cullen report, on May 10 2002, a down EMU commuter train derailed at 100mph on the southern main line approach to Potters Bar station whilst passing over facing points, causing seven deaths - six on the train and an elderly lady passer-by, fatefully in the wrong place at the wrong time, who was struck by falling debris, walking beneath a railway bridge.

It caused many in the industry to do a double-take when the *Guardian* for May 18 2002 reported that the contractor responsible for maintenance of the points, Jarvis, claimed that a sophisticated saboteur with informed engineering knowledge was likely to have deliberately tampered with the points, in order to cause the derailment. According to the *Guardian*:

Kevin Hyde, the company's chief operating officer, said: "These are three acts of commission - three things done deliberately."

He said they were carried out by an "informed" individual: "To have the biggest impact on trains moving through the points, this is probably the most dangerous set of changes which could take place. For that to be random would be difficult to imagine."

This unprecedented and outlandish theory, despite causing lots of damaging headlines, did not gain much traction and ultimately the cause of the Potters Bar derailment was determined to have been the poor installation, maintenance and inspection of the facing points. By Jarvis. This had, in turn caused a stretcher bar securing the switch blades the correct distance apart, to become detached, allowing the fateful train to jump off in the narrowing gap between the point

Inset, Facing Page: Looking north from the road overbridge south of the crash site. The immediate cause of the derailment was the shattering into 300 pieces of the high left hand rail on the super-elevated Welham Curve, owing to multiple and pre-existing fatigue cracks in the worn out steel. HSE concluded that maintenance contractor Balfour Beatty Rail Maintenance Ltd failed to effectively manage rail maintenance and that Railtrack had failed in its oversight and management of BBRML. The life-expired high rail shattered into 300 pieces over roughly 35m; beyond that the rail was intact, although pushed to the left for around 44m, followed by a further shattered length of 54m. This picture shows this damage, with the initial break in the foreground. *Nigel Harris.*

blades: the last bogie derailed at an estimated speed of around 98mph. Jarvis subsequently apologised for its initial allegation of sabotage - but went into administration before any prosecution could take place.

And yet it was not the rail accidents of these years that themselves ultimately led to the removal of HMRI from HSE. Rather, it seems, the final trigger was the industry's - and specialist media, notably *RAIL* magazine's - persistent criticism of HMRI as an out-of-touch regulator, compelled by its HSE masters to impose unnecessary regulatory burdens on an industry it simply did not understand. *RAIL* in particular campaigned relentlessly, claiming repeatedly that HSC/HSE were playing to the crowd and 'grandstanding' for the press and public and constantly seeking to transfer blame - or, as was more commonly said at the time, was guilty of 'covering its backside.' The war of words because increasingly intense, heated and unpleasant.

There was also a persistent grumble (muted from within HMRI but loud and clear in the industry and specialist media) that HSE had, post-Cullen, deployed many inspectors from non-railway backgrounds who were simply not sufficiently familiar with the industry. They were colloquially seen as 'factory inspectors' blundering about in the specialised environment of a railway they did not comprehend. This was also, by the way, an allegation also levelled at the British Transport Police of the day, who had given a very poor account of themselves in their investigations at Southall in particular, where crucial physical evidence was either not collected or was bulldozed into the ballast during clear-up. As with HMRI, BTP has also since reinvented itself and now both are rightly very highly regarded and respected.

The new and inexperienced railway inspectors were largely both unsympathetic to - and dismissive of - the industry's claims that transport is wholly different from other concerns and should not be regulated in the same way.

Industry and rail commentators were quick to highlight the relative safety of travelling by rail compared with road and argued that an intrusive regime was harmful to both industry and the country, and was actually disproportionate to the true risks.

RAIL magazine Managing Editor Nigel Harris had been a particular thorn in the side of the HSC/HSE and through a series of challenging Comment pieces had campaigned hard, articulating his perceived criticisms of HSC/HSE. He insisted consistently that HSE was entirely the wrong home for HMRI. *RAIL's* ongoing criticisms were unexpectedly and suddenly validated in November 2003 when HMRI Director of Rail Safety Alan Osborne, appointed in response to a Cullen post-Ladbroke Grove recommendation for fresh leadership, suddenly resigned after only 12 months, complaining about HSE intransigence, internal politics and the promulgation of costly safety intitiatives. His resignation letter was leaked to the *Economist* and was also reported by the BBC. Osborne's revelations detonated a political explosion which finally caused HSE's ownership of HMRI to implode.

Osborne had effectively 'blown the whistle' on HSE's internal politics and turf wars - giving endorsement to *RAIL's* campaigning, which had incensed the HSE/HSC leadership. Describing HSE/HSC as "grossly inefficient" and "dysfunctional", Osborne made clear his view that this proved that it was not possible to implement Lord Cullen's vision for the Railway Inspectorate.

Tellingly, the BBC news report of Osborne's resignation included the portentous words: "He concluded that the body should lose its responsibility for railway safety... Some ministers are understood to share his concerns about the authority. *The Economist* believes a shake-up may be on the way".

Having resigned on principle, Osborne then further validated *RAIL's* long campaign criticising HSC/HSE in a damning 'whistle blower' interview with *RAIL* Managing Editor Nigel Harris in December 2003 (*RAIL* 476). Harris recalls a number of subsequent high profile confidential ministerial lunch briefings and private conversations where HSC/HSE failings in their stewardship of HMRI were discussed at length and with considerable passion. It gradually became clear to Harris that the Department for Transport - and Secretary of State for Transport Alistair Darling in particular - had finally been persuaded by *RAIL's* long-running argument that HMRI should be freed from the troubled and ineffective grip of the HSC/HSE. Alan Osborne's damaging revelations from within left nowhere for the HSE/HSC to hide.

Above: The Welham Curve at Hatfield, 16.7 miles from King's Cross, where at 12.23pm on October 17 2000, Great North Eastern Railway Class 91 No. 91023, its nine Mk 4 coaches and a Driving Van Trailer (DVT) forming the 12.10pm King's Cross-Leeds train derailed at 115-117mph. A rail known to be long overdue for replacement shattered into 300 pieces beneath the train (see also pages 158-159) a half-mile south of Hatfield station. Four passengers died and more than 70 others suffered injuries; there were 170 passengers and 12 GNER staff aboard. The inset picture shows how the left hand rail did not merely break but shatter, the train wheels reducing the concrete sleepers beneath to rubble. The four fatalities occurred in the buffet car at the rear of the front section of the train. The buckeye at its rear parted in the crash and the rear two Mk 4s and the DVT came to rest a few hundred metres to the rear of the front section of the train. The penultimate Mk 4 rolled to its left and came to rest on its side in the cess. Aerial photographs were taken both by Hertfordshire Police helicopter and an RAF Tornado jet.

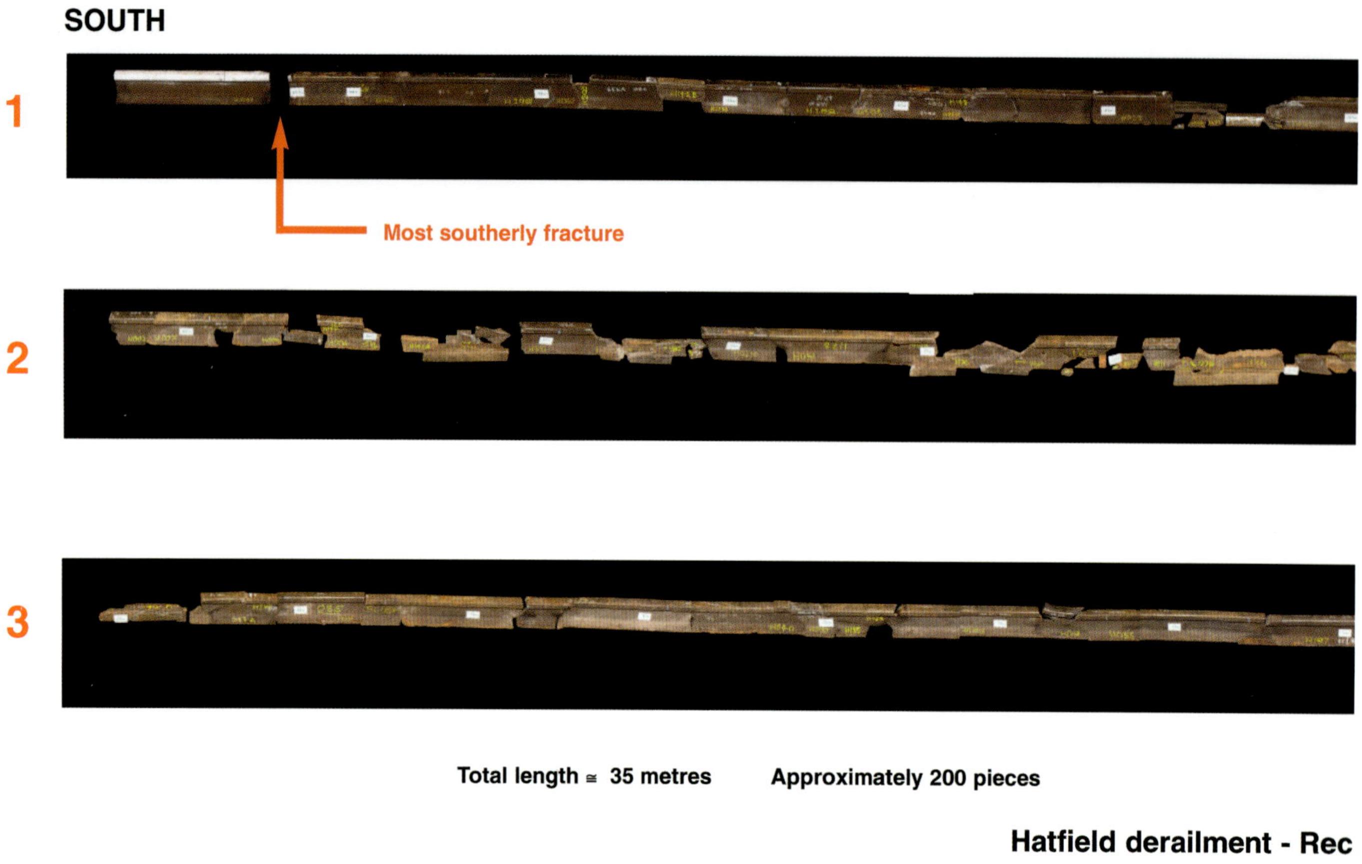

Adrian Shooter was Managing Director of Chiltern Railways at this time and has strong memories of HMRI behaviours under HSE. His words give a snapshot of how train operators experienced HSE railway safety regulation in the 1990s.

"The RI had been run, since the 19th century, by ex-Army officers who understood railways and were quite independent of the railway companies and, later, British Railways.

"I was fortunate in my BR career to accompany such officers on their inspections of yards and depots. They had a no-nonsense, common-sense approach. These former Royal Engineers were equally at home discussing details with ground level staff as they were in standing no nonsense from very senior managers.....as I discovered first-hand several times!

"Transferring RI to HSE might have worked but for the foolish decision to ignore the many years of continuous improvement that had been brought about by BR, often as a result of unseen prodding by RI.

"I clearly remember meeting a new inspector who joined HMRI from the agricultural industry, who proudly told me that she knew nothing about railways - and saw no need to learn. It soon became apparent that this was the culture that HSE was intent on creating. It tended to create unnecessary friction because, whilst the new breed of inspectors were undoubtedly trying their best to encourage the adoption of a more modern safety culture, this was undermined by a very powerful lack of credibility.

"What brought this to a head for me and many colleagues, was a meeting called by HSE at very short notice. Chief Executives and Managing Directors of every train operating and infrastructure company were left in no doubt that, whatever else they were planning that day, they would cancel it and answer this HSE summons.

"We were not impressed when HSE leaders turned up late. We were even less impressed to be subjected to a highly political speech about how appalling it was that the rail industry was now in private hands, when it should be nationalised. I can only describe this as a rant about how we would all be going to prison if we did not buck our ideas up.

"Straight after that meeting, I privately contacted Nigel, who for some time had been conducting a vociferous campaign in *RAIL*, seeking to prise HMRI from HSE's grasp and urged him to push even harder to have HMRI removed from HSE and placed in a new home, where it could build on its much-missed former strengths and make a really positive contribution to improving safety.

"I believe that *RAIL's* vociferous campaign to have HMRI removed from what came across as a politically-driven and very anti-privatisation HSE, stands as a real feather in the cap for both Nigel personally and *RAIL* as a magazine. On his Comment page, Nigel consistently repeated

Above: The East Coast Main Line into King's Cross was closed for three weeks for forensic examinations of the wreckage. This led to a debate about exporting passenger risk to the A1, where the likelihood of loss of life was much higher. One of the of the GNER Mk 4s, complete with its bogies, is lifted from the closed down fast, over the station (left) to a waiting low loader, for removal. *Nigel Harris*

Left to right 0012-095/1-15

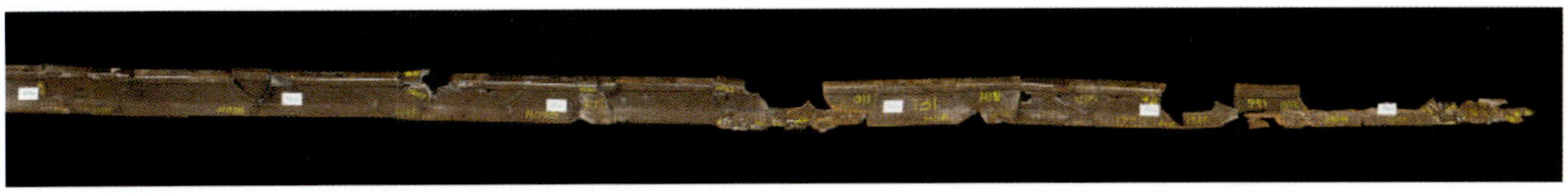

2

Left to right 0012-095/17-32

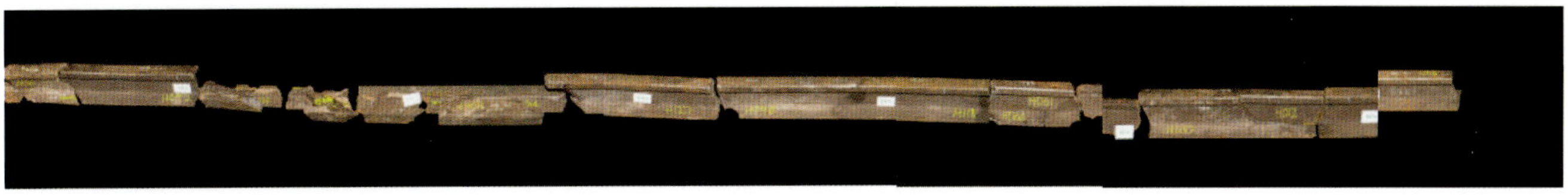

3

Left to right 0012-095/34-48

4

NORTH

econstruction of fractured rail.

Nearly 300 fragments of the shattered rail from Hatfield gathered during forensic investigation at the Welham Curve were 'reconstructed' by specialist investigators at what was then known as the HSE's Health & Safety Laboratory at Buxton. This has since been renamed the HSE Science & Research Centre, who kindly provided this astonishing photograph.

Above: All four fatalities at Hatfield occurred in this buffet car, which rolled onto its left side and whose roof was then peeled back by the vertical sharp edge of the I-section trackside steel catenary mast, as glimpsed on the left.

Above: Potters Bar from the air after the May 10 2002 accident. The last carriage of the non-stop West Anglia Great Northern (WAGN) four-car Class 365/5 25kV electric unit derailed at approximately 12.55pm at a speed of 96.9mph, around 150m south of the station on points No. 2182A (just off the top of this picture). It slewed to its left, partly demolishing the bridge parapet just beyond the platforms and launching the vehicle into the air, slewing it to around 45 degrees from its direction of travel. It then hit the southern ramp of the right hand platform, slewed further and came to rest as seen at right angles to its direction of travel, wedged beneath the canopy. The front three coaches ran on for around a quarter of a mile, notwithstanding full emergency braking, stopping 400m north of the station. Only the rear bogie of the third coach had been derailed, by the extreme force of the fourth carriage splitting the points and veering left. Six passengers died in the train and an elderly lady pedestrian was killed by falling debris as she walked beneath the bridge at the top of the picture. *HMRI/ORR.*

Above: The Potters Bar accident report was produced on March 18 2005 (after a preliminary report published on December 5 2002), not by HMRI but the Railway Safety & Standards Board and the Health & Safety Commission. The fourth coach jammed beneath the platform canopies. The cab end is to the left, the vehicle slewing in an anti-clockwise direction. The end on the right was coupled to the third coach in the train. Damage to the southern platform ramp is clear. The 1245 King's Cross-King's Lynn (1T60) is thought to have been carrying 130-150 passengers. Points No. 2182A had moved under the train as it passed over at speed, running under clear signals. The points were part of a crossover allowing trains stopping at Potters Bar to turn to the left from the down fast to the down slow line. RSSB concluded that the right hand switch rail of 2182A points closed against the stock right (running) rail as the third carriage passed over it. At the same time, the left hand switch was locked against the left stock rail meaning that "a number of wheelsets touched both switch rails simultaneously and were then squeezed into derailment." This happened because the lock stretcher bar, which holds the switch rails in position to ensure a clearance for the wheels whether the points are set for ahead or to the left, fractured at its right hand end. Held to the left under tension, the free end moved to the right once released, towards the stock rail, closing the gap required between them for the wheels to pass safety through. In effect, the point was set for straight ahead running and turning to the left at the same time. *HMRI/ORR.*

very important things that those of us in the industry wholeheartedly agreed with and would very much have liked to have said, but which we could not articulate openly.

"Without *RAIL's* relentless campaigning, I don't believe HMRI would have been moved out of HSE by the Government in the 2004 Rail Review."

Harris had been one of the most frequent and vocal critics of HMRI's treatment and approach under the HSC/HSE umbrella: he had been relentlessly critical of the HSE-driven philosophy and had repeatedly locked horns with its Chairman, Bill Callaghan.

In May 2004, Osborne wrote in *RAIL* magazine 487 criticising HSE under the headline "When safety stifles sense". In his reflections on the report of the Commons Transport Committee and "its message for Alistair Darling's rail review", Osborne stated that one of the few things on which the industry was united was that safety regulation should be taken away from HSE.

"Nearly 90% of industry people at the 2004 National Rail Conference felt that the HSE over the last few years had moved too far away from a cost effective and common sense approach. Just over 80% felt that the credibility of Her Majesty's Railway Inspectorate (HMRI) had been damaged by being part of the HSE over the past 14 years and 84% felt that HMRI should be removed from HSE control."

The foundation of Osborne's argument was that the application of the Health & Safety at Work Act, and in particular its safety case regime, were (as critics inside and outside HMRI had consistently been arguing) inappropriate and overly-burdensome in a transport sector they had never been designed for. His views echoed a pervasive and then persistent media narrative of burdensome and non-sensical (non-railway) health and safety (or as the media frequently mocked at the time, 'elf n 'safety') over-regulation. Osborne stated in his article "Risk averseness…eats away at the very fabric of our society".

Against a photograph of an Anglia Railways Class 86 passing over a foot crossing at Witham in Essex "where clear indication [miniature stop lights] advises pedestrians about the risks and whereabouts of trains" Osborne commented:

"We have to have a common sense approach to safety and the risks involved in being around the railway. Foot crossings, for example, are commonplace even on high speed lines, and if the public is sensible about using them, then accidents are exceptionally rare".

While this and his other comments may have been an industry view, it was not one held by HMRI, especially, in the aftermath of the double fatality of schoolgirls Olivia Bazlinton and Charlotte Thompson at Elsenham station in Essex using precisely such a foot crossing.

Nevertheless, the seeds had been sown in evidence to the Transport Select Committee for the removal of railway safety from HSE, and it seemed likely that Cullen's overall conclusion that railway safety should stay with HSE would not survive ministerial scrutiny.

Following a second highly-critical article in *RAIL* magazine, Osborne's spat with HSE finally boiled over when the HSE sent an unprecedented and rather sour letter to *RAIL* from Timothy Walker, HSE Director General, and Bill Callaghan, Chair of the Health and Safety Commission, in which they roundly condemned (and clearly

Above: Six passengers were ejected through windows in the Potters Bar crash; four died. A number of 40kg balance weights from the overhead 25kV line smashed into the fourth carriage, through broken windows. Four passengers sitting close to these windows all suffered fatal or serious head injuries. Investigation showed that even strengthened laminated glass would not have prevented this, given the energy involved in a 100mph impact with a 40kg weight. The driver reported that as he approached Potters Bar at nearly 100mph he felt a series of increasingly severe jolts after which all panel lights went out and there was an unsolicited full brake application, caused when the fourth coach broke free, rupturing the air brake system. No brake application was made by the driver, who had cut traction power as the jolts became serious. Damage to track triggered various alarms in the PSB (power signal box) at King's Cross and the signaller put all signals to danger to protect the area. *HMRI/ORR.*

Above: Looking south from the platform end on which the fourth derailed coach slewed around at right angles to the track, after being launched into the air when it collided with the damaged bridge parapets seen here. Falling debris from this impact killed the elderly lady who happened to be walking beneath. Points 2082A on which the adjustable stretcher bar securing the point blades failed and derailed the train are being examined by the investigators wearing HV. Note the kink immediately this side of the point, caused by the force of the derailment. Interviews with signalling maintenance staff revealed they had received no training specifically relating to adjustable stretcher bars, either before or after privatisation. The RSSB report was especially critical of the methods used to secure the positioning and locking of the main nuts on the stretcher bar which held the point blades in their correct position. *HMRI/ORR.*

Above: The aftermath of the very high energy, 142mph closing speed head-on collision of a GNER express and a coal train, at Heck (Selby) 11½ miles north of Doncaster, on Wednesday February 28 2001. Ten people died - including both drivers and two train crew - and a further 82 were injured, many seriously. An up Great North Eastern Railway express, derailed at 120mph-125mph after a collision with a Land Rover and trailer which had crashed off the M62 and came to rest obstructing the East Coast Main Line, collided with a northbound Freightliner coal train, just south of the Pollington Road overbridge (No. EC2/7) 167.18 miles from King's Cross. The Freightliner Class 66 (hauling 6G4, the 5.00am Immingham-Ferrybridge coal train) was thrown to its left and came to rest on its side in the foreground, narrowly missing a large lineside dwelling. The GNER express was also forced to its left and was wrecked in the lineside field, the Class 91 electric locomotive propelling it stopping just short of the road bridge. The Mk 4 on the grass in the distance (the first vehicle behind the DVT, Coach M) lost its bogies, bounced onto and flew over the remains of the DVT to land 130m beyond the road bridge. It started rotating in the impact such that its roof slid along the ground before rotating a further 180 degrees to land upright. Put simply, it performed a 360 degree anti-clockwise lengthwise roll before landing on its base with a large piece of the Class 66 bogie within its body shell. *HMRI/ORR.*

sought to undermine) Osborne's opinions, professionalism and credibility. Caustically, they noted dismissively that Osborne was "now working as a consultant."

HSE's representations that it should retain HMRI were destroyed by Osborne's bravely expressed revelations and on July 15 2004, Transport Secretary Alistair Darling launched the Rail Review White Paper, which included formal proposals to pass railway safety - in other words HMRI - to The Office of Rail Regulation (ORR).

Trade Unions were not supportive and Bob Crow stated: "RMT fundamentally disagrees with the proposal to transfer responsibility for passenger safety to the ORR [to be a combined safety and economic regulator] and away from HSE because of the economic conflicts of interest involved."

Prospect, the Union to which HSE inspectors generally belonged, also voiced its opposition to the proposal, for similar reasons.

These were spurious arguments - after all, the same criticisms are not levelled at the Civil Aviation Authority, where economic and safety considerations are also handled perfectly satisfactorily (and to a very high standard) under the same roof. The ORR/HMRI model has worked extremely well in practice. The resignation of Alan Osborne, the resources allocated fighting to keep HMRI within HSE and the very public - and unmistakably sour - rhetoric from Callaghan and Walker all backfired leading to reputational damage for both HSE and HSC. It was ironic that a few years later, Walker's wife Anna (a senior career civil servant) served as Chair of ORR from 2009 to 2015.

The transfer of railway safety regulation from HSE to ORR was legislated for in the Railways Act 2005 and on April 1 2006, following what had been possibly the most tumultuous period in its history, HMRI formally became part of the Office of Rail Regulation. This meant HMRI was in its third home.

Has it been successful since? Did Alistair Darling do the right thing? The evidence would suggest that the answer to both questions is 'yes'. In February 2017, the railway achieved a decade in which no passenger had died on a train (the last on-board fatality had been Margaret Masson, 84, in the Grayrigg Pendolino derailment of February 2007) and repeated surveys show our railway to be the safest in Europe, often quoted as 'by a factor of four.' Since Margaret Masson's tragic death in February 2007 at Grayrigg, no passenger has died on a British train. With 1.7bn passenger journeys a year by 2019, that is a significant achievement.

In 2014 we recorded the first year ever in which no passenger train derailed and in 2015/16 there was the first year ever in which no rail worker died doing their job. In 1990, when HMRI celebrated its 150th anniversary and acquired its royal status, around 30 workers a year were being killed doing their jobs. In 1990, former Deputy Chief Inspector Alan Cooksey (1975-2005) recalls great departmental satisfaction at HSE when the annual figures for railwaymen being killed fell below 30!

This was a tremendous team effort by everyone on the railway. ORR/HMRI had been 'front and the centre' of the effort leading to this achievement - and it remains thus committed today.

Above: An aerial view of the M62 crossing of the ECML (bridge EC2/8A), looking east, with the ECML running north-south from the left. Gary Hart's Land Rover and trailer drifted off the M62 to his left, just behind the last of the row of police vehicles parked on the hard shoulder. The Land Rover and trailer careered along and down the steep 3.5m embankment for fully 115m - the tyre tracks are just discernible passing between the two HV-clothed figures - demolishing 16.9m of wooden post and rail motorway boundary fence immediately to the right of the bridge parapet. The Land Rover then crashed through the railway boundary fence and dropped onto the railway. Almost immediately, the GNER express of nine Mk 4 coaches, a Class 91 and a DVT, running at 120-125mph, hit the Land Rover, whose front near side wheel was in the four foot. Had the 'Armco' protecting the bridge been just 50 metres longer, Hart's runaway Land Rover Defender 110 CSW 2.5 Tdi would have been deflected back onto the M62 and this would have remained a road accident. *HMRI/ORR.*

Right: The view from the eastern approach to Pollington Road bridge, near the point of collision, where the GNER DVT was wrecked and its train deflected down the embankment side and into the field. The DVT, derailed by the impact with Hart's Land Rover, travelled for a further 642 metres, roughly in line and upright, before hitting the Class 66, at about 88mph, on the down line. The Class 66 windscreen would have been half filled with the DVT front at the point of impact between the centre line of the DVT cab front and the leading right hand corner of the Class 66. The front of the DVT had been deflected into the path of the Class 66 (running at an estimated 54mph) when its derailed wheels ran through the trailing points leading to the Plamor industrial yard on the eastern side of the line, north of the Pollington Road bridge. The 127-tonne Class 66 over-rode the much lighter 45-tonne DVT, demolishing the vehicle. The DVT cab was severed from the main body and thrown clear, coming to rest 145m south of the road bridge. As the DVT slowed, the weight of the following train caused the Mk 4s to then over-ride the rear of the vehicle breaking the coupling and shearing the body from its chassis. Trapped beneath the front of the Class 66, the DVT started rotating clockwise, taking the leading end of Coach M with it. Eventually torn free from the Class 66 moving in the opposite direction, the remains of the DVT and Coach M careered down the embankment into the field and it was at this point Coach M started to rotate along its length. This was the highest speed head-on collision in British railway history and the masses and energy unleashed by the impact far exceeded all crashworthiness features of the DVT, which was destroyed. *HMRI/ORR.*

Above: Gary Hart's Land Rover came to rest astride the cess-side running rail, 11m south of the bridge and adjacent to the trailer and Renault Savanna saloon, with its front nearside wheel in the four foot. It was pushed into the position shown and wrecked by the 120-125mph impact with the DVT's front nearside buffer. Hart's speed had been sufficiently high to not only carry his Land Rover and loaded trailer 115m over steeply sloping rough ground from the hard shoulder and demolishing 16.9m of fence along the field boundary, but also to breach Railtrack's boundary fence along the railway before careering down the shallow cutting shown, to foul the up ECML. It is thought (but not verified) that GNER Driver John Weddle - who the official accident report described as "an experienced and competent driver" - would have seen the Land Rover in his path beneath the bridge and had time to make an emergency brake application. AEA Technology Rail investigated the DVT impact and concluded that "derailment was not a certainty, but an unfortunate combination of marginal circumstances and that a similar event may well not result in derailment." The conclusion was that a solid object of greater than 10mm in diameter passing between wheel and rail would be enough to lift and derail the DVT's leading wheelset. *HMRI/ORR.*

Above: Fifteen of eighteen bogies on the GNER train were torn off - in all cases the bolted connection between the central pivot and underframe mounting broke. This also happened at Hatfield and it matters because detached bogies can become either large obstacles or missiles capable of causing significant damage and injury, as do detached wheelsets. Of the 30 wheelsets from the detached bogies, eight were torn free, as shown here. All were from the front four coaches - M, H, G and F. None of the wheelsets were detached in the 115mph derailment at Hatfield, which is a powerful indicator of the severity of the forces unleashed at Heck. By coincidence, the Class 91 - No 91023 - was the same locomotive that had been involved at Hatfield, in 1999. *Nigel Harris*

Above: A truly shocking picture from the official report reveals the catastrophic damage inflicted on the DVT which led the GNER express and which was destroyed partly by the Class 66 smashing it from the front and partly by its own train over riding from the rear.

Chapter 11

All change at HMRI/ORR: Re-establishing leadership

By 2005, HMRI was emerging from a period of tremendous challenge, only to find itself on the threshold of yet more fundamental change. Turbulence continued. The rapidly shifting landscape of the privatised railway had tested not merely HMRI's capabilities and skills, but also its spirit, resilience and character. High profile accidents of the later 1990s/early 2000s (Southall 1997; Ladbroke Grove 1999; Hatfield 2000; Potters Bar 2002) had put Britain's railways and its regulators under political, public and media scrutiny.

The number of inspectors rose considerably from about 30 to 70 because the rail industry was under greater scrutiny than at any time in its history. HSE's approach to concentrating on safety management systems (enshrined in the Railways & Other Guided Transport Systems (Safety) Regulations 2006, known as ROGS) and treating rail as a high hazard industry (just as it did oil, gas and chemical installations) had brought both internal and external tensions. External capabilities, already under pressure, were stretched yet further because skilled inspectors were taken off front line inspections and used to train new inspectors from other industries who had little or no rail knowledge or understanding. HMRI's relationship with the rail industry - already strained - dipped further, to a worrying all-time low. Staff morale likewise slumped to a new low.

The fundamental nature of rail regulation was changing rapidly. No longer were changes to infrastructure subject to HMRI approval: the emphasis was now entirely on duty holders to assess risks surrounding changes and then manage those risks appropriately and safely. The fallout from the failure of Alan Osborne's appointment to

Above: In the first decade of the 21st century, tilting trains which Britain pioneered with the Advanced Passenger Train (APT) from the late 1960s to the 1980s and abandoned in 1985/86, finally came to Britain. On July 23 2002, the Class 390 Virgin 'Pendolino' trains, built by Fiat/Alstom, started running on the West Coast Main Line, initially between London Birmingham International and Manchester Piccadilly in 2002, to coincide with the Commonwealth Games in Manchester later extended to Euston in 2003 and Glasgow in 2004. Designed for 140mph, Railtrack's inability to deliver the moving block digital signalling required, in the badly-managed PUG2 (Passenger Upgrade 2) of the botched West Coast Route Modernisation meant that the '390' operational line speed was reduced to 125mph. Originally budgeted at £2.5bn, projected WCRM costs soared to more than £13bn before a combination of descoping and tough intervention by the Strategic Rail Authority (SRA, abolished 2004) reduced costs to less than £10bn. On February 23 2007, WCML passenger Margaret Masson, 84, died in the '390' wrecked at Grayrigg (pages 170-178) when the nine-vehicle train derailed at 95mph on a badly maintained facing crossover. At the south end of Carlisle Citadel, successive generations of railway photographers have photographed LNWR and LMS express steam locomotives at this spot; this was the 21st century scene on September 11 2012, with a pair of 'Pendolino' trains standing in the sun. ***Gavin Morrison.***

Above: In southern England, 140mph domestic UK passenger services were successfully introduced for the first time in 2009, when Hitachi's Japanese-built Class 395 'Javelin' EMUs - which the national media insisted on describing as 'Bullet trains' - were introduced between Ashford and St Pancras International. This picture shows one of these sleek and successful trains at St Pancras International on October 2 2015. *Gavin Morrison.*

lead HMRI accelerated momentum towards moving the Inspectorate out of HSE. Osborne's resignation and his subsequent *RAIL* magazine comments had powerfully validated and endorsed the increasing criticism of the last few years, largely led by *RAIL* magazine, whose trenchant criticism of HSE/HSC had played a key part in convincing Secretary of State Alistair Darling to move HMRI to ORR. Furthermore, there was about to be a new player - the Rail Accident Investigation Branch (RAIB) - which would in future undertake one of the major traditional roles of HMRI by investigating rail incidents. This was in part a response to EU legislation mandating an independent investigation body but also a political imperative and a Cullen recommendation, following the criticism in his Ladbroke Grove Public inquiry report of the combined approvals/investigation functions of HMRI.

HMRI moves to ORR

Dr Alan Sefton, who as HMRI Chief Inspector between October 2003 and December 2005 had overseen the further expansion of the HMRI within HSE and who had worked to embed a philosophy of concentrating on catastrophic risk and improving safety management systems, retired and was replaced from December 5 2005 by Linda Williams. This was a very significant and historic moment; Linda was the first woman to hold the post of Chief Inspector of Railways. She led and successfully managed the inevitably tricky transfer of HMRI from HSE (which bitterly opposed this transfer) into its new and hopefully less controversial home at the Office of Rail Regulation (ORR).

Linda Williams was initially seconded back to HSE to help implement HMRI's transfer to ORR. She was an HSE 'lifer' who had previously been Chief Inspector of Agriculture. She took on the task of ensuring a smooth transition from HSE to ORR. To everyone's credit - not least hers - this was largely achieved.

At first, however, the new arrangement emerged as a rather uneasy alliance between ORR and HMRI. ORR was the economic regulator for the main line railway and its board was unfamiliar with safety regulation, with which it had no experience. It took considerable dedication from both parts of the new organisation (and focussed determination by Linda Williams) to ensure that everything was in place to allow the formal launch of the joint safety and economic regulator on April 1 2006. Fully effective integration of those functions, however, would not materialise for several years.

ORR's principal function had been, until 2006, economic regulation of the main line railway. ORR translated government policy (as outlined in the High Level Output Specification statement - HLOS) into a determination of funds to allow Network Rail to deliver those outputs efficiently. Yes, there had always been a requirement to ensure that safety was taken into consideration - but this was very different from having an organisation where safety regulation comprised half of the activities and workforce of the office. In those early days, the merger felt rather more like a shotgun marriage than a happy union, as both sides struggled to understand and accommodate the unfamiliar role, work, approach and style of the other. This rather two-headed feeling, which stopped short of antagonism but which was certainly not integrated, was emphasised by HMRI's presence in regional offices across the country whereas ORR had been solely London-based until 2006. There was (perhaps inevitably) a definite feeling of 'us and them' which took some time to subside.

However, less than a year after the creation of the joint safety and economic regulator there came an event that crystallised how HMRI came to define its role in its new home. This event was the fatal Virgin 'Pendolino' near-100mph derailment at Grayrigg on February 23 2007, which caused one death and scores of casualties. We shall return to this.

Rail safety - the pre-Grayrigg landscape

We have already examined the significant weaknesses in safety management exposed by the fatal accidents of the later 1990s/early 2000s. In particular, Hatfield had brought into very sharp focus Railtrack's alarming lack of engineering expertise and the broken model of asset management it had pursued. Deep-seated post-Hatfield risk aversion demonstrated by Railtrack - which arose from it's ignorance of track condition nationwide - led to widespread 20mph speed restrictions that massively disrupted passenger services and caused national chaos.

The railway's reputation in general, and that of Railtrack in particular, were destroyed in seemingly endless, relentlessly critical, rolling TV news coverage. The late Sir Alastair Morton, first chairman

of the Strategic Rail Authority, accurately captured the mood when he described the industry as having suffered a "collective nervous breakdown."

The Prime Minister hosted daily meetings at 10 Downing Street, at the end of which Morton gave comments to waiting reporters. This challenging media focus was relentless and as safety regulator HMRI was at the heart of it. The irony is that the meltdown of Railtrack immediately after Hatfield resulted in greater risk transfer to other transport modes (primarily road) where people were several orders of magnitude more likely to suffer injury and death than aboard a train.

HMRI not only helped to restore some proportionality and calmer, more ordered thinking after the Hatfield crash, it also drove the crucial systemic improvements that were needed such as withdrawal from the approvals regime. Nevertheless, the Inspectorate was still too reactive at this critical time and it frankly missed some of the early signs of trouble that were the precursors to the Grayrigg derailment in February 2007. This would also be revealed to be particularly true of its handling of the lessons of the Potters Bar derailment. During its HSE period, which took a very different approach, HMRI had gradually but imperceptibly drifted away from having an ongoing effective dialogue with the industry and, therefore, it's influence in encouraging improvements had become weakened.

Having said that, by 2007 the risk profile of the main line railway was significantly improved compared with earlier years. This was almost entirely due to a single piece of legislation: The Railway Safety Regulations of 1999, which had a profound impact on improving railway safety by taking a step forward from the very basic Automatic Warning System (AWS). This had been first introduced by BR in 1956 but 50 years later it was still not installed on some main lines, leaving driver vigilance as the prime safety control. The 1984 rear-end collision between a Liverpool-Scarborough passenger train and a loaded oil tanker train at Eccles was a consequence of there being no AWS assistance for the driver and some appalling signal sighting. Bear in mind that this was effectively Britain's first and oldest intercity route, opened in 1830 and operated by Stephenson's *Rocket*! And yet there was still no AWS in 1984; this was very poor.

In a relatively short period of time, these 1999 regulations drove the industry to appreciably improve safety. The regulations arose from the work of the joint Cullen/Uff public inquiry into Train Protection Systems. Whilst accepting that full Automatic Train Protection was prohibitively costly, the regulations nevertheless required a train protection system to prevent or mitigate SPADs

Above: At one extreme, HMRI was supervising many 125mph - and even some 140mph - 21st century electric passenger trains - but at the other extreme it oversaw continued operation at around 25mph of otherwise life-expired ex-London Tube stock. These 1938-vintage trains had been re-purposed and refurbished for the Isle of Wight in 1992. In 2019, these trains were still running, at the incredible age of 81 years. In summer sunshine, one of these venerable units is at Ryde Pier Head station, on August 8 2015. It's worth noting that these 1938 trains had themselves replaced yet earlier Tube stock on the Isle of Wight, dating from 1923-34; they had been introduced in 1967 after the end of steam on the island. *Gavin Morrison.*

much more effectively than AWS. At first, the emerging technology was known as 'AWS-plus' but it later became Train Protection Warning System (TPWS).

For the first time, this AWS enhancement introduced overspeed protection and although it did not bring full automatic train protection (ATP) the industry pressed ahead and implemented Train Protection Warning System (TPWS) throughout the network. This action immediately and increasingly significantly reduced the risk of passenger harm arising from SPADs. At a fraction of the cost of ATP, TPWS delivered a reduction of approaching 85% in train accident risk from SPADs. It is impressive just how quickly installation was achieved: the network was fitted with full appropriate TPWS cover by 2006.

It is interesting to note that Cullen and Uff expected TPWS to be a short-term solution, because introduction of the European Train Control Systems (ETCS) was then, not unreasonably, judged to be imminent. In the event, TPWS has now been in full national service for 15 years and will be our core protection system for some years yet, as Network Rail's complex 'Digital railway' plans are prepared for implementation.

The 1999 regulations also introduced approach speed control, not only at terminal platforms but also at some permanent speed restrictions. Additionally, the legislation finally removed slam door rolling stock - or mandated the fitment of secondary Central Door Locking (CDL) as on the IC125 trains. This has virtually eliminated passengers being killed by falling from moving trains. This had been a major concern for the Inspectorate, given that 21 passengers had been killed falling out of trains as recently as 1990.

It had been one of the talismans of HMRI within HSE to challenge industry complacency about falls from trains. These regulations removed the last rolling stock still in service where it had not been possible to fit CDL. The exception was for heritage passenger charter

Mk 1 carriages, although potentially fatal risks here were managed by fitting doors with internal, manually-operated sliding bolts and procedures amended to ensure all doors were stewarded, to properly and effectively mitigate risk.

The elimination of passenger-operated doors also considerably reduced risk at what is now known as the 'Passenger Train Interface' (PTI) not only from injury to people seeking to alight or board whilst a train is moving, but by eliminating the risk of terrible injuries caused by open doors on moving trains striking passengers standing close to the platform edge.

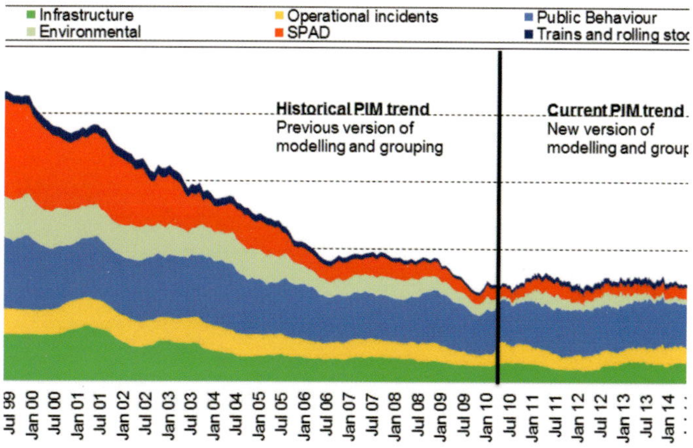

Long term graph change in the Safety Risk Mode that shows the impact on TPWS on SPAD risk reduction. ***RSSB***

Creation of the Rail Accident Investigation Branch

The creation of an independent 'no-blame' rail accident investigator had been advocated in the 2001 Cullen report into the Ladbroke Grove accident, where 31 people died. The same concept was also enshrined in the European Railway Safety Directive of 2004 and The Rail Accident Investigation Branch (RAIB) was duly established in October 2005 under the leadership of Chief Inspector Carolyn Griffiths. RAIB began modestly, in 'shadow' mode.

The creation of RAIB was yet another challenge for HMRI. Much of what HMRI had achieved over the years had been through its own inspectors investigating the causes of major incidents. Now another body was to investigate incidents on a no-blame basis, in order to establish root cause. This would not mean that HM Railway Inspectors would stop investigating, since it was still necessary to establish if a breach of the law had taken place and whether enforcement action, including prosecution, was necessary.

The idea was to share evidence between the organisations to avoid duplication of effort - but this was difficult in practice. In addition to an industry inquiry after an accident, plus possible BTP/HMRI investigations, there was now an added RAIB process. A fourth parallel investigation, in other words.

RAIB's role was to investigate occurrences and make recommendations to tackle the root causes it identified. However, the process of monitoring implementation of RAIB's recommendations or otherwise was left with the Health & Safety Regulator - HMRI. The Regulator's role is to decide whether or not to pass on any recommendation to the duty holder and then report to RAIB what is being done to satisfy the intention of the recommendation.
If the duty holder's response is not considered satisfactory, the Inspectorate might take enforcement action. Enforcement, though, has to be in line with both legislation and policy - both of which are predicated according to the 'so far as is reasonably practicable'

Above: In the early 1800s, railways rapidly developed in north east England, for moving coal from inland pits to coastal docksides, for shipment. The black rocks were transported in four-wheel wooden 'chauldron' wagons (see pages 16-17) - 200 years later, they had evolved into high-speed bogie hoppers of 100 tons capacity. Beeching, best known for his notorious extensive passenger route and station closures, had also proposed the non-stop, circular 'merry-go-round' trains which ran continuously between pithead and power stations, supplying coal to generate electricity. Increasing environmental awareness and public pressure about climate change brought about by carbon emissions caused coal to fall out of favour very rapidly in the 21st century. Coal by rail effectively collapsed in 2015-16, when carrying slumped by 54.6% to a 38-year low of 19.8m tons. Once upon a time, Toton yard alone handled 1m BR standard four-wheel 16-ton capacity coal wagons every year. The run-down of coal traffic happened very fast: this was the scene at Black Carr Sidings, south of Doncaster, on May 29 2015, the year coal traffic fell by over a half. A Virgin Trains East Coast HST races north on the East Coast Main Line. By 2020 even the HST, introduced in 1975, will be long gone from front line service on the ECML and GWML. ***Gavin Morrison.***

Above: On February 23 2007, at 8:12pm, the 5:15pm London Euston-Glasgow (1S83) Class 390 'Pendolino' derailed at 95mph, almost the maximum permitted 100mph linespeed, in the open fell country of Lambrigg Fell, north east of Kendal, near the Cumbrian village of Grayrigg. The leading driving car derailed on badly-maintained facing crossover No. 2B; all nine vehicles derailed, eight of the carriages rolling down the embankment. Five turned on their sides, with one coming to rest at almost 90 degrees to the running line. The driver of 1S83 recalls his cab 'leaping in the air' on points 2A, throwing him from his seat before he could even reach for the emergency brake. His driving car broke free and rotated horizontally through 190 degrees before rolling down the embankment, coming to rest facing in the opposite direction, facing south. *Phil Metcalfe/Telerail/RAIL.*

philosophy and guiding principle. RAIB recommendations, however, are not bound by this concept and this led to some tension between the two in the early days.

It would have been naive to believe that RAIB's arrival would not create such tensions, as its arrival put two players on the pitch where previously there had been only one. In particular, under the terms of the Memorandum of Understanding, RAIB had precedence at accident sites (unless there was evidence of a criminal act, which BTP would pursue) meaning it had first access to evidence. RAIB was obliged to share 'technical' evidence with HMRI, but not any of the formal witness statements. This inevitably led to much duplicated effort and occasional uncertainty about what information could even be shared. It was not a simple investigative landscape.

This was particularly evident when it came to the 95mph Virgin West Coast fatal 'Pendolino' disaster at Grayrigg, in Cumbria. This was the first major incident which RAIB investigated. This made it very clear that the most important thing for HMRI was to ensure it further developed a much stronger role regarding prevention, rather than reacting to things after they already gone wrong.

The Grayrigg derailment

At 8:15pm on February 23 2007, a Virgin West Coast Class 390 'Pendolino' service from Euston to Glasgow derailed at speed on a facing crossover on an embankment just after the Docker viaduct, in undulating, arable farmland near Grayrigg, in Cumbria. The '390' derailed on No.2B points while travelling at 95mph, within the 100mph limit. All nine carriages of the 'Pendolino' derailed. There were at least 105 passengers and four crew on board. One passenger was fatally injured, whilst 28 passengers, the train driver and one other crew member were seriously injured and 59 more people received minor injuries.

The immediate cause of the derailment was the deterioration of 2B points through a combination of failures of the three stretcher bars, the lock stretcher bars and their fastenings. This allowed the left-hand switch rail to move into an unsafe position close to its stock rail, without losing signalling detection - which would have alerted signallers to the problem. Vibration and impacts from passing traffic shook the points until they literally fell apart.

RAIB's Grayrigg report took nearly two years to produce and contained 29 recommendations which actually meant 50 actions, given that many recommendations had multiple parts. Many questions were asked about what had been learned by both Network Rail and the regulator from the relatively recent facing points fatal derailment in 2002, at Potters Bar (pages 160-162).

Superficially, Potters Bar and Grayrigg were similar. Both happened on facing points and in each case, derailment was caused by stretcher bar failure which led to the blades moving towards their stock rails and a train then 'bursting the points'. There were also significant differences but there was, nevertheless, major political, media and public criticism of HMRI for 'allowing it to happen again.' There were sufficient concerns to alert incoming Chief Inspector Ian Prosser (appointed in 2008) that greater effort and rigour was required to proactively and more effectively regulate NR.

Following Potters Bar (May 10 2002) NR had progressively brought contracted-out track maintenance back in-house. This progressively reversed the major change that had taken place at privatisation, when maintenance had been contracted out. The original intention of splitting-up of maintenance into contract areas and privatising them had been intended, partly, to contain the power of the rail unions.

This not only failed: the opposite happened. Terms and conditions had become extremely varied between contractors and this combined with the skills shortages caused after many people left the industry at privatisation, to trigger an escalation of wages, with inevitably higher industry costs. RMT and other unions successfully used fragmentation of the industry to ensure that its members wages kept well ahead of inflation, as was clearly later demonstrated by the McNulty Report.

Although the unions' public position is to continue to oppose privatisation, they also - entirely understandably - continue to use the current structure to ensure their members derive considerable benefit. One of the most successful exponents of this strategy was the late RMT General Secretary Bob Crow, who, despite his public posturing and rather belligerent image, was as skilled an RMT negotiator and 'do-er of deals' as any business leader. Senior rail managers always and openly readily agree and admit that behind Crow's public image, he was actually very good to deal with when it came to detailed negotiations.

The big failure by both Railtrack and Network Rail - particularly in their early days - was around asset management, specifically their knowledge of the age and condition of critical assets, such as the permanent way. This contributed considerably at the Hatfield, Potters Bar and Grayrigg incidents and was clearly reflected in RAIB's recommendations, post-2007. It is true to say that this was actually already on the Inspectorate's radar at the time - but it is also true to concede that it had not been driven anywhere near hard enough.

This approach changed and gathered momentum after Grayrigg, following Ian Prosser's appointment in September 2008 as Director of Railway Safety at ORR. The change in focus was actually initiated by Prosser's later deputy Sue Johnston, who led HMRI's Grayrigg investigation. This resulted in the successful prosecution of NR, ending with a £4m fine. It was a difficult task, though, navigating the problems created by having both RAIB and HMRI each independently investigating the same incident, to the subtly different ends outlined earlier.

HMRI's successful prosecution of NR was a significant achievement for Johnston, who had achieved a great deal to improve rail safety during her time in HMRI. Unfortunately, she developed a life-threatening illness from which she subsequently recovered but it nonetheless resulted in her early retirement from ORR. Her Improvement Notice regarding the lack of understanding NR had of the design performance of their point systems was a pivotal moment that started to change NR's mind-set towards Asset Management. NR started to move towards 'predict and prevent' thinking rather than 'find and fix'. Grayrigg had graphically and tragically illustrated what happens when there is a failure to find those problems in time - and then fix them before failure…and disaster.

ORR's follow-up to Grayrigg involved relentless challenge to encourage Network Rail to properly understand the condition and behaviour of its safety-critical assets. The Inspectorate pushed hard for improved fundamentals - a better asset register; better recording of asset condition and faults; a more systematic understanding of failures; a more rigorous assessment of risks and controls and improved analysis of designed function. HMRI was also instrumental in persuading NR of the benefits of adopting hand-held technology 'on the spot', to record defects in the field in real time, rather than retrospectively writing-up notes 'back at base.'

The Inspectorate further challenged the complexity and confusion of the vast number of written standards and instructions and helped NR commence its programme to simplify its highly complex, very detailed rules and make them more risk-based. This work also marked the beginning of truly joined-up successful activity between the two halves of ORR. Asset Management was an area of natural overlap and therefore became the focal point of developing relationships within ORR.

Meanwhile on London Underground

Alongside the intermittent but regular turmoil we have described on the privatised main line railway, a rather different picture had been emerging on LUL, which had a long-standing philosophy of continuously improving safety management. The catalyst for this commendable approach had been the fatal King's Cross fire on November 18 1987 (32 deaths; 100 injuries) and the subsequent Fennell Report. Under the leadership of Director of Safety Mike Strzelecki, LUL had successfully and effectively overhauled its entire safety management system. Consequently, by 2000, its safety indicators compared very favorably with the main line, despite decades of chronic under-investment.

Government's attempted (but ultimately doomed) solution to that lack of investment in LU infrastructure was the Public-Private Partnership of 2002 (PPP), whereby three infrastructure companies would manage the assets from trains to stations and track. LUL continued to manage day to day operations.

PPP was ultimately a commercial failure but it did nonetheless introduce desperately needed funds to renew and upgrade LUL lines. Despite the major organisational change it brought (accompanied later by uncertainty) it is important to note that safety improvements did actually accelerate during this otherwise troubled time commercially.

That said, there were still some significant incidents. In January 2003, before the start of the PPP contracts a Central Line train derailed and crashed into the tunnel wall at Chancery Lane, owing to a faulty gearbox. This was followed by a series of further derailments on points at Camden and Hammersmith, caused by track faults, not long after the new companies had taken over.

The contrast with the main line was the sharp thoroughness of investigations after these mishaps (identifying root causes) and the maturity of the relationship between LUL and HMRI. The Underground's senior team was receptive and responsive to the sometimes harsh feedback from the Inspectorate and there was always a good working relationship, despite some significant and (for LUL) painful enforcement.

The external climate, too, was difficult in the early days of PPP, with the threat of high-profile strikes from the RMT and hostility from the then Mayor Ken Livingston. However, together LUL and the Infrastructure Maintenance Companies began to improve maintenance and renewals over the next few years. At the time of going to press in 2019, there had been just one passenger train

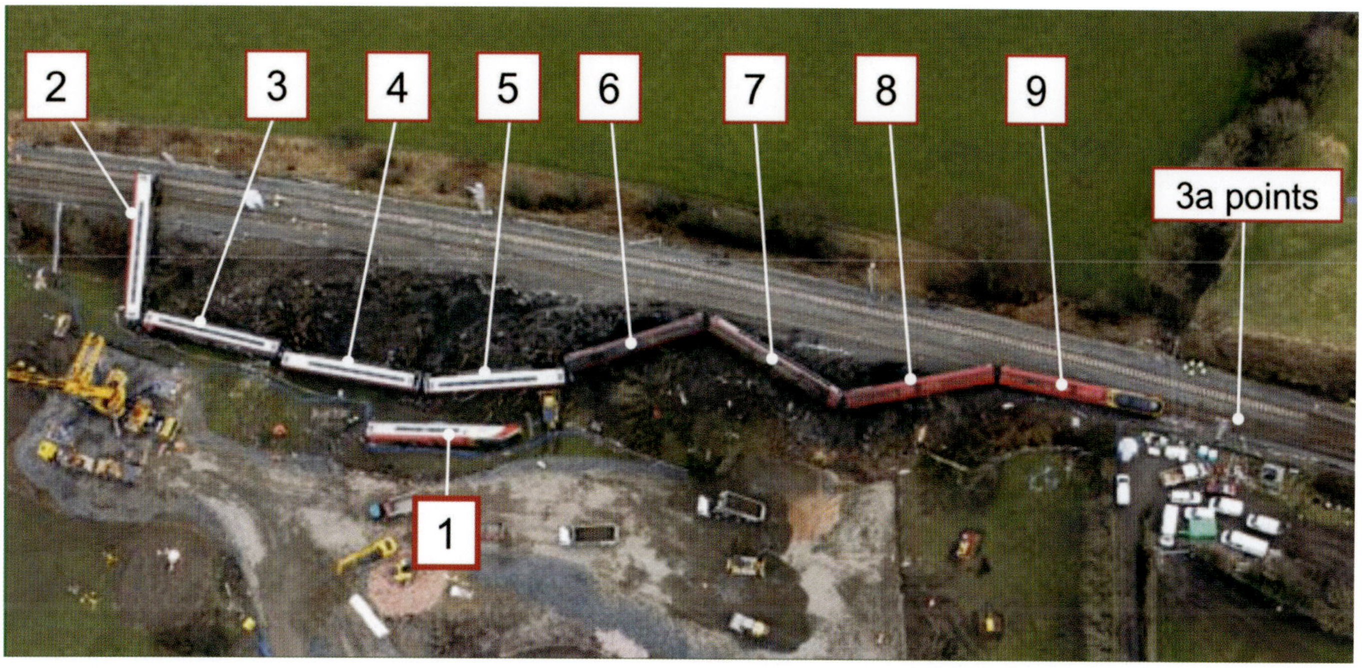

Above: The '390' travelled 320 metres from derailment on the toe of points 2B, just off the right of this view. The train came to rest from 95mph very rapidly in just 100m more than its own length of 217.4m. Damage to infrastructure by the derailing train caused all signals in both directions to immediately and automatically revert to danger and all approaching trains were stopped safely before the accident site.
Phil Metcalfe/Telerail/RAIL.

Above: A view clearly showing how the leading driving car rotated in its own length, coming to rest facing south, the rear end pushed round by the momentum of the eight derailed coaches behind. Eighty percent of the people in the train were hurt and there was one fatality Margaret Masson, 84, who was severely injured in the leading vehicle. Rescued by firefighters and paramedics, she died whilst being airlifted to hospital. The driver, one crew member and 28 passengers were seriously injured with a further 58 receiving treatment for minor injuries. The remaining 18 passengers and two crew were not physically injured. The line was closed until March 12 for recovery, investigation and infrastructure repairs. The train was eventually written off. The WCML was closed for 16 days and reopened to traffic at 7.45pm on March 11 2007. *Phil Metcalfe/Telerail/RAIL.*

derailment in 12 years. At the same time, performance and efficiency of the Underground has improved very significantly. For example, in 2018/19 despite increased use of the network with all night services there were only nine broken rails on the whole of the network.

Ian Prosser

In May 2008, Ian Prosser had been appointed with the formal title Director of Railway Safety at ORR/HMRI. However, Prosser understood the importance and powerful symbolism of his organisation's historical significance, going right back to 1840 and he continued to use the traditional title of 'HM Chief inspector of Railways'. Indeed, Prosser is only the 25th holder of this historic office (see page 12).

Prosser's ambitious strategy was to make the Inspectorate a pro-active driver of strategic change and improvement in national rail safety. With the creation of RAIB, the time was ripe for a shift to a more proactive approach. In short, Prosser's goal was to eliminate the potential for incidents and attempt to ensure they did not happen, rather than seek remedies 'after the event.'

In his interview for the post, Prosser had suggested that the regulator should have a clearer strategic vision - that it should be to aim for zero industry-caused fatalities within a context of ever-decreasing risk. One of his first acts was to ensure that this was enshrined in ORR strategy. It is a vision that ORR formally adopted for the entire industry which was still going strong in 2019.

This new concept of driving the industry towards excellence in Health & Safety management was launched by Prosser in 2008. HMRI was going to need to be more proactive than by just checking legal compliance: inspectors would need to be 'out there', more proactively and strenuously seeking to ensure that the conditions were in place to make sure that legal compliance was likely. This was done by influencing the industry to continually improve, so that it reduced harm to not only passengers, but also its workforce and the public.

'Pushing the industry towards excellence' is not a desire for 'gold-plating,' however. It's more about creating and framing the management system of a high performing company so that legal breaches are less likely. In simple terms, this is about doing things right first time, creating trust throughout an organisation from top to bottom and displaying clear, visible leadership.

From the end of 2008, Prosser and his team set about creating a structure that would deliver these improvements. Partly this was to create efficiencies - by merging engineering and information analysis resource with the rest of ORR - but it was mainly about creating a model that focussed on relationships with duty holders.

HMRI moved away from teams that dealt with the full range of industry players to a more dedicated team-based structure that ensured accountability specifically for key duty holders. Restructuring HMRI into teams focused on duty holders was a policy based on the successful Transport for London model established earlier by HMRI. This was led initially by Principal Inspector Caroline Wake OBE, who also later became a very well respected Deputy Chief Inspector and latterly UK head of the Channel Tunnel Safety Authority.

A division was created to concentrate solely on Network Rail - both centrally and regionally - with a further division for TOCs, FOCs, metros & light rail, trams and the small, but challenging, very specialist heritage sector. There was also a policy and central business functions arm.

This restructuring brought a welcome, very direct focus to the Inspectorate's activities - and it soon reaped rewards. For example, it became possible to bring significant pressure to bear to secure improvements in a number of areas such as level crossings, where risk halved between 2008 and 2018. Closure of more than 1,000 crossings made a significant contribution to this reduction.

In the heritage charter sector, which has very specific needs arising from the many grandfather rights and derogations which apply to older equipment, such as Mk 1 carriages. These vehicles are inherently less crashworthy and would not otherwise not be permitted to operate. HMRI has led and encouraged a more professional approach to safety management. This has sometimes required very strong enforcement, as in the case of West Coast

Railways, after one of its trains ran past a red danger signal with a loaded passenger 'special' of Mk 1 rolling stock, at Wootton Bassett on March 7 2015. West Coast's steam excursion, hauled by SR Bulleid 'Battle of Britain' class 4-6-2 No. 34067 *Tangmere*, passed the red signal protecting Wootton Bassett Junction and ran across the converging double track main line trailing in from the left. *Tangmere* ran across the double turnout just 44 seconds after a Great Westerm IC 125 had cleared the points, running at 85mph. A high speed flank collision in which there would almost certainly have been fatalities was avoided by less than a minute. It was a horrific 'near miss'. But what made this awful incident unforgivably worse was that the TPWS - which would almost certainly have prevented this near-catastrophic SPAD - had been isolated by the crew.

Following the potentially high consequence SPAD (signal passed at danger) at Wootton Bassett, West Coast Railway Company was given notice that a consultation was being launched which could result in the loss of the company's safety certificate, without which its business could not continue to operate. The shock waves of this potentially catastrophic near-miss, caused by deliberate equipment tampering, resounded around both the charter and the national railway industry.

Notwithstanding this very severe incident and penalty, a second instance of TPWS equipment being isolated was then discovered that had occurred at Hexthorpe Goods Chord near Doncaster. The consultative process whereby the company's safety certificate could be cancelled was thus launched to include this second unauthorised TPWS isolation. Meanwhile, the Chief Inspector imposed an immediate Prohibition Notice, which halted all West Coast operations for five weeks.

In order to lift this Prohibition Notice, West Coast Railways agreed in writing to implement improvements to a range of safety and governance processes and routines, and made a formal commitment to ongoing continuous improvement. The improvement actions were closely monitored by the Chief Inspector over the next year and once they were deemed complete, two detailed audits were undertaken by ORR specialist inspectors.

One audit focussed specifically on driver management, to ensure that the new arrangements put in place were working and were fully embedded, the other focussed on rolling stock maintenance. Both audits gave ORR assurance that significant improvements had been made. West Coast came extremely close to losing its business because of its very poor safety management and dubious operating practices. This was very clear proof that poor safety management and culture could easily and very rapidly extinguish a business.

Ongoing safety improvements were considered for all heritage main line charter operators and the Chief Inspector made it very clear in 2019 that significant improvements were needed to allow the 1950s-design MK1 passenger coaches a continuing and sustainable life on the main line. Such improvements included the fitting of controlled emission toilets to replace those which discharge directly onto the track, modifications to droplight windows, aimed at preventing people leaning out and central door locking preventing falls from doors.

HMRI has also offered crucial and important leadership to Britain's independent heritage railways which are operated by a mixture of limited numbers of full time staff, almost always outnumbered by numerous volunteers. It is very important not to under-estimate the significant regulatory and supervisory requirements of this sector. If laid end-to-end, our privately operated steam heritage railways - largely branch lines but also with the double track absolute block

Above: The seventh and eighth Grayrigg coaches, with the leading end of the rear driving car on the right. It was dark at the time of the derailment. Despite the massive strain placed upon it, the coupling did not fail, meaning the coaches remained virtually upright. Train brakes were fully applied four seconds after derailment when the leading vehicle separated from the rear eight coaches and the brake pipe ruptured, triggering a maximum brake application. The driver had been qualified for five years, knew the route well and had driven 'Pendolino' trains since their introduction in 2002. He had taken over 1S83 at Preston on February 23, having driven from Glasgow to Preston that morning. He suffered serious injuries and had to be cut free and rescued from his cab; he was hospitalised until March 20. The fatality and serious injuries occurred in the first five carriages, where many passengers were thrown out of their seats. *Phil Metcalfe/Telerail/RAIL.*

Above: Emergency services were called by passengers, train crew and nearby residents, but owing to the remote, rural and undulating landscape, it took some time to establish the exact crash location. The first ambulance/fire crews reached the wrecked Grayrigg train at 2046, 34 minutes after derailment. The last person was removed by 10.47pm, all injured passengers and crew being taken to hospital by helicopter and road ambulances by 12.11pm next morning. This picture was taken several days later, during recovery, which could not proceed until temporary infrastructure was provided to allow access by heavy plant and road transporters. Significant earthworks and temporary steel roadway were installed to connect with the nearest roads, some distance away. As this picture illustrates, despite the severity of this high speed, high energy derailment, damage to windows was limited and all but two passengers and all the crew were contained within the train whilst it same to rest. Injuries and the single fatality were caused by people and objects being thrown around within the train. A large crane is recovering one of the saloons ready for removal by contractor Allelys. *Phil Metcalfe/Telerail/RAIL.*

Above: The Allelys road transporter drivers faced challenges of their own at Grayrigg, created by the temporary roadways built to enable recovery. Lashed down but not yet covered for road removal, one of the saloons is edged away from the crash site on the specialist trailer. The driver is slowly taking his lorry very close to the edge of the earthwork roadway and is just starting a sharp right turn of around 90 degrees. Note the structural integrity of the carriage, whose crashworthiness protected passengers from a range of hazards which had caused deaths in previous accidents. This included multiple ejections through windows (Purley, 1989, pages 118-121) penetration of the passenger saloon (Hatfield, 2000, pages 157-159) and loss of survival space caused by external structures penetrating the vehicle (Southall, 1997, pages 146-150; Cowden 1994, pages 132-135). *Phil Metcalfe/Telerail/RAIL.*

Above: A picture which clearly illustrates the extremely remote and rugged nature of the Lambrigg Fell landscape in which the Grayrigg crash happened, and the difficulties this created for rescue, investigation and recovery. The crashworthiness of the carriage is again apparent - the laminated windows did not shatter, thereby containing passengers within the train in this 95mph derailment. Other features included very robust couplers which generally kept the vehicles together and helped keep the rear vehicles upright; anti roll bar links which kept most of the bogies attached to the train; penetration resistance and roll-over strength of the bodyshells. ***Phil Metcalfe/Telerail/RAIL.***

main line of the Great Central Railway which has some 70mph sections approved for testing purposes - would, it is said, stretch the entire 400 miles of the West Coast Main Line from Euston to Glasgow.

On the main line, historic steam locomotives which at their youngest (BR 'Standard' class engines designed after 1948 by Robert Riddles) are, despite being regarded as modern and 'new', are maybe 70 years old. The oldest operating main line locomotive in 2019 - Gresley 'A3' 4-6-2 No. 60103 *Flying Scotsman* - was built in 1923 and is therefore approaching 100 years old. After a £2m overhaul in the years after 2004 (when it was bought by the National Railway Musuem) it operates widely on NR main lines at up to 75mph. The UK's youngest operational main line steam locomotive - 'A1' 4-6-2 No. 60163 *Tornado* - was completed only in 2008.

All main line certified steam locomotives must meet the most stringent requirements in terms of safety management and operation. This gives HMRI very different challenges to regulating the modern railway, with its increasingly digital, high-tech approach.

The Inspectorate had publicly committed to promoting excellence in the rail industry and securing systemic improvements. It therefore needed a tool to measure this - one that went beyond traditional reactive, historic Key Performance Indicators (KPIs) and that would assist both duty holders and the regulator to properly understand all strengths and weaknesses. Hence, a new, powerful, proactive tool was created by the Inspectorate: the Rail Management Maturity Model (RM3).

RM3 rapidly established its usefulness throughout the industry and has been successfully used to develop a tool that the European Rail Agency (ERA) also now uses to determine the effectiveness of National Safety Authorities. ORR has worked closely with the sector to develop this model further through a combined programme board and relaunched the model in April 2019. It is a little-known (and even less appreciated) fact that the UK has always played a leading role in evolving and formulating European rail safety policy and that the EU held the UK in considerable respect for this.

HMRI's post-2008 restructuring and new approach quickly started to pay off, making life increasingly uncomfortable for Network Rail. The Inspectorate's new organisation ensured it soon started to 'get under the skin' of what was really going on inside NR. The first big push included tackling maintenance, level crossings, and workforce safety. This refocused organisation came into place at the same time as the beginning of Control Period 4 (CP4) in 2009 - the New Control Period for Network Rail's financial settlement. A benefit of the merger with HSE was that HMRI had been influential in making sure that the efficiency challenge imposed on NR was more realistic than the original proposal by the ORR's economists.

However, a key part of NR's response to the challenge posed by HMRI was to look very hard at its maintenance organisation. Maintenance had been brought back in-house from 2003 and during CP3, from a number of private contractors. The result, according to NR, was a very significant saving, which actually made up most of the savings for maintenance that were required by the old Office of the Rail Regulation for CP3. However, at the beginning of CP4, NR came to fully appreciate the true significant scale of the challenge and launched a major reorganisation of its maintenance function, known as 2B/2C. It followed a management reorganisation a few years earlier, which, in turn, followed reintegration of maintenance back into the main business, known as 2A.

This reorganisation ultimately led to a clash between the revitalised HMRI now known as the Railway Safety Directorate and NR, then run by Chief Executive Iain Coucher .

This NR reorganisation was sadly implemented with too much haste and consequently was not ready to be launched in the forecast timescales. The rail unions, led by RMT, were able to find flaws in

Above: Lambrigg is 18 miles south of Penrith, and the nearest station to the crash site was Oxenholme (junction for the Windermere branch) five miles south. The crash site was 24 miles and 12 chains north of Lancaster. The nearby road network consists largely of country lanes winding through undulating farmland, through which this temporary vehicular and plant access had to be created and connected, using temporary steel trackway. *Phil Metcalfe/Telerail/RAIL.*

some of the implementation plans and raised a number of issues with Labour Secretary of State for Transport Andrew (now Lord) Adonis. HMRI's new organisation enabled the inspectorate to quickly and effectively inspect the arrangements. It identified weaknesses which were consequently discussed with Adonis and re-presented in a more realistic implementation plan. This revised plan allowed one year more than originally intended by NR for full implementation, with subsequent reviews. Disagreements with NR remained but ORR's intervention resulted in some of these issues being better managed, thereby ensuring more effective risk control than would have been the case had HMRI not intervened.

This interaction with NR had, however, created friction and tension between the new ORR Railway Safety Directorate and the leadership at NR. This tension increased as the revitalised inspectorate, under its new name, dug ever more deeply into NR and came to better understand operational delivery weaknesses. It was worth the effort: over time this has led to greater mutual respect between the two organisations, with the benefit of improving safety.

A culture of fear

There had been growing concern at HMRI that personal injury statistics, as reported by NR under RIDDOR (Reporting of Injuries, Diseases and Dangerous Occurrences Regulations) in terms of normal Health & Safety procedures 'just didn't look right.' Bluntly, history, statistics and hard experience show that in big, safety critical industries, you can effectively predict the number of RIDDOR accidents that might be expected in any given period. What was furrowing brows was that NR's formally reported accident figures seemed way too low for a company of its size. This was of particular concern to the Chief Inspector, who checking the maths, noticed that not only was the ratio of major injuries to minor injuries very high compared with London Underground, for example - but that this ratio was actually worsening. This implied trend was in conflict with global experience in large, safety critical industries.

Inspectors also started to hear similar, increasingly worried concerns from the unions - and so looked in more detail at specific and individual cases. This confirmed the suspicion that the reported accident figures simply didn't conform to industry experience and statistics everywhere else, in terms of the ratios of minor to major injuries in hazardous industries of varying sizes. The numbers just 'didn't stack up.'

However, finding enough hard evidence to enable a successful prosecution was going to take considerable time and cost. Therefore, the Chief Inspector took a more novel approach for a regulator and used the return to producing an annual health and safety report as a platform in which to highlight this serious issue.

This very much had the intended effect, assisted by pressure from the unions and a couple of investigative features in *RAIL* magazine. NR was compelled to commission an investigation, which was carried out independently by RSSB. This exposed and highlighted a 'culture of fear' that had developed within parts of NR. Put simply, fear of consequence and the use of 'league tables' was deterring managers from properly recording and reporting RIDDOR accidents, leading to the disparity in the accident ratios spotted both by unions and HMRI.

This change started the journey towards a radically different approach of a more open and effective culture.

Elsenham

Following closely in the wake of governance issues about NR were the controversial developments around the double tragedy on December 3 2005 at the Elsenham level crossing. It was a Saturday afternoon and young teenagers Charlotte Thompson and Olivia Bazlinton were killed instantly when they were hit by a 75mph Cross Country express on the pedestrian strip bordering a road level crossing on their way to an afternoon of Christmas shopping in Cambridge. It was a horrific accident which was shown later in Court to have been avoidable.

On February 9 2011, *The Times* approached ORR with information that Tina Hughes, the mother of Olivia, had raised. Sifting through papers returned to her after the civil legal case against NR, she

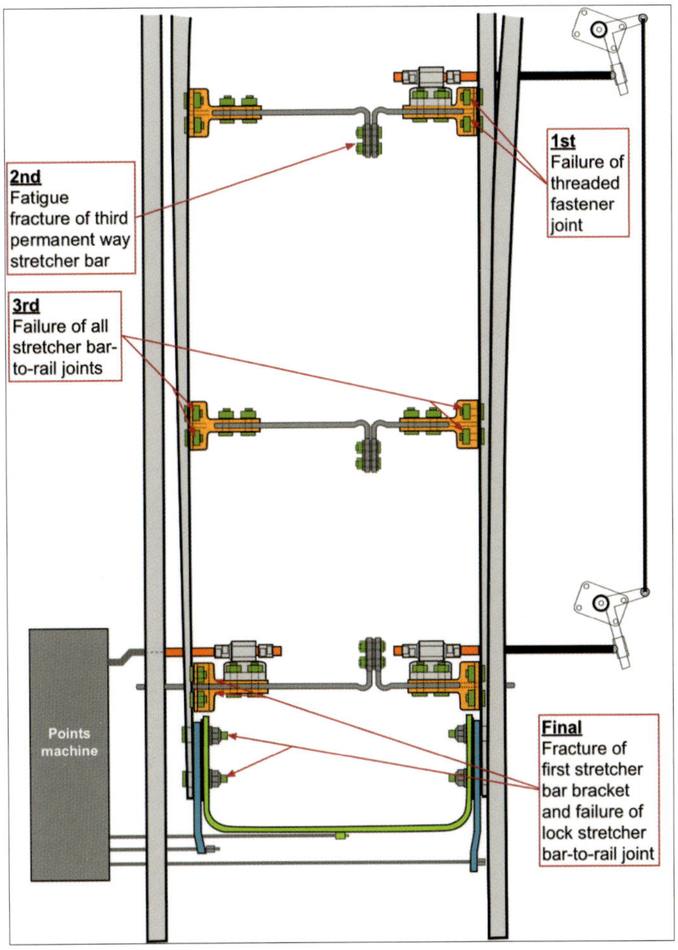

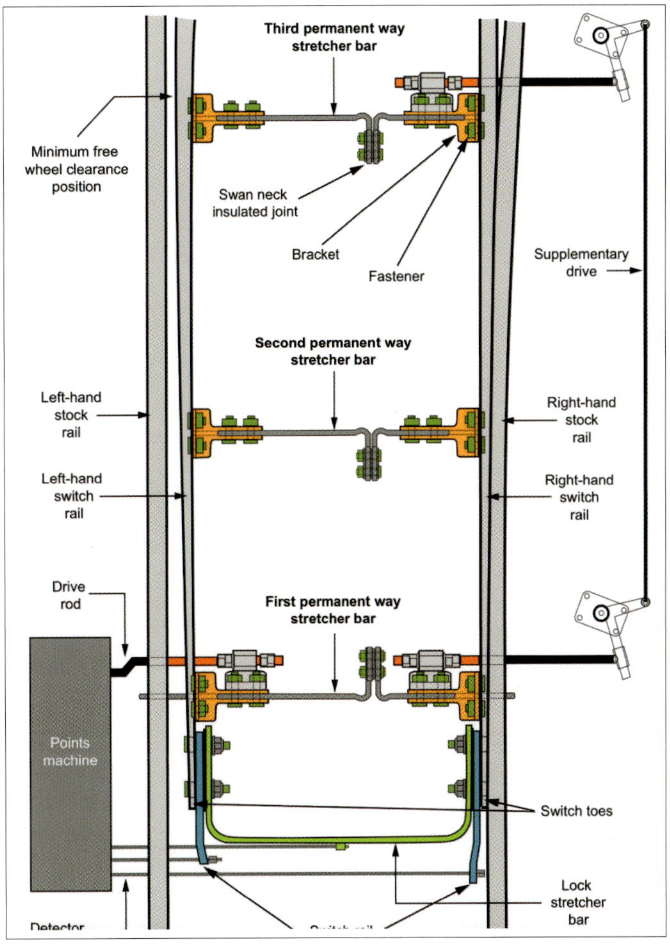

Above: As 1S83 passed over the unsafe 2B facing switch at 95mph, a combination of stretcher bar failures and fractured fastenings to the switch rails allowed the left-hand switch rail to move to the left, as tension in the rail tried to straighten it out. The left hand wheels of either the first or second bogie on the leading driving car (investigation was unable to ascertain which) passed on the wrong (right-hand) side of the switch rail, forcing the wheels into the narrowing space between the switch rails. The wheels then climbed the rails and derailed in the narrowing gap. All nine vehicles derailed this way. Bolts securing the third stretcher bar had loosened and fallen off their threads. The switch was also incorrectly set-up, with excessive residual switch opening: thus, the left hand switch rail flexed far enough to the left to be struck repeatedly by the inner flange faces of the wheels of passing trains, which caused rapid deterioration of the remaining stretcher bars and their fastenings. Had the switch opening been accurately set-up, the rail would have been held further to the right after failure of the third stretcher bar and wheel impacts would have been less severe, with slower deterioration. This would have made detection before disaster much more likely. Stretcher bars Nos. 1/2 ultimately failed and the left switch rail became completely unrestrained. This enabled it to move even further to the left as the tension relaxed - and derailment of the next train became inevitable. This process took place over at least 11 days before the accident and then an inspection due in February - which would in all likelihood have detected these failures - did not take place because of management confusion and failures. Disaster was now unavoidable. *RAIB*

Above: Grayrigg facing Points 2B, with all key components identified. *RAIB.*

discovered a document she had not previously seen. It was a Part B NR Risk Assessment from 2002. This RA was very important because it had recommended considering fitting Elsenham's level crossing pedestrian wicket gates with locks, operated from the nearby signalbox. If NR had actually fitted those gate locks as recommended in this 2002 document, then Charlotte and Olivia, excited to be off on that shopping trip, would have been prevented from dashing onto the crossing and losing their lives. This was brought to the attention of HMRI's Chief Inspector who discovered that even the inspectors involved in the original case had never seen this fundamentally important document. ORR's response was rapid and decisive: Prosser

Below: When Lambrigg's facing crossover had been installed by BR in 1971 (one of two installed around the same time, largely to enable single line working during WCML electrification) there were around 50 movements over the points each day, controlled by a signalbox nearby. By February 2007, this had risen to around 60 movements, including 34 express 'Pendolino' and Class 221 'Super Voyager' trains, and Class 220 'Voyager' units, plus 24 freight or engineering trains and two overnight sleeping car trains. The signalbox closed in 1993, after which the crossover was controlled by a ground frame, electrically released by the Carlisle power signal box (PSB). *RAIB.*

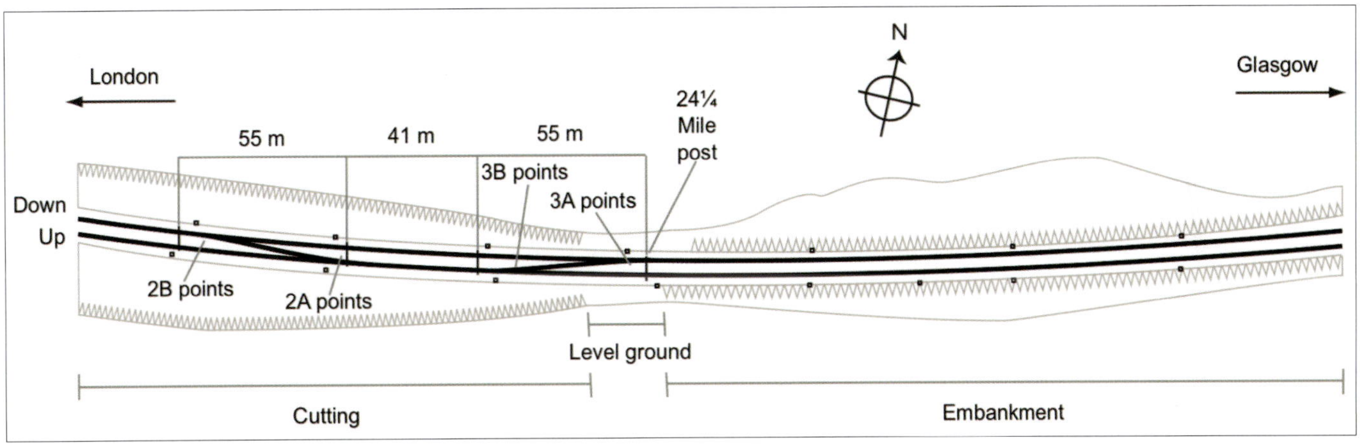

Above: Grayrigg facing points 2B, as photographed by the 'Doctor Yellow' converted IC125 NR Network Measurement Train train, on January 10 2007. *NR*.

instructed his inspectors to look at reopening the case in light of this new information.

This led to further information coming to light which paved the way for a successful prosecution of NR, on March 12 2012: it was fined £1m. This was a watershed in the way that the industry considered risk at level crossings. The oft-quoted industry mantra of 'perfectly safe if used properly' was consigned to the past.

NR Chief Executive Sir David Higgins (appointment announced September 28 2010) commendably showed great leadership after sentencing, by sending a powerful email to all Network Rail staff, explaining why the company had pleaded guilty. A degree of closure and vindication for the families was finally achieved, particularly for Tina Hughes, who had fought and campaigned tirelessly for safer level crossings (and indeed still does) following the terrible loss of her teenage daughter.

This case, as Prosser told the families when he had announced his decision to prosecute, had been made so that the names of Charlotte and Olivia would live on and thereby ensure level crossing safety improved consistently and permanently.

HMRI/ORR had been trying to progressively make NR improve in its understanding of risk generally and how it managed these risks specifically at every level crossing. Crossing closures had been already been gaining momentum, but a step-change occurred following Elsenham as NR allocated investment of more than £100m to improve level crossing safety. It set a target of reducing risk by 25% by April 2014 and further funds of around £100m were allocated in CP5 which enabled further closures and implementation of new tehnology. Consequently, in the last 10 years more than 1,100 level crossings have been closed with more to come.

Tina Hughes, Olivia's mother, did an incredible job in driving forward level crossing safety. By repeatedly telling her own tragic story, she has done more than anyone to ensure change both inside and outside NR. In recognition of her outstanding efforts and courage, Tina was appointed MBE in 2014. This was richly deserved. Prosser feels that many things have improved as a consequence of inspectorate intervention since 2006 but he regards his most influential legacy decision was his reopening the Elsenham case.

Since the 2008 reorganisation, there have been many examples of how focused the Inspectorate has become and how this has had a positive impact over the rail and tram sectors. As a consequence of much proactive enforcement against, and proactive engagement with, the heritage sector and its trade body, the Heritage Rail Association (HRA) we now see much stronger formal Safety Management Systems across this sector. There has also been much more effective safety leadership by HRA, which has helped to provide crucial safety guidance and leadership to more than 200 organisations, many run largely by volunteers.

The Inspectorate has taken a special interest in minor railways ever since Captain Tyler's days, back in 1877. At the dawn of what was then known as 'railway preservation' in the early 1950s (the Talyllyn was our first volunteer-run 'preserved' railway, re-opening in 1951) Inspectors gave considerable advice and guidance to specifically allow volunteers to operate and maintain railways in a professional and safe manner. The Middleton Railway, in Leeds, was actually the first British standard gauge railway to be taken over by volunteers, in June 1960, when it carried passengers for one week only. However, as it had been open continuously since 1758 it was not strictly a reopened heritage railway. Regular steam passenger operation only began in 1969, leading to a friendly rivalry between the Middleton and Bluebell Railways as to which was the UK's first heritage steam railway. Our first standard gauge closed branch line railway to reopen to carry passengers was the Bluebell Railway, which ran its first train on August 7 1960. This was less than three years after BR closed the line between East Grinstead and Lewes.

This supervision by HMRI continued to develop and extend as the number of what were then known as 'preserved railways' (which seems a rather odd expression today!) began to grow very rapidly, especially after the opening of the Keighley & Worth Valley Railway in 1968. In 1970 there were around a dozen standard/narrow gauge heritage railways, in 2019 there were more than 211. In the 1970s/80s, HMRI's very well known (and respected) Major Peter Olver spent most of his time dealing with reinstated and steadily lengthening heritage railways. Following Major Olver's retirement in 1989, the redoubtable former army officer Major John Poyntz took over the Inspectorate's oversight of minor railways. Poyntz retired in 2006 but is remembered with considerable respect.

Major Poyntz also enjoyed the great distinction of being the last Inspector to come from the British Army. He was formerly the Eisenbahnbetriebsleiter for the British Army on the Rhine, in command of all British rail movements in Germany. Major Poyntz, who was also a commanding officer at the late and much lamented Longmoor Military Railway, in Hampshire (closed 1969) was followed by David Keay as Deputy Chief Inspector. Keay was responsible for overseeing the development of our minor railways for 15 years, until 2017 using an appropriate and professional mix of persuasion where possible accompanied by carefully targeted legal enforcement where required, to encourage robust governance and an ever-deepening safety culture on all heritage railways. This is to his very considerable credit.

Our minor railways are some of the UK's best loved and premier tourist attractions and they create very significant economic benefits in the towns and villages through which they pass. Indeed, our larger railways such as the Severn Valley, North Yorkshire Moors and Great Central Railways, play a very significant part in their wider regional economies and as such require supervision from the Inspectorate to ensure on-going viability in the context of largely voluntary operation. They sometimes become stars in their own right - the NYMR not only was the fictional Aidensfield in the long-running 'Heartbeat' Sunday evening TV police drama, it has also featured in two series of Channel 5's fly-on-the-wall documentary 'The Yorkshire Steam Railway: All Aboard' in 2018/19.

Light rail and Network Rail

During the 1990s/2000s a welcome number of new light rail systems and extensions have been successfully delivered. The Inspectorate has continued to show leadership in this sector and with the move ahead from the previous reactive approvals approach, has been successful in persuading the industry to take the lead in producing its own guidance and standards - a service the Inspectorate had previously provided.

There has also been some very powerful work - backed by enforcement where necessary - that has led to a significant improvement in how NR manages its assets. The last ten years have seen significant improvements in how the main line manages and controls risks from earthworks, structures, drainage, track and switches and crossings, most dating from the Victorian era and all taking loads and traffic considerably higher then their original builders could have dreamed of. This has required persistent effort and relentless focus. ORR is constantly challenging Network Rail to demonstrate that it has the capability and resources to safely and sustainably manage its network. This extends to new works and enhancements where for example on electrification RSD has made repeated efforts to persuade the industry to embrace safety by design and to leave behind the 'like for like' mentality. This has sometimes been a struggle, leading, for example, to enforcement on electrification schemes to ensure that risks are more effectively controlled than in the past.

Occupational Health

Following completion of the Periodic Review 2008, and the reorganisation described earlier, ORR under the leadership of Chris Bolt overhauled it's corporate Strategy. One headline was the 'zero fatality' ambition and the push for excellence, but a further significant theme was occupational health.

This was, in many ways, a health and safety 'Cinderella'. For many years, the regulator's focus had, understandably, been identifying precursors to catastrophic events. However, it was clear that much could also be done to improve the health and well being of individual

Above: Four track workers from contractor Carillion died instantly and five others were injured (one seriously) on the West Coast Main Line at Tebay, when this runaway four-wheel engineers trolley of 15ft in length ploughed into them in the dark, at more than 40mph. The accident happened during a track possession at 6.00am on February 15 2004. The trolley ran away for 3¼ miles on the steep 1 in 76 falling gradient from Scout Green, on Shap Fell, where it was carrying 16 tons of scrap rail. A road-rail excavator using its hydraulic 'log grab' to unload the scrap rail by dragging lengths off the trolley, nudged it over makeshift wooden scotches under the wheels, intended to stop it moving. Attempts to stop the trailer failed and it rolled south with rapidly increasing speed on the falling gradient, towards the work gang just over three miles away, in a separate track possession. They could not be warned of the trolley running away towards them and they neither saw nor heard its 40mph approach: they were working in darkness, wearing safety helmets and ear protection to protect their hearing from the noise of heavy machinery, including a diesel generator nearby. "They would have known nothing, heard nothing, seen nothing until it was all too late," said a fellow trackman who had been close by. *Robert France.*

Above: The Tebay runaway trolley careered on for a further mile after killing the four men; it further collided with two other on-track trolleys before coming to a halt near where the A685 crosses the WCML. MAC Machinery chief Mark Connolly, 44, of North Wales and crane operator Roy Kennett, 29, of Maidstone, Kent were both subsequently convicted on majority verdicts on four counts each of manslaughter. Connolly was jailed for nine years and Kennett for two years, at Newcastle Crown Court, in March 2006. Kennett was also convicted of a single count of breaching health and safety laws: he had deliberately disconnected the trolley's automatic hydraulic brakes because it was cheaper than repairing them. He had then filled the brake hoses with ball bearings to give the impression they were functioning. British Transport Police Superintendent Alistair Cumming condemned Connolly's greed and "blatant and premeditated disregard for safety." On March 1 2007, the two jailed men's appeal seeking to overturn their convictions failed. Connolly later applied for a Heavy Goods Vehicle Licence after being caught driving a lorry without one in May 2016, but in January 2017 the Traffic Commissioners for Wales rejected his application because of the manslaughter convictions. One of the dead men was Gary Tindall, a married father of one from Tebay, who lived close to the scene of the accident. His son should have been working with him but he had taken the night off to go to a party. The other men killed were Colin Buckley, 49 and Darren Burgess, 30, both of Carnforth and Chris Waters, 53, of Morecambe. The track was being upgraded in readiness for the start of 125mph tilting 'Pendolino' services in 2004. *Robert France.*

rail workers. Consequently, a five-year programme was established under the leadership of John Gillespie and Claire Dickinson. At times, it has frankly been an uphill battle to encourage the industry to appreciate that making improvements in health management actually have good business cases. This was an area of proactive work pursued by the Inspectorate - putting together case studies to demonstrate these double benefits.

Much more is now known about areas where there was a lack of data and ORR can now prove that the industry is engaging with enthusiasm. The Inspectorate has worked with RSSB to create a long-term project to bring about a step change across the industry. The recent updated baseline review ORR has carried out across the industry has shown that this five-year programme has significantly shifted the industry in the right direction although there is still a way

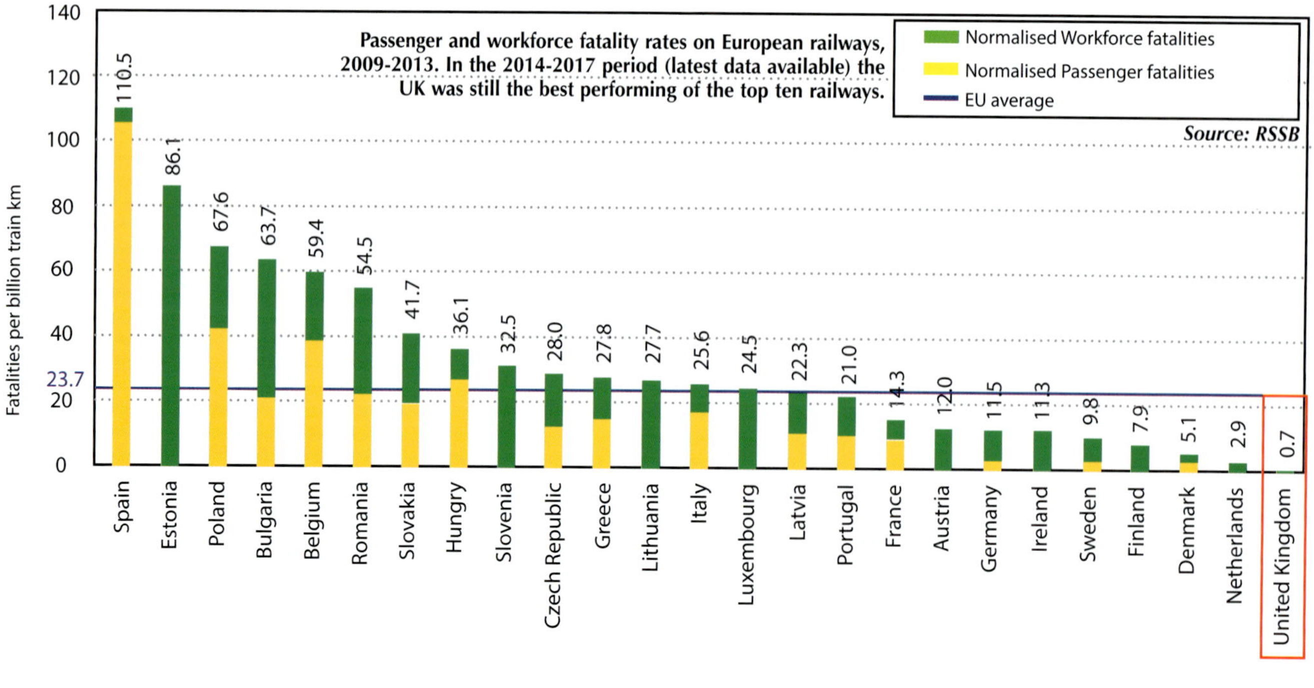

Passenger and workforce fatality rates on European railways, 2009-2013. In the 2014-2017 period (latest data available) the UK was still the best performing of the top ten railways.

to go before excellence is achieved across the industry as a whole. Examples being the improved control of Silca Dust and Hand Arm Vibration.

ORR's 2013 Periodic Review

In ORR's 2008 Periodic Review, which led to CP4, HMRI played a small part. It helped by moderating the efficiency challenge placed on NR by ORR's final determination. After the reorganisation of 2009, ORR's two sides worked more closely together. The benefits of this joint approach were illustrated in the 2013 Periodic Review, with Inspectors working alongside economists to analyse NR's plans.

ORR's economists were moving steadily away from 'light touch' regulation to much more proactive monitoring of what Network Rail would actually deliver. The Railway Safety Directorate (RSD) played an integral part in this - working with economic colleagues to evaluate not only asset policies but also business plan submissions. It had input into what required outputs and indicators might look like. Some specific safety and efficiency related projects were funded, such as the initiative to achieve safer and quicker power isolations on the electrified railway. There was also a ring-fenced level crossing budget to further reduce risks, with a target 25% reduction.

The Railway Safety Directorate reviewed Network Rail's Strategic Business Plan along with the rest of the office in a much more integrated way. This resulted in the Directorate being able to persuade the rest of its office colleagues that NR's aim of maintenance cost reduction profile was too aggressive and that the early years needed increased funding.

All in all, this periodic review proved that after seven years, the two original parts of ORR had finally come together to work in close harmony as a key plank of ORR economic regulation through NR's Periodic Review process. Culture is hard to change and requires sustained effort by everyone.

Britain's Railway Performance today

Britain's main line railway is now statistically the safest in Europe. This is a significant achievement and is clearly illustrated in the graphic below

LUL's safety performance also remains very strong and ranks along with the best in the world. However, we can never be complacent and everyone can rest assured that HMRI will remain ever-vigilant. There is no doubt that after 180 years HMRI has played an important and crucial role in encouraging and leading the British rail industry to its status today as the safest railway in Europe.

Railway Inspectors have fought continuously for improvements throughout their long history even though at times having only limited enforcement powers. ORR now uses its powers proportionately to help encourage and ensure continuous improvement in a very proactive way.

The Inspectorate is there to protect passengers, public and workforce from harm.

And in 2020, 180 years after 'Father of the Railways' George Stephenson triggered the establishment of the Railway Inspectorate, that will always be the first priority.

So in 2019, with continuous improvement in both health and safety on the railways as a whole, the ORR and the Railway Inspectorate celebrated its 180th anniversary. It was an important time to thank the team - numbering around 120 - for all their efforts over the last decade. In 2015, when 175 years old the ORR became the second oldest institution in the railways worldwide - only the British Transport Police is older, with its roots in 1826. A small celebration took place at the Annual Railway Safety Directorate Staff Conference in the October of that year, held at the Tower of London. A very large cake was provided with a number of retired inspectors attending along with other previous members of the HMRI, HSE and ORR. A keynote address was given by Ladbroke Grove survivor Pam Warren, who was terribly burned in the accident and barely survived. However, she did survive, chiefly as a result of her incredible determination and belief. She has become a key reminder to us all of the importance that passengers put their trust (and lives) in railways and expect them to provide a safe journey. Pam eloquently reminded everyone that we all "put [our] faith in the Railway Inspectorate to protect the interests of passengers, the public and the workforce."

Another piece of history that year was the recruitment of an army officer to HMRI's ranks. Colonel Johnny Schute OBE, whose last job in the army had been Head of Health & Safety and Environment. Schute was recruited by Prosser as one of his deputies focussing on Policy, Planning and Strategy before becoming deputy Chief Inspector. The leadership brought by military personnel was thereby recognised again - as had been the case throughout the history of the Inspectorate. Schute subsequently moved on to RSSB, as Chief Operating Officer.

The financial year 2015/16 has another special place in the history

In the last ten years safety has improved.......

Courtesy RSSB

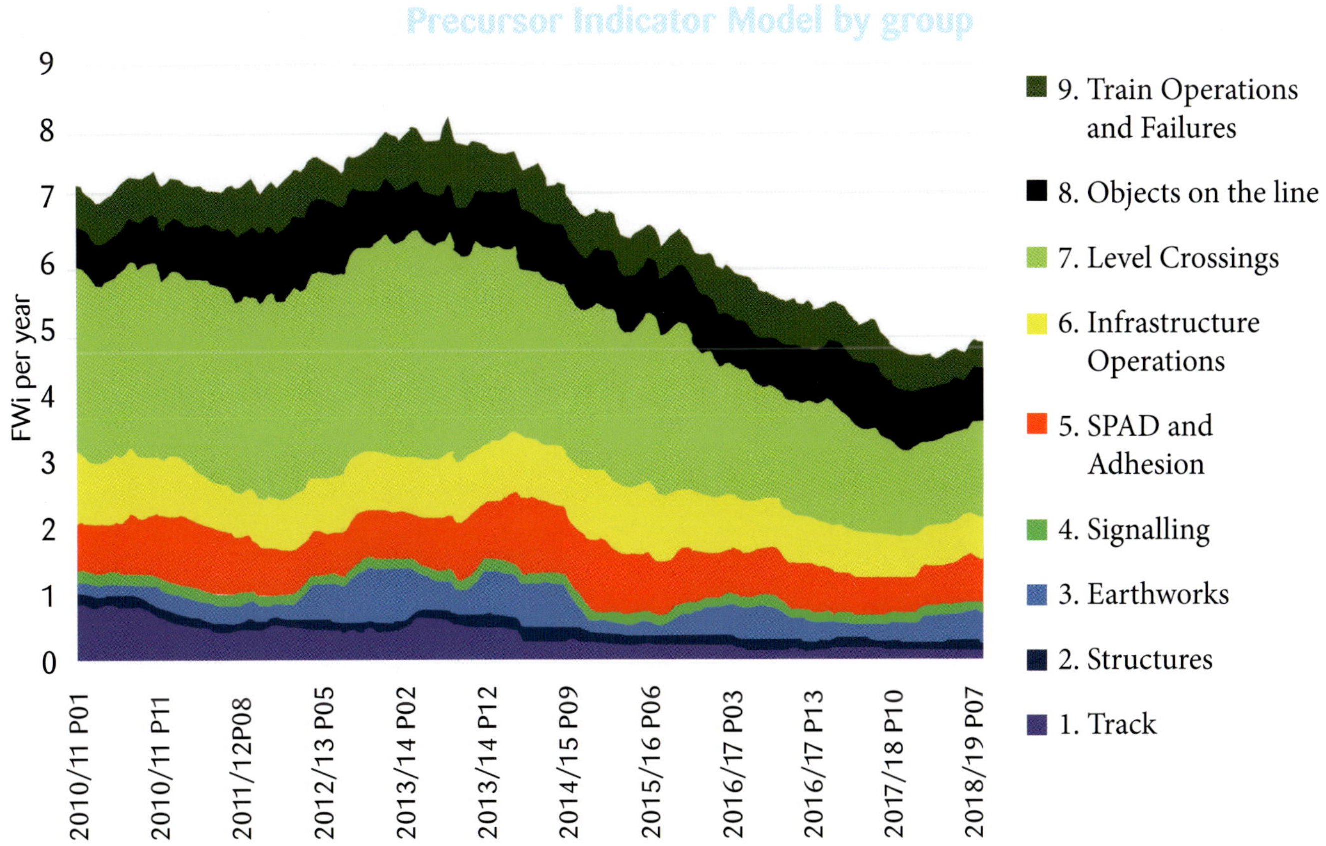

of HMRI/ORR. It was the first time there were no workforce fatalities on Britain's railways - which meant that the vision Prosser had established in 2008 was finally achieved. This sadly has not been repeated and later in 2016 there was a very sharp reminder of HMRI's need to remain vigilant. On November 9 a tram on the Croydon network derailed and overturned at Sandilands causing the deaths of seven people with a further 62 passengers injured.

This was a deep shock to both the industry and the Inspectorate. It had been nearly 10 years since the last fatal train accident at Grayrigg and there had not been a passenger fatality on board a UK tram since 1959, in Glasgow. RAIB - by this stage very well established - produced its report just over a year later. This has resulted in some important direct improvements in driver fatigue management. However, Croydon also produced some important learning for the sector as a whole, particularly around human performance and especially fatigue which in some cases may be hidden.

HMRI/ORR took a hard look at how it regulated this element of the sector and increased its resource to ensure its now-established tool RM3 was embedded in this part of the industry too. It also tried to secure closer collaboration between the individual systems particularly with regards to safety data and risk modelling. The other main move forward led by ORR has been the establishment of the Light Rail Safety & Standard Board. This is very much a baby version of the now well-established RSSB for the main line railway as it was set up following Cullen. The Chief Inspector took the lead in January 2018 at a conference in Manchester which by the end of the year saw the board established with funding from the DfT and the sector itself. This incident was a very sharp reminder for everyone that we cannot be complacent and it is vital we continuously improve.

The events of 2016 were a sharp setback but the sector continued to improve in other areas. At the end of the 2017/18 financial year, the main line railways RSSB's Precursor Indicator Model for train accidents risk achieved it's lowest ever level. Level crossing risks had halved in the preceding ten years, in part driven by the closure of more than 1,100 crossings. Infrastructure risk, particularly track, also significantly reduced following improvements driven by the Inspectorate and NR since the fatal Grayrigg derailment in February 2007.

2018 also saw two important landmarks for Chief

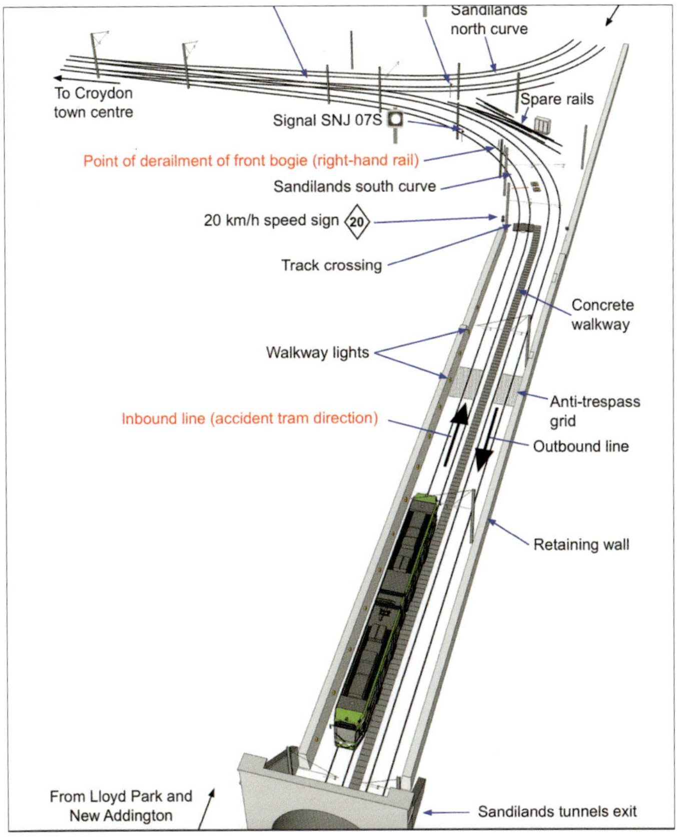

Facing Page & Above: Early in the darkness and heavy rain on the morning of November 9 2016, a total of 69 passengers who had boarded at the first five stops, were travelling into Croydon on the 5.53am tram from New Addington. They were about to be enmeshed in the worst UK tramway accident in more than 90 years. On a section of what was a former heavy rail route, tram No. 2551 emerged at 48mph from a tunnel onto 100m of plain, straight line leading to a 12mph, 90 degree left-hand bend, where the tramway leaves the rail formation. Although the driver braked at the very last moment, his tram hit the 112mph sharp left curve at 45mph and at 6.07am rolled immediately onto its right side. It was still dark, raining heavily and the curve was unlit. Passengers described the derailment as: "like being in a washing machine." Windows on the right side smashed and doors were torn off as the tram hit, and then slid, along the ground.

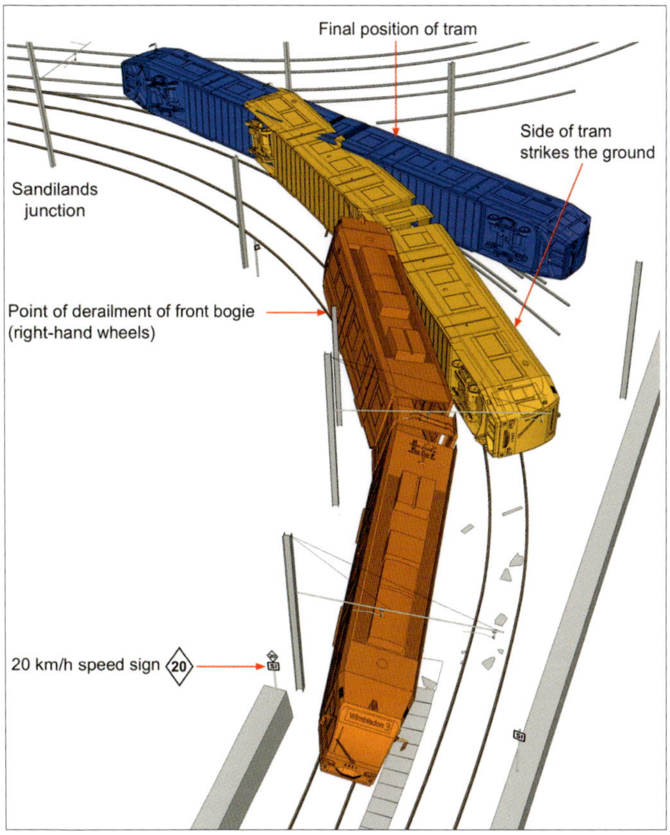

Around 34 passengers fell fully or partially through the openings in the broken glass and were crushed as the tram slid to a stop, three seconds after rolling off the track. It travelled about 18m on its side, of the 27m since it rolled. Seven passengers died, 19 were seriously injured and 43 (including the driver) had minor injuries. Investigations revealed that the tram would have rolled off the track at any speed greater than 30mph; it was travelling at 45mph. RAIB concluded that the experienced driver (a former bus driver) who had been driving since 2008, had suffered a temporary loss of awareness during a period of low workload on a long straight section of track, which caused him to 'microsleep'. He had driven around this bend on at least 693 occasions between January 2015 and November 2016. It was discovered that late braking and some 'near misses' had gone unreported on this curve. *Both: RAIB*

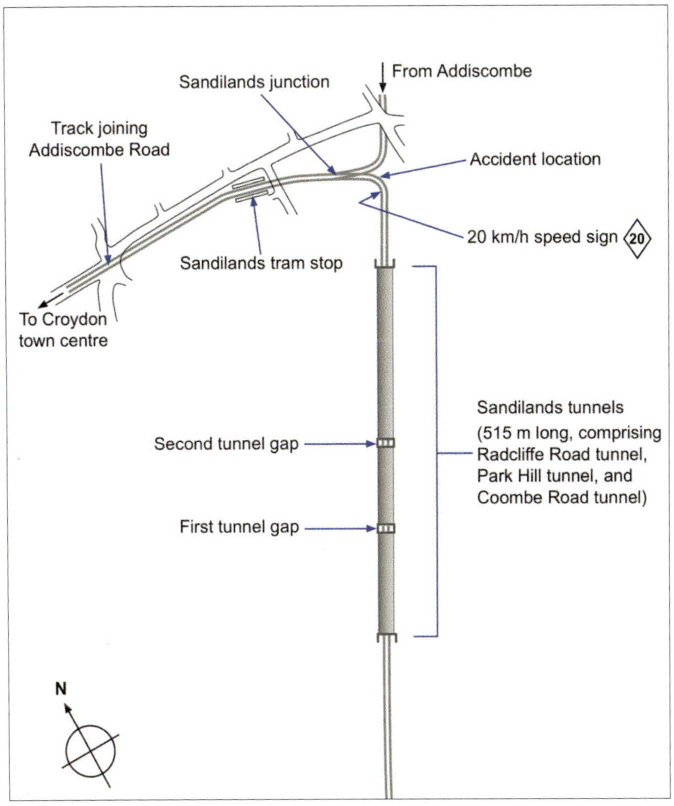

Inspector Prosser. First was the award of a CBE in the Queen's Birthday honours and second was that he celebrated his tenth anniversary in the role. Prosser's contribution was recognised by the National Rail Awards in September of that year with the Senior Outstanding Personal Contribution Award.

It is vital that the Inspectorate and ORR remain vigilant in the face of the many risks to be confronted as Inspectorate closed in on its 180th Anniversary. In its latest annual health and safety report ORR highlighted three key challenges.

1. Supporting its people: This brings many challenges to us all. Our people very often provide the last line of defence in ensuring our railway is safe. Health management needs to be improved further, particularly mental health. This will help improve further the industry's health and safety culture.

2. Pressure on the system: Our largely Victorian railway is busier than it has ever been, at the same time as being safer than it has ever been. This brings real challenges as do the significant changes in organisation being proposed. Very significant numbers of new vehicles are being introduced on to the railway - 6,000 in total - which is bringing real challenges to the Inspectorate.

3. Technology: This brings great opportunities to improve safety, as it has done throughout the history of the railway. However, it also brings challenges particularly in the modern digital world. Software integrity and it's security are vital. This requires new skills and processes for both the industry and the Inspectorate.

So, as it has done throughout its history, the Railway Inspectorate needs to continue to show leadership and ensure its own professional development. The Inspectorate itself is becoming increasingly diverse which adds to its strength as areas like human factors, culture and health management take it beyond its original engineering and safety management roots.

Hopefully, George Stephenson would have approved!

Acknowledgements & Index Information

A substantial history of this detail and complexity could not be produced without the help, support and expertise of a wide range of people and we are both grateful and privileged to have had a great deal of enthusiastic assistance.

Thanks first of all to our editor, Nigel Harris, for his skill and expertise in terms of his diligence and hard work with the book's words and pictures, many of which he sourced. We also benefitted from his in-depth knowledge of railway history and train operations, not least the challenges and responsibilities faced by drivers. Without Nigel's help, support and hard work over a number of years, a comprehensive and complete book such as this would not have been possible.

Our sincere thanks and appreciation to former HMRI/RAIB rail accident investigator Chris Hall, whose late father Stan Hall was also a career railwayman. Stan specialised in rail safety and accident investigation and he chaired more than 100 accident inquiries for BR. A prolific and very well known rail writer, Stan produced several rail safety and accident books including *Railway Detectives: 150 Years of the Railway Inspectorate*, published in 1990 – the year the Railway Inspectorate became Her Majesty's Railway Inspectorate. Our early chapters are based closely on Stan's 1990 book and we are very grateful for Chris's permission to use his father's work as the core of the first section of this new history, published to mark the RI's 180th anniversary, in 2020.

Thanks also to ORR particularly former Chief Executive Richard Price and Director of Corporate Operations Tom Taylor, who were both in-post when this project was launched in 2014 and without whose enthusiastic support this book would not have happened. Others at ORR whose expertise and enthusiasm were also much appreciated: Head of Media Relations Simon Belgard; former PA to Ian Prosser, Nigel Nevis; HMRI Principal Inspector Ian Raxton; HMRI Inspector Simon Smith; HM Assistant Chief Inspector Anna O'Connor; former HMRI Principal Inspector Stephen Firth; ORR Senior Executive Paul Wilkinson and former HMRI Assistant Chief Inspector Gerald Kerr. Thanks also to former Assistant Chief Inspector of Railways Stan Hart and ORR Development & Competency Manager Lee Collins.

Retired Railway Inspector Major John Poyntz has been an invaluable source of historical, technical and engineering expertise and advice. 'The Major' was the last of many generations of Royal Engineers to be recruited to the RI as an Inspector in 1989 and so we were delighted when John agreed to contribute a Foreword. He speaks on behalf of the very many former army engineers who faithfully served the RI and then HMRI continuously from 1841 to 2006, when John retired. He brought to a close a very noble and distinguished tradition.

Our thanks also to Chief Inspector of Railway Accidents Simon French at the Rail Accident Investigation Branch, for permission to use artwork and graphics from RAIB reports, notably Grayrigg and Croydon.

Great Western Managing Director Mark Hopwood, the National Railway Museum's Bob Gwynne and railway historian/writer Chris Leigh all happily and enthusiastically enriched the book's historical detail. RSSB Lead Operational Feedback Specialist Greg Morse was not only a cheerful source of otherwise elusive technical and historical detail, he also did us a great service by helping to proof read the entire book.

Thanks to Simon Bradley, joint editor of the celebrated *Pevsner Architectural Guides* for invaluable help with some important historical financial details. Simon's 645-page tour de force *The Railways: Nation, Network & People* (published by Profile Books 2015) is one of the most important and enjoyable railway books of the last couple of decades. Anyone with an interest in railways (passing or serious) should read this superb book. It tells a great story and sets a very clear social and cultural context against which our own book will be all the more accessible, meaningful and – hopefully - enjoyable.

Renowned railway photographer Gavin Morrison provided numerous superb photographs to lead Chapters 7-11, to illustrate the character and traffic of the railway which RI/HMRI was dealing with in the years covered by those chapters. Thanks to Lorraine Gavin, at the HSE Science & Research Centre, at Buxton, for the superb picture of the Hatfield broken rail, on pages 158-159.

The Railways Archive (https://www.railwaysarchive.co.uk) was an invaluable online research tool, especially for the large number of full RI/HMRI reports it hosts. Readers are urged to dip into these superb documents as a source of further reading. These, by the way, are generally scanned versions of the original documents, which enhances their historical impact considerably.

We acknowledge the hard work and considerable patience of AT Graphics Designer Lucy Carnell, in Peterborough, for sharing and supporting, with both diligence and good humour, our relentless pursuit of detail in order to produce very best book possible. At *Steam World*, office manager Caroline Kingdom provided seamless administrative support, not least in dealing extensively with photo-libraries Getty and Alamy, to secure the high resolution digital images we needed. In the *RAIL* office, Nigel's PA Ellie Johnson also provided invaluable communications support.

Thanks to *RAIL* Deputy Editor Stefanie Foster for helping pull the entire manuscript together, ready for despatch to the printer, at the end of a very long and complex production process. The running text (78,000 words, approx) and captions (36,000 words, approx) were worked on by four people and Stef's legendary thorough approach and unblinking eye for detail has helped create a consistent style and 'voice' within these 184 pages. Anmarie Landi also assisted with proof reading.

Finally, thanks to Clive Nicholls at Steam World Publishing, for taking on this project and doing such a top quality job producing this book.

Ian and I are very proud of this volume and any errors or omissions are ours alone – we hope you enjoy the story of RI/HMRI.

Ian Prosser CBE, Cambridge,
Eur Ing David Keay, Penkridge.

August 2019.

INDEX

Time constraints made it impossible for us to complete an index for this book before publication. A downloadable full index PDF is available from the *Steam World* magazine website (https://steamworldmag.co.uk) which will be printable for insertion in this book.